THE THIRD
REFORMATION?

The Third Reformation?

CHARISMATIC MOVEMENTS AND THE LUTHERAN TRADITION

by CARTER LINDBERG

Institute for Ecumenical Research
Strasbourg

MERCER UNIVERSITY PRESS
MACON, GEORGIA 31207

ISBN 0-86554-075-6

ALL BOOKS PUBLISHED BY MERCER UNIVERSITY PRESS ARE
PRODUCED ON ACID-FREE PAPER THAT EXCEEDS THE
MINIMUM STANDARDS SET BY THE NATIONAL
HISTORICAL PUBLICATIONS AND RECORDS COMMISSION.

LIBRARY OF CONGRESS CATALOGING IN PUBLICATION DATA

Lindberg, Carter, 1937-
The third reformation?

Bibliography: p. 327.
Includes index.
1. Pentecostalism—Lutheran Church.   2. Lutheran
Church—Doctrinal and controversial works.   I. Title.
BX8065.5.L56   1983   248.1'09   83-11371
ISBN 0-86554-075-6

TABLE OF CONTENTS

DEDICATION

To Alice, Anne, Erika and Matthew

Let us thank God, therefore, that we have been delivered from this monster of uncertainty and that now we can believe for a certainty that the Holy Spirit is crying and issuing that sigh too deep for words in our hearts. And this is our foundation: The Gospel commands us to look, not at our own good deeds or perfection but at God Himself as He promises, and at Christ Himself, the Mediator. . . . And this is the reason why our theology is certain: it snatches us away from ourselves and places us outside ourselves, so that we do not depend on our own strength, conscience, experience, person, or works but depend on that which is outside ourselves, that is, on the promise and truth of God, which cannot deceive.

Martin Luther, *Commentary on Galations*, 1535.
LW 26, 387; WA 401, 589, 15-19, 25-28.

PREFACE

There is an increasing need for historical-theological analysis and response to the challenges and contributions issuing from the charismatic renewal movements. This study originated in the context of expressions of this need by Lutheran churches and leadership both within and without the Lutheran World Federation and by the leadership of the Lutheran charismatic renewal itself. The history of much of Protestantism's oft-times neuralgic reaction to emphasis upon religious experience is rooted in Luther's vehement response to the renewal movements of his day. Therefore this study begins with the Reformation, moving then to examine the successive claims of selected post-Reformation renewal movements and on to the completion of the Reformation itself.

Since I began this research nearly three years ago there has been no abatement of concern and literature with regard to the person and work of the Holy Spirit and the gifts of the charismata. The manuscript was completed too early to incorporate the most recent developments such as the June 1982 International Theological Consultation of Lutheran charismatic theologians at Schloss Craheim and their projected volume of studies, or the growing number of scholarly dissertations and theses by Pentecostal scholars and their recently created society of theologians. At the time of this writing a four-day meeting is in progress here in Strasbourg titled "Pentecôte sur l'Europe." Some 20,000 Pentecostal and charismatic participants from throughout Europe are not only celebrating their faith but also involving themselves in a wide range of study sessions including such "new" topics as theology, social and political engagement, and ecumenics. It is not within my competence or gift to prophesy the outcome of the renewal's growing sensitivity to the theological and doctrinal aspects of the faith which are traditional concerns of the ecumenical church. Nevertheless I hope that the following study may serve as a contribution to these beginning dialogues and the growing theological awareness between and among charismatic and non-charismatic alike. I have attempted to be fair but the reader will quickly note that I am not neutral. I have written a critical study of the renewal from the standpoint of Lutheran theology and tradition because I am convinced that only a critical approach will facilitate the dialogical confrontation necessary for the integrity of both the renewal and the churches. Uncritical rejection or mere toleration of the renewal is the first step toward its isolation.

I hasten to add that I have had the privilege of meeting many of the international leaders of the Lutheran charismatic renewal. I have always been most graciously received, especially at their international meetings in Helsinki and Schloss Craheim. In spite of our differences I have been invited and encouraged to participate in the theological discussions of these meetings. In this process of personal dialogue I have learned that there is a more nuanced, sophisticated, and pluralistic theology in the renewal than is evident in many of the writings I criticize in this study. Nevertheless the publications of the renewal are its "public face" and I would do a disservice to the renewal and the churches if I did not take these published expressions seriously and critically. I have also come to appreciate the deep commitment of the charismatic leadership to the church. Thus I hope this study will be accepted in the spirit it is offered—that of respectful but critical dialogue.

It is my happy privilege now to publicly thank a number of people who have encouraged and supported me in my work. To Dr. George W. Forell I owe my first awareness of and enthusiasm for Luther's theological genius. Dr. E. Kent Brown and other colleagues in the School of Theology, Boston University, were instrumental in supporting my successful request for a leave of absence to join the staff of the Institute for Ecumenical Research, Strasbourg. The staff here at the Institute has been exceedingly helpful personally and academically in ways too numerous to recount so I must limit myself to a simple expression of gratitude with the hope that each person remembers his or her daily assistance. Dr. Vilmos Vajta, recently retired director of the Institute, suggested this study project to me. Both Dr. Vajta and Dr. Harding Meyer, present director, have consistently encouraged and supported my work. However, I must hasten to claim the traditional authors' absolution of all of the above for any responsibility for errors of fact and judgment on my part. Dr. Yoshiro Ishida, director of the Department of Studies of the Lutheran World Federation, has been of great help through personal encouragement as well as provision for my participation in two international consultations of Lutheran charismatic leadership in Helsinki, 1981, and Schloss Craheim, 1982. I wish to express special gratitude to Ms. Patricia Williams of the Institute who has patiently "Englished" my Americanisms, and provided editorial assistance and suggestions during the long process of researching and writing. She has typed and retyped this study from its initial proposal to its final draft, the excellence of her work being matched by her grace and good humor. Last but not least I wish to thank my family for their patient understanding during my immersion in this study and their courageous spirit in adjusting to a new life in France.

—Carter Lindberg
Institute for Ecumenical Research, Strasbourg
Pentecost 1983

INTRODUCTION

Ever since Luther's violent explosion against his former colleague, Karlstadt, whom he characterized as "he who has devoured the Holy Spirit feathers and all,"[1] subjective religious experience has been a neuralgic point in the Lutheran tradition. With the exception of Pietism, sometimes termed the second Reformation, Lutheran worship, theology, and life have been highly suspicious of personal claims for direct experience of the Holy Spirit. Thus until recently, the question, "Can the Pentecostal experience be harmonized with Lutheran theology?,"[2] was answered in the negative by charismatic and non-charismatic alike.

In recent years, however, mutual anathema has been gradually giving way to mutual concern for understanding and dialogue. Lutheran churches throughout the world from the parish level to the international level have been confronted by both the phenomenal growth and missionary power of the Pentecostal churches without, and the disconcerting if not anxiety-producing rise of charismatic movements within. The vigor

---

[1]Against the Heavenly Prophets, 1525, in Helmut T. Lehman and Jaroslav Pelikan, *Luther's Works* (St. Louis and Philadelphia: Condordia and Fortress Presses, 1955ff.) 40:83 (cited as *LW* vol., p.).

[2]Erling Jorstad, *Bold in the Spirit. Lutheran Charismatic Renewal in America Today* (Minneapolis: Augsburg Publishing House, 1974) 101.

and almost universal presence of what Bishop Newbigin called "the third stream of Christian tradition"[3] have compelled serious attention by the churches.

This was recognized clearly in 1970 by the Fifth Assembly of the Lutheran World Federation which called upon its Commission of Studies to "undertake a study of Pentecostalism." Acknowledging both the contemporary importance of the Pentecostal churches and charismatic renewal movements as well as confessing the mutual ignorance which hitherto hindered development of positive relationships, the Assembly stated:

> The Lutheran churches have long neglected the questions posed by Pentecostal brothers in the faith. The road toward fruitful dialog has seemed to be strewn with insurmountable obstacles. Professor Nils Bloch-Hoell has claimed that "no other non-Catholic church is further removed from the Pentecostal churches than the Lutheran." One great impediment for such dialog has been the fact that Lutherans and Pentecostals know very little about each other.... We therefore believe that the time has come for the LWF to take measures to initiate a dialog between Pentecostalism and Lutheranism. . . . [4]

At approximately the same time Lutheran charismatics began to express concern for "a clearer grasp of their own identity. Without this, Lutheran charismatics would tend to drift toward the Pentecostals on one side, or toward the Catholics on the other."[5] It is of ecumenical interest that the challenge to develop their Lutheran identity came in 1973 from leaders in the Catholic Charismatic Renewal.

It was within this context that four Lutheran charismatic pastors and teachers, participants in a major study project begun in 1974 by the Division of Theological Studies of the Lutheran Council in the USA, addressed their concerns to the Lutheran churches. "Does the Lutheran heritage have room for this testimony of possibly widened (or deepened or broadened) spiritual horizons or are there fundamental motifs in the Lutheran tradition which would call some or all of these interpretations

---

[3]Leslie Newbigin, *The Household of God* (London: SCM Press Ltd., 1953) 87. In these Kerr Lectures given in Glasgow, 1952, Newbigin characterized this stream (the other two being Catholicism and Protestantism) in terms of its central "conviction that the Christian life is a matter of the experienced power and presence of the Holy Spirit today," and called for its inclusion in the ecumenical movement. Cf. his chapter four, "The Community of the Holy Spirit."

[4]*Sent into the World.* Proceedings of the Fifth Assembly LWF (Evian, 1970) 79-80.

[5]Larry Christenson, *The Charismatic Renewal Among Lutherans* (Minneapolis: Bethany Fellowships, Inc., 1976) 9 (hereafter cited as *CRAL*).

of religious experience into question?" The Lutheran charismatic leaders not only challenged the Lutheran Church to remember her task of "continual self-reformation," they also expressed the need to test their own experience by "the historic norms of Scripture and the Lutheran Confessions." "Charismatics who explicitly continue to identify themselves as Lutheran are eager to assume the responsibility of witnessing to charismatic experiences in a way consistent with their commitment to the Lutheran theological heritage . . . and they solicit the help of fellow Lutherans in working through this task."[6] This concern was evident among many of the charismatic leaders assembled at the "International Lutheran Renewal Leaders' Conference '81" held near Helsinki in August 1981. Two special ad hoc sessions were devoted to discussing the need for historical and systematic theological reflection on the charismatic renewal and a committee was formed to coordinate theological work among Lutheran charismatic leaders. The above references could be multiplied by others but these are sufficient to indicate the Lutheran concern—both charismatic and non-charismatic—for an examination of the present experiences of charismatic renewal. In short, there is an in-house impetus for such a study.

However, it is important to emphasize that the following study is motivated not only by intramural concerns, but by extramural ecumenical responsibilities as well. Innumerable studies and popular works testify to the fact that charismatic renewal is not only a major ecumenical force today, but that in one form or another it may become a permanent part of the churches' life. There is no major denomination which is untouched by this remarkable phenomenon. Thus in 1975 the WCC established a sub-unit on Renewal and Congregational Life. Indeed the facility of charismatics in placing personal experience (the so-called baptism of the Holy Spirit) prior to ecclesial and doctrinal demarcations gives the charismatic movement itself a transconfessional character which is sometimes compressed into the slogan "doctrine divides, experience unites." This transconfessional aspect holds both the promise of increased openness among churches plus the problem of a double loyalty to the church on the one hand and the charismatic community on the other.[7] Regard-

---

[6]Paul D. Opsahl, ed., *The Holy Spirit in the Life of the Church: From Biblical Times to the Present* (Minneapolis: Augsburg Publishing House, 1978) 232, 235ff.

[7]Cf. Gassmann and Meyer, eds., *Neue transkonfessionelle Bewegungen* (Frankfurt am Main: Lembeck, 1976) 19ff., 28f., 93f.; and Kilian McDonnell, *The Charismatic Renewal and Ecumenism* (New York: Paulist Press, 1978) 81ff.

less of one's evaluation of the charismatic renewal as a transconfessional movement, its relevance to continuing multilateral ecumenical dialogue among all churches is quite significant and requires serious study as well as engagement.

Finally, in terms of ecumenical dialogue we refer again to the desire expressed by the LWF to begin a bilateral dialogue with the Pentecostal churches. Since the main object of ecumenical dialogue is to overcome division between the churches then the theological, historical, exegetical, and other issues which are included in the reasons for this division must be dealt with thoroughly. It may be argued that the Lutheran Church has a particular responsibility here in regard to the Pentecostal churches and to the charismatic movements because the initial and predominant critiques of the charismatic experience arose in the first decade of the Lutheran Reformation. For good and for ill these critiques have continued to be influential today. For example, a recent study on "The Pentecostal Experience and the New Testament Witness"[8] credits Luther in his controversy with the spiritualists for major theological assistance.

The motivations for this study with its specific concern for relating the Lutheran tradition to charismatic movements may be summarized as including the worldwide impact of charismatic renewal on all churches, the rapid growth of international and transdenominational charismatic organizations and their influence, the 1970 LWF recommendation for a study of Pentecostalism, intra-Lutheran concerns regarding the rise of Lutheran charismatic movements, and preparation for bilateral dialogue with the Pentecostal churches.

In light of the above motivations this study hopes to achieve the following goals:

1. To assess charismatic movements in light of selected elements of Lutheran tradition. The major points of orientation will be Luther, the

---

[8]The subtitle of Frederick D. Bruner's *A Theology of the Holy Spirit* (Grand Rapids MI: Eerdmans, 1970) 344: "Finally it should be mentioned that the person who provided the largest general theological assistance to us was—somewhat unexpectedly—Martin Luther. We took up the reading of Luther in Germany mainly as a kind of avocation and as a means of acculturation. Soon Luther had become our theological tutor. Luther's understanding of the gospel and his important controversy with the Protestant spiritual-movement of his time were very impressive to us. After the New Testament we feel we owe the most to our acquaintance with Luther and with those materially influenced by him for the understanding of the meanings of Christian theology." Bruner is a United Presbyterian.

Confessions, and Lutheran Pietism. The limitations of time and space preclude major emphasis upon other foci and influences such as Lutheran Orthodoxy, Zinzendorf and the Moravians, nineteenth-century confessionalism, or modern biblical criticism. As with any selection process there is a certain arbitrariness involved here and good arguments may be raised for including one or another historical-theological "focus" beyond those chosen as essential for an adequate assessment of charismatic movements. Certainly no rationale is required for the choice of Luther and the Confessions. Pietism is an important element in this study because of its interest in the young Luther and his religious experience as well as what appear to be analogies to if not continuities with charismatic movements. Furthermore Pietism clearly regarded itself as an international and interconfessional movement.

2. To assess Lutheran tradition in light of charismatic movements. A study written by one person is obviously not a dialogue, especially since the author himself is not a charismatic. Nevertheless, I hope to provide charismatic Lutheran critiques and assessments of Lutheran tradition as they see it in its own pluriform development.

3. To contribute historical and theological analyses of the traditional responses and reactions of the Lutheran tradition to charismatic movements and vice versa. We have already indicated a special Lutheran responsibility to reevaluate charismatic movements because of the formative influence of the early Reformation perspectives on later evaluations of renewal movements. Stereotypes and caricatures however exist on both sides—if Luther referred to the renewal leaders of his day as fanatics, they referred to him as a scribe and neo-papist. A critical evaluation of the source and perpetuation of distortive perspectives on theological sophistication, ecclesiology, ethics, and social class may contribute to healthier, more constructive dialogue.[9]

4. To describe and analyze selected charismatic movements and their relationship to Lutheran churches. The selection of "case studies" has been determined both by the availability of information and the desire to have a wide geographical and cultural representation. Particular atten-

---

[9]Remigius Bäumer has suggested the ecumenical value of such a study on the historical influence of Luther's view of the papacy. Cf. his *Martin Luther und der Papst* (Münster: Aschendorff, 1970) 100. Adolf Herte helped clear Roman Catholic polemical air by such a study on the historical influence upon Catholic scholarship of Cochläus's biography of Luther. Cf. A. Herte, *Das katholische Lutherbild im Banne der Lutherkommentare der Cochläus,* 3 vols. (Münster, 1943).

tion will be directed toward their "Sitz im Leben," and their social-ethical perspectives and praxis as well as theology.

5. To assess contemporary Lutheran responses to and official church statements about charismatic movements. This will be done from the perspective of the material developed in the above points.

6. Finally, it is hoped that this study will contribute to Lutheran understanding of charismatic movements in history and in the present ecumenical and transconfessional relationships, and to Pentecostal and charismatic movements' understanding of Lutheran concerns. To the extent that these goals are realized, this study may contribute to the development of guidelines for ecumenical dialogues with the Pentecostal churches and also for the relationship of Lutheran churches to charismatic movements.

The method of approach to the vast amount of material involved in this study will be historical-critical. The autobiographical reason for this is that my own training and profession is in the field of church history and historical theology. Apart from personal predilections, however, there are sound reasons for choosing a historical approach to this study. One is that a historical-theological method provides the possibility of a more faithful interaction with the material than a systematic-theological method. The subject matter at hand is that of personal experience viewed in historical perspectives from Luther to the present. The subject of this study then is biographical as well as historical and theological. No one reading Luther can avoid being struck by the autobiographical vividness of his theology and work as Reformer. Pietism, also, because of its concern for religious experience, was concerned with both history and biography. To the extent that history took on the aspect of a history of piety (Gottfried Arnold's *Unparteiische Kirchen- und Ketzer-Historie,* 1699-1700) and an emphasis upon biographies of outstanding Christians and twice-born people, Pietism not only formed the soil for charismatic movements but also contributed to the development of modern psychologizing biographies and novels.[10] The literary parallels to this in charismatic literature are striking.[11] In short, the historical method more

---

[10]Cf. Christof Ziemer, "In und neben der Kirche. Charismatische Bewegung in den Kirchen der DDR," *Die Zeichen der Zeit* 6 (1979) 224; Martin Schmidt, "Pietismus" in *RGG,* 5:370ff.

[11]The sources for studying the Pentecostal churches are frequently in biographical form. Cf. Walter J. Hollenweger, ed., *Die Pfingstkirchen* (Stuttgart: Evangelisches Verlagswerk, 1971) 312.

accurately will reflect the Pietist, Pentecostal, and charismatic interests as well as the sources available.

We are not searching for the "essence" of the charismatic movement. This is precluded not only because of the great variety of Pentecostal and charismatic movements but also because as Troeltsch pointed out quite succinctly some years ago, "To define the essence is to shape it afresh."[12] Our concern is not with a theory of religion but with religious self-understanding. Also, along the same line, the historical method provides the opportunity to take into consideration the "Sitz im Leben" of the movements and persons under consideration. As Hollenweger has pointed out, the self-presentation of Pentecostal piety is to be distinguished from pentecostal piety itself. Kilian McDonnell, who has extensive personal knowledge of both charismatic communities and their leaders, makes the same point. He claims that it is important to realize that charismatic life-patterns and worship are more in conformity with denominational traditions than is evident from their writings. The twofold reason for this is that many charismatic authors are not trained theologians and that their writings tend to emphasize their differences with the tradition. The Lutheran charismatic researcher of the renewal, Tormod Engelsviken, makes a similar point when he says, "Although the Charismatic Movement differently from the Classical Pentecostal Movement has produced or attracted some outstanding theologians, the Charismatic Movement can hardly be adequately understood by the employment of literary tools alone. Any fair presentation of the charismatic experience must be made on the basis of personal observation."[13] Research must be conscious of this to avoid false conclusions. Because we take seriously the orientation of scholars such as McDonnell, Hollenweger, and Engelsviken, it is appropriate to clarify our own methodology in relation to theirs.

I have already mentioned personal and professional interest in historical theology as a factor contributing to the orientation of this study. Very practical reasons for not using the recommended participant-observer approach include the fact that I am myself not a charismatic and that my

---

[12]"What Does 'Essence of Christianity' Mean?" in R. Morgan and M. Pye, eds., *Ernst Troeltsch: Writings on Theology and Religion* (Atlanta: Knox, 1977) 162.

[13]Tormod Engelsviken, *The Gift of the Spirit. An Analysis and Evaluation of the Charismatic Movement from a Lutheran Theological Perspective.* Unpublished dissertation. (Aquinas Institute School of Theology, Dubuque IA, 1981).

time available for research was too limited to facilitate the extent and depth of personal contacts with charismatic communities that would be necessary for personal substantive analysis. I have attempted to supplement my own literary approach by correspondence with Lutheran charismatic leaders. With but one or two notable exceptions these persons have responded to my inquiries in a positive and helpful manner.

My own participation and observation of charismatic services of worship and meetings is limited to some local gatherings but I wish to gratefully acknowledge here the hospitality shown me by my inclusion and welcome into the "International Lutheran Renewal Leaders' Conference '81" which met in Finland in August 1981. During the five days of this conference I had the opportunity to meet and discuss this study with leading participants in the Lutheran charismatic renewal movement as well as to participate in the total range of the meetings, lectures, and worship services. The effect of this personal experience confirmed for me the orientation and results of this study. I also hope that the limitations of my methodology will be balanced by the extensive use of materials by those persons who themselves have used a participant-observer method, such as McDonnell and Hollenweger, or are themselves Lutheran charismatics, like Bittlinger and Engelsviken. Thus with the balance provided by these resources I do not believe the method of analysis we are using is inadequate to the material.

Methodology in itself, of course, is no guarantee of the adequacy of the results of any study. It is quite possible to carefully utilize the participant-observer methodology and develop critical conclusions about the charismatic movement.[14] More to the point is the fact that interested laity, theologians, and the leadership of the churches will gain much of their understanding of the charismatic movement from its own writings as well as personal exposure to the renewal itself. Since charismatic literature is an expression of the movement's own self-understanding it seems highly appropriate to take it seriously enough to provide a basis for our analysis of the movement. Where possible we have attempted to take into consideration sociological studies.[15] It is hoped that the historical meth-

---

[14]Cf. for example Francoise van der Mensbrugghe, *Les Mouvements de Renouveau Charismatiques. Retour de l'Esprit? Retour de Dionysos?* Dissertation (Faculté Autonome de Théologie, Université de Genève, 1978) 70ff.

[15]Hollenweger, *Die Pfingstkirchen,* 314, 331ff. A model study for this orientation is that by Gerd Theissen, *Studien zur Soziologie der Urchristentums* (Tübingen: J.C.B. Mohr, 1979).

od will also avoid the typological history of ideas orientation which overlooks the social and political contexts in which religious self-understanding has its place. To neglect the concrete social relationships which contribute to the rise and power of the Pentecostal churches and the charismatic movements would unbalance our study in the direction of a normative theological critique of endorsement which would delimit its usefulness as well as its integrity.[16]

It should be made clear at the outset that this is a limited study. The charismatic movement as a whole will not be studied. Because it "contains different and partly contradictory theologies of the Charismatic experience, any theological validation of the Charismatic *Movement* as such is impossible. It is always necessary to evaluate concrete Charismatic theologies."[17] Only selected aspects of the Lutheran tradition and selected models of charismatic movements will be studied. Furthermore this does not intend to be a historical-dogmatic study of the doctrine of the Holy Spirit. These limitations are understood not as a burden or embarrassment but as freedom to relate major expressions of the Christian faith to contemporary uncertainties, concerns, and developments. In this limitation there is comfort in Harnack's statement that history assumes the character of falseness according to the degree of accuracy that tells of all circumstances and motives.[18]

The charismatic material and sources covered in this study are international in scope. However a brief word may be expressed at the outset about what may be regarded as unevenness in the analysis and a perhaps too-heavy dependence upon the American expression of the charismatic movement. There are basic reasons for this. One is that, as the dean of Pentecostal-Charismatic studies, Walter Hollenweger, points out, "There is no reliable overview of the charismatic renewal in the Third World."[19] Another reason is that modernization and pluralism, specific

---

[16]This has been a problem in Reformation studies dealing with the sixteenth century Anabaptists and Spiritualists. Cf. for example Klaus Deppermann, *Melchior Hoffman* (Göttingen: Vandenhoeck & Ruprecht, 1979) 11f., and the Symposium "Problems of Anabaptist History" in *Mennonite Quarterly Review* 53/3 (1979) (hereafter cited as *MQR*).

[17]Engelsviken, *The Gift of the Spirit,* 481.

[18]Adolf von Harnack, "Was hat Historie an festen Erkenntnis zur Deutung der Weltgeschichte zu bieten?," *Reden und Aufsätze* NF 4 (Giessen: Töpelmann, 1923) 173.

[19]Walter Hollenweger, "Roots and Fruits of the Charismatic Renewal in the Third World: Implications for Mission," *Theological Renewal* 14 (1980): 11-28, 11.

contextual stimulants for the rise of the charismatic movements, have advanced further in America than anywhere else.[20] We may further note the abundance of charismatic literature issuing from the United States.

As a final note to avoid possible misunderstandings at the outset, it should be noted that our title, "The Third Reformation?," is in the form of a question, not a statement. This should indicate clearly that our orientation toward the claims of the charismatic movement is critical. I have endeavored to be fair but this should not be interpreted as either neutrality or endorsement. The title is also intended to convey my heuristic organization of the historical-theological resources for this study. Again, this is not a claim or inference that the charismatic renewal *is* the "third reformation" of the church or a reformation at all. The title is also an attempt to convey what I perceive to be the Lutheran charismatic movement's self-understanding of its place in the history of the church. It goes without saying that this self-understanding does not brook the question mark! It is of interest that following the completion of this study, a major leader of the international Lutheran charismatic movement used almost exactly the same terminology to express his conviction of God's present purposes. "God, by his Spirit, in this century is causing a third church restoration. He has done so before through the 16th century Reformation and again through the 18th and 19th century Pietistic revival and mission movements. Today the Lord is bringing the full blessing of Pentecost to his churches, regardless of secular opposition and ecclesiastical resistance."[21]

Finally, I wish to emphasize once again that our purpose is to present a historical-theological analysis of the present charismatic renewal in light of prior renewal movements. Our primary concern is not to document the glories and disasters of the renewal. The former are amply proclaimed in much of the literature published by charismatics themselves. The latter are painfully obvious to those persons who have been hurt by the renewal in many different ways as well as to congregations and their leaders who have been divided over charismatic issues and concerns. Our concern is with theological analysis in light of historical resources rather than with testimonies pro or con. This is not to gainsay

---

[20]Cf. Peter Berger, *The Heretical Imperative: Contemporary Possibilities of Religious Affirmation* (New York: Doubleday, 1979) 58.

[21]W. Dennis Pederson, "Pentecost Challenge for the 20th Century," *Lutheran Renewal International* 2/2 (1981): 19-21, 19 (hereafter cited as *LRI*).

Christian witness but to claim that without a fully reflective examination of that witness its claims may be unintelligible if not deficient or even false. Our focus then is not on the results—joyful or painful—of charismatic theologies but rather on the theologies themselves as sources for these effects.

LITERATURE REVIEW

The number of studies on pentecostalism and the charismatic movements staggers the imagination. Already in his 1971 publication, *Die Pfingstkirchen*, Walter J. Hollenweger included a bibliography of seventy pages plus four additional pages of selected Pentecostal journals.[22] What is striking when reading through this as well as other bibliographies is that there is almost no attempt to discuss pentecostalism and the charismatic movements in a church-historical context. When one looks to the field of church history itself there is, of course, literature on Luther and the sixteenth-century spiritualists, Pietism, and the turn-of-the-century origins of the Pentecostal churches. But even here it is exceedingly rare to find an effort to relate contemporary spiritual experience to the continuities and discontinuities of post-Reformation developments. Interestingly enough the few exceptions to this are mainly by charismatics.

There will be ample opportunity to discuss the secondary literature as well as primary sources during the course of the study. However a brief overview of studies at this point will serve to illustrate the lack of church-historical studies and the type of literature available.

According to Hollenweger, the only scholarly attempt to relate the Pentecostal movement to the spiritualists of the Reformation period is Karl Ecke's *Schwenckfeld, Luther und der Gedanke einer apostolischen Reformation*.[23] Ecke himself was a leader of the German Pentecostal movement and a Lutheran pastor. Ecke's original interest in Schwenckfeld was a scholarly one stimulated by Heinrich Boehmer; however he

---

[22]Hollenweger, *Die Pfingstkirchen*, 392-466. For an annotated review of selected literature cf. "Scholarly Investigation" the Appendix to Richard Quebedeaux, *The New Charismatics: The Origins, Development, and Significance of Neo-Pentecostalism* (New York: Doubleday and Co., 1976) 199-210.

[23]Berlin: Martin Warneck, 1911, 345 pp. Edited and abbreviated by O. S. von Bibra, it is in its third edition under the title, *Fortsetzung der Reformation: Kaspar von Schwenckfelds Schau einer apostolischen Reformation* (Gladbeck: Schriftenmissions-Verlag, 1978). Cf. Hollenweger, *Die Pfingstkirchen*, 416.

came to see in Schwenckfeld's connection of primitive Christianity and the living church community the key to contemporary problems in the churches. He viewed the revision of the prior assessments of Schwenckfeld not only as a scholarly necessity but as an act of justice:

> For we are actually dealing here with the exposure of a spiritual scandal. This is that the Reformers through massive lies and defamations—which even according to the most ordinary use of the Sermon on the Mount are at all times sinful abuse—committed the most brutal defamation of a noble, faultless character whose deep biblically based testimony to Jesus would take a leading position in today's believing community on the basis of his fullness of spiritual power and divine attestation.[24]

Along similar lines Otto Weber wrote to Ecke in 1951 that his work on Schwenckfeld "helps somewhat to compensate for the historical guilt that our Reformation fathers related to the so-called *Schwärmer* not as brothers but as judges."[25]

As the title suggests, the Reformation did not take seriously the ethical and spiritual content of the New Testament proclamation; it preached only half of Christ and his salvation. Therefore the importance of Schwenckfeld both in the sixteenth century and the present is in his life and call to continue toward an apostolic Reformation—to recover the church of the apostolic period with its gifts of grace and power.[26] Ecke's thesis that Schwenckfeld was a forerunner of German Pietism receives some confirmation from E. Hirsch, but his claim that Schwenckfeld completed Luther's ecclesiology is corrected by G. Maron's study, *Individualismus und Gemeinschaft bei Caspar von Schwenckfeld.*

The massive surge of the charismatic movement since the 1960s has stimulated at least two other scholars to relate it to Reformation developments. Bengt R. Hoffman's *Luther and the Mystics* attempts to validate contemporary charismatic renewal by arguing for the centrality of experienced grace (sapientia experimentalis) in Luther and persons of piety in the history of Lutheranism.[27] Hoffman, obviously influenced by the charismatic movement, polemicizes against modern scholarly

---

[24]Ecke, *Fortsetzung der Reformation,* edited by von Bibra, 141f.

[25]Ibid., 8.

[26]Ibid., 121, 140.

[27]Bengt R. Hoffman, *Luther and the Mystics: A Re-examination of Luther's Spiritual Experience and his Relationship to the Mystics* (Minneapolis: Augsburg Publishing House, 1976) 218.

minimization and neglect of "mystical theology" in Luther's writings. We have been blinded to the mystical and spiritual elements in Luther by our rationalist and intellectualist preclusion of the "paranormal."

> *The thesis of the present study is that Martin Luther's faith consciousness was significantly moulded by mystical experience and that western dependence on rationalism has obscured or eclipsed this mystical light.*[28]

Hoffman argues that the confessional-orthodox interpretations of Luther were unable to deal with Luther's mysticism because of their repristinating rationalism, whereas more recent liberal-neo-orthodox interpretations, under the aegis of natural science presuppositions and historical criticism, have resorted to an empirical frame of reference to communicate Luther's faith to the common sense of "modern man." Hoffman's review and criticisms of the history of Lutheran scholarship's neglect of the mystical in Luther is the first part (128 pages) of his book. The next part (fifty pages) reviews "Luther's Views on God, Man and Salvation." Part three is titled "Luther on the Reality of the Invisible" (thirty pages). Here Hoffman discusses Luther's views of angelic and demonic powers; his personal psychic experiences; occultism, healing deliverance, and life after death. Only in the last chapter does Hoffman treat "Luther and the Mystics" (nineteen pages). In short, the book's title is a misnomer; its concern is not with medieval mysticism but with paralleling Luther to contemporary "parapsychological," "transhuman," charismatic experiences.

> The mystical dimension of faith is the essence of the charismatic renewal. Unbiblical and unspiritual aberrations in this "movement" provide no adequate reason for Christian believers not to take it seriously. Martin Luther's mystical-charismatic consciousness and his practice of the presence is a reminder of the Third Article of the Creed which many of us have intellectualized and institu-tionalized. Luther would no doubt have recognized and greeted with joy the current evidence of the power of the Holy Spirit, both in Protestant and Roman Catholic circles.[29]

From the Evangelical perspective, a historian known for his Anabap-tist studies has published two articles delineating charismatic elements in historic Anabaptism.[30] Kenneth Davis argues that Anabaptist origins are

---

[28]Hoffman, *Luther and the Mystics,* 18. Author's emphasis.

[29]Hoffman, *Luther and the Mystics,* 231f.

[30]Kenneth Davis, "The origins of anabaptism: Ascetic and charismatic elements exemplifying continuity and discontinuity," in Marc Lienhard, ed., *The Origins and Characteristics of Anabaptism* (The Hague: Martinus Nijhoff, 1977) 27-41; and

more accurately to be found in late medieval asceticism than mysticism. Here is the element of continuity between Anabaptism and medieval Christianity. But there is also discontinuity—"the charismatic factor." In his first article Davis gives qualified assent to John J. Yoder's comment " . . . that the major contemporary charismatic movement, Pentecostalism, is in our century the closest parallel to what Anabaptism was in the 16th.' "[31] He goes on to say that "The Anabaptists should be characterized essentially as, apart from their own creativity, a radicalization and Protestantization . . . of the lay-oriented ascetic reform vision of which Erasmus is the principal mediator."[32]

It is of interest to note that in Davis's second article he concludes that:

> Clearly sixteenth-century Anabaptism was a charismatic movement, and while in the larger Radical Reformation there are abundant examples of the extreme heretical-mystical brand . . . the core of Anabaptism from the beginning held firmly to a Tertullian version—moderate, "orthodox," and biblical—which complements the Anabaptists' ascetic emphases on brotherhood, lay participation and holy living.[33]

From the Roman Catholic perspective J. Massyngberde Ford, herself a Catholic charismatic, has suggested an "unconscious" modeling of the two major Catholic charismatic communities upon a theology "not dissimilar to that of the Radical Reformation."

> The fact that Anabaptist, or rather Hutterian, patterns are now significant for the Ann Arbor—South Bend Pentecostals is confirmed by their adoption of the book *The Joyful Community* by B. Zablocki (Maryland, 1971), and their patterning of leadership of community according to the principles found therein. These include a strong and rigid hierarchy to whom absolute obedience is required, a non-professional teaching body which purports to speak directly through the inspiration of the Spirit, a complicated exclusion system, the subordination of women and withdrawal from the world.[34]

"Anabaptism as a Charismatic Movement," *MQR* 53/3 (1979): 219-34. Davis is associate professor of history at Waterloo University; his M.A. thesis was "A Study of the Charismatic Phenomenon: To the End of the 2nd Century" (Wheaton College IL, 1955).

[31]Lienhard, *The Origins and Characteristics of Anabaptism*, 37. The Yoder quotation is from "Marginalia" in *Concern for Christian Renewal*, no. 15 (1967) 78.

[32]Ibid., 41.

[33]Davis, "Anabaptism as a Charismatic Movement," *The Origins and Characteristics of Anabaptism*, 233.

[34]"Neo-Pentecostalism within the Roman Catholic Communion," *Dialog* 13/1 (1974): 45-50, 47. Cf. "Response to Dr. J. Massyngberde Ford: An Interview with Steve Clark," *New Covenant* (April 1978) 14-20.

In the third part of our study we shall see how these elements also run through the Lutheran charismatic community. What is of interest here is that Professor Ford refers to the neo-Pentecostal similarities to the Radical Reformation, and she also refers to other writings influential upon it, including *The Christian Family* by the Lutheran charismatic leader Larry Christenson.

We should not be surprised by the paucity of church-historical studies concerned with studying pentecostalism in light of earlier movements in the church or vice versa.[35] Church historians like other scholars are people of their times and reflect the concerns of their contexts. Even a cursory review of the history of Reformation studies makes clear the role of cultural and theological perspectives in scholarship.[36] At its best, historical research is increasingly sensitive that it functions with its own form of Heisenberg's "indeterminacy principle," in that the observer influences the material under consideration. Insofar as pentecostalism and charismatic movements are attracting more attention from scholars of a variety of disciplines as well as church leaders, we may expect a growing number of studies which attempt to place the current phenomenon in its larger historical context both in terms of broadening our understanding and providing resources for analyzing current relationships. That is, contemporary issues may provide a hermeneutic for understanding past issues in church history just as these same past events may provide insight for the present.

Given the commitments of the persons involved, some of these studies will have a controversial as well as dialogical nature. For example, the Lutheran church historian Scott Hendrix places the charismatic movement "in a longstanding tradition in Christianity which under-

---

[35]Perhaps because of pentecostalism's evident appeal to the early church, there is some interest in parallels or analogies in early church history. Cf. for example, R. Joseph Hoffman, "Meméristai ho Christós? Anti-Enthusiast Polemic from Paul to Augustine," *Studia Theologica* 33 (1979): 149-64; John Koenig, "From Mystery to Ministry: Paul as Interpreter of Charismatic Gifts," *Union Seminary Quarterly Review* 33/3 & 4 (1978): 167-74; Edward Schweizer, "Was ist der Heilige Geist? Eine bibeltheologische Hinführung," *Concilium* 15/10 (1979): 494-98, and others.

[36]Cf. for example, Heinrich Bornkamm, *Luther im Spiegel der deutschen Geistesgeschichte*, 2nd ed. (Göttingen: Vandenhoeck & Ruprecht, 1970); Abraham Friesen, *Reformation and Utopia: The Marxist Interpretation of the Reformation and its Antecedents* (Wiesbaden: Steiner, 1974); Horst Stephan, *Luther in den Wandlungen seiner Kirche* (Berlin: Topelman, 1951), and others.

stands *renewal as restoration of the New Testament* church." As such this is not merely the call for continuing reform of the church but a demand for duplicating the experience of the primitive church which implies that "existing structures are illegitimate insofar as they deviate from the New Testament pattern which serves as normative."[37]

The charismatic Lutheran theologian, Theodore Jungkuntz, was quick to respond that Hendrix may know something about the history of Christian thought, "but he does not have a grasp or even a handle on what is going on in the contemporary charismatic renewal as a whole and in Lutheranism in specific. His thesis can only stand on the basis of carefully selected evidence." Jungkuntz strongly objects to the thesis that "charismatic renewal and restoration ideology necessarily go hand in hand."[38] As we shall see charismatic Lutherans have good reason to dissociate themselves from the sixteenth-century spiritualists who received violent polemical and theological attacks from Luther. In a brief counter-response Hendrix sees no reason to retract his earlier judgment and reaffirms his view that charismatics seek out and make normative extraordinary signs of God's power. "They also appeal to the presence of these phenomena in the Bible as the authority for their views in addition to their own religious experience. This historical judgment was the point of my article. . . . "[39]

One of the reasons that articles like Hendrix's provoke a sharp response from charismatic Lutherans is because they are concerned to show not only that the charismatic movement is not antithetical but even in some cases that it continues elements Luther himself embodied. We have already mentioned in this regard the book by Bengt Hoffman which argues, among other things, that Luther had clairaudial, clairvoyant, and precognitional experiences.[40] Jungkuntz himself argues on the level of more concrete historical theological data that Luther's Smalcald Articles cannot be legitimately used against charismatics but rather support the

---

[37]"Charismatic Renewal: Old Wine in New Skins," *Currents in Theology and Mission,* 4/3 (1977) 158-66, 158, 165. For a typological study of this perspective which does not take into account modern developments, cf. Ronald Knox, *Enthusiasm: A Chapter in the History of Religion* (Oxford, 1950).

[38]"A Response to Scott H. Hendrix's 'Charismatic Renewal: Old Wine in New Skins,'" *Currents in Theology and Mission* 5/1 (1978): 54-57, 54, 57.

[39]"Reply to Jungkuntz," *Currents in Theology and Mission* 5/1 (1978): 58, 60, 59.

[40]Hoffman, "Meméristai ho Christós?," 186-91.

charismatic position.[41] Elsewhere he expresses the concern of Lutheran charismatics to be faithful to the Lutheran Confessions[42] and has given this concern form by publishing *A Lutheran Charismatic Catechism.*[43]

The only full-length study that seeks to analyze the charismatic movement from a Lutheran theological perspective is the recently completed dissertation by Tormod Engelsviken, himself a charismatic Lutheran. The Reverend Engelsviken very graciously shared a copy of his dissertation with me. Although the manuscript arrived following the completion of my study I have attempted to incorporate its contributions wherever possible. Itself a lengthy study (498 pages), it is divided into two major parts. The first part analyzes charismatic experience and doctrine as it has found expression in Norway. This is a valuable contribution not only for its description and analysis of leading Norwegian charismatics but also because it makes available materials which are not accessible to those unable to read Norwegian The second part of the study is an evaluation of charismatic experience and doctrine in light of the Scriptures. The two major parts are about equal in length. Engelsviken shows how the charismatic movement has its historical roots both experientially and doctrinally in the Pentecostal movement.[44] His purpose is "to give an objective account of the *salient features of the Charismatic experience,* regardless of the ecclesial and theological context in which it is found, and also of some representative Norwegian interpretations of the Charismatic experience with the aim of delineating a *common fundamental theology of the Charismatic experience,* also regardless of ecclesial and theological context." He concludes in the first major part of his study that "The unifying factor within the international charismatic movement is therefore not merely a common experience or reality but also a common doctrinal framework."[45] This is an important point to which we shall return in our own third section. Although Engelsviken

---

[41]"Sectarian Consequences of Mistranslation in Luther's Smalcald Articles," *Currents in Theology and Mission* 4/3 (1977): 166-67.

[42]"A Response," *The Cresset* (occasional paper, 2) 1977, 9.

[43]New York: Bread of Life Ministries, 1979. This is being translated into Swedish and will be published by Interskrift Förlags.

[44]Cf. also James H. Smylie, "Testing the Spirits in the American Context. Great Awakenings, Pentecostalism, and the Charismatic Movement," *Interpretation* 33/1 (1979): 32-46.

[45]Engelsviken, *The Gift of the Spirit,* 251.

analyzes the experience and doctrine of Lutheran leaders of the charismatic movement in Norway he does not attempt to do so by comparison to the specific theology of Luther and the Lutheran Confessions, but nevertheless regards this as an urgent and challenging task which he plans to take up in the future.[46] Although I regret not having Engelsviken's study available during the writing stage of my own study I shall try to incorporate it wherever possible. On important points I think Engelsviken's research corroborates my own work, but certainly it should be clear that Engelsviken is not responsible for conclusions which I may make.

The official response of Lutheran churches to the rise of the charismatic movement shares the concern expressed previously—that being "charismatic" and "Lutheran" are not mutually exclusive. "There is no cause for Lutheran pastors or people to suggest either explicitly or implicitly that one cannot be charismatic and remain a Lutheran in good standing."[47] Nevertheless all the statements issuing from Lutheran church bodies voice concern over division, both actual and potential, resulting from the charismatic movement within the churches and also emphasize the traditional Lutheran understanding of the Word and sacraments as *the* means of grace.[48] The most intensive study so far is that of the Theological Study Department of the Bund der Evangelischen Kirchen in the German Democratic Republic.[49] From 1977 to 1979 this study department produced over two hundred typed pages of documentation, analysis, and reports. It is the most thorough church study of the charismatic movement of which I am aware.

All of the statements by the various Lutheran churches refer to Luther and the Confessions as norms for evaluation of the charismatic movements. However the theology of Luther and the Lutheran Confessions are

---

[46]Ibid., 482.

[47]"The Charismatic Movement in the Lutheran Church in America: A Pastoral Perspective" (New York: LCA, 1974) 13.

[48]Cf. the reports of the Lutheran Church-Missouri Synod (USA); "The Charismatic Movement and Lutheran Theology" (1972) and "The Lutheran Church and the Charismatic Movement: Guidelines for Congregations and Pastors" (1977). Brief descriptions and guidelines have been written by the American Lutheran Church, "The American Lutheran Church and Neo-Pentecostalism" (1973) and the Church of Norway, "Factors for the Perception of the Charismatic Movement in Norway" (1979).

[49]"Charismatische Bewegung in der DDR" (Beiträge A3, 1978) and "Kirche und charismatische Erneuerung: Über Chancen und Probleme einer Bewegung in unseren Kirchen" (Beiträge A4, 1979).

presented in these documents without any reference to their original contexts. Thus their appeals for dialogue[50] do not explicitly take into account the original setting of the Lutheran tradition's animus against charismatic movements. Of course, this was not the intention of church statements designed to provide guidelines for pastors and parishes to use in relating to a frequently disturbing "new" phenomenon in their midst. Nevertheless as long as the personal and historical roots of Lutheran-charismatic conflict remain unexplored, stereotypes and prejudices will continue to haunt contemporary efforts toward dialogue both with the Pentecostal churches without and Lutheran charismatics within. Whether the ghosts of prior Lutheran encounters with charismatic-type movements in the Reformation and in Pietism need to be exorcised or resurrected, or a bit of both, remains to be seen. At the very least a study of past tensions in Lutheran tradition should help all of us to better understand the values and problems of our tradition in forming our present identity as Lutherans and/or charismatics. It is to this task that we now turn.

---

[50]In "Kirche und charismatische Erneuerung," 67ff., "dialogical plurality" is seen as the possibility with the most promise to guard the Church against stultification and impoverishment; the dilution of the movement and particularly its exodus into isolation, separation, and total ecclesial inefficacy. The report here refers to the above-cited *Neue transkonfessionelle Bewegungen,* 41f., and H. Meyer, "Transkonfessionelle Bewegungen—Hoffnung oder Gefahr?," *Beiheft zur Okumenischen Rundschau* 32 (1978): 55f.

1

THE REFORMATION
OF THE
SIXTEENTH CENTURY

To sketch the context of the Reformation in a few pages is an impossible task. The embarrassment of the following oversimplification is alleviated only by the conviction that it is necessary for our purposes and that numerous textbooks and monographs by major scholars are readily available for balance and correction.[1] This is a necessary sketch because it is important for our purpose to make clear that Luther and the Reformation did not just suddenly descend from heaven one sunny day in

---

[1]A useful essay which discusses the use of periodization and historical interpretations to make Luther and the Reformation understandable in the present is that by Heiko A. Oberman, "Reformation: Epoche oder Episode," *Archir für Reformationsgeschichte* 68 (1977): 56-111 (hereafter cited as *ARG*). For a discussion of recent historical studies of the Reformation in terms of socialist historiography, cultural history, the history of ideas, and the social and political principles behind the development and spread of Reformation religious forms, cf. the "Prolegomena" chapter of Thomas A. Brady, Jr., *Ruling Class, Regime and Reformation at Strasbourg 1520-1555* (Leiden: E.J. Brill, 1978). Brady is concerned to apply the norms of modern historical criticism to his subject. For recent developments in the social history of the Reformation cf. the report by Thomas A. Brady, Jr., " 'Social History of the Reformation,' 'Sozialgeschichte der Reformation,' A Conference at the Deutsches Historisches Institut, London, May 25-27, 1978," *Sixteenth Century Journal* 10:1 (1979): 89-92 (hereafter cited as *SCJ*). An extensive list of sources would serve no purpose here, thus the following are mentioned as specific resources for this section: A. G. Dickens, *The German Nation and Martin Luther* (London: Arnold, 1974); G. R. Elton, *Reformation Europe 1517-1559* (London: Collins, 1963); Harold J. Grimm, *The Refor-*

October 1517. Here and in the following major sections enough bare bones of historical and social data will be provided to support the contention that religious movements do not arise without intimate connections to the anxieties and aspirations of their times. This is no less true for modern charismatic movements or medieval mystical movements than for the Reformation. By setting aside metahistorical or divine causation as explanations for the rise and progress of the Reformation, Pietism, and Pentecostalism, we are not rejecting the validity of a theology of history. Rather, we would stress that only a historical understanding of these movements could take seriously the incarnation and, by rejecting all quasi-gnostic secret insights into history, remain open to the possibilities of rendering these movements intelligible to those who stand outside of them. At the same time an awareness of historical contexts may reveal prototypical elements operative in, with, and under particular religious orientations. This will remain to be seen in the course of our study and we hasten to add that we do not wish to emphasize continuity at the expense of discontinuity.

If it is possible to express in one word the most characteristic aspect of the social, cultural, economic, political, psychological, and religious context of the late medieval and Reformation era, it is the word *crisis*.

> The most obvious and pervasive factor in our period is the phenomenon of crisis. There exists a consensus on the significance, although not on the exact effects of the Black Death, which reached its highpoint in England around 1349. Preceded by an extended food crisis on the continent, we notice in its wake both a relatively striking acceleration of urbanization and a strikingly rapid expansion of existing urban centers. . . . The deflation of wheat prices and the decline in agrarian self-sufficiency led to a dramatic trek to the cities, which left behind ghost villages and whole ghost areas. . . . The agrarian crisis did not only affect the lower aristocracy and the payroll agrarian workers. It also hit the town communities in thrusting upon them a fast-growing urban proletariat which did not find—and was not granted!—access to the guilds or representation in the city government. The monetary crisis is clearly reflected in the increasing protest against the threat to existing reliable value systems and against the arbitrary manipulation of coinage values.[2]

---

mation Era 1500-1650 (New York/London: Collier-MacMillan [Student's Edition], 1965); Lewis W. Spitz, *The Renaissance and Reformation Movements* (Chicago: Rand McNally, 1971); G. Strauss, ed., *Manifestations of Discontent in Germany on the Eve of the Reformation* (Bloomington IN, 1972). The bibliographies in these works will direct the reader to further literature.

[2]Heiko A. Oberman, "The Shape of Late Medieval Thought: The Birthpangs of the Modern Era," *ARG* 64 (1973): 13-33, 16.

For most people life was grim. As a result of poor diet, repeated outbreaks of the plague, and feudal warfare, life expectancy was not much over forty years, and many men of that age referred to themselves as "old men." The Germans, moreover, stood directly in the line of the advance of the fearful Turks as they pressed up the Danube. A somber mood predominated, perhaps best illustrated in Albrecht Dürer's woodcut of the four grinning horsemen of the Apocalypse riding roughshod over humanity, or in his portrait of the knight in armor accompanied by death and the devil.[3]

In short, the social context of the Reformation was characterized by widespread cultural crisis and social upheaval. Late medieval conceptions and institutions were breaking down along with social relationships under the pressures of economic and technological developments as well as natural causes and the concomitant social changes effected by both. The development of mining technology and metallurgy led to a vastly increased production of silver which among other things contributed to inflation. Those hardest hit were, of course, the people on fixed incomes—as the landowners set about to increase taxes. The peasants' incomes were thereby decreased while at the same time their costs increased, thus opening the series of peasant revolts which culminated in the rebellion of 1524-1525.

The mining industry also fed the weapons industry which, with the development of gunpowder and cannon, found a ready market in the incessant wars of the period. This of course led not only to the obvious results of the suffering and insecurity of war but also to the obsolescence of an entire social class—the imperial knights—whose fighting style was ineffectual with the advent of guns. Many of these people attempted to preserve their accustomed style of living by turning to crime and the exaction of tribute and/or becoming leaders of mercenary soldiers. The unrest of the knights also erupted in a revolt, the Knights' War of 1522-1523.

The rapid increase in industrial production after the mid-fifteenth century and the power of the profit-motive in this period of early capitalism eroded the social and economic security which had been developed by the medieval merchant and craft guilds. These guilds responded to their own crises by becoming increasingly reactionary and monopolistic. Journeymen soon found it difficult to become masters; therefore when they tried to establish their own guilds, they were frequently suppressed and forced by these circumstances to become day

---

[3]Lewis W. Spitz, *The Renaisance and Reformation Movements*, 325.

laborers. The growth of entrepreneurial markets with their transference of goods between cottage industries led to large numbers of workers becoming dependent upon conditions over which they had no control.

> The emergence of a strong and ambitious class of townsmen under the aegis of territorial princes and kings was well under way by 1500. This tendency threatened to disrupt that social stratification which medieval man had considered ordained by God for all eternity. The medieval conception that the clergy constituted the head, the nobility the arms, and the peasants the feet of the medieval body could not long persist in the face of those economic and political changes which were disrupting the medieval way of life. There was no place in this conception for that class which felt no compunctions of conscience about accumulating money by profiting from man's needs and using this wealth to gain social prestige and political power.[4]

The larger political scene was equally unstable. The old three-cornered struggle between the Papacy, France, and the Holy Roman Empire continued unabated even in the face of the Turkish threats to Europe. Within the Holy Roman Empire, the limitations of which were already being acknowledged by the addition of the phrase, "of the German nation," successive Diets enumerated national grievances against the Papacy. These *gravamina,* reiterated from the mid-fifteenth century, included 102 papal abuses at their presentation at the Diet of Worms (1521), the very Diet that condemned Luther.[5] The centuries-old struggle to create a German nationalism was intimately related to anti-papalism.

But the criticisms and questions addressed to the church were far more profound than moral critiques or abuses. The issue was whether human society had its foundation in the sacred. The Papacy was an expression of "the urgent medieval belief that there must be some agency through which the divine law is brought into human order, by which divine law becomes positive legal codes."[6] This perspective which had received its summary in Boniface the VIII's bull, Unam Sanctam (1302) derived political and social consequences from a hierarchy of being rooted in the sacred. "Without the *vera iustitia* of the Church, the Augustinian

---

[4]Harold J. Grimm, *The Reformation Era 1500-1650,* 13.

[5]Cf. A. G. Dickens, *The German Nation and Martin Luther,* 7-8.

[6]Michael Wilks, *The Problem of Sovereignty in the Later Middle Ages* (London: Cambridge University Press, 1963) 163-64; cf. also 469-70.

'Unam Sanctam' tradition holds that the State has to disintegrate, can only become a *latrocinium,* a robber-state—as St. Augustine put it."[7]

The theoretical context of the role of the Papacy in the medieval world may be expressed along the lines of Peter Berger's *The Sacred Canopy.* Berger argues that every human society is involved in an ongoing task of structuring a meaningful world for itself. In the face of the precariousness of personal and social life, society strives to shield itself from chaos, formlessness, meaninglessness, and the terror of the void by structuring a meaning which can deal with the marginal situations of life. Faced by the constant possibility of personal and cultural collapse into anomie, humankind has perpetually grounded social structures in the cosmos and thereby given ontological status to institutions. "Put differently, religion is the audacious attempt to conceive of the universe as being humanly significant."[8]

The aftermath of the Avignonese "captivity of the Church" (1309-1377) confronted the world with the horror of rival popes—each legitimately elected by the same college of cardinals—excommunicating each other. It is this ecclesiastical crisis stemming from the Western Schism and the abortive attempts at solution by the following councils which is "The context in which the unsettling effects of all these crisis factors could have their full impact. . . . The Western Schism . . . called the sacred basis of existence into question to an extent hitherto unknown." ". . . there have been few times in which the awareness of crisis has reached and encompassed all social classes, and pervaded—though admittedly with *Phasenverschiebung*—such extensive areas of Western Europe."[9]

LUTHER AND EXPERIENCE: GERMAN MYSTICISM

It was in this context of crisis, a crisis of the very symbols of security, that Luther struggled with the question of his experience of God. As he was to say later in the face of the "establishment's" attacks on him, "It is through living, indeed through dying and being damned that one becomes a theologian, not through understanding, reading or specula-

---

[7]Oberman, "The Shape of Late Medieval Thought," 27.

[8]Peter Berger, *The Sacred Canopy: Elements of a Sociological Theory of Religion* (New York: Anchor Books, 1969) 28.

[9]Oberman, "The Shape of Late Medieval Thought," 17, 20.

tion."[10] The quest for security in the face of the insecurity of an age in crisis finds its path in an experiential epistemology. Luther was not the first nor the only person of this era for whom the normal tradition and practice of the church as conveyed by "understanding, reading or speculation" failed to bring peace and security to that most crucial crisis area of medieval life—the relationship with God.

Therefore, before we outline the major theological motifs in Luther's thought, we shall construct an overview of late medieval mysticism. The advantage of this procedure is twofold: it allows us to clearly see the initial influence of mysticism upon Luther, an influence which also is important for his later spiritualist opponents; and it helps us to understand that when Luther departs from mystical theology he is not rejecting it out of hand but on the basis of intimate knowledge and theological conviction.

It has been said that "An abstract formula for mysticism is impossible because this phenomenon exists only in its historical appearances. . . ."[11] It is of interest to note that a recent World Council of Churches Consultation on charismatic renewal makes a similar statement: "Nowhere have we said what we essentially understand by 'charismatic renewal.' Is that surprising? The fact is, 'it' must be experienced. A binding definition is not possible—each individual can only define it from his personal perspective."[12] However, it may be said that the mystic does not deny historical revelation or externally change the "letter" but only individually transcends its sense in quest for direct contact with divinity. "Mystical anthropology and reflection on man's union with God made possible direct communication with that Power and Authority to whom pope, council, tradition, and holy book must necessarily cede. Mystical theology, with abundant scriptural proofs, promoted the view that the individual heart and conscience, not traditional institutional structures or historical

---

[10]Operationes in Psalmos (1519-1521). (Weimar: Hermann Böhlau, 1883ff.) 5, 163, 28-29 (hereafter cited as WA vol., page, line).

[11]L. Richter, "Mystik" RGG, 4:1237. "The greatest methodological hindrance is without doubt the fact that the concepts 'mysticism' and 'mystical theology' have varying meanings from author to author." Heiko Oberman, "Simul Gemitus et Raptus: Luther und die Mystik," in Ivar Asheim, Kirche, Mystik, Heiligung und das Natürliche bei Luther (Göttingen: Vandenhoeck und Ruprecht, 1967) 20-59, 21.

[12]"Die Bedeutung der charismatischen Erneuerung für die Kirchen, Bericht einer Konsultation in Bossey (8.-13.3.1980)," Una Sancta 36/1 (1981): 5-10, 5.

writings, was the immediate locus of this Power and Authority."[13] From its beginning the Reformation was accompanied by mysticism operative in persons such as Karlstadt, Müntzer, Schwenckfeld, and others, persons whom Luther labeled *Schwärmer* and recent historians refer to as "radical Reformers" or the "left wing" of the Reformation. One of the ironies of history is that it was Luther who made available to these "spiritualists" the basic medieval mystical writing, the *Theologia Deutsch*.

We have already alluded to the stresses and strains of the late medieval period; it would be a mistake to understand mysticism solely in terms of a response to spiritual and ecclesiastical crisis. There is a valid sense to Tillich's apt expression that mysticism was "scholasticism experienced." Not to mention, of course, the continuity of the contemplative-mystical tradition vividly expressed by the "Father of Western Theology," St. Augustine: "My mind in the flash of a trembling glance came to Absolute Being—That Which Is."[14] Also to be considered is the view that mysticism was a theory of dissent and protest as Ozment expressed it. Or in Gordon Rupp's inimitable style: "The Protestant left was the heir of the medieval underworld, to categories of thought and a vocabulary emerging from late medieval heresies, Waldensianism, the spiritual Franciscans, the German mystics, the modern devotion, the revival of Platonism, a varied vocabulary which pre-existed the Reformation and had its own power and momentum quite apart from Luther and Wittenberg."[15] Nevertheless "the more immediate source of mysticism was the intensification of religious feeling in the fourteenth and fifteenth centuries, a

---

[13]Steven E. Ozment, *Mysticism and Dissent. Religious Ideology and Social Protest in the Sixteenth Century* (New Haven and London: Yale University Press, 1973): 59. Cf. also Spitz, *The Renaissance and Reformation Movements,* 38: "Mysticism is based on the assumption that the ultimate nature of reality or the divine essence may be known by the mystic through immediate apprehension, insight, or intuition. The mode of perception differs from all ordinary sensation and ratiocination, for the mystic experiences union or intercourse with divine being in vision, in trance, or by absorption. Since the experience is unattainable by the natural intellect, it cannot be communicated or analysed by ordinary linguistic tools, and a sense of its nature can best be suggested by symbols. Within the Western Christian tradition all mystics agree that true beatitude consists of union with God and that this union is attained through ecstatic contemplation. The nature of this contemplation is love, and this love is made possible by the life of discipline and order regulated to that end."

[14]*Confessions,* 7:xvii, 23; as quoted in Ray C. Petry, ed., *Late Medieval Mysticism* (London: SCM Press, Ltd., 1957) 18. See also 27ff.

[15]Gordon Rupp, "Word and Spirit in the First Years of the Reformation," *ARG* 49/1 (1958): 13-22, 14.

direct product of the crisis in spirit that accompanied the medieval institutional breakdown and the accelerated pace of historical change."[16]

To Luther the importance of German mysticism, especially the sermons of Tauler and the *Theologia Deutsch,* was its stress upon the priority of God's activity in salvation over human merit.[17] Furthermore he was positively disposed toward this mysticism as a *sapientia experimentalis,* a practical wisdom according to which the person does not speculate theoretically from without about religious reality but rather stands and lives within it.[18]

One of Luther's earliest references to Tauler is in his scholia or commentary on the passage in Romans 8:26: "In the same way the Spirit comes to the aid of our weakness. We do not even know how we ought to pray, but through our inarticulate groans the Spirit himself is pleading for us . . . " (NEB). Here Luther reflects upon the response of God to our prayers which contravenes our conceptions and "renders us capable of receiving His gifts and His works. And we are capable of receiving His works and His counsels only when our own counsels have ceased and our works have stopped and we are made purely passive before God, both with regard to our inner as well as our outward activities." God thus patiently works with us as an artist with new material. "Concerning this patience and endurance of God see Tauler, who has shed more light than others on this matter in the German language."[19]

In a letter to his father-confessor, Staupitz, himself a great influence upon him, Luther wrote: "Now what I have done is that I follow the theology of Tauler and of that book which you recently gave to Christian Düring to print; I teach that men should trust in nothing save in Jesus only, and not in their own prayers, or merits, or works, for we shall not be saved by our exertions but by the mercies of God. . . . "[20]

---

[16]L. W. Spitz, *The Renaissance and Reformation Movements,* 43.

[17]Cf. Bengt Hägglund, "Luther und die Mystik," in Asheim, *Kirche, Mystik, Heiligung,* 84-89, 93ff.

[18]Erwin Iserloh, "Luther und die Mystik," in Asheim, *Kirche, Mystik, Heiligung,* 60-83, 60f. Cf. WA 6, 291, 30; WA 9, 98.

[19]Lectures on Romans. Glosses and Scholia, 1516. LW 25, 365, 368. WA 56, 376, 378. Cf. also WA 9, 102, 17-27; Luther's marginal notes on Tauler's *Sermons* which were perhaps written at the same time.

[20]WA Br. 1, 160, 8. To Staupitz, 31 March 1518. Quoted from the "General Introduction," p. lvi of W. Pauck, ed., *Luther: Lectures on Romans,* Library of Christian Classics, 15 (London: SCM, 1961).

"That book" which Luther mentioned in the letter to Staupitz refers to his edition of *Eyn theologia deutsch* for which he wrote a preface. The first edition, titled "A Spiritually Noble Little Book," was published in 1516 on the basis of an incomplete manuscript. In June 1518 Luther published the complete work after having found a complete manuscript. This he titled "A German Theology." In his 1518 Preface he praises the divine wisdom expressed in the text's "simple German language." "...no book except the Bible and St. Augustine has come to my attention from which I have learned more about God, Christ, man, and all things.... It is obvious that such matters as are contained in this book have not been discussed in our universities for a long time, with the result that the Holy Word of God has not only been laid under the bench but has almost been destroyed by dust and filth." Luther concludes by saying, "Let anyone who wishes read this little book, and then let him say whether theology is original with us or ancient, for this book is certainly not new."[21] While this latter statement "was made in the context of a sustained effort *to blunt the charge of innovation*"[22] against a reform movement now spread far beyond the confines of the Wittenberg theology faculty, it should be clear that Luther agreed with various themes in Tauler and the German Theology. These mystical writings confirmed Luther's stress on the hidden activity of God which gives the Christian life "bitterness" to the selfish human nature and reason which try to flee suffering. They deepened Luther's understanding of faith in terms of passive resignation and conversion from self-reliance to trust in the incarnate and crucified Lord. On the other hand their ontological anthropology with its call for the annihilation of "creatureliness" and the soteriological quest for "deification" are rejected by Luther.[23]

Although we cannot pursue in depth the relationship of Luther to late medieval mysticism it is nevertheless possible to make some concluding observations. First of all this is a manifestly complex field of inquiry with such a diversity of definitions, sources, and chronological breadth that pursuit of even the methodological issues involved in a thorough study is

---

[21]Preface to the complete edition of *A German Theology*, 1518. LW 31, 75-76. WA 1, 378f.

[22]Ozment, *Mysticism and Dissent*, 20.

[23]Cf. Ozment, *Mysticism and Dissent*, 21-24; Jared Wicks, *Man Yearning for Grace. Luther's Early Spiritual Teaching* (Wiesbaden: Steiner, 1969) 143-52, 357n. 71.

beyond the scope of our purpose.[24] We have attempted to minimize this problem by limiting our references to Tauler and the German Theology—the sources Luther himself explicitly refers to in his formative period.[25]

Secondly, on the basis of contemporary research it is clear that Luther's relationship to the mystics was both positive and negative; as Oberman says, this was a "sic et non" dimension.[26] From 1516 on Luther rejected the speculative and ascent-oriented mysticism typical of the Dionysian school. On the other hand he affirmed Roman mysticism's emphasis upon the earthly Christ and the place of experience in faith. The German development was most amenable to Luther's own development in its understanding of *Anfechtungen* and acceptance of God's judgment upon the sinner to the point of the *resignatio ad infernum*. The mystical language of Tauler, for example, provided a vehicle for expressing Luther's understanding "the destruction of human self-righteousness and the establishment upon this of what is *extra nos in Christo* as the experiential movement away from all self-concern and inner complacency (*complacentia interior*) toward the grace of Christ."[27]

Since this "extra nos" dimension of Luther's theology will exercise a critical function in Luther's later conflicts with the Schwärmer,[28] it is pertinent to emphasize here its connection to Word and faith. Luther transferred the mystical function of ecstatic love (*amor extatiens*) to faith using the notion of being outside or beyond oneself (*extra se*) to characterize justification by faith. In oneself the person is nothing but a sinner, but outside oneself in faith in Christ the person is at the same time

---

[24]For an introduction to this problem cf. Oberman, "Simul Gemitus et Raptus," 21ff.

[25]For a list of Luther's positive references to Tauler over the years 1515-1544, cf. Bernd Moeller, "Tauler und Luther," in *La mystique Rhénane: Colloque de Strasbourg, 16-19 mai 1961* (Paris, 1963) 157-68, 158. For a wider analysis one can begin with the studies of Erich Vogelsang, "Luther und die Mystik," *Luther Jahrbuch* 19 (1937): 32-54, and "Die unio mystica bei Luther," *ARG* 35 (1935): 63-80. For a review of more recent literature cf. Karl-Heinz zur Mühlen, *Nos Extra Nos. Luthers Theologie Zwischen Mystik und Scholastik* (Tübingen: J.C.B. Mohr, 1972).

[26]Oberman, "Simul Gemitus et Raptus," 24ff.

[27]Zur Mühlen, *Nos Extra Nos. Luthers Theologie,* 94f. For the significance of mysticism for the formulation of the formula *extra nos* cf. 101-16. Cf. also Oswald Bayer, *Promissio: Geschichte der reformatorischen Wende in Luthers Theologie* (Göttingen: Vandenhoeck und Ruprecht, 1971) 57ff., 295f.

[28]Cf. Bayer, *Promissio,* 59.

righteous. For Luther this moving outside oneself is not a silent interior event but rather occurs in the knowledge of faith in which the person's being is disclosed before God (*coram Deo*) by the Word. Thus the mystic *extra nos* is a key to the correct understanding of the forensic understanding of Luther's doctrine of justification.[29]

> ... a Christian lives not in himself, but in Christ and in his neighbor. Otherwise he is not a Christian. He lives in Christ through faith, in his neighbor through love. By faith he is caught up beyond himself into God. By love he descends beneath himself into his neighbor. Yet he always remains in God and in his love, as Christ says in John 1. . . ."[30]

The Word is central to Luther's theology because God is so hidden in the cross of Christ that even the mystical way of moving in God from outside to within (*ab extra ad intra in deum*) may not attain God. God is revealed nowhere but in his Word which simultaneously is judgment and promise. This Word unmasks the person as sinner and at the same time transfers the person outside the self into God through faith in the promise.[31]

> For where there is the Word of the promising God, there must necessarily be the faith of the accepting man. It is plain therefore, that the beginning of our salvation is a faith which clings to the Word of the promising God, who, without any effort on our part, in free and unmerited mercy takes the initiative and offers us the Word of his promise.[32]

Third, in concluding this section, we should be aware that Luther's "sic et non" stance to the mystics and his creative use of the concepts of German mysticism to develop his theology of the Word[33] precludes apologetic usage of selected Luther statements to support current interest in charismatic experience and/or the "mystical-charismatic consciousness" of Luther himself.[34] In a recent study of the marginal notations in

---

[29]Zur Mühlen, *Nos Extra Nos. Luthers Theologie,* 114.

[30]The Freedom of a Christian, 1520. LW 31, 371; cf. also 351. WA 7, 38, 6ff.

[31]Zur Mühlen, *Nos Extra Nos. Luthers Theologie,* 203.

[32]The Babylonian Captivity of the Church, 1520. LW 36, 39.

[33]O. Scheel, "Taulers Mystik und Luthers reformatorische Entdeckung," in *Festg. J.F. Kaftan* (Tübingen, 1920) 298-318; 316 claims that Luther's conception of the righteousness of God cannot be attributed to Tauler but that Luther "creatively misunderstood" Tauler's mysticism in this regard. Reference in Zur Mühlen, *Nos Extra Nos. Luthers Theologie,* 96, nr. 16. For alternative view cf. Oberman, "Simul Gemitus et Raptus," 25.

[34]Bengt Hoffman, *Luther and the Mystics: A Re-examination of Luther's Spiritual Experience and his Relationship to the Mystics* (Minneapolis: Augsburg Publishing House, 1976) 232.

Luther's edition of the "German Theology," Martin Brecht states that the author of the notations was neither a mystic nor a spiritualist in spite of the repeated introduction of "Spiritual" concepts. Humility and resignation (*Gelassenheit*) are essentially not human virtues but rather Christian attitudes in keeping with God's justifying action.[35] At the same time we are aware that the late medieval "democratization" of mysticism[36] influenced the development of piety. "In any case the quintessential which Luther understood from the 'German Theology' is certainly not mystical: '. . . the person shall rely upon nothing other than Jesus Christ alone, not upon his prayers, merit or works. For we are not saved by our strivings but rather by God's mercy.' "[37]

LUTHER'S THEOLOGICAL MOTIF: JUSTIFICATION

We are not saved by our own strivings but by God's mercy! The story of Luther's struggle to find a merciful God is too well-known to be reviewed here. But because the theological motifs which developed out of that struggle articulated both his own new-found certainty of salvation and his later opposition to spiritualist contemporaries, they merit a systematic overview.[38]

Luther entered the Augustinian Eremite cloister in Erfurt in 1505 in order to resolve the crisis of his life—the desire for a right, personal relationship to God. It was not long before the monastic regimen of introspection profoundly deepened this crisis. The pastoral care of his superiors directed him to the sacrament of penance which was designed to mediate God's assistance and solace to sinners. Even though his turn to confession and penance bordered on the obsessive,[39] certainty of forgiveness continued to elude him. He had a guilty and terrified conscience which to him was hell itself.

---

[35]"Randbemerkungen in Luthers Ausgaben der 'Deutsche Theologie,' " *Luther Jahrbuch* 47 (1980): 10-32, 32. Brecht argues for Luther's authorship of these notes, cf. 27-29.

[36]Heiko Oberman, *The Harvest of Medieval Theology* (Cambridge MA: Harvard University Press, 1963) 341ff. and Oberman, "Simul Gemitus et Raptus," 38f.

[37]Oberman, "Simul Gemitus et Raptus," 39f. Cf. WA Br. 1, 160, 10-12.

[38]For Luther's own brief synopsis of theology cf. his Preface to the Epistle of St. Paul to the Romans, 1546 (1522), LW 35, 365-80. WA DB 7, 3-27.

[39]One of his confessors remarked to him: "Martin, God is not angry with you, you are angry with God." Cf. Gordon Rupp, *The Righteousness of God. Luther Studies* (London: Hodder and Stoughton, 1953) 117.

> ... I learned from my own experience in the monastery about myself and about others. I saw many who tried with great effort and the best of intentions to do everything possible to appease their consciences. . . . And yet the more they labored, the greater their terrors became.
>
> When I was a monk, I made a great effort to live according to the requirements of the monastic rule. I made a practice of confessing and reciting all my sins, but always with prior contrition; I went to confession frequently, and I performed the assigned penance faithfully. Nevertheless, *my conscience could never achieve certainty but was always in doubt* and said: "You have not done this correctly. You were not contrite enough. You omitted this in your confession."[40]

Numerous other examples of Luther's spiritual conflict and struggle for certainty could be selected from his writings. As Gordon Rupp says: "That Luther underwent acute spiritual conflict as a monk is a fact more solidly attested in his writings than any other single fact of his career."[41] Given the spiritual struggles of Luther, it is surprising that more attention has not been given to him by modern Pentecostals and charismatics. This is probably due mainly to the foreshortened historical consciousness of the present.

The ecclesial theory and praxis of Luther's time was unable to resolve his anxiety; in fact it was this theology and pastoral care that was the source and exacerbation of the anxiety of Luther and others. Without a grasp of the late medieval theological and penitential system it is difficult to understand the relief, liberation, and joy Luther experienced in his rediscovery of the Pauline theology of justification by faith alone.[42]

We can avoid exploring all the nuances and theological schools behind late medieval ecclesial theory and practice by framing Luther's context with the questions of where and how fellowship with God may occur. Put quite simply, the medieval answers to these questions stated that fellowship with God occurred on God's level and thereby the sinner must somehow ascend to God. As we shall see, Luther turned these

---

[40]Lectures on Galatians, 1535. LW 27, 13 WA 40², 14f. (my emphasis). Cf. also LW 27, 73. WA 40², 91f.; WA 10³, 192, 15; Rupp, *The Righteousness of God*, ch. 5: "The Bruised Conscience," 102ff.

[41]Rupp, *The Righteousness of God,* 102.

[42]The words of the Jesuit Luther scholar, Jared Wicks, are of interest here: " . . . the Catholic scholar probably has a sense for Luther's theological and ecclesial milieu which his Protestant colleague gains only with great effort. The Catholic can grasp more easily the mentality of the men who posed the momentous questions we find Luther laboring to answer," *Man Yearning for Grace*, vii.

answers upside down, claiming that fellowship with God occurred on the human level through God's descent to us.

The dominant architect of the theological perspective throughout the Middle Ages was St. Augustine, whose doctrine of charity (*caritas*) became the heart of medieval Christianity. Charity is love directed toward God. Because Augustine understood love in fundamental terms of seeking the good, he could describe both the ascent to God and descent in sin in terms of love.[43] Thus in his famous definition of the two cities, the heavenly and the earthly, Augustine says:

> . . . two cities have been formed by two loves: the earthly by the love of self, even to the contempt of God: the heavenly by the love of God, even to the contempt of self.[44]

The personal and cultural complexities of Augustine's struggles with Cicero, Manichaean dualism, Neoplatonic philosophy, and the Christian faith cannot be outlined here, but at the risk of oversimplification we may describe his theology in terms of ascent to God. He viewed being in terms of a hierarchy, the apex of which is God; the highest good being itself. This metaphysic conceives of God as the eternal, absolute, immutable being; all beings below God are relative, temporal, transient, and incomplete. He begins his autobiography with the confession: "Thou makest us for Thyself, and our heart is restless, until it repose in Thee."[45] Thus in seeking God we are seeking our ultimate good, but in turning toward the creation—anything less than God—we are seeking destruction. This is expressed in his definition of sin as being "curved or directed toward the inferior" (*curvatus ad terra*).[46] This theology of ascent is graphically expressed in the image of the traveler journeying to his or her homeland. The world may be used (*uti*) as a ship aids the traveler—as an aid on the way of love (*caritas*) up to God. But if we enjoy (*frui*) the voyage, then that love (*cupiditas*) drives downward, away from God, to the earth.[47] The earthly city then is a foreign land; here we are pilgrims, travelers on our

---

[43]Cf. the exposition of Augustine by Anders Nygren in his classic study of the Christian idea of love, *Agape and Eros* (Philadelphia: Westminster, 1953).

[44]Augustine, *De civitate Dei*, PL 41, 436 (Book 14, ch. 28). English translation from *The City of God* (New York: Modern Library, 1950) 477.

[45]St. Augustine, *Confessionum*, PL 32, 661 (Book 1).

[46]Luther also speaks of sin in terms of *curvatus* but it is being turned in upon oneself (*incurvatus in se*) not turned toward the world of the senses.

[47]St. Augustine, *De doctrina Christiana*, PL 34, 20-21 (Book 1, ch. 4).

way to the heavenly city, our homeland. Here, in capsule form, are the great medieval themes of pilgrimage, renunciation, alienation, and asceticism incorporated into the heart of Christian theology, love.[48]

This Augustinian theology of ascent found expression, albeit with variations upon the theme, in medieval mysticism and scholasticism. What was common to the various theologians of Luther's context was an order of salvation (*ordo salutis*) which placed the burden of proof for the relationship with God upon the person. Certainly Luther was initially attracted by Augustine's emphasis upon the grace of God which renews and supports the sinner's *caritas,* but Luther soon came to realize that this theology was oriented to a process of achieving holiness and fellowship with God. To Augustine the person was always "partly righteous and partly sinner" while striving for inner renewal and obedience to the Christ *in me, in nobis.* The impact of Augustine's anti-Pelagian writings was not enough to keep Luther within the Augustinian theological orbit.[49] So Luther says, "See then how great a darkness is in the books of the Fathers about faith! . . . Augustine writes nothing special about faith, except when he disputes against the Pelagians. They woke Augustine up and made him into a man."[50]

We have already referred to Luther's attraction to German mystical theology with its experiential dimension of faith. However in terms of a theological understanding of justification, mysticism also was marked by the motif of ascent to God. The mystical order of salvation presupposed

---

[48]Cf. David Herlihy, "Alienation in Medieval Culture and Society," in Frank Johnson, ed., *Alienation: Concept, Term and Meanings* (New York and London: Seminar Press, 1973) 125-41; and G. Ladner, "Homo Viator: Medieval Ideas on Alienation and Order," *Speculum* 42/2 (1967): 233-59.

[49]On Luther's relationship to Augustine cf. Leif Grane, *Modus Loquendi Theologicus: Luthers Kampf um die Erneuerung der Theologie 1515-1518* (Leiden: Brill, 1975) 23-24, 26; and Bernhard Lohse, "Die Bedeutung Augustins für den jungen Luther," *Kerygma und Dogma* 11 (1965): 116-35.

[50]WA Tr 4, 55-56: no. 3984. Re. his exegesis of Galatians 2:16 and the distinction between justification by faith and by the works of the law, Luther remarked: " . . . because this passage seems absurd to those who have not yet become accustomed to Paul's theology, and because even Saint Jerome wearies himself no end trying to understand this, we shall expand the comments we began to make about the traditions of the fathers. Among the extant authors, I fail to find anyone except Augustine alone who treats this thought in a satisfactory manner; and even he is not satisfactory everywhere. But where he opposes the Pelagians, the enemies of God's grace, he will make Paul easy and clear for you." Lectures on Galatians, 1519. LW 27, 219/ WA 2, 489, 14-20.

"an inalienable and irrepressible 'spark of the will and reason' (*synteresis voluntatis et rationis*) or 'ground of the soul' *(Seelengrund)*—an indestructible orientation to God, which one can speak of simply as the direction of the heart or the testimony of conscience. . . . It is a receptacle for more intimate communications from God than those which the eyes and ears behold in the sermons, sacraments, ceremonies and writings of the Church."[51] This "spark" within the soul is an unquenchable thirst for God.[52] How this thirst is quenched is by the sinner's turning away from everything which is not God through self-resignation (*Gelassenheit*) and will-lessness *(willeloskeit.)*[53] Here, too, there is the process which is designed to diminish sinfulness and increase righteousness.[54] Thus in spite of the role of grace in creating the sinner's receptivity for God, the burden of proof remains on the sinner to "achieve" resignation and self-condemnation. "Even in the subtle mystical form of passive resignation—a 'doing' which is a 'doing nothing'—this is still allied to that semi-Pelagian *facere quod in se est* which Luther overcame theologically in his first lectures on the Psalms (1513-1516) and attacked explicitly in writings against the nominalists in 1516-1517."[55]

Facere quod in se est—to do what is in you—here is the scholastic formulation which most sharply expresses the responsibility of the sinner for the ascent to God. By doing one's very best—all that is within the person's natural power (*ex puris naturalibus*)—it is possible to love God above all things and thereby earn (*meritum de congruo*) the infusion of first grace. Here the *synteris* concept has an ethical rather than a mystical focus. The sinner, longing for salvation, turns toward God through the performance of good works and thereby receives grace necessary for "full merit" (*meritum de condigno*)—the infusion of first grace.[56] The sinner, longing for salvation, turns toward God through the performance of good works and thereby receives the grace necessary for

---

[51]Ozment, *Mysticism and Dissent,* 3; cf. also 5-9.

[52]Cf. *Die Predigten Taulers,* Ferdinand Vetter, ed., (Berlin: Weidemann, 1910) 137, 1-5.

[53]Vetter, *Die Predigten Taulers,* 138, 28ff.; 348, 27ff.; 8-11; 21.

[54]Ozment, "*Homo Viator:* Luther and Late Medieval Theology" in Ozment, ed., *The Reformation in Medieval Perspective* (Chicago: Quadrangle Books, 1971) 145, 149.

[55]Ozment, *Mysticism and Dissent,* 24; and Ozment, *Homo Spiritualis: A Comparative Study of the Anthropology of Johannes Tauler, Jean Gerson and Martin Luther (1509-16)* (Leiden: Brill, 1969) 159ff.

"full merit" (*meritum de condigno*) and divine acceptation. The doctrine that God does not withhold grace from those who do their very best (*facientibus quod in se est Deus non denegat gratiam*) developed in a pastoral climate the intention of which was to provide assurance and security for the anxious sinner.[57] In fact however, the effect upon many of the medieval penitential systems was greater insecurity. In spite of the promise that God gives so much for so little, how do I know the little I do is enough? How do I know if I have done my very best? The absolute demand of God is relativized to correlate with human ability, but in this process the sinner is thrown back upon him or herself. No matter how much you do and how well you do it, the tormenting question remains: is this my very best? Thus Luther recalls that as a monk "My conscience could never achieve certainty but was always in doubt and said: 'You have not done this correctly. You were not contrite enough. . . . ' " Human efforts could not stand before the righteousness of God. In this context the gospel could only appear as bad news.

Luther's breakthrough to a new understanding of the righteousness of God was the discovery that this righteousness is a gift not a demand.

> Though I lived as a monk with reproach, I felt that I was a sinner before God with an extremely disturbed conscience. I could not believe that he was placated by my satisfaction. I did not love, yes, I hated the righteous God who punishes sinners, and secretly, if not blasphemously, certainly murmuring greatly, I was angry with God. . . . At last, by the mercy of God, meditating day and night, I gave heed to the context of the words, namely, "In it the righteousness of God is revealed, as it is written, 'He who through faith is righteous shall live.' " There I began to understand that the righteousness of God is that by which the righteous lives by a gift of God, namely by faith. And this is the meaning: the righteousness of God is . . . the passive righteousness with which merciful God justifies us by faith. . . . Here I felt that I was altogether born again and had entered paradise itself through open gates.[58]

Here the burden of righteousness is shifted from the person to God:

> . . . this most excellent righteousness, the righteousness of faith, which God imputes to us through Christ without works, is neither political nor ceremonial nor legal nor works-righteousness but is quite the opposite; it is merely a passive righteousness, while all the others, listed above, are active. For here we

---

[56]Cf. Heiko Oberman, *The Harvest Of Medieval Theology*, 459-76: "A Nominalist Glossary."

[57]Heiko Oberman, ed., *Forerunners of the Reformation* (New York: Holt, Rinehart & Winston, 1966) 123-40, 129.

[58]Preface to the Complete Edition of Luther's Latin Writings, 1545, LW 34, 336f.

work nothing, render nothing to God; we only receive and permit someone else to work in us, namely, God. Therefore it is appropriate to call the righteousness of faith or Christian righteousness "passive."[59]

Justification is not contingent upon an *inner* change in the sinner, no matter how stimulated by the grace of God, but rather justification occurs *outside* the sinner, that the situation of the sinner before God (*coram Deo*) is changed.[60] "In short, the term 'to be justified' means that a man is considered righteous."[61]

God does not want to redeem us through our own, but through external, righteousness and wisdom; not through one that comes from us and grows in us, but through one that comes to us from outside; not through one that originates here on earth, but through one that comes from heaven. Therefore, we must be taught a righteousness that comes completely from the outside and is foreign.[62]

This is succinctly expressed in Luther's marginal gloss on Romans 2:13: " 'To be righteous before God' is the same as 'to be justified in the presence of God.' A man is not considered righteous by God because he is righteous; but because he is considered righteous by God, therefore he is righteous. . . . "[63]

The emphasis upon God's descent to and acceptance of the sinner by grace alone is vividly expressed by Luther's images of the marriage between Christ and the sinner and the last will and testament of God. In his 1520 tract, "The Freedom of A Christian," Luther describes the benefit of faith as the union of the soul with Christ as a bride is united with her bridegroom. But unlike the medieval use of this image wherein the bride is purified for this union, Luther depicts the bride as a "poor wicked harlot."

Now let faith come between them and sins, death, and damnation will be Christ's, while grace, life, and salvation will be the soul's; for if Christ is a bridegroom, he must take upon himself the things which are his bride's and bestow upon her the things that are his.[64]

---

[59]Lectures on Galatians, 1535. LW 26, 4-5. WA 40¹, 41, 15-21.

[60]For a concise discussion of this point cf. Gerhard Ebeling, *Luther: Einführung in sein Denken* (Tübingen: J.C.B. Mohr, 1964) 175f.

[61]Disputation Concerning Justification, 1536. LW 34, 167. WA 39¹, 98, 13-14.

[62]Lectures on Romans, 1516. LW 25, 136. WA 56, 158, 10.

[63]Ibid., LW 25, 19. WA 56, 22, 24.

[64]The Freedom of a Christian, 1520. LW 31, 351. WA 7, 55, 26; 55, 1ff.

In Luther's German translation of this tract he calls this a "joyous exchange" (*fröhlich Wechsel*).[65]

Justification is a change *extra nos,* outside of us, of our situation before God; this is also expressed by Luther's discussion of inheritance rights and the certainty which a will provides the heir. Luther interpreted Hebrews 9:17 as the new testament (a new will) in Christ already given as "the forgiveness of sins and eternal life."[66] "What for medieval theology was future and belonged only to the realm of hope and love, Luther regards a reality in the present. Faith is not of one's own doing or of one's own nature, yet it is really one's own possession."[67]

> A testament, as everyone knows, is a promise made by one about to die, in which he designates his bequest and appoints his heirs. A testament, therefore, involves, first, the death of the testator, and second, the promise of an inheritance and the naming of the heir. Thus Paul discusses at length the nature of a testament in Rom. 4, Gal. 3 and 4, and Heb. 9. We see the same thing clearly also in these words of Christ. Christ testifies concerning his death when he says: "This is my body, which is given, this is my blood, which is poured out" (Luke 22:19-20). He names and designates the heirs when he says "For you (Luke 22: 19-20; 1 Cor. 11:24) and for many" (Matt. 26:28; Mark 14:24), that is, for those who accept and believe the promise of the testator. For here is a faith that makes men heirs, as we shall see.[68]

> Let someone else pray, fast, go to confession, prepare himself for mass and the sacrament as he chooses. You do the same, but remember that this is all pure foolishness and self-deception, if you do not set before you the words of the testament and arouse yourself to believe and desire them. You would have to spend a long time polishing your shoes, preening and primping to attain an inheritance, if you had no letter and seal with which you could prove your right to it. But if you have a letter and seal, and believe, desire, and seek it, it must be given to you, even though you were scaly, scabby, stinking and most filthy.[69]

These images of the "joyous exchange" and God's testament clearly illustrate Luther's understanding of how radical is God's justification of the sinner. There is nothing which the sinner can bring to God in order to attain forgiveness . . . except his or her sin! It is only the ungodly, only the

---

[65]Von der Freiheit eines Christenmenschen, 1520. WA 7, 25, 34.

[66]WA 57³, 212, 4-7.

[67]Kenneth Hagen, *A Theology of Testament in the Young Luther. The Lectures on Hebrews* (Leiden: Brill, 1974) 82.

[68]The Babylonian Captivity of the Church, 1520. LW 36, 38. WA 6, 513, 22-514, 10.

[69]*A Treatise on the New Testament,* 1520. LW 35, 88. WA 6, 361, 3-7. Cf. also, Lectures on Galatians, 1519. LW 27, 268. WA 2, 518-21.

sinner, who is acceptable to God. Paradoxically, to acknowledge sin is to justify God and thereby oneself.[70]

The good news is the unconditional promise of the gospel. This is the origin of religious ecstasy for Luther, the unconditional promise of God grasped by faith. Thus, while Luther can utilize mystical terminology about religious experience, the crucial point of distinction between him and his tradition is that he emphasizes the priority of faith over love. For Luther religious ecstasy has its origin not in *synderesis,* nor in ascetic discipline, nor in doing what lies within one, but rather in faith alone. Religious ecstasy is not based on ascent to God, nor like being known by like, but to the contrary, on the promise of God to real sinners.

The significance of Luther's theology for contemporary dialogue with Pentecostal and charismatic theologies is precisely in his linking of justification and faith. Union with Christ in faith is the basis for the "joyous exchange" of sin for righteousness. This is the foundation rather than the goal of Christian life. Rapture, ecstasy, and the depths of religious experience are not excluded but are expressions of faith, not love; the descent of God to the sinner, not the ascent of the sinner to God. Thus "Religious ecstasy is not merely affective for Luther; it is cognitive. But the cognition is granted to faith and is mediated by the Word of God. The believer suddenly perceives that what God says is true, though reason and sense may contradict it, and trusts that Word rather than his own resources or the aid of people who stand around him. . . . Faith elevates and exalts the self *coram Deo.* What earlier mystics and teachers, including Staupitz, had attributed to divine love is now attributed by Luther to faith."[71]

It cannot be overemphasized that the foundation of the relationship with God is not religious experience but the Word. To the person terrified by sin and plagued by doubts, Luther says:

> You are not to be conscious of having righteousness; you are to believe it. And unless you believe that you are righteous, you insult and blaspheme Christ, who has cleansed you by the washing of water with the Word (Eph. 5:26) and who in His death on the cross condemned and killed sin and death, so that through Him

---

[70]Cf. for example the Dictata super Psalterium, 1513-1516. WA 3, 298, 6ff.; 291, 26-28; 55², 24, 6-12; 33, 1-4. "This stress on being a real sinner and on justifying God is an accent which one finds first in Staupitz, and there is every reason to think that Luther takes these themes over from him. . . ." David Steinmetz, "Religious Ecstasy in Staupitz and the Young Luther," *SCJ* 11:1 (1980): 23-27, 34.

[71]Steinmetz, "Religious Ecstasy," 35.

you might obtain eternal righteousness and life. You cannot deny this, unless you want to be obviously wicked, blasphemous, and contemptuous of God, of all the divine promises, of Christ, and of all His benefits. Then you cannot deny either that you are righteous.

Let us learn, therefore, that amid great and horrible terrors, when the conscience feels nothing but sin and supposes that God is wrathful and Christ is hostile, we must not consult the consciousness of our own heart. No, then we must consult the Word of God. . . .[72]

Thus Luther used the mystical terminology available to him but redefined it in light of his understanding of justification by faith. "The truly spiritual person, as Luther points out in his marginal notes on John Tauler (1516), is the person who relies on faith. That is a theological shift of great importance in the history of Western Christianity."[73]

ANTHROPOLOGY

The radical understanding of justification described above brings with it a radical understanding of the person *coram Deo*. To proclaim that justification occurs *extra nos* (outside of us) reflects Luther's mystical heritage. But once again we wish to emphasize that Luther is not repeating but rather redefining and co-opting this heritage. The union with God is not the raising of like to like by love but rather the acceptance by faith of God's judgment upon the unlike. There is therefore no avenue of access to God other than faith. Here Luther departs from all anthropologies which divide the person whether it be body and soul; body, soul, and spirit; flesh and spirit; inner and outer. There is no special human faculty, however defined, which sufficiently "like" God, will enable the person to ascend to union with God.[74]

For Luther, the person is always the whole person. He could continue to use traditional terminology, but once again he has redefined and co-opted it. Thus the distinction between "flesh" and "spirit" is no longer dualistic and anthropological but now biblical and theological. The terms are not used to differentiate parts of the person but the person's relationship with God. Both terms, "flesh" and "spirit," refer to the *whole person*

---

[72]Lecture on Galatians, 1535. LW 27, 26f. WA 40², 32f.

[73]Steinmetz, "Religious Ecstasy," 37.

[74]Cf. Zur Mühlen, *Nos Extra Nos. Luthers Theologie*, 273ff. Scholasticism defined *synteresis* as a "natural inclination," "an inextinguishable spark of reason," "an inborn habit," "a power tending naturally to the good."

as he or she relates to God. "The cause of their error is that... they make a metaphysical distinction between flesh and spirit as though these were two substances; however, it is the total man that is flesh and spirit, spirit insofar as he loves the law of God and flesh insofar as he hates the law of God."[75]

There is, therefore, no "higher power" or intrinsic capacity of the person which can warrant God's relationship. Indeed, we humans are characterized by the ability to distort the best in us. "... wisdom is not of itself evil, nor is the law to be evaded; but without the theology of the cross man misuses the best in the worst manner."[76] The whole person is a sinner not just some "lower" portion of him. "There is simply nothing in us that is not sinful."[77] Sin is not merely being curved away from God toward inferior things, *curvatus ad terrenum* as Augustine defined it. Sin is being curved in upon the self, *incurvatus in se*.[78] Sin is the egocentric compulsion of the person to assert his own righteousness against God— the refusal to allow God to be God. This is succinctly stated in the Disputation Against Scholastic Theology (1517):

4. It is therefore true that man, being a bad tree, can only will and do evil (cf. Mt. 7:17-18).

13. It is absurd to conclude that erring man can love the creature above all things, therefore also God.

16. One ought rather to conclude: since erring man is able to love the creature it is impossible for him to love God.

17. Man is by nature unable to want God to be God. Indeed, he himself wants to be God, and does not want God to be God.[79]

In Luther's view sin is so radical that only God's gracious imputation of Christ's righteousness can overcome it. "This is a peculiar righteousness: it is strange indeed that we are called to be righteous or to possess a righteousness which is in us but is entirely outside us in Christ and yet becomes our own, as though we ourselves had achieved and earned it."[80] It is the sinner's willingness to accept God's judgment which enables him to live as righteous in spite of sin.

---

[75] WA 2, 415, 6-10.

[76] Heidelberg Disputation, 1518. LW 31, 41; thesis number 24.

[77] WA 40², 322, 6-11 (Psalm 51, 1532; LW 12, 307).

[78] Lectures on Romans, 1515-1516. LW 25, 222. WA 56, 237.

[79] LW 31, 9ff.

[80] Sermons on the Gospel of St. John, 1537-1538, LW 24, 347; WA 46, 44, 34-38.

By "letting God be God" the sinner is allowed to be what he was intended to be—human. The sinner is not called to deny his or her humanity and seek "likeness" (*similitudo*) with God. Rather, the forgiveness of sins occurs in the midst of human life. The Christian's position before God, therefore, is at one and the same time righteous and sinful, *simul justus et peccator*. The Christian ". . . is at the same time both a sinner and a righteous man; a sinner in fact, but a righteous man by the sure imputation and promise of God that He will continue to deliver him from sin until He has completely cured him. And thus he is entirely healthy in hope, but in fact he is still a sinner. . . . "[81]

The importance of this perspective for Luther's relationship to both the Augustinian tradition and his contemporary spiritualist opponents is that it precludes a progressive sanctification that attributes a growth in righteousness *coram Deo* to the Christian.

LAW AND GOSPEL

The theological motif which related the perspectives on justification and the whole person (*simul iustus et peccator*) is the dialectic of law and gospel. Here too Luther moved beyond his received tradition in a manner that had a significant bearing upon his theological relationship to the spiritualists of his day. Luther replaced the traditional antithesis of "spirit and letter" by the dialectic of "law and gospel."

The dialectical distinction of law and gospel is the essential nerve of theological thinking; it is that which makes a theologian a theologian: "Nearly the entire Scripture and the knowledge of all theology depends upon the correct understanding of law and gospel."[82] "The person who knows how to correctly distinguish the gospel from the law may thank God and know that he is a theologian."[83] "You often already have heard that there is no better way to hand on and preserve pure doctrine than that we follow this method, namely to divide Christian teaching into two parts, namely, into law and gospel."[84] Throughout his career Luther never tired of emphasizing the dialectic of law and gospel as *the* key to

---

[81]Lectures on Romans, 1515-1516. LW 25, 260; WA 56, 70, 272. Cf. also WA 57, 165; WA 2, 496-97.

[82]WA 7, 502, 34f. (1521).

[83]WA 40¹ 207, 17f. (1531, 1535).

[84]WA 39¹, 361, 1-4 (1537).

correct theology. It is only by making the proper distinction between law and gospel that human judgment and the Word of God may be distinguished:

> To put it clearly, this means that as often as the Word of God is preached, it renders consciences joyful, expansive, and untroubled toward God, because it is a Word of grace and forgiveness, a kind and sweet Word. As often as the Word of man is preached, it renders the conscience sad, cramped and full of fear in itself, because it is a Word of the Law, of wrath and sin; it shows what a person has failed to do and how deeply he is in debt.[85]

As Gerhard Ebeling has pointed out, "Luther presents the decisive issue in the form of a distinction."[86] This is remarkable because one would tend to think that the center of theology should be a particular idea or doctrine to which everything else is subordinate, such as the kingdom of God, love, and the forgiveness of sins. Even with all his emphasis upon justification by faith Luther does not make this a doctrine by which all other doctrines are ordered. Even justification by faith may be understood in its true significance only in light of "the decisive standard of theological judgment"—the distinction between law and gospel.[87]

From the outset it should be made clear that the law and gospel distinction is *not* a division or an "either-or" relation. Neither can replace nor exclude the other. Nor are they complementary—the gospel needing the addition of the law for fulfillment or vice versa. The law is not the gospel and the gospel is not a new law.

The centrality of this distinction for theology, the reason that it is constitutive for being a theologian, is because it is not a theoretical distinction but a practical one. The distinction between law and gospel is not a process of logic but rather involvement and commitment in proclaiming the Word of God. "Christian proclamation—that *is* the event of distinguishing law and gospel."[88] Preaching is not instruction concerning correct theological procedure but the proclamation, the enactment of salvation. Thus the distinction between law and gospel is not incidental but central to the event of preaching. "If however the process of preaching is that which it claims to be, namely a salvation process, then it comes

---

[85]Lectures on Galatians, 1519. LW 27, 164; WA 2, 453.

[86]Gerhard Ebeling, *Luther*, 125. Much of what follows is dependent upon Ebeling's incisive chapter "Gesetz und Evangelium."

[87]Ebeling, *Luther*, 124.

[88]Ebeling, *Luther*, 128.

to pass through the distinction between law and gospel. Their confusion is not a small misfortune, a regrettable failure but rather in the strict sense against salvation itself."[89] Confusion of law and gospel is not merely preaching a partial gospel or preaching the gospel without sufficient clarity, it is rather the loss of the gospel itself and the preaching of law.

> Therefore we always repeat, urge and inculcate this doctrine of faith or Christian righteousness, so that it may be observed by continuous use and may be precisely distinguished from the active righteousness of the Law. (For by this doctrine alone and through it alone is the church built, and in this it consists.) Otherwise we shall not be able to observe true theology but shall immediately become lawyers, ceremonialists, legalists and papists. Christ will be so darkened that no one in the church will be correctly taught or comforted. Therefore if we want to be preachers and teachers of others, we must take great care in these issues and hold to this distinction between the righteousness of the law and that of Christ. This distinction is easy to speak of; but in experience and practice it is the most difficult of all, even if you exercise and practice it diligently. For in the hour of death or in other conflicts of conscience these two kinds of righteousness come together more closely than you would wish or ask.[90]

This brings us back to our earlier discussion of justification. The distinction between law and gospel is the distinction between two fundamental kinds of speech. The law is the communication of demands and conditions; it imposes an "If . . . then" structure on life. The scholastic formula of doing your best (*facere quod in se est*) exemplifies this condition—if you do your best, God will continue to support your pilgrimage. All law communication presents a future contingent upon the person's works. The gospel, however, is the language of promise, the pattern of "because . . . therefore."[91] It is a promise which is unconditional because it is made by Christ who has already satisfied all conditions including death. In this sense then, justification is not a content item of the gospel along with other content items. Rather justification is the type of language which always is that of unconditional promise.

> The gospel tolerates no conditions. It is itself unconditional promise. And when it is rightly spoken, it takes the conditions we put on the value of our life as the very occasions of its promise. This is the first and fundamental Lutheran

---

[89]Ebeling, *Luther,* 129.

[90]Lectures on Galatians, 1535, LW 26, 10; WA 40¹, 49. This entire introductory section to the Lectures (pp. 4-12) treats the distinction of law and gospel.

[91]For Luther's discussion of these language patterns cf. for example his *The Bondage of the Will,* 1525. LW 33, 132ff., 158.

proposal of dogma. When it is practiced consistently, the Lutheran Reformation has succeeded, whatever else may happen. When it is not practiced, other departures from medieval Christianity represent only sloth and lack of seriousness.[92]

Before concluding this section we need to make a further clarification about the law itself. The gospel is univocal; its only use is the proclamation of unconditional promise. The law, however, has two uses: the civil or political use (*usus civilis* or *politicus*) and the theological use (*usus theologicus*). At the same time the law is always the one law through which God deals with persons in two ways.

The civil use of the law is to build up society through the encouragement of good and the discouragement of evil. This is accomplished through civil government.

> For the law was given for two uses. The first is to restrain those who are uncivilized and wicked. In this sense the statement, "He who does these things shall live by them," is a political statement. It means: If a man obeys the magistrate outwardly and in the civil realm, he will avoid punishment and death. The civil magistrate has no right to impose punishments upon him or to execute him but permits him to live with impunity. This is the civil use of the Law, which is valid for the restraint of the uncivilized.[93]

This, of course, applies to the Christian as well as to the non-Christian for the Christian being simultaneously sinner as well as righteous needs the rule of the civil use of the law.

The theological use of the law is to reveal sin, destroy self-sufficiency, and drive the person to Christ. Neither civic restraint nor civic good works justify the person before God. "This civic restraint is extremely necessary and was instituted by God, both for the sake of public peace and for the sake of preserving everything . . . but it does not justify."[94]

> The other use of the Law is the theological or spiritual one, which serves to increase transgressions. This is the primary purpose of the Law of Moses, that through it sin might grow and be multiplied, especially in the conscience. . . . Therefore the true function and the chief and proper use of the Law is to reveal to man his sin, blindness, misery, wickedness, ignorance, hate and contempt of God, death, hell, judgment and the well-deserved wrath of God. . . .
>
> Hence this use of the Law is extremely beneficial and very necessary. For if someone is not a murderer, adulterer, or thief, and abstains from external sins,

---

[92]Eric W. Gritsch and Robert W. Jenson, *Lutheranism. The Theological Movement and Its Confessional Writings* (Philadelphia: Fortress Press, 1976) 44; cf. also 41-44.

[93]Lectures on Galatians, 1535. LW 26, 274f.; WA 40¹, 429f.

[94]Ibid., LW 26, 309; WA 40¹, 479-81.

as that Pharisee did (Luke 18:11), he would swear, being possessed by the devil, that he is a righteous man; therefore he develops the presumption of righteousness and relies on his good works. God cannot soften and humble this man or make him acknowledge his misery and damnation any other way than by the Law.[95]

The law then poses the question for which the gospel is the only proper answer. Without the question the answer seems to be a trivial non sequitur. Without the answer the question creates presumption or despair.

Hence God says through Jeremiah (23:29): "My Word is a hammer which breaks the rock in pieces." For as long as the presumption of righteousness remains in a man, there remains immense pride, self-trust, smugness, hate of God, contempt of grace and mercy, ignorance of the promises and of Christ. The proclamation of free grace and the forgiveness of sins does not enter his heart and understanding, because the huge rock and solid wall, namely, the presumption of righteousness by which the heart itself is surrounded, prevents this from happening.[96]

The dialectic of law and gospel runs through all of Luther's work for it is the form by which the gospel is proclaimed. The distinguishing of law and gospel is not a theoretical abstraction but the dynamic proclamation of the gospel by which the presumptuous are terrified and the terrified consoled.

THE THEOLOGY OF THE CROSS

Soon after the 95 Theses, Luther began to speak of justification in terms of God's descent to the level of the human under the rubric "theology of the cross." Conversely, all theologies of human ascent to God he labeled "theologies of glory."[97]

In his famous 1518 Heidelberg Disputation, Luther argued that only in the crucified Christ is revealed authentic theology and true knowledge of God. The theology of the cross is sharply juxtaposed to the theology of glory:

19. That person does not deserve to be called a theologian who looks upon the invisible things of God as though they were clearly perceptible in those things which have actually happened (Rom. 1:20).

---

[95]Ibid., LW 26, 310; WA 40[1], 481f.

[96]Ibid.

[97]Cf. Walter von Loewenich, *Luther's Theology of the Cross,* trans. by W. Bowman (Minneapolis: Augsburg, 1976). Original edition, 1927.

20. He deserves to be called a theologian, however, who comprehends the visible and manifest things of God seen through suffering and the cross.

21. A theology of glory calls evil good and good evil. A theology of the cross calls the thing what it actually is. . . .

24. . . . wisdom is not itself evil, nor is the law to be evaded; but without the theology of the cross man misuses the best in the worst manner.[98]

Luther was attacking what he considered the great vice of contemporary religion—false security and false peace. Against the false certitude promised by the indulgences of the establishment on the one hand and the dreams and revelations of the spiritualists on the other, the theology of the cross "made clear and certain the gospel's bidding of a continuing and inward penance, not as the 'good news' of the deliverance from the human experience of suffering, negation and abandonment in the world that God has given, but as the clarion call to enter into that experience."[99] Already in the 95 Theses Luther had exclaimed: "Away then with all those prophets who say to the people of Christ, 'Peace, peace,' and there is no peace! (Jer. 6:14). Blessed be all those prophets who say to the people of Christ, 'Cross, cross,' and there is no cross!"[100]

The theology of the cross opposes all efforts to ascend to God whether they be speculative, ethical, or experiential. Once again this is the affirmation that God deals with sinners on their level, on the basis of their sin not on the basis of their achievement no matter how inspired. The theology of glory fails to comprehend that God is hidden under the cross and that faith is not based on empirical verification or signs and wonders. "God's gifts and benefits are so hidden under the cross that the godless can neither see nor recognize them but rather consider them to be only trouble and disaster. . . ."[101] The theology of the cross reveals God in his concealment in Jesus and the cross whereas the theology of glory conceals God in his revelation.

Already in his first Psalms lectures Luther was developing this theology of the revelation which occurs under its contrary:

---

[98]LW 31, 53; WA 1, 362, 28f.; LW 31, 40f.

[99]Jerome King del Pino, *Luther's Theology of the Cross as Reflected in Selected Historical Contexts of Social Change from 1512-1525*. Unpublished dissertation (Boston University, 1980) 142.

[100]LW 31, 33.

[101]WA 31¹, 51, 21-24.

If under the glory of the flesh God gave the glory of the Spirit, and under the riches of the flesh the riches of the Spirit, and under the graciousness and honor of the flesh gave the grace and honor of the Spirit, then the latter would rightly be described as profoundly concealed. . . . For who could realize that someone who is visibly humbled, tempted, rejected and slain, is at the same time and to the utmost degree inwardly exalted, comforted, accepted and brought to life, unless this was taught by the Spirit by faith?[102]

"But the Holy Spirit is not given except in, with and by faith in Jesus Christ. . . . Faith, moreover, comes only through God's Word or gospel which preaches Christ, saying that he is God's Son and a man, and has died and risen again for our sakes. . . ."[103] Because faith relates to what is not seen, that which is believed must be concealed.[104] This is precisely the opposite of all theologies of glory which attempt to ascend to God for it looks to the God who is submerged in humans; it is deeply incarnational. "True Christian theology" always begins " . . . where Christ began—in the Virgin's womb, in the manger, and at his mother's breasts. For this purpose He came down, was born, lived among men, suffered, was crucified, and died, so that in every possible way He might present himself to our sight. He wanted us to fix the gaze of our hearts upon Himself and thus to prevent us from clambering into heaven and speculating about the Divine Majesty." The world does not see God in Christ because it looks at him only as a weak man.[105]

In short, the Word of God is always contrary to us. When we are self-assured and confident, the word of the law destroys our self-righteousness; when we are depressed and anxious, the word of the gospel declares us righteous. Here the Christian is drawn into the cross of Christ and becomes realistic about the world: "A theology of the cross calls the thing what it actually is." "True theology is a 'theology of the cross' resting on the faith that the source of the most realistic vision of life is the death of God. False theology is a 'theology of glory,' resting on the speculation that man's effort guarantees divine forgiveness. . . . God cannot be perceived by mystical introspection or scientific observation—ways by which sinful men try to know what is true; rather, God is

---

[102]WA 4, 82, 14-21 (1513-1515). (As quoted in Ebeling, *Luther,* English translation, 236.)

[103]Preface to Romans, 1546 (1522). LW 35, 368.

[104]Cf. De Servo Arbitrio, WA 18, 633, 7-15.

[105]Lectures on Galatians, 1535. LW 26, 29f.; WA 40¹, 77.

comprehended through his self-revelation in the Jesus of Israel."[106] The realism of the theology of the cross is manifest in its rejection both of all flight from the world through speculation and religiosity, and triumphalist programs to establish the kingdom of God by works. The criticism of the theology of glory with its self-chosen crosses of religious works is that it makes human aspirations appear significant in direct proportion to their personal and social irrelevance. The theology of the cross, however, propels personal engagement where God wills to be found rather than where persons desire to find him; this cruciform shape of life precludes all spectator stances in relation to the world.[107]

THE CHURCH

Where does God will to be found? Where is God for me, for us (*pro me, pro nobis*)? Our prior references from Luther have already indicated his answer: in Jesus of Nazareth. If we want to know where God is for us we "must put away all speculations about the Majesty, all thoughts of works, traditions and philosophy—indeed, of the Law of God itself. And you must run directly to the manger and the mother's womb, embrace this Infant and Virgin's Child in your arms and look at Him—born, being nursed, growing up, going about in human society, teaching, dying, rising again, ascending into the heavens and having authority over all things. In this way you can shake off all terrors and errors, as the sun dispels the clouds."[108]

The continuing incarnation of this Word occurs in the church. Indeed, the church is that community which is constituted by the Word, by speaking the gospel:

> . . . thank God, a seven year old child knows what the church is namely, holy believers and sheep who hear the voice of their Shepherd. So children pray, "I believe in the one holy Christian church." Its holiness does not consist of surplices, tonsures, albs or other ceremonies of theirs which they have invented over and above the Holy Scriptures, but consists of the Word of God and true faith.[109]

---

[106]Gritsch and Jenson, *Lutheranism,* 47f.

[107]Cf. Loewenich, 112f.; Del Pino, 130f.

[108]Lectures on Galatians, 1535. LW 26, 30; WA 40¹, 75-77.

[109]Smalcald Articles, 1537. T. Tappert, ed., *The Book of Concord* (Philadelphia: Muhlenberg Press, 1959) 315.Cf. Lectures on Romans, 1515-1516. LW 25, 145; WA 56, 165.

The church thus is not so much an institution as it is an event, Luther liked to call it a *Mundhaus* ("mouth house"),[110] for faith comes by hearing *(fides ex auditu)*. Certainly the church is an institution and not some platonic ideal—an incarnation without concrete forms is a chimera. But the point we are emphasizing here is that the unity and marks of the church are not the like-mindedness of the community but the proclamation of the gospel—the unconditional promise of God embodied in Word and sacrament. The human structures of the church, of course, exhibit the same life as the church's members—a life under the cross which is simultaneously sinner and righteous. Thus the church, like its members, also lives by the continuous encounter with the Word of God which is why it needs constant reform. This is another way of saying that the church is not specified by the character of its members but rather by the character of the assembly—the preaching of the gospel. This is the basis upon which the church stands or falls.[111] The church too is an article of faith.[112]

> Indeed by what signs can I recognize the church? There must somehow be given visible signs by which we shall be gathered to a place in order to hear God's word. I answer: a sign is necessary and we also have it, namely baptism, the bread, and above all else, the gospel. These three are the true signs of the Christian, they are the marks and characteristics. Where you see that baptism, bread and the gospel are, there is—entirely irrespective of the place and the people—without doubt the Church.[113]

The Word is the foundation of the church and the sacraments are the Word made visible.[114] Since our concern is with the relationship of the Lutheran tradition to the Pentecostal and charismatic churches and movements, the pertinent theme for us in Luther's theology of baptism and the Lord's Supper is his emphasis upon God's promise made visible in these sacraments. "In the New Testament baptism and the Lord's

---

[110]WA 10 1/2, 48.

[111]Smalcald Articles. Tappert, *The Book of Concord,* 292; WA 30², 632f., 636f., 640-43. " . . . If we lose the doctrine of justification, we lose simply everything. Hence the most necessary and important thing is that we teach and repeat this doctrine daily. . . . " Lectures on Galatians, 1535. LW 26, 26; WA 40¹, 71, 8-9.

[112]Cf. Preface to the Revelation of St. John, 1546 (1533). LW 35, 410f.

[113]WA 7, 410f.

[114]"The Word and the rite have the same effect, as Augustine said so well when he called the sacrament 'the visible word,' for the rite is received by the eyes and is a sort of picture of the Word, signifying the same thing as the Word." Apology of the Augsburg Confession, 13:5, Tappert, *The Book of Concord,* 212.

Supper are, as it were, God's clothes, through which he reveals himself to us and deals with us."[115] The sacraments are instituted "in order to nourish faith."[116] This nourishment is always through earthly means.

> Now when God sends forth his holy gospel he deals with us in a twofold manner, first outwardly, then inwardly. Outwardly he deals with us through the oral word of the gospel and through material signs, that is, baptism and the sacrament of the altar. Inwardly he deals with us through the Holy Spirit, faith and other gifts. But whatever their measure or order the outward factors should and must precede. The inward experience follows and is effected by the outward. God has determined to give the inward to no one except through the outward. For he wants to give no one the Spirit or faith outside the outward Word and sign instituted by him, as he says in Luke 16 (:29), "Let them hear Moses and the prophets." Accordingly Paul can call baptism a "washing of regeneration" (Titus 3:5). And the oral gospel "is the power of God for salvation to every one who has faith" (Rom. 1:16).[117]

This "external word, preached orally by men like you and me . . . is what Christ left behind as an external sign, by which his church, or his Christian people in the world, should be recognized."[118] "Even the Holy Spirit is bound by the limit and standard of Christ's word."[119] God veils himself in these earthly means because we could not endure a direct encounter with God. "No, he (God) wants to work through tolerable, kind, and pleasant means, which we ourselves could not have chosen better. He has for instance, a godly and kind man speak to us, preach, lay his hands on us, remit sin, baptize, give us bread and wine to eat and to drink. Who can be terrified by these pleasing methods, and would rather delight in them with all his heart?"[120]

As we emphasized in the discussion of justification so also here in his theology of the sacraments, Luther stresses salvation *extra nos* which is always and only mediated to us by external means of hearing, feeling, and

---

[115]WA 25, 127, 41-42. Luther dealt with the theology of the sacraments in two distinct periods, the first (1517-1520) in relation to his critique of the scholastic doctrine of the sacraments, and the second (1525-1529) in response to the sacramentarian and spiritualist positions from Karlstadt through Zwingli. Our interest focuses mainly on this second period.

[116]WA 529, 36.

[117]Against the Heavenly Prophets, 1525. LW 40, 146.

[118]On the Councils and the Church, 1539. LW 41, 149.

[119]Ian Siggins, *Martin Luther's Doctrine of Christ* (New Haven and London: Yale University Press, 1970) 70. Cf. WA 12, 576, 1ff.; 18, 137, 13; 21, 445, 13ff.; 468, 35.

[120]LW 41, 171.

tasting. The unconditional promise of God is the gift of himself to us which, therefore, is not contingent upon any qualities we have. Thus Luther rejected any position which made Word and sacrament dependent upon human faith such as an emphasis upon "believer's" baptism to the exclusion of infant baptism and any understanding of the Lord's Supper univocally contingent upon the recipient's remembrance of Christ's sacrifice. Both cases shift justification from an event outside of us to a process within us which, no matter how grace-assisted, is a form of works-righteousness. This posits that the recipient brings to the sacrament something which, however minimal, nevertheless characterizes him or her as worthy of the sacrament. This may be characterized as, to paraphrase an old heresy, a donatism of the believer. That is, the sacraments of baptism and the Lord's Supper depend upon the faith and "remembrance" of the recipient. For Luther this was to thrust the Christian back into the never-never land of insecurities and uncertainties generated by seeking righteousness in religiousness.

> Justification by my own righteousness is overcome only by a word that both declares my justification and is clearly and permanently not my own word. Justification by faith can only be opened by a word addressed *to* me, from outside of me. The gospel is intrinsically an "external" word; it is a word with a home out there in the world that stands against my subjectivity, and that is to say, out there in the world of objects, of bodies and places for bodies. It is, therefore, intrinsically a word "with" a body, with an undetachable nonverbal or more than verbal manifestation.[121]

In summary, Luther opposed all spiritualization of the sacraments because the desire and effort for an unmediated relationship with God as he is in himself is a theology of glory which can lead only to idolatry, despair, or atheism.[122] "But these are not fundamentally different alternatives."[123] The reason for this is that a spiritualizing of the sacraments and the Word shifts justification from *extra nos* to *in nos*. But inner repentance, cognizance of a worthy remembrance of Christ, and level of belief are ambiguous and intrinsically uncertain. The modern psychological question of how do I know I have believed my best is not far removed from the medieval ethical doubt of knowing when I have done my best.

---

[121]Gritsch and Jenson, *Lutheranism*, 81. Cf. also, Wilfried Joest, *Ontologie der Person bei Luther* (Göttingen: Vandenhoeck und Ruprecht, 1967) 416ff.

[122]Cf. Lectures on Galatians, 1535, LW 26, 28ff.; WA 40¹, 75ff.

[123]Ebeling, *Luther* (English translation), 264; Gritsch and Jenson, *Lutheranism*, 107.

"Let us thank God, therefore, that we have been delivered from this monster of uncertanity. . . . And this is the reason why our theology is certain: it snatches us away from ourselves and places us outside ourselves, so that we do not depend on our own strength, conscience, experience, person, or works but depend on that which is outside ourselves, that is, on the promise and truth of God, which cannot deceive."[124]

---

[124]Lectures on Galatians, 1535. LW 26, 387; WA 40¹, 589.

2

LUTHER
AND THE
"SPIRITUALISTS"

Luther, of course, was not the only person concerned about certainty in an uncertain age. A company of people whom we, for heuristic purposes, shall label individually "spiritualists" and collectively as the sixteenth-century "renewal movement," were also concerned to find certainty. The upheaval of the Reformation quickly spawned groups and individuals whose diverse theologies and programs for reform have taxed the categorizing ingenuity of a number of modern scholars.[1] We are not so interested in these modern typologies as we are in selecting persons whose work and thought both roused the critical ire of Luther and foreshadowed contemporary Pentecostal and charismatic developments. To avoid a false impression of uniformity we shall, as much as possible, allow each of the "spiritualists" to speak for himself. Indeed it would take a protean bed to lodge Karlstadt, Müntzer, Hoffman, Franck, Schwenckfeld, and Weigel without sharp complaints. Nevertheless, these men do share enough

---

[1]The seminal works by Max Weber, Ernst Troeltsch, and Karl Holl are well known. More recent efforts include George H. Williams, *The Radical Reformation* (Philadelphia: Westminster Press, 1962); F. H. Littell, *The Origins of Sectarian Protestantism* (New York and London: Macmillan, 1964); Hans-Jürgen Goertz, ed., *Umstrittenes Täufertum, 1525-1975: Neue Forschungen* (Göttingen: Vandenhoeck & Ruprecht, 1975); Marc Lienhard, ed., *The Origins and Characteristics of Anabaptism* (The Hague: Nijhoff, 1977); and "Problems of Anabaptist History: A Symposium," *MQR* 53/3 (1979); to mention but a few.

common concerns as Reformers and prototypes of the present to provide at least an initial overview of their perspectives. At the very least it is clear that they were united in one issue—dissatisfaction with Luther's Reformation.

The particulars of this dissatisfaction varied in relation to the personal and social alienation as well as the theology of Luther's critics; ranging from the harsh polemics of a Thomas Müntzer to the irenic tones of a Caspar Schwenckfeld. Overall, the concern was to free Christianity from all forms of externalization. This was first formulated by Luther's Wittenberg colleague, Andreas Bodenstein von Karlstadt, in his attacks upon images and Luther's theology of the Lord's Supper. To Karlstadt the idolatry of images in the church and the misunderstanding of the Lord's Supper are intimately related. By 1525 his eucharistic tracts were attacking the new "papists" at Wittenberg. At best Luther was accused of caution and compromise in instituting true reform;[2] at worst he was the author of a "fictitious faith" which displaced the Law of God by an insufficient "faith alone."[3]

Spiritual religion is superior to historical religion and is the means and essence of the true church whether this church be the restoration of the past prophetic and apostolic community or the future church of the Spirit. In both cases the goal of the Christian life is sanctification which at least initially included the drive for a regenerated church and a godly state. The church and its ministry is to be recognized by its fruits which varies among its exponents from a theocratic world rulership to an interiorized form of piety. In all these areas Luther appeared to be singularly lacking. As Gordon Rupp says, "There is at work a restiveness against the tidy pieties of Wittenberg, too slow moving, too tied to hierarchical obediences. If the radicals played to the gallery almost all the time, they were perhaps more sensitive to what was going on in the minds of common men."[4] But now it is time to let them speak for themselves. In doing so we

---

[2]Cf. C. Lindberg, "Karlstadt's 'Dialogue' on the Lord's Supper," *MQR* 53/1 (1979): 35-77; Ronald Sider, ed., *Karlstadt's Battle with Luther* (Philadelphia: Fortress Press, 1978).

[3]Cf. C. Lindberg, "Theology and Politics: Luther the Radical and Müntzer the Reactionary," *Encounter* 37/4 (1976): 365-71; and "Conflicting Models of Ministry—Luther, Karlstadt and Muentzer," *Concordia Theological Quarterly* 41/4 (1977): 35-50.

[4]Gordon Rupp, "Word and Spirit in the First Years of the Reformation," *ARG* 49/1 (1958): 13-15, 14.

shall devote the most space to Karlstadt for it was he who had the greatest impact on the development of Luther's anti-renewal stance which has been so influential down to our day.

ANDREAS BODENSTEIN VON KARLSTADT (c. 1480-1541)

Karlstadt[5] was trained as a Thomist, joining the Wittenberg faculty in 1505. By the time Luther began his first lectures at Wittenberg in 1508, Karlstadt was gaining a name for himself through the publication of two studies in Thomist logic. His prominence at Wittenberg is also evident in his role as archdeacon of the Castle church (with a staff of sixty-four clergy including professors of canon law) and his numerous terms as dean of the faculty.[6]

Karlstadt was also interested in law—both canon and civil. A natural reason for this interest is the fact that the archdeacon's office was also a locus for ecclesiastical law. It has also been argued that Karlstadt's interest in law was motivated by his ambition for advancement to the office of provost, which was not only a highly paid position in the Castle church but also ranked third in the hierarchy of the university. This would seem to be an ad hominem view but for the comments and suspicions about Karlstadt's character which were voiced by his colleagues on occasion. At the same time we need to recall that since the thirteenth century complaints had begun surfacing that theologians were switching to jurisprudence out of ambition and greed for higher incomes and social

---

[5]Unfortunately Karlstadt has received little attention from Reformation scholars until very recently. The major biography is still that of Hermann Barge, *Andreas Bodenstein von Karlstadt*, 2 vols. (1905; reprint Nieuwkoop: De Graaf, 1968). Barge attacked Luther's assessment of Karlstadt as a legalistic spiritualist. In turn Karl Müller attacked Barge's study in his *Luther und Karlstadt: Stücke aus ihrem gegenseitigen Verhältnis* (Tübingen, 1907). Recent contributions to our understanding of Karlstadt include Ronald J. Sider, *Andreas Bodenstein von Karlstadt: The Development of his Thought 1517-1525* (Leiden: Brill, 1974)(hereafter cited as ABK). Ulrich Bubenheimer, *Consonantia Theologia et Jurisprudentiae: Andreas Bodenstein von Karlstadt als Theologe und Jurist zwischen Scholastik und Reformation* (Tübingen: J. C. B. Mohr, 1977); Gordon Rupp, *Patterns of Reformation* (Philadelphia: Fortress Press, 1969); Hans J. Hillerbrand, "Andreas Bodenstein of Carlstadt, Prodigal Reformer," *Church History* 35 (1966): 379-98; James S. Preus, *Carlstadt's "Ordinaciones" and Luther's Liberty: A Study of the Wittenberg Movement 1521-1522* (Cambridge MA: Harvard University Press, 1974).

[6]Cf. Rupp, *Patterns,* 50ff.

prestige.[7] Incurring some hard feelings from his colleagues, Karlstadt managed to obtain a leave of absence to make a pilgrimage to Italy. He overstayed his leave in order to earn degrees in both canon and civil law. One good reason for the faculty's displeasure was that Karlstadt had not provided a substitute for his lecture responsibilities.[8] Regardless of the circumstance and personal feelings, by the time Karlstadt sided with Luther he had made no mean personal investment in scholastic theology and canon law. The momentousness of Karlstadt's theological conversion should not be underrated for it meant not only a major turn in his theology, but also the repudiation of at least ten years of scholarly labor and publications. The latter would be a stumbling block to a professor in any age!

Karlstadt's theological conversion from Thomism and Scotism to an intensive study of Augustine is usually dated from the time of the promotion disputation for Bartholomew Bernhardi, 25 September 1516. Luther presided at this disputation and during the debate he attacked the authenticity of a major authority for the medieval theology of penance, the pseudo-Augustinian *De vera et falsa poenitentia*. Karlstadt was incensed by this and took up Luther's challenge to study Augustine and determine the issue for himself.[9] In January of 1517 Karlstadt bought his own edition of Augustine's works and proceeded to prepare himself to refute Luther. The result was just the opposite and on 26 April 1517 he published his own manifesto of Augustinian theology: the 151 Theses. He followed this by a lecture course on Augustine's *On the Spirit and the Letter,* the first part of which was printed in early 1518[10]. Although Luther was delighted by Karlstadt's theological shift, in retrospect these works seem to anticipate Karlstadt's later spiritualism. His theology

---

[7]Cf. Bubenheimer, *Consonantia Theologia et Jurisprudentiae,* 20 n. 43. For a discussion of the circumstances of Karlstadt's trip to Rome for his law degrees, cf. 11-32.

[8]Karlstadt's interpersonal difficulties prompt Rupp to say: " . . . he had not a bruised conscience, but he had a bruised personality, and no doubt found comfort in the thought that the things which had happened to him in his series of humiliations and failures had fallen out to the progress of 'Gelassenheit'," *Patterns,* 120. Sider, *Andreas Bodenstein von Karlstadt,* 12-15, discusses Karlstadt's inferiority complex.

[9]Cf. LW 48, 115 n. 2; WA 1, 142-51; and Luther's letter to Lang of mid-October 1516, WA Br. 1, 65-66.

[10]The theses and commentary are in Ernst Kähler, *Karlstadt und Augustin: Der Kommentar des Andreas Bodenstein von Karlstadt zu Augustins Schrift De Spiritu et Litera* (Halle [Saale]: Niemayer, 1952).

forms around the motifs of letter and spirit, inner and outer, Law and Spirit, good and evil, love and the regeneration of the sinner as compared to Luther's motifs of Law and Gospel, righteous and sinner, and forgiveness through faith alone. This is exemplified by the following selections from the 151 Theses:

8. The outer man is corrupted either by the advance or failure of the inner man.

9. The outer man is able to become a temple of God.

10. The inner man considers the outer man and sees himself as foul in comparison.

11. The inner man consists in the soul itself.

13. Through the sacrament of regeneration guilt is absolved but the law of sin remains.

104. That (law) written by the finger of God is a ministry of the freedom of the Spirit and of grace.

105. The law of faith written on the fleshly tablets of our hearts is love itself, diffused in our heart through the Holy Spirit.

138. The righteous man, therefore, is simultaneously good and evil. . . .[11]

Along with the discovery of the thought of Augustine came that of the German mystics. The influence of Tauler or the *Theologia Deutsch* is evident in the earliest recorded sermon of Karlstadt's (2 February 1518):

This is our peace: tranquility in strife, love in suffering, sweetness in bitterness, cheerfulness in affliction, oneness in dissension, endurance in danger or temptation (Anfechtung), contentment in opposition, forbearance in assault (Anfechtung), light in darkness, goodness in evil, completeness in weakness.[12]

The mystical influence is clearly expressed in his 1520 tract "Missive von der aller hochsten tugent gelassenheit" (open letter about the very highest virtue of resignation) where the concept of *Gelassenheit,* which will become central in Karlstadt's theology, is for the first time developed. Here in the period of his conflict with the Papacy, Karlstadt seeks comfort in unity of will with God. Here too is the beginning of a new hermeneutic, an important shift from the outer word to an inner, unmediated word of God: "In the 'gelassenen' person as the temple of Christ the

---

[11]Kähler, *Karlstadt und Augustin,* 8*-37*.

[12]Cited by Bubenheimer, *Consonantia Theologia et Jurisprudentiae,* 178 n. 81 with reference to a similar expression in Tauler's sermons, edited by F. Vetter (Berlin, 1910), 85, 33.

word of Christ rings out, and thus is God born."[13] We shall return to the discussion of *Gelassenheit,* its role in the resignation and self-renunciation, and its importance to Karlstadt's order of salvation when we discuss the development of his theology at Orlamünde. For now we need only note the presence of this mystical concept in his early development.

In regard to our concern for the early interaction of Lutheran thought and spiritualism, the next major event of importance is what is known as the Wittenberg Movement of 1521-1522.[14] Following the 95 Theses in 1517 there was a rapid escalation in the confrontation between Luther and his colleagues on the one hand and the Papacy and its theologians on the other. In 1519 both Luther and Karlstadt were threatened with excommunication unless they recanted.[15] The papal bull *Exsurge domine* which condemned both reformers arrived in Wittenberg on 10 October 1520. Luther's response was to publicly burn it along with a copy of the canon law. This was civil as well as ecclesiastical disobedience with a vengeance which invited the death penalty. Not many months later Luther was face to face with the Emperor at Worms. The well-known result was that Luther and his followers were put under the imperial ban by a rump diet which ordered them seized. The penalty for continued writing against the Roman establishment was execution. Prince Frederick, the Elector of Saxony, had Luther "kidnapped" and put in protective seclusion in his Wartburg castle. Karlstadt left soon afterward for Denmark but unexpectedly reappeared in Wittenberg to put into practice the now condemned new theology.

Karlstadt stepped into the leadership vacuum left by Luther's absence and Melanchthon's vacillation. The following months in Wittenberg were significant in many ways, not least in the introduction of a spiritualism which stressed charismatic leadership and efforts to compel social and ecclesiastical reform. The former is associated with the arrival of three radicals from Zwickau known as the "Zwickau Prophets."[16] These

---

[13]Bubenheimer, *Consonantia Theologia et Jurisprudentiae,* 177. *Missive,* Bl. B lv.

[14]The most recent detailed study of this is that of James S. Preus, *Carlstadt's "Ordinaciones."* For a critique of Preus's thesis that the issue dividing Luther and Karlstadt was tactical not theological cf. my review in the *MQR* 52 (1978): 273-75.

[15]Karlstadt's first writing on *Gelassenheit,* his *Missive,* was a letter to his family and friends explaining why he could not accept their advice to submit to the pope. Cf. ABK, 100ff.

[16]Cf. the study by Paul Wappler, *Thomas Müntzer in Zwickau und die "Zwickau Propheten"* (Gütersloh: Gerd Mohn, 1966).

men, Stübner, Storch, and Drechsel, had been connected with Thomas Müntzer in Zwickau before his own flight in April 1521. They themselves fled to Wittenberg around Christmas 1521. They claimed that since infants lack faith, infant baptism should be rejected. They claimed special revelations through dreams, visions, and direct conversations with God. "The Scripture," they announced, "is not powerful enough to teach man: 'Man must be taught by the Spirit alone. For if God wanted man to be taught by Scripture, he would have sent down the Bible to us from heaven.' The inward voice of God has no connection with Christ or the Gospel. Their commission to teach came via a 'clear voice of God.' They claimed prophetic insight into the near future which was to see a great Turkish invasion, the destruction of all priests and the end of the world. They even anticipated using the sword against the godless."[17]

In response to the claim that these prophets had a significant influence upon Karlstadt,[18] Sider convincingly argues on the basis of extant accounts of the prophets' stay in Wittenberg that Karlstadt did not share their views.[19] At this point in time Karlstadt did not reject infant baptism nor engage in promoting Reforming innovations on the basis of the literal words of the Bible. However, this is not to deny that Karlstadt regarded himself as driven by the Spirit of God to proclaim the divine word: "The word has fallen upon me with great suddenness; woe is me if I do not preach."[20]

What was Karlstadt driven to preach at this time? First he held an academic disputation advocating the abolition of clerical celibacy. He published his views in two tracts, one in German, "Von gelubden unterrichtung" (Instruction Concerning Vows), and the other in Latin, "Super coelibatu, monachatu et vidvitate axiomata" (Concerning the celibate, monastic, and widowed estates).[21] Here we see Karlstadt's penchant for

---

[17]ABK, 161f. with textual references.

[18]Cf. Rupp, "Word and Spirit," 20, and *Patterns*, 101, 113.

[19]ABK, 162-65.

[20]Karlstadt to Einsiedel, 4 February 1522. *Corpus Reformatorum, Melanchthons Opera*, 1:2, 545. A central biblical passage to Karlstadt was Gal. 1:8f. He referred to this frequently from 1520 on. For the texts cf. Bubenheimer, *Consonantia Theologia et Jurisprudentiae*, 291.

[21]For the bibliographical references cf. E. Freys and H. Barge, "Verzeichnis der Gedruckten Schriften des Andreas Bodenstein von Karlstadt," *Zentralblatt für Biblio-*

the biblical "letter," especially the Old Testament, in his long and strained exegesis of Numbers 30. His argument that priests should be married, persons under sixty should not enter the monastery, and monks and nuns under sixty should be given freedom to live in wedlock in the monasteries was derived from his exegesis of 1 Timothy 5:9f.

However, as mentioned earlier, Karlstadt's major concern was the externalization of religion. He now attacked this head-on with his proposal to reform the Mass and to demand communion for the laity in both kinds. From the time of the Leipzig Debate (1519), he had repeatedly exposed the uselessness of externals under the rubric of John 6:63: "It is the spirit that gives life; the flesh is of no avail." "God is a Spirit and should be worshipped spiritually. 'All visible and external acts of worship are useless.' God esteems only the spirit."[22] Nevertheless side by side with his emphasis upon the Spirit, Karlstadt retained a biblical literalism which began increasingly to verge on legalism. Thus he rejected the elevation of the sacrament on the basis that this was part of the Old Testament sacrificial ritual. Whereas Luther had condemned the withholding of the cup from the laity, Karlstadt now condemned as sinful anyone who did not receive the wine as well as the bread: "Those who partake of the bread and wine are not Bohemians but true Christians. He who receives only the bread, in my opinion, commits sin."[23]

The theological developments had by now stimulated a large number of clergy and laity to press for their enactment in practice. The Augustinians ceased to celebrate Mass, anticlerical violence began, and a crisis was at hand. At first Karlstadt counseled caution but later advocated mandatory reforms. In the following weeks the elector expressed his view that this was not a propitious time or place for innovation. However, the pressure for change continued to increase and on 22 December, Karlstadt announced his intention to innovate at his next Mass, scheduled for 1 January. The elector sent word he was to do no such thing. Karlstadt's response was to move his Mass up to Christmas day! This may have been less overt rebellion than the attempt to forestall another riot. Clearly,

---

thekwesen 21 (1904): 153-79, 209-43, 305-31. Reprint Nieuwkoop (1965), Numbers 50-53, 59-62.

[22]This is argued in his tract against vows, *Gelubden*, EivV-FV; cf. Sider, ABK, 149ff., especially 150 n. 11.

[23]Theses 9-10 of the 19 July 1521 theses. Cf. Barge, *Karlstadt*, vol. 1, 291 n. 118, and 486-87.

however, what was most important for Karlstadt was that the mandates of God take precedence over the concerns of the authorities, including any "false" compassion on the part of the pastor for his congregation's weakness. To Karlstadt, grace was "costly," for it meant being in step with Jesus and biblical norms rather than with the culture. Christmas day he celebrated communion without vestments. Dressed as a layman, he pronounced the consecration in German and distributed communion in both kinds. To say the least, it was a sensation! It was a hard act to follow, but in his zeal to translate theory into practice he at least equaled it. The next day he was betrothed to a sixteen-year-old girl.[24]

The changes in the Mass as well as Karlstadt's call for the elimination of images were endorsed by the Wittenberg Town Council on 24 January 1522. Karlstadt had been preaching that the Old Testament law forbade images. When the council named a day for their removal from the churches there was more violence and disorder. This was the occasion for one of Karlstadt's most influential tracts, "On the Abolition of Images." On page after page he emphasized that images are against the first commandment. There is no excuse in the claim that an image, even the crucifix, points beyond itself to God. Christians are to abolish images no less than robbery, murder, adultery, and the like. Since the priests have perverted God's law and hindered the faithful, the magistrates should follow the example of King Josiah and forcibly reform the church.[25] Elector Frederick's response was less than enthusiastic; he was not about to begin emulating Josiah. Karlstadt was ordered to stop preaching. Melanchthon appealed to Luther to return and restore order.

Luther arrived in early March and immediately delivered a week-long series of powerful sermons[26] which distinguished between an evangelical "may" and a legalistic "must"; he argued that forced reform changes the gospel into law. Furthermore, the weak and unconvinced consciences need to be gradually led and not forced to Christian freedom. Order was restored, innovations ceased as did the violence. Karlstadt's significant

---

[24]Cf. Lindberg, "Theory and Practice: Reformation Models of Ministry as Resource for the Present," *The Lutheran Quarterly* 27/1 (1975): 27-35, 31f.

[25]Von Abtuhung der Bilder und das keyn Bedtler unther den Christen seyn sollen, 1522. Hans Lietzmann, ed., *Kleine Texte*, No. 74 (Bonn, 1911). Passim but especially, 20ff.

[26]Eight Sermons at Wittenberg, 1522. LW 51, 70ff.

role in the Wittenberg Reformation now came to an end at the same time that his rift with Luther began.

Whether or not Karlstadt had a religious conversion as a result of this experience, he certainly had a change of life-style: he renounced academe and took up the life of a peasant! " . . . Karlstadt may have had an inferiority complex which led to a desperate search for tangible signs of success and status. Apparently, Karlstadt interpreted his fall from power as divine chastisement for this intense love of honor and status."[27] In our day of egalitarianism and the low prestige of academics we may not appreciate the dramatic nature of Karlstadt's renouncing acedeme and embracing the role of peasant. However, to the sixteenth century the shock was so great that initially even Luther, who was rarely at a loss for words, was stunned into silence. The result was the promotion in 1523 of two doctoral students after which Karlstadt appealed to the injunction in Matthew 23 to call no one master or father and stated that henceforth he would no longer participate in such unscriptural activities. He preferred to take up instead the role of peasant and be called "brother Andrew"; this he understood to be more in keeping with Christ's example than academic degrees, titles, and costly dress.[28] Karlstadt now moved to Orlamünde and became pastor of the village church which was incorporated in the Wittenberg archdeaconry. There he dabbled in farming, called himself "the new layman," and proceeded to introduce immediately the reforms he had attempted in Wittenberg. Images were removed from the church, he refused to baptize infants, and the Lord's Supper was interpreted as a memorial of Christ's death.[29]

These activities, including the tracts he was publishing, his neglect of his teaching position at Wittenberg, and the question of the legality of his taking the Orlamünde church,[30] led to Karlstadt's banishment from electoral Saxony in September 1524. At a famous confrontation in the Black Bear Inn at Jena, Luther challenged Karlstadt to write openly against him.[31] Karlstadt obliged with a series of tracts on the Lord's

---

[27]ABK, 176f.

[28]Cf. Barge, *Karlstadt*, vol. 2, 12 n. 24; ABK, 176ff.

[29]ABK, 188f.

[30]Re. these issues, cf. ABK, 181ff.; Rupp, *Patterns*, 131ff.

[31]The account is in WA 15, 334.40; English translation in Sider, *Karlstadt's Battle with Luther*, 36ff.

Supper as well as a polemic against Luther's concern for the weak in faith. The five tracts on the Lord's Supper illustrate his adaptation of mystical terminology, spiritualist leanings, and a vigorous concern for a regenerated life of obedience to the Lord.

The years after his expulsion included near disaster during the Peasants' War from which he was saved by the intervention of Luther who took Karlstadt and his family into his house; more wanderings to Zürich and finally to Basle where, ironically, he taught theology in the university until his death in 1541.

KARLSTADT'S THEOLOGICAL MOTIFS

We have mentioned the influence of mysticism in the late medieval and Reformation period. Karlstadt seems to have discovered this orientation about the same time that he began to work with Augustine's writings. We have already mentioned his use of the central term of the German mystics, *Gelassenheit*; this deserves further development.

For Tauler, *Gelassenheit* is the key step in his conception of the order of salvation. The very ground of the sinner's soul has been corrupted and poisoned by the original sin of self-love and love of creation. This is manifest in the sinner's attempt "to grasp God and all created things as his own possessions." The attack upon this sin is directed at its active manifestations "by psychologically blunting and stripping away the self-affirming inclination of the will (*eigen willen*) and methodologically immobilizing its world-seeking activities. . . . Thus, the repeated exhortations to 'resignation' (*gelossenheit*) and 'will-lessness' (*willeloskeit*)." "In this process all alien, external, temporal things must enter 'forgetfulness.' The less nature and its joy live, the more God and His Will live; the more one wishes to live in Spirit, so much more must he teach natural things to die. He who would follow Christ must give nature its 'walking papers.' "[32]

The term *Gelassenheit* has been variously defined as "resignation," "yieldedness," "abandon," "a way of renunciation for the soul seeking union with God," "detachment of the soul from creatures," and "joyful endurance and patience in the face of adversity." Henry Suso (+1366) gives a brief definition of *Gelassenheit:* "love bodily discomfort, suffer

---

[32]Steven Ozment, *Homo Spiritualis: A Comparative Study of the Anthropology of Johannes Tauler, Jean Gerson and Martin Luther (1509-16)* (Leiden: Brill, 1969) 27-29.

evil willingly, desire contempt, renounce thy desires, and die to all thy lusts."[33]

Rupp argues that this key term of south German "inward religion" conveys for Karlstadt "the whole path of our santification, the purging from fleshly (self-centered), desires, the learning to forsake our own will and cleave to the will of God, an abandonment so complete of ourself that there must be a 'Gelassenheit in Gelassenheit'; that is, we may not make a work, or virtue, of our surrender to God."[34]

Rupp's assessment that Karlstadt's development following the Wittenberg disturbances arose from a "bruised personality" gives a psychological insight into the emphasis in his Orlamünde period on the doctrine of regeneration and sanctification. One of Karlstadt's favorite texts during this time was Paul's statement in Galatians 2:20: "It is no longer I who live, but Christ who lives in me." The central theme becomes "the divinely wrought supernatural rebirth of the egocentric self."

> The place where love, delight, affection and the life of our soul and all concupiscence dies . . . is the baptism in the death of Christ. That means to hang the old natural life on Christ's cross, to stab and murder it, to be buried with Christ through baptism, and to arise not with the old natural life, but rather with the new supernatural life (Romans 6) so that you may truly say, "I do not live, but Christ lives in me" (Galatians 2).[35]

Sider gives an even stronger assessment than Rupp of the personal factor in Karlstadt's order of salvation: " . . . Karlstadt knew, as Luther did not, what it means to begin with a petty, intensely egocentric personality which badly needs God's regenerating grace. Thus his Orlamünde theology represented a response not only to Luther, but also to himself."[36] With this personal equation in mind we may turn to Karlstadt's themes of inwardness, and the role of the law and Spirit in the development of the regenerate sinner and Christian community.

---

[33]"The Little Book of Eternal Wisdom" in Ray C. Petry, ed., *Late Medieval Mysticism,* Library of Christian Classics 13 (London: SCM Press, 1957): 258. Cf. also George Williams, ed., *Spiritual and Anabaptist Writers,* Library of Christian Classics 25 (London: SCM Press, 1957): 89, 272; and Rupp, *Patterns,* 118 n. 4.

[34]Rupp, *Patterns,* 119.

[35]*Sich Gelassen,* e.V. Quoted by Sider, ABK, 212.

[36]ABK, 303.

THE STRUGGLE BETWEEN THE INNER AND THE OUTER PERSON

Since salvation is the goal, the process by which it is reached is of great significance. That process is the mortification of the outer person for the sake of inner regeneration. On the basis of Jesus' words on cross-bearing for discipleship, "Karlstadt declared that a surrender of self and a circumcision of delight in creatures must precede regeneration or love of God."[37] Christ demands of his disciples far more skill than a master of his apprentice. "He desires that we should renounce everything that we possess and that we allow no creaturely thing in our soul and that the soul should overcome all things."[38] Since Karlstadt's understanding of sin is Augustinian and mystical—turning away from the Creator to the creatures and the self—the self-denial of *Gelassenheit* is the path toward salvation.

> This renunciation is an amputation of all love, desire, concern, trust and fear which we have for ourselves and our own things. In short, this renunciation is the annihilation of all that you are and a turning away from all things that you might desire.[39]

The danger to salvation posed by misplaced love of creatures explains Karlstadt's horror of idolatry and images. Already in his 1522 tract on the abolition of idols he was speaking in terms of a flesh/Spirit dichotomy with reference to John 6:63, the spiritualist *locus classicus*. Since idols are of the flesh they profit nothing; only the Word of God is spiritual and profits the faithful.[40] Later in the tract Karlstadt gives an autobiographical acknowledgment of how deeply externals have affected his inner self:

> I will confess with sighing my secret thoughts before the entire world, and acknowledge my guilt that I am of little courage. I know that I should fear no image. . . . But . . . my heart was trained and reared from my youth up to offer honor and worship to images, and a destructive fear was produced in me which I desire eagerly to rid myself of, but cannot. Thus I stood in fear that I might burn no idols. . . . Although I have and know the Scripture (in part) that images do not have influence nor life nor blood . . . nevertheless . . . fear held me and made me stand in fear of a painted devil, a shadow, bushes, a light little leaf, and cause me to flee that which I should seek in a manly way. . . . I know how I, in this case, stand vis-à-vis God and the images, and how strong and deep images sit in my heart.[41]

---

[37]ABK, 216.

[38]*Sich Gelassen*, biiV, ABK, 217 n. 78 (my translation).

[39]*Sich Gelassen*, ciiiV. ABK, 218.

[40]Lietzmann, *Von Abtuhung* (1522), 25-27.

[41]Ibid., 41.

In his concern to overcome the power of such externals, Karlstadt emphasized thorough mortification of the flesh for the goal of inner regeneration. In his emphasis upon the necessity of the circumcision of the heart, he sometimes stated that this was beyond human ability and solely the activity of God, and at other times suggested that love and righteousness are contingent upon the extent that the person's heart is circumcised.[42] However, with the death of the self-will and the spiritual birth, there comes a new life of obedient conformity to Christ. This conformity is shaped by the law.

THE LAW

The category of the law in the life of the regenerate Christian was so important to Karlstadt that his major sympathetic biographer, Barge, subtitled the second volume of his Karlstadt study, "Karlstadt as the pioneer of lay Christian puritanism." The entire Scripture is for Karlstadt a divine law book in the strict sense of the phrase. As such, the biblical texts provide the patterns for the Christian and the church. Bubenheimer calls this "juridical biblicism,"[43] and Sider refers to the significance of "the fact that Karlstadt thought the proper understanding of Christian freedom pertained not primarily to the Christian's freedom apropos laws, but rather to the regenerate man's ability to obey them."[44] Thus the law of Moses and the law of Christ are continuous:

> For Christ proves his teaching out of Moses and the prophets, and says that he has come not to break the law but rather to fulfill it. He also taught his disciples how he must live and suffer that the Scriptures might be fulfilled. Christ did not break even the smallest letter of Moses. He also made no addition and no subtraction from the law of Moses. In short, Christ pulled down nothing that pleased God in the old law. Christ stood fast in the will and content of the old law.[45]

All areas of the Christian life are oriented about the law, whether it be the abolishing of images, care for the poor,[46] or keeping the sabbath.[47]

---

[42]Cf. ABK, 220ff.

[43]Bubenheimer, *Consonantia Theologia et Jurisprudentiae*, 244.

[44]ABK, 282.

[45]*Von Abtuhung* Lietzmann, (1522) 44.

[46]". . . das keyn Bedtler unther den Christen seyn sollen," 1522. Lietzmann, *Kleine Texte*.

Those weak in the faith must be paternalistically guided to the truth. In response to Luther's advocacy for reform through persuasion by the preached word, Karlstadt insisted on compulsion:

> ... I will show you that he who would forcibly break the will of fools would manifest toward them the brotherly love which is genuine and best. . . . Therefore, I ask whether, if I should see that a little innocent child holds a sharp pointed knife in his hand and wants to keep it, I would show him brotherly love if I would allow him to keep the dreadful knife as he desires with the result that he would wound or kill himself, or when I break his will and take the knife? You must always say that if you take from the child what brings injury to him, you do a fatherly or brotherly Christian deed. For Christ has depicted for us genuine Christian and brotherly love in the passages where he says: "If your hand offends you, cut it off and throw it from you."(Matt. 18:8)[48]

Before his expulsion from Saxony, Karlstadt had hoped to see the regeneration of the entire civil community (or at least its mortification) through the imposition of biblical law. Thus, for example, in a manner which foreshadows Müntzer's famous "Prince's Sermon," Karlstadt called upon the magistrates and all civil authorities to imitate the Old Testament King Josiah. But Karlstadt's hope for a Christian commonwealth, as indicated on the title page of some of his tracts,[49] was disappointed. "Would to God that our lords were as the worldly pious kings of Judaism were whom the Holy Spirit praises. They indeed put into effect the Holy Scripture and acted in the Church, and abolished that which scandalized and hindered the faithful." Since, however, the magistrates are not reforming the church according to God's will they "shall be punished, for the Scriptures do not lie."[50]

This failure of the civil authorities to enact God's law turned Karlstadt's energies toward the development of a holy community, the church of the regenerate.

---

[47]Von dem Sabbat und gebatten feyertagen, 1524, in Erich Hertzsch, ed., *Karlstadts Schriften aus den Jahren 1523-1525,* 2 vols. (Halle [Saale]: Niemayer, 1956-1957): 1:21-47.

[48]"Whether One Should Proceed Slowly and Avoid Offending the Weak in Matters that Concern God's Will," 1524. In Sider, *Karlstadt's Battle with Luther,* 50-71, 65.

[49]For example, "Carlstadt in the Christian City of Wittenberg, "Lietzmann, *Von Abtuhung,* 1522.

[50]Lietzmann, *Von Abtuhung,* 42f.

THE CHURCH

As Sider points out, Karlstadt did not develop a systematic doctrine of the church.[51] His emphasis upon the law and the Spirit did lead to significant developments of his understanding of the church as a holy community, the ministry, baptism, and the Lord's Supper.

One becomes a member of the church through the inner experience of regeneration, an experience which is recognized by the life that he or she leads. But the community itself is to manifest such fruit and thus to wait for no one in proceeding to reform itself according to God's Word.[52]

> God has given a general law to which the whole believing people, and each congregation and each person should hold and conform. The same law, which God also calls covenant, was rightly recited or read to the whole people.... Thus Moses bound his people so firmly to God's doctrines, practices, laws and to the work of the law that they could neither teach nor do otherwise than as they heard. . . .
> That God's covenant concerns every individual community and in addition each household . . . is shown so often in Deuteronomy alone that I think it unnecessary to adduce evidence.[53]

Karlstadt's ecclesiology rests upon a covenant theology which highlights congregational and individual responsibility. Here may lie the nascent seeds of later congregational discipline for Karlstadt makes it clear that there are instances when persons should be excluded from the church and Christian association.[54]

MINISTRY

Karlstadt's "Dialogue" on the Lord's Supper clearly shows the importance he attached to the priesthood of the faithful for the central character "Peter the Layman" is the one who most represents Karlstadt's views. The layperson clearly has the right to preach and expound the biblical text and indeed even conduct the Lord's Supper. But this does not mean that the role of the minister is abolished for Karlstadt. Rather, public

---

[51]ABK, 283.

[52]By almost half a century, Karlstadt foreshadowed English Puritanism: "Each congregation however little or great it may be should see for itself that it acts properly and well and waits for no-one." Cf. Rupp, *Patterns,* 138.

[53]"Whether One Should Proceed Slowly . . .," 1524. In Sider, *Karlstadt's Battle with Luther,* 56f.

[54]Cf. Rupp, *Patterns,* 137f.; ABK, 285ff.

preachers were necessary and should evidence divine, regenerating grace and have an inner call. Karlstadt's emphasis here calls to mind the Donatist position but it is not clear whether Karlstadt desires to go that far. Nevertheless, the minister must be holy to proclaim God's holy word. "For the proclamation is a speech of faith which proceeds from the heart through the mouth. Therefore the outward confession or preaching of the death of Christ is a sign or fruit of the inner righteousness...."[55] "He who wants to handle pure and holy things blamelessly should be as pure and holy as the things which he grasps and handles."[56]

The clear inner call of God comes to the preacher through the Spirit. In Wittenberg in 1522 Karlstadt responded to a challenge to his call to preach by asserting, "The word has fallen upon me with great suddenness; woe is me if I do not preach." In his work on Malachi that year he declared that anyone "driven" by the Spirit of God to preach is a divine messenger.[57] Two years later in his "Dialogue" Karlstadt says that just as "the apostles who were assured inwardly through the testimony of the Spirit and thereafter preached Christ externally," so "The Spirit alone leads us into knowledge of the sayings of God." The minister is "engaged to his (God's) Spirit" and "gives God's living voice a creaturely form."[58]

"It is certainly true that the Spirit is important in Karlstadt's ecclesiology, for the Holy Spirit provides a direct inward call to the minister and a similar inward awareness of the same to the congregation. Nevertheless, the regeneration of the candidate and the congregation's observance of his actual righteousness are equally important. Karlstadt joined a spiritualist element to an essentially regenerationist ecclesiology."[59]

BAPTISM AND THE LORD'S SUPPER

Karlstadt rejects the term sacrament because it has no biblical basis and misleads and hinders the people. Baptism and the Lord's Supper should instead be called "signs."[60] "The sacraments are external signs of

---

[55]Lindberg, *"Karlstadt's 'Dialogue,' "* 58f.

[56]"Ursachen das And. Carlstat ein zeyt stil geschwigen . . ., " 1523. Hertzsch, *Karlstadts Schriften,* 1:1-19, 15. Quoted in ABK, 288.

[57]ABK, 290f.

[58]Lindberg, *"Karlstadt's 'Dialogue,' "* 50, 49.

[59]ABK, 290f.

[60]Lindberg, *"Karlstadt's 'Dialogue,' "* 42f. Cf. also Rupp, *Patterns,* 143.

the grace already received rather than an external medium for its communication."[61]

Thus external baptism may only follow inner regeneration. "He who wants to receive baptism properly and be baptized in the name of Jesus must repent, forsake the old life, and take up a new life."[62] It follows therefore that infant baptism must be rejected because only believing adults who have experienced an inner change may be baptized.

While there are only a few scattered references to baptism in Karlstadt's writings, he wrote numerous tracts on the Lord's Supper. Once again the major themes revolve around inner regeneration and the presence of the Spirit. Karlstadt rejects both transubstantiation and the "new papalism" of Wittenberg whose affirmation of the real presence led to neglect of the historical cross of Christ. The sacrament is not a means of grace because forgiveness may be found only in the cross of Christ.[63]

In the "Dialogue" Karlstadt rejected Luther's doctrine on the basis of an idiosyncratic interpretation of Luke 22:19 ("This is my body") and on John 6:63 ("It is the Spirit that gives life, the flesh is of no avail"). He interpreted the words of institution to mean that Christ referred to himself, not to the bread, by arguing that *touto* (this) is neuter while *artos* (bread) is masculine, thereby making reference to bread impossible.[64] This grammatical effort to separate the bread and wine from the body and blood of Christ was less than impressive to his contemporaries. Indeed Erasmus Alber commented that if Jesus also pointed to his blood then he must have had a nosebleed or a cut finger.[65] Regardless of the ridicule occasioned by his exegesis Karlstadt presented "the first public statement of a purely symbolic understanding of communion, oriented by a radically spiritualistic concept of faith."[66]

> He who has a passionate remembrance of the delivered up body of Jesus Christ and desires to prove that externally in the congregation . . . he is worthy to

---

[61]ABK, 291.

[62]Erklerung, CivV. Quoted in ABK, 291.

[63]Cf. Hillerbrand, "Andreas Bodenstein of Carlstadt," 391; Barge, *Karlstadt*, 2:563; ABK, 293-99.

[64]Lindberg, *"Karlstadt's 'Dialogue,' "* 48f.

[65]Cf. Barge, *Karlstadt*, 2:170 n. 62. For Luther's extensive attack on this exegesis see *Against the Heavenly Prophets*, LW 40, 161-76.

[66]Hillerbrand, "Andreas Bodenstein of Carlstadt," 393. Cf. also Rupp, *Patterns*, 147.

receive the Lord's bread. He who does not have the right remembrance of Christ is not fit as Christ wants him to be fit.[67]

It is also in his "Dialogue" that Karlstadt gives the most radical spiritualist expression of his faith. Peter the layman, who represents Karlstadt in the "Dialogue," says, "I do not need the external witness for my own sake, for I desire to have my testimony of the Spirit inwardly as Christ has promised." When asked who taught him his interpretation of the Lord's Supper, Peter responds, "He whose voice I heard yet did not see; I also knew not how he came and went from me. . . . Our Father in heaven." When further pressed as to why he had not explained his views earlier, Peter says, "The Spirit did not impel me quickly enough. If he had sufficiently impelled and mastered me I would have concealed or hidden much less than when I have a consuming fire in my bones. At times one must conceal the Spirit for the sake of his honor. . . . I know quite well that you and the world, especially the 'Scripture-wise,' would have laughed at me and said, 'He raves,' if I had burst forth earlier."[68] It is of interest to note here that this experience of Karlstadt as expressed by Peter is echoed by contemporary charismatic testimonies of initial reluctance to profess being "filled by the Holy Spirit."

CONCLUSIONS

We have sketched Karlstadt's theology and activity in terms of his legalism and spiritualism, twin growths of his encounters with Augustine and German mysticism which he held together in his theological order of salvation. This order of salvation was an ongoing process of sanctification in the life of the Christian posited upon inner regeneration. It is not possible in the current state of Reformation scholarship to neatly summarize Karlstadt's work in formulas such as "justification by grace alone" or the dialectic of "law and gospel." A major scholar of Karlstadt, Ernst Kähler, said in 1952 that "in spite of the scholarly endeavours of the last decades concerning Karlstadt's history and theology . . . the essential key for understanding his theology and activity has not yet been found."[69]

---

[67]Lindberg, "Karlstadt's 'Dialogue,' " 56.

[68]Ibid., 49, 50-51.

[69]Kähler, Karlstadt und Augustin, 1*.

Many streams of thought fed Karlstadt's theology and much remains to be done in analyzing him.[70]

Nevertheless, Luther was certainly clear enough in his own mind to pen the vehement and often acute tract, "Against the Heavenly Prophets, in the Matter of Images and Sacraments," the subtitle of which pinpoints the twin foci of Karlstadt's concern to reform the Christian faith from all externalization. We shall explore these views of Luther after we have sketched the rest of our selected "spiritualists"; it suffices for now to say that Luther's experience with his former colleague Karlstadt was formative for his later opinions of other spiritualists. What Luther attacked in 1525 and continued to see in other "Karlstadtians" was a mixture of law and spirit which subverted the good news of God's forgiveness into the bad news of human legalism. We have stressed that Luther's turning point was in his experience of existential freedom from the compulsion of the law through the gospel. Thereafter, Luther always had an aversion to legal forms of the Christian life. However, at the very time (1515-1516) that Luther was working this out in his Romans commentary, Karlstadt was obtaining his degrees in canon and civil law! The fundamental question for Karlstadt was not "How do I find a gracious God?" but rather "How can man fulfil the law of God?"[71] This is a basic orientation which we shall see running through consequent renewal movements. The fundamental concern of Pietism and the charismatic renewal is not the unconditional forgiveness of sins but a quest for the power to fulfill the will of God. Karlstadt continued to work on this issue through the last decade of his life, the Swiss period of 1530-1541. The true sense of the law is first understood by the spiritually reborn man whose freed spirit now understands the spirit of the law. The gospel is understood in the sense of a new law *(Nova Lex)*, a law of the spirit and life *(lex spiritus et vitae)* mediated by Christ. The Christian is thus given the power to do good works. These are the presuppositions for a second justification, a justification by the law which is an advancing sanctification through fulfillment of the law. Whereas for Luther, justification meant freedom from the law, for Karlstadt it meant freedom for the law.[72]

---

[70]Bubenheimer, *Consonantia Theologia et Jurisprudentiae,* 10, 287.

[71]Kähler, *Karlstadt und Augustin,* 37*; Bubenheimer, *Consonantia Theologia et Jurisprudentiae,* 285.

[72]Bubenheimer, *Consonantia Theologia et Jurisprudentiae,* 275-76, 286.

THOMAS MÜNTZER (c. 1489-1525)

Thomas Müntzer was and continues to be one of the most controversial figures in a controversial age.[73] It was Luther's judgment that Müntzer was a bloodthirsty rioter who, possessed by the devil, was bent upon destroying both church and state. Müntzer was "a man born for heresies and schisms."[74] Variations on this theme dominated opinion until the publication in 1850 of Friedrich Engels's *Peasant War in Germany,* which presented Müntzer as the first democratic socialist. With some important variations on this theme Marxist Müntzer research continues to present Müntzer as a social revolutionary, a prophet of a still-to-be-born class, and a fighter against social and economic oppression.[75] However, since the famous essay by Karl Holl, "Luther und die Schwärmer,"[76] which presented Müntzer as the wayward disciple of Luther struggling to complete what Luther had begun, reformation studies have recognized the central importance of Müntzer's theology in understanding his life and work. "The greatest progress in recent Müntzer studies has been in winning a religious understanding of the whole career, instead of dismissing the revolutionary activities as a deviation."[77] We shall turn to his theology after a brief sketch of his career.

Müntzer was born around the year 1488 or 1489 in Stolberg which lies in the Harz mountains of Saxony.[78] Little is known about his family or Thomas himself until he matriculated at Leipzig University in October 1506. Like Karlstadt, Müntzer's introduction to theology was by the Thomistic *via antiqua.* There is no record of his graduating from Leipzig,

---

[73]For a recent discussion of Müntzer research see A. Friesen and H. J. Goertz, eds., *Thomas Müntzer. Wege der Forschung* (Darmstadt, 1978).

[74]"Letter to the Princes of Saxony Concerning the Rebellious Spirit," 1524. LW 40, 45-59; WA 15, 199-221; WA Br. 2, No. 412; 345f.

[75]Cf. Abraham Friesen, *Reformation and Utopia: The Marxist Interpretation of the Reformation and Its Antecedents* (Wiesbaden: Steiner, 1974).

[76]Karl Holl, *Gesammelte Aufsätze zur Kirchengeschichte* 1 (Tübingen, 1948 [7th edition]: 420-67.

[77]James Stayer, "Thomas Müntzer's Theology and Revolution in Recent Non-Marxist Interpretation," *MQR* 43 (1969): 142-52, 152.

[78]The following biographical sketch is dependent largely upon the monumental study (842 pages!) by Walter Elliger, *Thomas Müntzer. Leben und Work,* 2nd ed. (Göttingen: Vandenhoeck & Ruprecht, 1975).

but he did enter the University of Frankfurt on the Oder in 1512. He was ordained a priest some time thereafter. It appears that he did not earn a theological degree and Elliger suggests that this could have created a certain inferiority complex which would partially explain his later polemics against the "literalistic" manners of "the scribes."[79] Be that as it may he nevertheless had a hunger for theological learning and spent a good portion of his income on amassing an impressive library.[80]

In 1516 he became provost of a nunnery at Frohse. Sometime in 1519 when already acquainted with some of Luther's Reformation writings, he became assistant to the Martinian preacher at Jüterborg, Franz Günther. From there he went on to Zwickau to be a supply preacher. By this time he was acquainted with Luther's edition of "The German Theology" and had apparently received Luther's endorsement during the Leipzig disputation to be the temporary substitute in Zwickau for Egranus who wished a leave of absence.[81]

Egranus left Müntzer a legacy of conflict with the local Franciscans which the new preacher quickly took up in his first sermons. The Franciscans' counterattack forced Müntzer to appeal to Luther for counsel and support. When Egranus returned to his post, Müntzer was transferred to St. Catherine's in Zwickau which provided him with a more sympathetic audience of workers and weavers. Müntzer's growing anticlericalism was now directed against Egranus as well as the Franciscans for their dead, inexperienced, and external faith and soft lives. Among other things Egranus is attacked for teaching that "the church has had the Holy Spirit only during the time of the Apostles."[82] Some scholars argue that now Müntzer was under the influence of the Zwickau prophets while others say Müntzer influenced them.[83] Regardless of the critical question of who influenced whom, by the spring of 1521 Müntzer was the center of enough turmoil and civic crisis that he was forced to flee

---

[79]Ibid., 38.

[80]Cf. Rupp, *Patterns,* 252f., for his book list.

[81]Elliger, *Thomas Müntzer,* 68, 76.

[82]Letter to Hausmann, 15 June 1521. Franz, Günther, ed., *Thomas Münzter. Schriften und Briefe. Kritische Gesamtausgabe* (Gütersloh: Gerd Mohn, 1968) (hereafter referred to as Franz) 372, 16-17. Cf. also 513-15 and Steven E. Ozment, *Mysticism and Dissent. Religious Ideology and Social Protest in the Sixteenth Century* (New Haven and London: Yale University Press, 1973) 66-68; Elliger, *Thomas Müntzer,* 163ff.

[83]Cf. Ozment, *Mysticism and Dissent,* 65f.

Zwickau. His concern for an impassioned and experienced faith had fallen on all too fertile ground.

From Zwickau Müntzer traveled to Prague. It is not precisely clear what Müntzer's intent was in going to Prague though various conjectures have been advanced regarding possible hopes for a favorable reception from Martinians there and from its Hussite background. (Luther had given the impression at both the Leipzig Debate and the Diet of Worms that all true Christians were Hussites.) At any rate even though he continued to present himself as a Martinian, the so-called "Prague Manifesto" of November 1521 is a break from Luther. The Bohemians are called not to a human, created theology but rather to a direct living word of God from God's own mouth:

> Yet all the days of my life (God knows, I lie not) I have never been able to get out of any monk or parson the true use of faith, about the profitableness of temptation which prepares for faith in the Spirit of the Fear of the Lord, together with the conditions that each elect must have the sevenfold Holy Ghost. I have not learned from any scholar the true order of God. . . . For whoso cannot discern God's Spirit in himself, yea, who has not the assurance of this, is not a member of Christ, but of the devil. . . . The children have asked for bread, but there were many then, as there are now today, who have chucked bread at them, that is the letter of the Word, without breaking it to them. . . . They have not explained the true Spirit of the Fear of the Lord which would have taught them they are irrevocably God's children.[84]

God's will and law are manifest in the elect through the Spirit. Thus Spirit, Law, and Word at times appear identical. "This identity of conceptualizations is typical of the thought of Müntzer. No doubt it has its roots finally in the *unio mystica* and may serve as evidence of the extent to which Müntzer's theological thinking is determined by a mystical experience of reality beyond all conceptualization."[85] This theme of the Spirit of the Fear of the Lord remains in Müntzer from the "Prague Manifesto" through to his last tract against Luther.

The Bohemians, however, did not rally around Müntzer, so he returned to Germany. By this time his friends, the Zwickau prophets, had left their mark on Wittenberg and his Martinian friends were leery of giving him much support especially in light of his role in the rebellion at Zwickau and rumors about him from Prague. Karlstadt did invite him to

---

[84]Rupp, *Patterns*, 175-76; Franz, 491, 7-492, 26.

[85]Hans-Jürgen Goertz, *Innere und Aussere Ordnung in der Theologie Thomas Müntzers* (Leiden: Brill, 1967) 116.

join him in farming. However, the misery of Müntzer's exile was ended by his obtaining the position of preacher in the parish church of St. John in Allstedt in Electoral Saxony. From the spring of 1523 to August 1524, Müntzer developed his ministry and theology in Allstedt.

"The Prophet of Allstedt," as Rupp calls him, was incredibly busy. He developed the first thoroughgoing liturgical experiments in Saxony. "Not only was he among the creative pioneers, but his stresses . . . were strikingly modern, and not least in his emphasis on worship as the common action of the whole People of God."[86] He translated Psalms into the vernacular and wrote hymns. Between his new liturgy and his preaching Müntzer began attracting crowds, large enough to disturb the local Count Ernest of Mansfeld. The count's attempt to prohibit his subjects from listening to Müntzer aroused the preacher's wrath to a degree that he challenged the count to bring the bishop and theologians to test his teaching. This request was fulfilled a year later. In the meantime Müntzer's tongue and pen remained active. In his tract "Of False Faith" ("Von dem Gedichteten Glauben") he emphasizes the necessity of the true faith which experiences suffering and the "bitter Christ." In his "Protestation or Defence of Thomas Müntzer" (*Protestation oder Entbietung*) and in his "Exposition of Psalm Nineteen," Müntzer made it clear that "justification by faith alone"—the center of Wittenberg theology—was an "invented" doctrine, for Christ had come to fulfill the law. The sinner is to be converted into a willing instrument of God (Müntzer referred frequently to himself as the hammer or sickle of God against the godless). He proceeded to put this view into action by organizing a secret military league of the Elect which on 24 March 1524 destroyed the small Mallerbach chapel outside town.

The subsequent investigation of this incident by Duke John, the Elector's brother, was indecisive. For, while insisting upon the punishment of the guilty, both Frederick and John also heeded Luther's underestimation of Müntzer's influence. Luther did not "perceive any particular fruit of the Allstedtian spirit except that he wants to do violence and destroy wood and stone; love, peace, patience, goodness, gentleness, have been very little in evidence so far." Luther was still convinced that this was a battle of the Word, not princely force, and was convinced that "the Antichrist shall be vanquished without human hand."[87]

---

[86]Rupp, *Patterns*, 305. Cf. Elliger, *Thomas Müntzer*, 252ff.

[87]Letter to the Princes of Saxony, July 1524. LW 40, 56-58.

Thus Duke John decided to visit Allstedt to find out for himself about Müntzer. This is the context for the famous "Princes' Sermon." Preaching to Duke John and his advisors in the electoral castle near Allstedt, Müntzer used King Nebuchadnezzar just as Karlstadt had used King Josiah as a model for the conduct of rulers. As Nebuchadnezzar made Daniel his adviser, so the Saxon rulers should place him, Müntzer, in charge of ushering in the new order. In this appeal to the rulers, Müntzer remained within the classic framework of civil obedience in requesting protection and support, but his unique focus was on verses 3-4 of Romans 13 in order to present the ruler as the servant of God's wrath upon the ungodly. "For the godless person has no right to live when he is in the way of the pious. . . . The sword of the rulers . . . is bestowed on them for the retribution of the wicked as protection for the pious."[88]

There is no evidence of this sermon's immediate effect upon the princes, but it was not long before Müntzer and others were summoned to Weimar. Within a week of his return, Müntzer fled Allstedt. It was clear to him that Luther's "false faith" promoted and supported princely tyranny. To Müntzer, Luther was a preacher of a "honey-sweet Christ" who called only for belief without works. This "cheap grace" avoids the "bitter Christ" and the discipleship of the cross.[89]

Müntzer was now in his final stage of development. His desire to christianize the world[90] had led him to become a "reformer without a church."[91] He now fled to Mühlhausen and from there to Nürnberg and elsewhere, then back again to become involved in the Peasants' War. The latter provided him with what he interpreted as the context for the eschatological battle of the Lord. In his famous exhortation to his old disciples at Allstedt, he called on them to join this battle: "It is time to hunt the knaves down like dogs . . . have no mercy. . . . Let not your sword

---

[88]"Princes' Sermon," in Williams, ed., *Spiritual and Anabaptist Writers,* 66-68; Franz, 259-61.

[89]"Protestation," paragraphs 5, 13. Franz, 228, 9; 234f. Cf. also Franz, 222f.

[90]Cf. Goertz, *Innere und Aussere Ordnung,* 148-49; Thomas Nipperdey, "Theologie und Revolution bei Thomas Müntzer," *ARG* 54 (1963): 145-81; Gottfried Maron, "Thomas Müntzer als Theologe des Gerichts," *Zeitschrift für Kirchengeschichte* 83 (1972): 193-225; Lindberg, "Theology and Politics."

[91]The insightful title of Erich Gritsch's study of Müntzer (Philadelphia: Fortress Press, 1967). Cf. also Elliger's small volume, *Aussenseiter der Reformation: Thomas Müntzer* (Göttingen: Vandenhoeck & Ruprecht, 1975).

grow cold . . . for it is not your battle but the Lord's."[92]

On 14 and 15 May 1525 Müntzer preached encouragement to his peasant troops at Frankenhausen before their bloody slaughter by the troops of Duke George. Müntzer fled but was found hiding in his bed feigning illness. Under torture he recanted and was executed.

MÜNTZER'S THEOLOGY

Like Luther, Thomas Müntzer was and remained a theologian and preacher: "Through my office I seek to proclaim the name of God, to bring comfort to the troubled, and destruction and sickness to the healthy."[93] Unlike Luther, his major work was compressed into the few years between Zwickau and Frankenhausen (1521-1525). These years were marked by polemical and physical violence culminating in his execution. Thus the controversial nature of his person and work make him a difficult person to assess. Certainly his theology was concerned for an experienced faith which grasped the "bitter Christ." In the exposition of his plan of salvation there is a blending of a biblical piety, a mystical plan of sanctification, with an apocalytic messianism.[94] God's will and law are manifest in the elect through the Spirit. Thus, Spirit, law, and Word of God at times appear identical.[95]

Goertz has persuasively argued that the key to Müntzer's theology is a mystical spiritualism and that when this is grasped we will see a cohesiveness hitherto hidden.[96] This is a mystical theology of an experiential self-disclosure of God to the person. As we have noted above, Müntzer states, "I have not learned from any scholar the true Order of God. . . . For whoso cannot discern God's Spirit in himself, yea, who has not the assurance of this, is not a member of Christ, but of the devil."

"THE TRUE SPIRIT OF THE FEAR OF THE LORD"

"The Spirit is for Müntzer not so much one of the notes as the key-signature at the side of the music determining the mood in which the

---

[92]Franz, 454f.

[93]Franz, 332, 5-6.

[94]Rupp, *Patterns,* 303.

[95]Cf. for example Franz, 264ff.; 226, 25-327, 17.

[96]Rupp, *Patterns,* 277 n. 2, agrees with Goertz that mysticism is more important than apocalyptic in Müntzer's thought.

whole is written."[97] Thus in discussing Müntzer's theology of the Spirit we may include his perspectives about the "fear of God," faith, Scripture, and the living Word of God, mortification and sanctification. The Spirit, in other words, is at work in every stage of salvation.

However, scribes such as Luther consistently attempt to block the work of the Spirit through the dead letter of Scripture. This is not to say that Müntzer remained within the Augustinian letter-Spirit dichotomy, rather he opposed the Scripture-hearing correlation of Luther by the correlation of Spirit-heart. "It is not the preacher speaking to the ears but the Spirit of God working within the heart that makes true believers. Müntzer has adroitly used Scripture against Scripture to place Scripture on his side."[98] It is the Spirit, not Scripture, that makes true believers. True faith is always directly experienced and thus is possible even without the Bible.

> If a man had neither seen nor heard the Bible all his life, yet through the teaching of the Spirit he could have an undeceivable Christian faith, like all those who without books wrote the Holy Scripture.[99]

> Even if you had eaten the entire Bible, it does not help you for you must suffer the sharp plowshare. If you have no faith, God himself then gives it to you and himself teaches you.[100]

However, Scripture and the direct revelation of God are related in the sense that Scripture affirms revelation. So when accused of deriving his views from Joachim of Fiore, Müntzer said, " ... my teaching is from a far higher authority—I get it not from him but from the God who speaks to me, as I will show with all the writings of the Bible, at the proper time."[101]

A witness to the Word of God does come from books but the Word itself comes from God.[102] This Word is not "contained" in Scripture in the sense of being an enclosed and concluded revelation. God's revelation

---

[97]Rupp, *Patterns*, 276.

[98]Ozment, *Mysticism and Dissent*, 89.

[99]Ausgedrückte Entblössung, 1524. Franz, 277, 25-33. Translation by Rupp, *Patterns*, 273.

[100]Protestation oder Erbietung, 1524. Franz, 234, 2-5.

[101]Letter to Hans Zeiss, 1523. Franz, 398, 16-18. Translation by Rupp, *Patterns*, 257.

[102]Letter to Melanchthon, 1522. Franz, 380, 11-13.

continues. However, scribal emphasis upon *sola scriptura* is the clerical tool for exploiting the poor. God's people have been deceived by those who subvert the living Word by the appeal to Scripture by those who lack experienced faith. However, the elect who have suffered and experienced the Fear of the Spirit of the Lord are able to read the Scriptures as a witness to their faith. "The Son of God has said, the Scripture gives testimony. There, our scribes say, it gives faith."[103] Müntzer develops this theme in his 1524 tract, "A Special Exposé of False Faith, drawn forth from the witness of Luke's Gospel and set before the unfaithful world in order to remind weak, pitiable Christendom of its error."[104]

Müntzer contrasts the difficult, true faith of the biblical examples of Zachariah and Mary to the cheap and easy faith of Luther:

> Zachariah and Mary did not attain their faith in the rosy way believed today by this insane world. They did not one day say: "Yes I will simply believe that God will make it all right." With such an easy advent (of faith) this drunken world concocts a faith more deadly than that of Turks, heathens, and Jews. Mary and Zachariah were frozen in the fear of God until the faith of a mustard seed overcame their unbelief. Theirs was a faith attained only through great fear and trembling.[105]

This true faith is difficult because it is filled with the "fear and trembling" caused by God's presence. This true fear of the Lord is what creates the possibility for the work of the Holy Spirit. "He who believes easily has a shallow heart; but fear of God creates a place for the Holy Spirit."[106]

Religious authority is shifted here from Scripture to the person as the "temple of the Holy Spirit."

> Every man should look closely at himself and mark his own movement[107] how he himself is a holy temple, 1 Cor. 3:16f. and 6:19, a temple authorized by and responsible to God from eternity; that it is created nowhere else for he has the Holy Spirit as the schoolmaster of his faith and is to perceive all His works, John 14:26; 16:13; Rom. 8:14. And this very same temple is laid waste by the ignorant clergy.[108]

---

[103]Ausgedrückte Entblössung, 1524. Franz, 276, 34ff.

[104]For much of the following cf. Ozment, *Mysticism and Dissent,* 79ff.

[105]Franz, 272. 1ff.; Ozment, *Mysticism and Dissent,* 81f.

[106]Franz, 273, 30ff. Ozment, *Mysticism and Dissent,* 82. Cf. also Rupp, *Patterns,* 327, 284 for a discussion of the influence of Tauler and the concepts of *Gelassenheit* and *Langweil.*

[107]"Movement" (*Bewegung*) is a technical term, cf. Rupp, *Patterns,* 280-82.

[108]Franz, 292, 33-293, 8.

That the problem with the clergy, however, is not just ignorance is clearly expressed in Müntzer's last writing against Luther, "Highly Provoked Defense and Answer Against the Spiritless Soft-Living Flesh at Wittenberg, Which Has Befouled Pitiable Christianity in Perverted Fashion in its Theft of Holy Scripture."[109] One might think the title says it all, but that is to underestimate Müntzer's rhetorical and theological skill. Luther is denounced as "Dr. Liar," "Cousin Steplightly," "the pope of Wittenberg," "Virgin Martin, the chaste Babylonian virgin," "raven," "archdevil," and "rabid fox." Luther is all this—and more!—to Müntzer because he has perverted the gospel into a spurious fictitious faith by displacing the Law and Spirit of God by an insufficient "faith alone." Müntzer argued that emphasis upon *sola scriptura* avoids the power of the Spirit and thus the scholars, theologians, and clergy disqualify themselves as messengers of God.

> Therefore just before speaking to the pious people, Christ says to the scribes: "My word is not with you." And why? Because [their] unbelief gives absolutely no room to the true roots of sincere faith. Mt. 13:1ff.; Mk. 4:1ff.; Lk. 8:4-15; Ju. 9:39-41; Jer. 6:9f.[110]

> Their teaching sets absolutely nothing free except the freedom of the flesh. So they poison the Holy Spirit with the Holy Scripture.[111]

Müntzer sets forth what I would call a kind of "higher donatism" for even if the lives of the preachers are morally exemplary, they are still false teachers because they depend upon Scripture alone rather than direct, unmediated communion with God.

> The Son of God has said that Scripture gives a witness [to faith]. The learned theologians say that it gives faith itself. O no, my dear friends. . . . The truth that has been so long suppressed and so long asleep must now come boldly to the light of day, and to such an extent that, should a Christian among the poor masses say that he has learned the Christian faith from God himself, he is not to be believed [as we are now prepared to do] unless, in his report, he agrees with what Scripture says is the way the elect should be taught by God [viz. as set forth in] John 6 (:45), Isaiah 54 (:11ff.), Jeremiah 31 (:33-34), Job 35 (:10-11), Psalms 17 (18:29), 24 (25:14), 33 (34:12-23), 70 (71-17), 93 (94-10), and many other passages of Scripture, each of which emphasizes that one must be taught by God alone.[112]

---

[109]1524. English translation and commentary by Hans J. Hillerbrand, "Thomas Muentzer's Last Tract Against Martin Luther," *MQR* 38/1 (1964): 20-36; Franz, 321-43.

[110]Franz, 276, 12-22. Cf. Ozment, *Mysticism and Dissent*, 87.

[111]Franz, 306, 17-21. Cf. Ozment, *Mysticism and Dissent*, 87.

[112]Franz, 276, 34-277, 24. Ozment's translation, *Mysticism and Dissent*, 87f.

This direct teaching of God is a living, active working in the hearts of men, a plowing up of the weeds of the heart. Through mortification and *Gelassenheit* the person grows in conformity to the "bitter Christ" sharing his trials and losing creaturely desires. Here we may see the relationship of the law to the work of the Spirit.

LAW

Müntzer was quite fond of the image of the sharp plowshare preparing the heart for its crop of faith. "No, dear man, you must suffer and know how God sorts out of your fruitful land the weeds, thistles and thorns, that is, out of your heart. . . . You must suffer the sharp ploughshare."[113] The key to this process is the law. At first it appears that the law works here in a manner similar to Luther's concept of the theological use of the law; that is, it works internally as mortification. Both inner and outer suffering is necessary to the *unio mystica*.[114] Outer suffering has a preparatory function for salvation, leading to inner suffering, attacking the conscience and the heart, breaking the opposition of the fleshly person to inner suffering and the work of the Spirit.

Müntzer's understanding of the law is finally, however, not that of Luther's distinction and dialectic of law and Gospel, rather it seems to be a continual process of purification through suffering. Müntzer's "preaching of the Law is determined by a strong ascetic-puritanical ethos."[115] God is always the working, judging God driving the world from the heart through suffering. The "cheap grace" of a faith without works is attacked as the proclamation of a "honey-sweet Christ" which avoids the discipleship of the cross. Only when our heart is emptied of the world can God enter. Suffering is the presupposition for the preaching of the living Word of God's judgment upon the person in order to anticipate the Last Judgment. This is necessary because persons have turned from fear and worship of God to fear and worship of persons and creatures.[116]

---

[113]Protestation, 1524. Franz, 233, 29-234, 4. See also 277, 7-8, and Von dem gedichteten Glauben, 1524. Franz, 218, 5-13, 21-28.

[114]"Tauler, significant for Luther, was for Müntzer of catastrophic importance. Strobel tells us that Müntzer carried round with him Tauler's sermons, bound in a double volume. In them Müntzer found that pattern of sanctification which supplied the lack of such description in what he knew of Luther." Rupp, *Patterns,* 255.

[115]Thomas Nipperdey, "Theologie und Revolution," 172.

[116]Ausgedrückte Entblössung, 1524. Franz, 284, 32-285, 37. Cf. Lindberg, "Theology and Politics," 366f.

Rupp states that the clue to Müntzer's "doctrine of Christian beginnings" is the verse: "The fear of the Lord is the beginning of wisdom." The references to this verse "are manifold at every level in his writings."[117] In his exposition of Psalm 19 he writes:

> There it is told you through the Holy Spirit how you must learn through suffering the Work of God declared in the law so that your eyes may be opened for the first time. You must lay one word alongside another . . . for a man must walk every moment in mortification of the flesh, but especially so that our name stinks in the mind of the godless, and then a tried (*versuchten*) man may preach the name of God, but the hearer must first have heard Christ preached in his heart through the Spirit of the Fear of the Lord, and then a true preacher can give him sufficient witness. But the Work of the Hands of God must have first shown him Reverence (*Verwunderung*) before God, otherwise all preaching and writing is vain.[118]

This emphasis upon actualization of God's will through the law expressed in manifold variations by Müntzer is his opposition to Luther's doctrine of justification. The divine command to fulfill the law is presented as the verification of the faith. It is the decisive criterion to prove genuine faith. "Christ began from the beginning like Moses and declared the law from beginning to end."[119] The law must be fulfilled with the utmost seriousness.[120]

THE CHURCH AND THE KINGDOM OF GOD

It is difficult to develop an ecclesiology from Müntzer's writings. Indeed were it not for his German Mass and liturgical experiments,[121] one would be tempted to say he had no ecclesiology at all. Among the more plausible reasons for his lack of writings on this topic is the fact that he had an extremely short and tumultuous career as a reformer (1521-1525). Furthermore, his self-understanding was that of a prophet—a chiliastic

---

[117]Rupp, *Patterns*, 276f. with an extensive list of references to Müntzer's writings.

[118]Franz, 402, 8ff. Rupp's translation, *Patterns*, 277. Cf. also Elliger, *Thomas Müntzer*, 531f.

[119]Hochverursachte Schutzrede, 1524. Franz, 326, 13-14. Cf. Elliger, *Thomas Müntzer*, 601ff.

[120]Franz, 328, 10-13.

[121]Cf. Franz, 25-215; Rupp, *Patterns*, 305ff.

one at that[122]—whose covenantal theology was oriented increasingly toward a theocratic christianizing of the world rather than renewal of the church.

In the "Prague Manifesto," Müntzer appeals to his "dear Bohemians": "For the sake of Christ's blood, help me to fight against such high enemies of the faith (meaning the stupid parsons!). Before your eyes in the spirit of Elijah, I will make them a disgrace. For in your land there will begin a new apostolic church...."[123] His self-comparison to Elijah and the destruction of the priests of Baal (1 Kings 18:17ff.) is not merely rhetoric; his numerous references to the Old Testament prophets indicate his conviction of a new salvation situation. Müntzer based his prophetic consciousness upon the Spirit of the living Word of God in distinction from the dead word of the Bible; upon an ongoing revelation to the elect. From June 1521, Müntzer characterized himself in one way or another as the "servant of God's elect,"[124] and by the "Princes' Sermon" he unequivocally stated that "the godless have no right to live." The famous chapter 14 of 1 Corinthians in which Paul exhorts the church to build up the community rather than become divided and confused over ecstatic and prophetic experiences, Müntzer understands to mean that "a preacher should have revelation otherwise he cannot preach the Word of God."[125]

Thus as we have seen, Müntzer reproached Luther as a preacher of a "sweet Christ" and a denier of the divine Law. Müntzer's concern for the formation of the Christian faith in the elect and the relationship of this inner faith to outer norms was focused in the law. Everyone who desires to believe must suffer the law interiorly, in the "ground of his soul" as the "piercing sword" of the "bitter Christ." This inner *Anfechtung* of the law through the Spirit of God purifies and elects the person to be the instrument of God for the establishment of the new visible covenant.[126] In this new covenant there is a sharp emphasis upon the third use of the law as preparation for the eschatological battle for the genuine theocracy.

---

[122]Cf. Reinhard Schwarz, *Die apokalyptische Theologie Thomas Müntzers und der Taboriten* (Tübingen: J. C. B. Mohr, 1977) 84f.; Erwin Mülhaupt, "Martin Luther oder Thomas Müntzer—Wer ist der rechte Prophet?" *Luther* (1974) 55-71; and Günther List, *Chiliastische Utopie und Radikale Reformation* (München: W. Fink Vl., 1973) 120ff.

[123]Franz, 504, 27-30.

[124]Franz, 371, 14.

[125]Franz, 493, 15f. Cf. Mülhaupt, "Martin Luther oder Thomas Müntzer," 61.

[126]Cf. Ausgedrückte Entblössung. Franz, 318, 22f.

With this orientation it is understandable that for Müntzer, external norms such as the Bible, sacrament, and church order are always secondary. He shifted the dialectic of Word and Spirit to that of "spiritual" and "creaturely." Those who refuse the inner assault of the law and the Spirit (because they are still in the tyranny of creatureliness) must suffer outwardly the *Anfechtung* created by the theocratic sword. The rebellion of the peasants against the princes was for Müntzer the opportunity to apply this militarily. Justification through the law alone *(sola lege)* thus became the justification of the peoples' revolt and the foundation of a revolutionary program. "The new law creates not only a 'puritanical church community' but also a theocratic world rulership which for Müntzer is the first stage of the Parousia."[127] "The purification of the church is an obvious procedure, the result of which is the earthly form of a 'new apostolic church.' "[128]

Baptism is important to Müntzer as the symbol of tribulation and judgment. Yet while he seems to have wanted to abolish infant baptism he does make provision for it in his liturgy. Of prime importance is the suffering of the baptism of the Spirit.[129] The Lord's Supper similarly is associated with temptation and suffering on the part of the disciples as participation in Christ's own tribulation and surrender of his will. Furthermore, the Eucharist is no longer celebrated as a memorial of Christ's passion but rather for Christ's victory. The righteous of the Lord shall be full of joy because following the period of suffering they will have experienced the victory of Christ. The communion with the Lord is connected to chiliastic ideas whereby the final turning of history from the contemporary suffering to the future period of joy is vindicated in the sign of the Eucharist.[130]

CONCLUSIONS

Müntzer had a twofold plan and pattern of salvation—initiation into true faith and conformity with Christ. Central to this entire order of

---

[127]Erich Gritsch, "Luther und die Schwärmer: Verworfene Anfechtung?" *Luther* 47 (1976): 105-21, 118. Cf. also Lindberg, "Theology and Politics," 366ff.

[128]Schwarz, *Die apokalyptische Theologie Thomas Müntzers,* 68.

[129]Schwarz, *Die apokalyptische Theologie Thomas Müntzers,* 120; cf. Rupp, *Patterns,* 296-98.

[130]Schwarz, *Die apokalyptische Theologie Thomas Müntzers,* 98; Rupp, *Patterns,* 296-98.

salvation is the regenerating work of the Spirit. In his discussion of the Spirit as the key-signature of Müntzer's theology, Rupp discusses his emphasis on Christian initiation and says, "Indeed, somewhere here is the non-sacramental doctrine, which through radical Protestantism and Puritanism, was to become a main emphasis in evangelical Christianity: the doctrine of conversion, and of the sanctifying work of the Holy Spirit in heart, life and doctrine."[131]

Yet the "blind religious fanaticism under the return to his earlier theological arguments concerning the inner Word, cross-theology and the bitter Christ"[132] of the last months of his life sealed his fate as "one of the most fascinating and tragic of God's delinquent children."[133] Müntzer's streak of violence reinforced Luther's suspicion of the potential danger in Karlstadt's theology just as Karlstadt's emphasis upon spiritualist hermeneutics reinforced Luther's opinion of Müntzer's reliance upon the Spirit cut free from the Scripture. (Karlstadt wrote to Müntzer in December 1522, "I lecture more about visions and dreams than any of the other professors.")[134] It is well known that Luther formed his views of the Reformation spiritualists from his contacts with Karlstadt and Müntzer; thus dialogue in a modern ecumenical sense was precluded almost from the beginning. Gritsch raises the question whether, in the historical context, Luther knew what the concerns of the Spiritualists really were. If that is indeed the case then the significance of Luther and Lutheran tradition for contemporary dialogue with Pentecostal and charismatic churches and movements must be investigated anew in light of modern research on the *schwärmer* and their heirs.[135] We continue this task now with briefer sketches of Melchior Hoffman, Sebastian Franck, and Caspar von Schwenckfeld.

MELCHIOR HOFFMAN (c. 1495-1543)

The disastrous defeat of the peasants at Frankenhausen and the execution of Thomas Müntzer contributed to the apocalyptic atmosphere

---

[131]Rupp, *Patterns,* 272; Rupp continues, "It is perhaps not accidental that in the hymnology of the Methodists . . . there is a rich doctrine of the Holy Spirit. . . . Some of the finest verses of Charles Wesley could be used to underline what Müntzer and his friends have said (about the regenerating work of the Holy Spirit)."

[132]Mülhaupt, "Martin Luther oder Thomas Müntzer," 65.

[133]Rupp, *Patterns,* 250.

[134]Franz, 387, 15f.

which had roots in pre-Reformation visions and prophecies. The cruel persecution of Anabaptists strengthened chiliastic tendencies and stimulated Pentecostal manifestations of dancing and speaking in tongues. Radical circles arose in the south German cities; an example was a Karlstadt-Müntzer community in Nürnberg which in the fall of 1524 proclaimed and awaited the coming kingdom of God upon earth.[136] This historical situation had a controlling influence upon the form of theology developed by Melchior Hoffman and others. The expectations of the lower classes, poor artisans as well as peasants, that the Reformation would renovate society were deeply disappointed. People whose poverty and social standing excluded them from the rights of citizenship and membership in guilds could no longer accept either Müntzer's revolutionary program or Luther's advice to work within the imperfections of the social order. To these disappointed masses Hoffman opened up two new horizons of expectation: a total transformation of the world by the datable (1533), imminent return of Christ; and a vision of a new, perfected humanity realizable through suffering and persecution.[137]

Melchior Hoffman was born about 1495 in Schwäbisch Hall. A furrier by profession and a lay preacher by conviction, he "has long been known as 'the Father of Dutch Anabaptism,' but the nature of his influence must still be defined with precision."[138] After becoming acquainted with Lutheranism he became a lay preacher in Livonia from 1523 until his banishment in 1526. While he held himself to be a Lutheran in this period, the beginnings of his later alienation from Wittenberg were already evident. He opposed the Livonian clergy as an inspired prophet capable of freeing the "spiritual sense" of the Bible from its letters. At the same time he advocated the rights of the simple laity in the congregation

---

[135]Cf. Gritsch, "Luther und die Schwärmer," 113, 120f.

[136]For an overview of the leaders and their locations see F. H. Littell, *Das Selbstverständnis der Täufer* (Kassel: J. G. Oncken Verlag, 1966) 39ff. (English original: *The Anabaptist View of the Church.*) Cf. also Klaus Deppermann, *Melchior Hoffman. Soziale Unruhen und apokalyptischen Visionen im Zeitalter der Reformation* (Göttingen: Vandenhoeck und Ruprecht, 1979) 20ff.

[137]Klaus Deppermann, "Melchior Hoffmans letzte Schriften aus dem Jahre 1524," *ARG* 63 (1972): 72-93, 90f.; Deppermann, *Melchior Hoffman,* 32ff., 336; and Deppermann, "Melchior Hoffmans Weg von Luther zu den Täufern" in Hans-Jürgen Goertz, ed., *Umstrittenes Täufertum 1525-1975,* 173-205, 173ff.

[138]Calvin Pater, "Melchior Hoffman's Explication of the Songs (!) of Songs," *ARG* 68 (1977): 173-91, 173.

to elect their pastors and deacons, to "prophesy," and to judge doctrine. He understood the church as a charismatic community of brothers with equal rights. His spiritualistic doctrine of the Lord's Supper was already divergent from Luther's doctrine of the real presence of Christ. A major source of conflict with the clergy was his prophecy that the day of judgment would arrive in seven years, 1533. His claim of possessing a higher wisdom than the theologians, his faith in a new outpouring of the Holy Spirit especially upon the lower classes, and his model of a deified "gelassenen" humanity along with his doctrine of the "unforgivable sin" were major steps away from Luther.[139]

He left for Stockholm in 1526 where he became more imbued with eschatological ideas. When the king saw the danger of political discord in Hoffman's apocalyptic spiritualism, he persuaded Hoffman to move on to Schleswig-Holstein. By this time it was clear that his theology could no longer be characterized as Lutheran. Indeed, in 1529 in Flensburg he and Karlstadt were in a disputation with Bugenhagen, one of Luther's close associates. In this disputation Hoffman denied the Lutheran doctrine of the Lord's Supper claiming that it was a mere sign. Consequently he was banished from Denmark and moved on to Strasbourg where he met and shared ideas with various Anabaptist and spiritualist groups and individuals. Between 1530 and 1533 he preached in Strasbourg, East Friesland, and the Netherlands.

Hoffman's preaching was well received in the Netherlands partly due to the context which included prior spiritualist attacks upon the Roman Catholic theology of the sacraments, and factors of social discontent. Hoffman now believed himself to be the executor of the great missionary command of God (Mt. 28:18-20). In the name of the bridegroom, Christ, he preached repentance and conversion; the church is to be gathered through baptism as the unspotted bride for the bridegroom. Baptism was the covenant sign by which the converted engaged himself to the bridegroom, Christ; the Lord's Supper was the marriage ring; and church discipline was the means to separate the unworthy from the covenant. One of Hoffman's converts, Jan Matthys from Haarlem, became the influential preacher who chose Münster in Westphalia as the place for the arrival of the New Jerusalem and the elimination of the godless thus

---

[139]Deppermann, *Melchior Hoffman,* 77f.

precipitating a bloody religious conflict throughout the city in 1535.[140]

In 1533 a prophetic Anabaptist from Friesland similar to Hoffman prophesied that Hoffman should return to Strasbourg, be imprisoned there, and after a half year in prison the Lord would return and Hoffman would then lead an Anabaptist procession through the entire world. Hoffman returned to Strasbourg as "Elijah" where it took over two months to convince the authorities to imprison him. He remained in prison until his death in 1543, still awaiting the establishment of the New Jerusalem.

HOFFMAN'S THEOLOGY

We have already referred to the growing importance of prophecy to Hoffman which led him after 1530 to identify himself with the role of Elijah redivivus. Here along with the tradition of the Zwickau prophets and Müntzer was the view that the elect shall study the living Word of God from God's own mouth. Thus Hoffman's hermeneutics and conception of history belong inseparably together. "He conceived of the history of salvation as a process of advancing spiritualization, and the task of the 'witnesses of God' to consist of bringing to consciousness this process of spiritualization through the interpretation of history. As the interpreter of history the 'testimony of the Most High' himself enters the point of development in which he sets free the latent, existing spiritual potential in historical 'figures' through his typological (allegorical) interpretation and thereby propels forward the process of spiritualization."[141]

Hoffman's understanding of justification, the church, and the sacraments was governed by four major conceptions: the certainty that in the immediate future the earth would be transformed into the Kingdom of God; the advancement of revelation through "figural" interpretation of the Scriptures (by the rise of the "inner word" in the soul of the believer); the divinization of persons; and the unforgivableness of sin after enlightenment.[142]

---

[140]Cf. Richard von Dülmer, *Reformation als Revolution: Soziale Bewegung und religiösen Radikalismus in der deutschen Reformation* (Münich: Deutscher Taschenbuch, 1977).

[141]Ibid., 212. On Hoffman's hermeneutics cf. Pater, "Hoffman's Explication," and Depperman, "Melchior Hoffmans Weg."

[142]Ibid., 340.

JUSTIFICATION

Under the influence of Hans Denck, a disciple of Müntzer and Karlstadt whose "manifest concern . . . is to dehistoricize and deinstitutionalize 'Truth' absolutely,"[143] Hoffman rejected the Lutheran doctrines of predestination and justification. The doctrine of predestination blasphemously blamed God for evil and exonerated persons from responsibility for their sin; and the doctrine of justification made Christ an idol, displacing a life of discipleship to Christ by lip service.

In his 1530 tract *Die Ordonanntie Godts,* Hoffman set forth the universality of grace in place of predestination. Christ died for everyone and has eradicated the consequences of Adam's fall. As soon as human understanding is enlightened by the divine Word that persons are not condemned for an "original sin" for which they were not responsible, they have the free will to be disciples of Christ. This leads to a distinction between two justifications. The first justification, the eradication of the consequences of original sin by the merit of Christ, is a pure gift of grace. The second justification which leads to eternal blessedness is earned by persons through their voluntary cooperation with God. The first justification returns the person to his "natural human condition" after having been a servant of Satan. By the second justification he becomes a sinless "heavenly" person. Only he who overcomes and sanctifies himself will acquire the crown of life.[144] "If faith is to be of any value, justification by faith must lead to justification by works."[145]

The new "spiritual man" now has free will through the birth of Christ in his soul and therefore must work toward divinization which is the goal of all Christians. Like the people of Israel he must leave the fleshpots of Egypt and wander in the desert.[146] This conflict between "flesh" and "Spirit" is given vivid expression through the ascetic morality and repressed sensuality of the visions and dreams of the Strasbourg prophets with whom Hoffman associated.[147]

---

[143]Ozment, *Mysticism and Dissent,* 126; cf. also 116-36.

[144]Deppermann, "Melchior Hoffmans Weg," 190.

[145]Deppermann, *Melchior Hoffman,* 210.

[146]Ibid., 208, 202. For a text behind the above summary see "The Ordinance of God" in Williams, ed., *Spiritual and Anabaptist Writers,* 184-203.

[147]Ibid., 156f., 184ff. For selections of Hoffman's edition of these dreams and visions see Heinold Fast, ed., *Der Linke Flügel der Reformation* (Bremen: Schünemann, 1962), 298-308.

THE CHURCH AND SACRAMENTS

The beginnings of Hoffman's charismatic ecclesiology are evident in his writing on the Song of Songs. The power of God first of all falls upon the "apostolic shepherds" who then pass it on to the assembly of the faithful.[148] This is further reinforced by the Strasbourg prophets whose hope rests on the raising up of a charismatic leader who will lead the people out of servitude into freedom and a new spiritualized life.[149] In this charismatic milieu of Strasbourg, Hoffman developed a theory of the hierarchy of offices in the Christian community. First of all there are the "multitude of apostolic messengers" or the "temple of God" who resemble Christ after the resurrection, are completely righteous, and can no longer sin. They possess nothing, traveling through the land proclaiming the gospel. Second in the hierarchy are the "first born" who lead the "office of prophet." They stand in the "forecourt of the temple" and are subject to the apostles as the house of Levi was to the house of Aaron. Thirdly, "the entire multitude of the pastors" act as the supervisors of the community and whose relationship to the community is like that of a husband to his wife. Finally, the simple members of the community take their place on the bottom rung of the hierarchy, and as a rule have no unmediated contact with the "apostolic messengers."[150]

The critical point in this teaching was the subordination of the prophets under the power of the "apostolic messengers." Hoffman distinguished the prophets between those who received their visions in the day with complete consciousness and those to whom the secrets of the future were revealed in dreams. Since dreams could also come from Satan they must be subject to spiritual judgment. Only the "apostolic messengers" are able to recognize the hidden meanings of visions and voices and to decide whether they proceed from the Spirit of Christ. The community therefore is dependent upon their apostles. "This ecclesiology also determined praxis. Hoffman and his 'apostolic messengers' widened the circle of leaders of the Melchiorite movement through cooptation. They were considered as sent by God and their appearance

---

[148]Ibid., 96; Pater, "Hoffman's Explication."

[149]Deppermann, *Melchior Hoffman,* 184. The following description of Hoffman's ecclesiology is dependent upon pp. 233ff. ibid.

[150]Cf. Deppermann, "Melchior Hoffmans Weg," 198f.

was accordingly charismatic-authoritarian."[151] Following the tragedy of the Münster attempt to bring in the kingdom of God, the Melchiorite groups expected no other reign of Christ upon earth than that present in the suffering community of the truly baptized. They rejected the conception of a progressive revelation in the present and moved toward a puritanical congregationalism. The preachers should be elected by the congregation and know the Scriptures. They rejected the structure of the church as a hierarchy of charismatics.[152]

The idea of human cooperation with God as expressed in his understanding of the second justification led Hoffman to a strong emphasis upon a covenant theology which was expressed in his doctrine of baptism. In baptism he saw the conclusion of God's covenant with man in which both partners pledge their mutual faithfulness. The expression of this on man's side is the renunciation of the world. Thus here is both the foundation for his emphasis upon a faith or adult baptism and the third use of the law (*tertius usus legis*) for purification. In his 1529 explication of the Song of Songs Hoffman refers to baptism as an internal rebirth attendant on purification through the blood of Christ.[153] Thus no one should be baptized by water until he is purified and renewed by the "inner, spiritual water."[154] Baptism thus had no sacramental meaning for Hoffman nor was it connected with the reception of the Holy Spirit or the forgiveness of sins. Rather, water baptism followed baptism by the Spirit as a public sign of the subjective appropriation of the first justification.

Like baptism, the Lord's Supper was also a sign of the individual's relationship with God and had little or no significance for the building up of the community.[155] On the basis of his spiritualist impulse Hoffman replaced the Lutheran doctrine of Christ's real presence in the sacrament by the spiritual communion of Christ with the believing soul. The earthly elements of bread and wine are only signs for the spiritual food.

---

[151]Deppermann, *Melchior Hoffman*, 234.

[152]Ibid., 313.

[153]Ibid., 341; Pater, "Hoffman's Explication," 184, 186, 188. He understood "believer's baptism as the conclusion of the first phase of progressive sanctification." G. H. Williams, "Sanctification in the Testimony of Several So-Called Schwärmer," in Ivor Asheim, ed., *Kirche Mystik, Heiligung und das Natürliche bei Luther* (Göttingen: Vandenhoeck & Ruprecht, 1967) 194-211, 198f. (hereafter referred to as Asheim).

[154]Ibid., 192.

[155]Ibid., 204.

Hoffman viewed the Lutheran view of the Lord's Supper as a blasphemous misunderstanding of the divine essence by its confusion of spirit and matter, and as both an expression of cheap grace without works and a clerical ruse to control the community.[156] It is the first point which is closely related to his monophysite christology and fusing of the first and second persons of the trinity to the point where he commanded that only the Father, not the Son, should be addressed in prayer. "The consequence of Hoffman's monophysite christology was finally here the return to the God of the Old Testament."[157]

This monophysite christology was expressed in terms of the notion of Christ's "heavenly flesh" and was advocated by the Strasbourg prophets and Caspar Schwenckfeld as well. "This doctrine is as old as Christian theology itself, and its intention is twofold. First, it seeks to exempt divinity from the weakness and sinfulness of the humanity it assumes in Christ. How can a holy God be embodied in sinful human flesh? Secondly, it seeks to insure that the God who does take flesh and dwells among men is truly God. For how could men be saved by one as weak and sinful as they themselves? The indirect social relevance of the doctrine lies in its basic problem: how to maintain the perfect in the midst of what is imperfect."[158] Although Hoffman grounded his doctrine that Christ could have eradicated the sins of humanity only if he was free from being stained by the sinful daughter of Adam, Mary, his christological speculation may be rooted above all in the spiritualist conviction that the divine Spirit cannot be bound to earthly creatures. This is certainly expressed in his teaching on the Lord's Supper,[159] as well as reflected in the judgment of the Strasbourg reformer, Martin Bucer, that Hoffman was not an innovator but a Montanist and Manichaean.[160]

SEBASTIAN FRANCK (1499-1542)

Sebastian Franck is of interest for our concern to relate the Lutheran tradition to Pentecostal and charismatic movements because he himself

---

[156]Ibid., 340.

[157]Ibid., 201.

[158]Ozment, *Mysticism and Dissent*, 229. Cf. Deppermann, *Melchior Hoffman*, 197ff.; Williams, "Sanctification in Testimony," 198.

[159]Deppermann, *Melchior Hoffman*, 341.

[160]Deppermann, "Melchior Hoffmans letzte Schriften," 91.

was a Lutheran pastor who turned against the Lutheran church and
theology to become one of the most significant representatives of the
mystical spiritualism of the sixteenth century. He not only dealt inten-
sively with the Lutheran Reformation but he also was influential in the
development of Pietism.[161]

Born in the small imperial city Donauwörth, he studied at the universities of Ingolstadt and Heidelberg. It cannot be historically verified
whether or not he met Luther at the Heidelberg Disputation (1518), but
if he did it would have been his first and only personal meeting with
Luther. He left the priesthood to become a Lutheran pastor about 1525
and by 1529 had given up his pastoral position and had moved to
Nürnberg to work as a translator and author. Thus his development from
Lutheran Reformation follower to opponent took place within a few
years. He expressed his "pox" on all houses in his 1530 "hymn," *Von vier
zwieträchtigen Kirchen,* which rejects the papists, Lutherans, Zwingli-
ans, and Anabaptists. His rejection of the Reformation because of its
"sparse ethical fruits"[162] is expressed in the stanza "I will and may not be a
Lutheran": "The freedom which it teaches is deception and pretence. It
builds not the house of God but demolishes it. The people become more
perverted. It teaches 'faith!' 'faith!' And thereby makes deaf and work-less
people. It is as clear as day that it is deaf to improvement."[163] As with
Caspar Schwenckfeld, Hans Denck, Ludwig Hätzer, and other spiritualists, Franck felt the disappointing experience that the Reformation
movement did not lead to a *restitutio christianismi.* In their eyes the
Reformation resulted in an ethical degeneration which led them to
become critics of the Reformation.[164] As we have noticed, a consequence
of this orientation is an emphasis upon a progressive sanctification in
imitation of Christ over against justification through faith in the redemptive work of the historical Christ.

---

[161]Horst Weigelt, *Sebastian Franck und die lutherische Reformation* (Gütersloh: Gerd
Mohn, 1972) 12, 69. Cf. also, Gertraud Zaepernick, "Welt und Mensch bei Sebastian
Franck," in Andreas Lindt and Klaus Deppermann, ed., *Pietismus und Neuzeit* (Bielefeld:
Luther Verlag, 1974) 9-24, 9f.

[162]Ozment, *Mysticism and Dissent,* 138.

[163]Von vier zwieträchtigen Kirchen, deren jede die die andre hasset und verdammet,
(ca. 1531), in Fast, *Der Linke Flügel,* 246-48, 247.

[164]Weigelt, *Sebastian Franck,* 16.

In Nürnberg Franck composed his *Chronicle of World History* which was published in Strasbourg in September 1531.[165] In this and in his letter to his friend John Campanus he scathingly indicts religious and secular authorities, maintains that the church fell with the death of the original apostles, and proclaims that inner experience is the key to Scripture.[166] The consequent displeasure of the authorities led to Franck's dismissal from Strasbourg. After brief stays in Kehl and Esslingen he managed to obtain citizenship in Ulm. He was excluded from Ulm in 1539 and moved to Basel where he died in 1542. Throughout his productive career as writer and printer[167] he continued his *Auseinandersetzung* with the Lutheran Reformation, being especially critical of the doctrine of justification, the understanding of the church, and the interpretation of Scripture.

JUSTIFICATION

Franck's criticism of the Lutheran doctrine of justification was that it did not bring about either individual or corporate ethical renewal. Lack of ethical improvement clearly indicates a dead faith. "Now where works do not follow (faith), it is a certain sign that there exists neither word nor faith nor spirit, indeed no Christian."[168] This argument runs through all his writings.[169] He does not, like Luther, understand faith as the confidence and reliance upon God's promise which justifies the person. Rather, Franck viewed faith as the coinage and payment for the acquisition of grace which the inner word actualizes. Thus faith is a means to the renewal of the good essence of persons.[170]

God, Christ, and the Holy Spirit are the inner word, present in all creatures but especially in persons. The fall buried this inner word but did not destroy it. Thus the propaedeutical function of Jesus is to lead us to the inner word. This is an inner activity of God because even the passion of

---

[165]Cf. André Seguenny, "Histoire Magistra Vitae. Quelques Remarques à propos de la Chronique de Sébastien Franck," in M. Kroon and M. Lienhard, eds., *Horizons Européens de la Réforme en Alsace* (Strasbourg: Istra, 1980) 107-18.

[166]Cf. Ozment, *Mysticism and Dissent*, 141-51.

[167]Cf. Weigelt, *Sebastian Franck*, 73-80, for a list of his printed works.

[168]Diallage, 1528. A 3 V. Quoted by Weigelt, *Sebastian Franck*, 22 n. 80.

[169]Weigelt, *Sebastian Franck*, 22.

[170]Ibid., 34.

Jesus is an external event of no saving significance in itself. The actualization of the inner word or the birth of the inner Christ in the soul is "rebirth." Through the birth of the inner Christ there arises a new man whose life is characterized by discipleship to Christ. This is visibly expressed in the overcoming of the self, in *Gelassenheit,* and in the imitation of Christ. But conformity to Christ is not the final goal; the goal is deification, a process which grasps the whole person.[171] From Franck's point of view there is a singular lack of such justifying faith:

> For I believe and am certain that at the present time not a single true and natural word of the Lord Jesus Christ, the Son of God, is acknowledged on earth, yea, that no one has begun to recognize the righteousness of faith. No one, I say, in the whole of Germany, nay, more, in the whole world—I speak of those who sound forth their falsified word from their pulpits to the common people, that is, of the swine and the dogs—no one has been called or sent. Of this I have absolutely no doubt. Therefore, they preach without any fruit, for they are not sent of God but instead retch out the Word solely according to the letter, soiled with human filth, not according to the divine sense. For they also don't know another word to say but what is Scriptural, and of no other teachers except their evangelists.[172]

SCRIPTURE

Thus Franck rejected the Reformation doctrine of *sola scriptura.* In doing so he used Scripture itself, appealing to John 5:39 ("You study the Scriptures diligently, supposing that in having them you have eternal life; yet although their testimony points to me, you refuse to come to me for that life.") and 2 Corinthians 3:6 ("The qualification we have comes from God; it is he who has qualified us to dispense his new covenant—a covenant expressed not in a written document, but in a spiritual bond; for the written law condemns to death, but the Spirit gives life.") The only binding authority is God's inner word and, so as to drive men directly to this inner word, God himself wrote contradictions into the texts of Scripture.[173]

> For this reason the Scriptures are called a book closed with seven seals, and the Word of God is so formed that no one understands it except his children. He speaks with them in parables and in a hidden manner so that no one under-

---

[171]Cf. Weigelt, *Sebastian Franck,* 23-34.

[172]Letter to Campanus, 1531. Williams, *Spiritual and Anabaptist Writers,* 158.

[173]Cf. Franck's *Paradoxa,* 1534; *Das verbütschierte, mit sieben Siegeln verschlossen Buch, das Niemand recht auftun, verstehen oder lesen kann als das Lamm. . . . ,* 1539; selections of which are in Ernst Staehelin, ed., *Die Verkündigung des Reich Gottes in der*

stands him except those who are born of him. This incomprehensible language is closed to all who are outside, that is, all the world.[174]

Since the Spirit inspired the Scripture, it is only the Spirit who can interpret it. Although contemporary charismatic literature lacks Franck's polemics, its emphasis upon the necessity of the Spirit for the disclosure of the true meaning of Scripture is a striking parallel to Franck's position. "Now as God is a spirit, he deals with our spirit only through the like spiritual means of his Word or Spirit."[175] Luther and others are caught in the dead letter of Scripture which they make into an idol.[176]

> In brief, all that we have learned since childhood from the papists, we must all of a sudden again unlearn. Again, the same for what we have received from Luther and Zwingli—all must be abandoned and altered. . . . For the veil of Moses hinders them, that is, the death-dealing letter of Scripture, which they receive as life and as life-giving Spirit. I, however, hold completely that the intention of the Lord does not reside precisely in the ring of Scripture. . . . I would sooner believe that it were locked with seven seals and knowable to none but to the lamb. For to such an extent does God hide his wisdom under the covering of likeness and literary parable of letters that none but those who are taught of God himself can understand them. And (he) does not so lightly expose his secret to the godless world and all scamps but rather conceals it beneath the rind so that only the instructed of God, as I have said, may be able to grasp it.[177]

Ozment points out that Franck is critically applying the principle of likeness, "the crucial rule of medieval epistemology and soteriology that only like can truly know and relate to like." This means that personal experience is the medium for the covenant with God.[178] With this emphasis it is easy to move toward donatism and a radical anti-institutionalism. In his *Paradoxa* Franck says that "God gives and works his light, kindness, Holy Spirit, life, etc., only through similarly illumined, kind, living, spiritual people. The Holy Spirit will not grace anyone through the Devil, but will rather work like through like." In response to

---

Kirche Jesu Christi. Zeugnisse aus allen Jahrhunderten und allen Konfessionen 4 (Basel: Reinhardt, 1957) 349-54.

[174]Chronica, Zeytbuch und Geschychtbibel, 1531. Fast, *Der Linke Flügel,* 239.

[175]Quoted by Ozment, *Mysticism and Dissent,* 161.

[176]Chronica, Fast, *Der Linke Flügel,* 245f. Letter to Campanus, Williams, *Spiritual and Anabaptist Writers,* 159.

[177]Letter to Campanus, Williams, *Spiritual and Anabaptist Writers,* 160.

[178]Indeed, Scripture is the confirmation of one's conscience; "it testifies to the heart and not against it." Letter to Campanus, Williams, *Spiritual and Anabaptist Writers,* 159.

his inquisitors in Ulm, Franck asked: "How can one who is not in God's house build something within God's house? How can one who is blind preach about colors and talk about light which he does not see? How can a minister who is the Devil's slave, graceless and standing in disgrace, be an instrument of grace? How can one who does not have the Holy Spirit preach the Holy Spirit?" Ozment concludes:

> The issue raised by Franck finally transcends the heresy of Donatism (or perhaps drives it to its most extreme conclusion). While his critique of the imperfection of social institutions suggests Donatism to his judges, his metaphysical presuppositions suggest a kind of theological nihilism. Ultimately, the problem is not the imperfection of institutions but institutions themselves.[179]

CHURCH AND SACRAMENTS

In light of the above it is no surprise that in opposition to the Lutheran Reformation Franck develops a purely spiritual understanding of the church. "The most important characteristic of the *ecclesia spiritualis* is its invisibility."[180]

> Therefore, I believe that the outward church of Christ, including all its gifts and sacraments, because of the breaking in and laying waste by Antichrist right after the death of the apostles, went up into heaven and lies concealed in the Spirit and in truth. I am thus quite certain that for fourteen hundred years now there has existed no gathered church nor any sacrament. For this is proved along with experience by the work, outward behaviour, and misuse with which Antichrist has besmirched and spoiled everything.
>
> Moreover, since the holy and omniscient Spirit anticipated that all these outward ceremonies would go under because of the Antichrist and would degenerate through misuse, he gladly yielded these tokens to Satan and fed, gave drink, baptized and gathered the faithful with the Spirit and the truth in such a way that nothing would be lost to truth, although all outer transactions might pass away. Therefore even as the Spirit of God is alone the teacher of the New Covenant, so also he alone baptizes and alone avails himself of all things, namely in the Spirit and in truth. And just as the church is today a purely spiritual thing, so also is all law, promise, reward, spirit, bread, wine, sword, kingdom, life—all in the Spirit and no longer outward, etc. Therefore the unitary Spirit alone baptizes with fire and the Spirit all the faithful and (all) who are obedient to the inner Word in whatever part of the world they be. For God is no respecter of persons but instead is to the Greeks as to the Barbarian and the

---

[179]Ozment, *Mysticism and Dissent,* 163; 160-63. Fast, *Der Linke Flügel,* 218, suggests that Franck anticipates modern historical relativism since his view that the Holy Spirit can only be known by the Holy Spirit fosters a deep skepticism about who can know the Spirit.

[180]Weigelt, *Sebastian Franck,* 43.

Turk, to the lord as to the servant, so long as they retain the light which has shined upon them and gives their heart an eternal glow.[181]

Thus the invisible spiritual church is truly ecumenical and includes not only pious Christians but enlightened heathens from the Greeks through Islam. All pious persons are in Christ even if they don't know it—a position which seems to anticipate the modern phrase "anonymous Christians." God "circumcises the hearts of his own with the Spirit and fire and in truth (which are not wiped away). With these also he causes them to sacrifice and makes and builds out of them at length a temple of God, baptizes scattered Israel, feeds and gives them to drink without hands and external elements."[182]

From his first writing (*On the Detestable Vice of Drunkenness*, 1528) to his last, Franck was pessimistic about the world and the church. He could not accept the claims of any one church not only because of their rival and mutually exclusive claims but because they did not bring about the fruits of faith. Thus he awaited the future assembling of the true God by the Spirit, convinced that until then faith, penitence, and self-denial could be realized by all in the Spirit whether in or out of organized Christianity. Quite logically, he wanted no following, for the way to the restitution of Christianity was not through sacraments, preaching, and church discipline but the interior and ethical renewal of the individual. Faced by the fallibility of the institutional church he found refuge in the interiority of the Spirit.

CASPAR VON SCHWENCKFELD (1489-1561)

We shall conclude our brief sketches of selected sixteenth-century "spiritualists" with Caspar von Schwenckfeld. He is of interest not only because like our other figures he began his reforming career under the influence of Luther and like Hoffman was a lay preacher, but also because he is the only figure of this period who has received scholarly attention from a modern Lutheran with a "charismatic" orientation, Karl Ecke.

Schwenckfeld was born at Ossig in Silesia of an old noble family. He studied at the universities of Köln and Frankfurt an der Oder. While he himself made no reference to the subjects studied, it is probable that he

---

[181]Letter to Campanus, Williams, *Spiritual and Anabaptist Writers*, 149, 150.

[182]Ibid., 152. Cf. also Franck's *Paradox*, 231; Staehelin, *Die Verkündigung des Reich Gottes*, 351.

was engaged in the liberal arts and law. From 1518-1523 he was a councillor to Duke Frederick II of Liegnitz. He was forced to give up this position due to deafness, but he continued to assist the Duke in introducing the Reformation through his activities as a lay preacher and writer of devotional literature.

He experienced a religious awakening from reading Luther's writings some time before the end of 1519. His indebtedness to Luther was felt so strongly that years after Luther's rejection of him, he confessed his thankfulness for Luther. The irenic and friendly personality of Schwenckfeld stimulated a wide response among the pastors and nobles of Silesia. Because his evangelization had a stong ethical tint to it from the beginning, the question of the ethical fruit of the Reformation became decisive for him; he wondered whether the "ineffectiveness" of the preaching of the gospel was related to an overemphasis of the doctrine of justification. He was already familiar with Karlstadt's writings on the Eucharist when he went to Wittenberg to have a conference with Luther in 1525. It was here that differences on the Lord's Supper, justification, the nature of the church, and christology became clear.

Schwenckfeld's consequent attempt to find "the royal way" between conflicting Reformation perspectives managed to antagonize the major Reformers and lose the sympathy of his Duke. Thus in 1529 he left Liegnitz for Strasbourg where he came into conflict with Bucer. In 1533 he went to Augsburg, then Ulm in 1535. Condemned in the Schmalkald Articles (1540), he spent the last decades of his life as a homeless wanderer.[183]

SCHWENCKFELD'S THEOLOGY

Up to 1525 Schwenckfeld was a follower and a student of Luther and, as a layperson, was less interested in sharply defined theological concepts than in renewed piety. In this respect Luther's 1517 exegesis on the seven penitential Psalms was influential upon Schwenckfeld. At the same time he gained from this writing a fundamental orientation for his own later theological development which included the antithesis of Adam and Christ, the growth of faith from bitter repentance, and the miraculous gift

---

[183]Gottfried Maron, "Schwenckfeld," *RGG* 5 (1620-1621); Horst Weigelt, *Spiritualistische Tradition im Protestantismus: Das Schwenckfeldertum in Schlesien* (Berlin: De Gruyter, 1973) 3-30; Emmanuel Hirsch, "Schwenckfeld und Luther," in his *Lutherstudien* 2 (Gütersloh: Bertelmann, 1954) 35-67.

of faith and new life. Nearly all the motives of Schwenckfeld's piety are reminiscent of Luther's 1517 writing. On the other hand Luther's distinction and dialectic of Law and Gospel did not make much sense to Schwenckfeld nor did it become so evident to him as it was to Luther that the conscience needs strong divine acceptance in order to be joyous and stand before God. This is a clue to why, for Schwenckfeld, the question of the ethical fruits of justification became decisive.[184]

JUSTIFICATION

As early as 1522 Schwenckfeld was expressing a growing unease about the absence of the ethical renewal he expected from the Reformation. He was disappointed by the ethical laxity not only of the people but also of many evangelical preachers who only polemicized against works and emphasized faith. His disappointment over the absence of the hoped for *renovatio christianismi* parallels the contemporary development of Hans Denck and, most notably, Sebastian Franck in southern Germany. This was an important theme in his December 1525 consultation with Luther.

As Schwenckfeld and his followers became more distressed by what they saw around them they began to ask whether perhaps the Lutheran doctrine of justification might itself be at fault. According to Schwenckfeld the absence of ethical improvement lay first of all in the misunderstood and misunderstandable *sola fide*. The people will neither hear nor learn that the prerequisite for the reception of grace is, according to Schwenckfeld, cross and suffering, mortification of the flesh, and flight from the world. Secondly, he criticized the doctrine of justification for completely negating human free will. Both Melanchthon's *loci* and the Luther-Erasmus exchange on free will had an impact on Schwenckfeld which was expressed in his 1528 tract, *Vom glauben in Christum,* by the formula: "The old man had free will for evil, the new man a free will for good."[185] Thirdly, in his *Ermanung Dess Missbrauchs* he criticized the doctrine of justification for completely eliminating the significance of works from the event of justification. Certainly the work of Christ is the fundamental ground for the reception of grace but works are not irrele-

---

[184]Hirsch, "Schwenckfeld und Luther," 37f.

[185]*Corpus Schwenckfeldianorum,* 3:560, 18-19. Quoted by Weigelt, *Spiritualistische Tradition,* 36.

vant. Here he distinguishes between the works of the natural man and those of the person reborn.[186]

From this point Schwenckfeld moved to develop what Weigelt terms a doctrine of "sanative making righteous" (*sanative Gerechtmachung*). This begins with repentance which purifies the heart and prepares it to receive the gospel. This purification occurs through suffering and asceticism; the elect may come to heavenly joy in no other way than Christ himself took. This is a process which is to become visible in a new life. Schwenckfeld's description of this new life borders on perfectionism.[187] However, human weakness remains, even a real fall back into mortal sin may occur, for which the Christian needs forgiveness. However, the weakness must be seen as the weakness of a growing new person, and a fall, from which the new becoming person must quickly arise, must be seen as an exception. Thus the certainty that Christ has entered into us and the new man is growing toward perfection is not destroyed. Here Schwenckfeld departs from Luther's fundamental position that justification is always the *iustificatio impii* throughout the life of the Christian. For Schwenckfeld the justification of the godless is limited to the initiation of the new man. Thus the certainty of communion with God rests not upon God's word of forgiveness but rather upon the fruit of the renewing work of the Spirit in the heart.[188]

SCRIPTURE

Schwenckfeld's understanding of justification and rebirth, and his view of the inner and outer man are intimately related to his reading of Scripture. Running throughout his theology is a thoroughgoing dualism that placed in antithesis the old and new man, Spirit and flesh, Spirit and letter. Faith does not come from hearing Scripture but is rather the indwelling of Christ through the Holy Spirit. God works faith directly by dwelling within the person. He does not need any mediation, not even Scripture, for this would limit divine liberty. Only the Spirit can produce the spiritual, thus something material as the Scripture cannot produce faith.[189]

---

[186]*Corpus Schwenckfeldianorum*, 2:72ff.; Weigelt, *Spiritualistische Tradition*, 36.

[187]Weigelt, *Spiritualistische Tradition*, 36ff.

[188]Hirsch, "Schwenckfeld und Luther," 54.

[189]For this and much of what follows see R. Emmet McLaughlin, "Spiritualism and the Bible: The Case of Caspar Schwenckfeld (1489-1561)," *MQR* 53 (1979): 282-98.

The purpose of the Bible is to inspire the outer man to a righteous life in conformity to the inner man who is really Christ. In practice this approximates the donatism that has been indicated in Franck and others—for any use of Scripture that does not produce righteousness must be false. A preacher's proclamation and doctrine then is to be judged by his own life and the life of his congregation. Here again is an aspect of Schwenckfeld's disappointment with the Reformation which he explained by saying the Reformers preached on the letter not the Spirit. Furthermore, the outer man could no more understand the true inner gospel than a man blind from birth could understand color. "The faithful, then, were *theodidacti,* those taught by God. In practice, the revelation given to believers was not an addition to Scripture, but rather a new understanding of what Scripture really said."[190] A central example of this is Schwenckfeld's doctrine of the heavenly flesh of Christ and the Eucharist.

CHRISTOLOGY AND THE LORD'S SUPPER

God's plan of salvation was for a progressive deification of man to overcome the gap between creature and Creator. Here again we note the theme of like being known only by like. Adam's fall prevented the Old Man from reaching this "divine status" of being the New Man. Christ, however, was born of Mary as the new noncreated man and now reigns in heaven as the new deified man. By partaking of this Heavenly Flesh we become New Men ourselves.

Schwenckfeld's theology of the Lord's Supper thus identifies believing and eating (*credere* and *edere*) in a spiritualist understanding of the Eucharist. The true Christian partakes of Christ's body and blood within the depths of his being. This inner supper is the increasing participation in Christ's glorified Flesh, and therefore the growth of the faith which is the New Man. "To this inner Supper corresponded an external ceremony which was a rite of remembrance and thanksgiving. Since the external sacrament was merely a remembrance, and not the efficient cause, Schwenckfeld was able to call for a suspension of its observance (*Stillstand*) until a better understanding would prevail among the various Protestant parties."[191] The Lutheran connection of the proclamation of the forgiveness of sins to the Lord's Supper was for Schwenckfeld as

---

[190]Ibid., 289.

[191]Ibid., 288, n. 28; Weigelt, *Spiritualistiche Tradition,* 50.

conducive to moral laxity as was their doctrine of justification. The Lutheran *extra nos* was opposed by a thoroughgoing *in nos*. Over this issue Luther and Schwenckfeld parted ways in 1525.

By conflating 1 Corinthians 11:24 ("This is my body") with John 6:51 ("the bread which I give is my own flesh") Schwenckfeld argued that,

> ... it is essential that the divine work of the Lord Christ, that is, the feeding and the inner, spiritual eating in faith, be properly distinguished from the external, sacramental eating ... that the inner, spiritual precede and be contemplated, but the external, sacramental eating follow and be observed in proclaiming the death of the Lord. . . .[192]

This spiritual feeding of the soul can only be given by Christ and not at all by ministers of the church. To believe otherwise, as Luther, is to make an idol out of the sacrament and promote false confidence.

> In reality the Supper or sacrament of the Altar has become not only a snare for the conscience and an offense to the Christ-believing soul, but a cloak for all error, all sin, and godless being, as well as a furtherance to and confirmation of the old unrepentant life and accursed way of the flesh (like the Mass). May God be merciful! Do what you will (say the Lutherans), only go to the Supper and everything will be simple; and as soon and as often as you come again after falling, everything will be forgiven you![193]

Schwenckfeld's dualism and dichotomy between inner and outer, Spirit and flesh, Old Man and New Man is further expressed in his christology which of course is intimately tied to his understanding of the Lord's Supper. By the spiritual feeding on Christ's heavenly flesh, Christians become New Men themselves. While Schwenckfeld vehemently denied the charges that he was repeating the ancient monophysite and Eutychian heresies,[194] he clearly asserted that Christ's human nature was not human according to the old order of Adam. "According to his human nature, he was an uncreaturely creature. The Holy Spirit conceived 'pure uncreaturely flesh' in a pure, reborn virgin. Christ's body belonged therefore to 'the new order of recreation or rebirth.' During his lifetime on earth this new flesh was progressively deified, so that by the time of his glorification and session in heaven it was virtually identical with his divine nature. It is upon this 'heavenly flesh' that the believer now feeds

---

[192]"An Answer to Luther's Malediction by Caspar Schwenckfeld," 1544. Williams, *Spiritual and Anabaptist Writers,* 163-81, 167. Cf. also 175.

[193]Ibid., 173. Cf. also 168f., 171, 178.

[194]Ibid., 179ff.

in faith."[195] "I recognize nothing of creation or creatureliness in Christ but rather a new divine birth and natural sonship (*kindtschafft*) of God. Wherefore I cannot consider the Man Christ with his body and blood to be a creation or a creature."[196]

CHURCH

Schwenckfeld's order of salvation proceeds from the death of the Old Man to the deification of the New. The Old Man experiences death under the judgment of the Holy Spirit who awakens the knowledge of our sinfulness with sorrow and remorse. The New Man is resurrected through the reception of the Spirit and the implantation in Christ. However, this is a process which may be analyzed in a series of experiences. First of all there is the "awakening" of the New Man: the Spirit instills the gospel of the grace of God in Christ and creates a transformation of the soul. Thus faith is born out of the eternal Word. Thereupon the following occur by degrees: change of life and essence, the essence, the knowledge of Christ and the perception of his sweetness, certainty of one's faith. Thereby faith and the incorporation into membership in Christ is completed and the height of the Christian estate is reached in the reception of the heavenly sacrament. This sacrament opens the next step which is the sealing by the Spirit. Next to spiritual baptism and the Lord's Supper of the heart, Schwenckfeld calls this the confirmation or assurance of the perseverance of salvation. However, the rebirth is not completed upon earth for we continue to bear our mortal and sinful flesh. Thus the task remains to continually mortify the Old Man and his desires. The process is finally completed by death and resurrection at the Last Day. The rebirth is completed with the glory of the resurrection-body. This process from beginning to end is described as one taking place in the inner solitary soul outside the human community.[197] Thus, along with the Scriptures and the sacraments, the visible church is directed to the moral reformation of the Outer Man. "Schwenckfeld's conception of the visible

---

[195]Ozment, *Mysticism and Dissent,* 299; Weigelt, *Spiritualistiche Tradition,* 159-68. For the relationship between Schwenckfeld and Hoffman in the development of this monophysite Christology, cf. Deppermann, *Melchior Hoffman,* 186ff. Cf. also Hirsch, "Schwenckfeld und Luther," 63ff.

[196]Williams, "An Answer to Luther," 180.

[197]Hirsch, "Schwenckfeld und Luther," 55.

church developed from that of a purely eucharistic community maintained by use of the Ban, to a pure individualism in which no external church played a role, but only prayer sessions and individual exhortation and comforting were foreseen."[198]

CONCLUSIONS

Toward the end of his life Schwenckfeld provided a summary of the "Difference between Caspar von Schwenckfeld and the doctrines of the Preachers"[199] which is useful for our conclusion. Here he sharply expressed his dualism between visible and invisible, outer and inner, Spirit and Scripture, heart and letter. The visible may only be understood from the viewpiont of the invisible. All external means for the goal of overcoming human sinful creatureliness and becoming equal (*Gleichwerden*) with the heavenly Christ are only a hindrance. The heavenly Christ calls his own directly to himself.

WAS THERE A CHARISMATIC MOVEMENT IN THE REFORMATION?

Our purpose in reviewing selected "charismatic" opponents to Luther has been to present some of those voices and ideas which stimulated and formed Luther's opinion about the *Schwärmer*. Beginning with Luther, the term *Schwärmer* has been a pejorative label for those whom Luther believed to have turned the gospel inside out, replacing the external Word of promise and forgiveness with the internal Word of religious experience and deification or self-fulfillment. Since the Reformation those persons and movements whose theology and practice have emphasized or gravitated toward an emphasis upon religious experience have been dubbed *Schwärmer*. Recent efforts by scholars and ecumenists to substitute other terms such as "left-wing" or "radical" Reformers and to provide more sophisticated discrimination in analysis of the *Schwärmer* have mitigated the problem somewhat but not resolved it.[200]

---

[198]McLaughlin, "Spiritualism and the Bible," 288. Cf. Gottfried Maron, *Individualismus und Gemeinschaft bei Caspar von Schwenckfeld* (Stuttgart, 1961).

[199]18 Theses, ca. 1556. Fast, *Der Linke Flügel,* 206-209.

[200]Roland Bainton's "The Left Wing of the Reformation," *Journal of Religion* 21 (1941) was one of the first efforts in this direction. One of the most ambitious typologies of the different positions is that of George H. Williams, *The Radical Reformation.* We

Thus if this term is to be demoted from its rank of shibboleth, with all its emotive currents and imprecise condemnations, we need to have an awareness of whom and what it was used against as well as why. Thus we have briefly surveyed some persons and their positions which elicited Luther's response. In the next section we shall survey this response and why it was so important to Luther and his heirs.

First however, it will be useful to pull together the views we have surveyed and ask not only whether there are common strains running through them but also whether they present a phenomenon at all analogous to contemporary Pentecostal and charismatic movements. This latter task is a provisional effort for as we stated at the outset we are not proceeding from the standpoint of a set definition of the essence of the charismatic movement. The question is how the persons and groups Luther denounced as *Schwärmer* differed from him in their religious self-understanding.

We do not want to imply that there is a genetic connection or a historical line of influence running like some red thread from the Zwickau prophets to contemporary charismatics. To do so would only be an anachronistic continuation of Luther's condemnation of the *Schwärmer*. However, it is important in light of the contemporary use of Luther's writings to consider whether or not Luther was confronted with phenomena at all analogous to contemporary Pentecostal and charismatic movements. If so, the tendency to use the Lutheran heritage as an arsenal against modern parallels—however insensitive and unecumenical—is not without some awareness of the central issues. On the other hand if the major targets for Luther's epithets were unique expressions of a particularly stressful, indeed apocalyptic era, then it is illegitimate to universalize his context and judgments to critique present expressions of religious experience which may be discomforting to the churches.

---

need to remember that in the upheaval of the Reformation period the differences among theologies were not always so apparent as they sometimes seem to us with the vantage point of time and relative stability. As late as 1958 Gordon Rupp could say, "The radical pedigree is still a dark side of the moon in Reformation study." "Word and Spirit," 14. Cf. also Bernhard Lohse, "Die Stellung der 'Schwärmer' und Täufer in der Reformationsgeschichte," *ARG* 60/1 (1969): 5-26. For a review of terminology developed in modern historiography to replace *Schwärmer* cf. J. F. G. Goeters, "Spiritualisten, religiöse," *RGG*, 255f.

Our choice of Karlstadt, Müntzer, Hoffman, Franck, and Schwenck-feld is a selection and is, therefore, not entirely arbitrary. We chose persons who were without any doubt very influential in the development of Luther's anti-spiritualist responses. Furthermore, our subjects include both pastors and laymen who were markedly influenced at the beginning of their careers by Luther himself. There are of course numerous other Schwärmer or "left-wingers" whom we have not mentioned. They range from bizarre parallels to the modern experience with the James Jones cult in Guyana to "closet spiritualists" like the Lutheran pastor Valentin Weigel. However, while we may have opportunity to refer to these people, the subjects we have chosen are sufficient for our purposes and limitations of space. There is already an extensive and growing body of multilingual literature on the Radical Reformation to which the interested reader may turn for more information.

From what we have seen so far it should be clear that our spiritualist subjects "are not obsessed with pneumatology, but more concerned with the contrast between the 'outer' and 'inner Word,' or between 'spirit' and 'letter,' or the 'inward' and 'outer man.' There is not nearly as much said as we might expect about the Person and Work of the Holy Ghost."[201] Thus if we look to the sources themselves with the hope of finding the designation "charismatic" we will be disappointed as this was not a term used in the sixteenth century. Nevertheless, realities are not eliminated nor created by the lack of or application of a label. We are concerned with a thought pattern not just a term. We have referred to our subjects as "spiritualists," a term now used in Reformation studies. In the narrow sense of the term this has been defined "as a protest against the church as a legitimately constituted institution of salvation, the exclusive mediation of grace through Word and sacraments, and the use of Scripture as the only source and norm for Christian faith and life."[202] This is a definition which Luther would have to qualify for it implies an equation of the Word with "pure doctrine" on the one hand and Spirit as the cover for human subjectivism on the other. In spite of Reformation controversies, Luther never wished to divorce Word from Spirit and neither did the spiritualists.[203]

---

[201]Rupp, "Word and Spirit," 13.

[202]Goeters, "Spiritualisten, religiöse," 256.

[203]Cf. Rupp, "Word and Spirit," 13; ABK, 205.

A more carefully nuanced definition of spiritualism still argues that spiritualism is an "underlying principle that directs itself against the externalization of religion" and that the Holy Spirit "does not necessarily need media through which to work on and in the human heart." In this sense the Lutheran pastor Valentin Weigel has been quoted in a recent critique of the charismatic movement as an example of a sixteenth-century "charismatic."

> For after one hour with the Spirit a peasant graduates to doctor (of theology). The Spirit teaches him languages and explains the meaning of Christ, why Christ came, died, descended into hell, and ascended into heaven. Any man who gives the Spirit room to work in him learns perfectly all the articles of faith.[204]

However, this does not necessarily mean a separation of Spirit from the written Word: "It must, however, be understood that this separation is not antipodal in the sense of a complete severance, but tensional; and that by consequence there can be only degrees of spiritualization, the tensions between Scripture and Spirit increasing in direct proportion to the Spiritualization."[205]

Two foci for the rise of this spiritualist tendency are the problem of authority and the mediation of grace. The persons we have surveyed exhibit spiritualist orientations on both points, sometimes in the same person. Thus Hoffman, for example, can claim leadership authority both in terms of special revelation and spiritual illumination in exegesis. As we saw in Karlstadt, there was the conviction both of the Spirit's inner call to the minister as well as to the congregation, and the sole sufficiency of the inner witness of the Spirit in exegesis. In Franck we saw the conviction that the Bible was contradictory precisely to facilitate the spiritual communication of grace apart from the Word. Both Müntzer and Hoffman posited new revelation in the outpouring of the Spirit: "For if Christendom is not to become apostolic (Acts 2:16ff.) in the way anticipated in Joel, why should one preach at all? To what purpose then the Bible with (its) visions?"[206]

The Baptist Reformation scholar, Kenneth Davis, sharply distinguishes the Reformation Anabaptists from what he calls the "extreme

---

[204]Hendrix, "Charismatic Renewal: Old Wine in New Skins,"*Currents in Theology and Mission* 4/3 (1977) 164; cf. Ozment, *Mysticism and Dissent,* 228.

[205]Walter Klaasen, "Spiritualization in the Reformation," *MQR* 37 (1963): 67-77, 70-71, 76, as quoted in ABK, 205.

[206]"Princes' Sermon." Williams, *Spiritual and Anabaptist Writers,* 62.

heretical-mystical brand" of charismatics represented by most of our figures, but he insists forcefully that "Clearly sixteenth-century Anabaptism was a charismatic movement. . . . " He argues that as a charismatic movement Anabaptism "arose not as a challenge to the sole authority of Scripture but as a challenge to institutionalized, politicized, rigorously structured ecclesiastical authority in advocacy of the freedom of the Spirit, the spiritual nature of the Church and lay participation."[207] What is of interest to us here is the claim that the sixteenth-century Anabaptists may be understood in the contemporary sense of the expression "charismatic movement." That Davis distances this from Müntzer and Hoffman is a way of saying that they embodied a more extreme expression of a diverse charismatic movement not unlike that of Montanism in the second and third centuries which had its fanatics and moderates. George Williams reinforces this perspective by actually labeling our selected persons "charismatic" in light of their experience of the Spirit as "a driving power."[208]

It now seems fair to say that the persons with whom Luther had his most intense disagreements over the Spirit and Word, inner and outer, the persons and movements he called *Schwärmer*, we may refer to as charismatic. This provides us with a more consistent vocabulary as we attempt to relate the Lutheran tradition to contemporary charismatic movements and expressions. Also by using the term "charismatic" instead of "Schwärmer" and "spiritualist," we hope to minimize the pejorative content of the latter terms and to free the religious-theological issues from a sometimes distorting sociological-phenomenological perspective.[209] At the same time there are two caveats to be emphasized. One is that the charismatics with whom Luther dealt were one or another extreme and only one expression of sixteenth-century charismatics. The second is that by the use of the term charismatic we are not suggesting that Luther's responses to them can be simply repristinated in the present situations. Before Luther's responses to the charismatics in his day may be a resource for today they have to be analyzed. It is to this task that we now turn.

---

[207]Kenneth Davis, "Anabaptism as a Charismatic Movement," *MQR* 53/3 (1979): 233, 221f.

[208]Williams, *Spiritual and Anabaptist Writers*, "Introduction," 29, 32.

[209]Cf. for an example Karl Steck, *Luther und die Schwärmer* (Zürich: Zollikon, 1955) 6f.

CONFLICTING VIEWS OF
SALVATION AND SANCTIFICATION

In what follows we shall be concentrating upon Luther's response to the charismatic challenges to his understanding of the gospel. To a great extent we shall be relying upon the treatises which Luther wrote between 1524 and 1528. These polemical works, directed mainly against Karlstadt and Müntzer, include the following: *Letter to the Princes of Saxony Concerning the Rebellious Spirit*, 1524,[210] in which he counsels the princes to act against Müntzer before Müntzer instigates open rebellion; *Letter to the Christians at Strassburg in Opposition to the Fanatic Spirit*, 1524,[211] in response to a formal request from the evangelical preachers in Strasbourg for a clarification of Luther's postion vis-á-vis Karlstadt following the latter's visit to the city in the fall of 1524; *Against the Heavenly Prophets in the Matter of Images and Sacraments*, 1525,[212] which is Luther's most thorough attempt to respond to Karlstadt's writings against him following their confrontation at Jena; *How Christians Should Regard Moses*, 1525,[213] which deals with how the law is understood in opposition to the positions of Karlstadt and Müntzer; *That These Words of Christ, "This Is My Body," Etc. Still Stand Firm Against the Fanatics*, 1527,[214] which is directed against the eucharistic theologies of Zwingli and Oecolampadius as well as Karlstadt and Schwenckfeld; *Concerning Rebaptism*, 1528,[215] rejects the Anabaptists' emphasis upon believers' baptism; and finally, *Brief Confession Concerning the Holy Sacrament*, 1544,[216] stimulated by Caspar von Schwenckfeld as well as the need to once again clarify his sacramental theology in light of confused reports circulating among pastors in Hungary. References to these writings shall be by volume and page whereas references to other tracts will be given in full including title and date.

---

[210]LW 40, 45-59; WA 15, 210-21.

[211]LW 40, 61-71; WA 15, 391-97.

[212]LW 40, 73-223; WA 18, 62-125, 134-214.

[213]LW 35, 155-74; WA 16, 363-93.

[214]LW 37, 3-150; WA 23, 64-283.

[215]LW 40, 225-62; WA 26, 144-74.

[216]LW 38, 279-319; WA 54, 141-67.

We are very appreciative of Regin Prenter's point that all too often Luther's conception of the person and work of the Holy Spirit is presented only in the context of his polemical statements against Karlstadt and others. "It is natural that Luther's testimony is not heard in all its strength by simply studying his polemic against the enthusiasts. The polemic which emphasizes but a single part of Luther's view of the Spirit's work has its background in Luther's total concept of the Spirit, and it must be interpreted on this background and not detached from it."[217] Thus while we shall refer in the conclusion of this chapter to Luther's theology of the Spirit, we wish at this point to draw attention both to the presence of the classical study by Prenter (especially Part One: "Before the Controversy With the Enthusiasts") and to recall that our purpose is primarily to explore Luther's response to the charismatic challenge of his day and not to write a study of Luther's theology of the Spirit.

The relationship of salvation and sanctification was central to the conflict between the charismatics of the Reformation and Luther. This is a broad and complex issue for it includes ethical and social as well as theological issues. "Accordingly, in dealing with the problem of sanctification in the radical opponents of Luther one may speak of penitential transformation of character; of participation in the holiness of the whole Christ in suffering and glory; of inheriting the resurrection of Christ in one's flesh; of becoming free from the rule of sin; of the experience of Christ not only *pro nobis* but also *in nobis*; of regeneration, renewal, divinization, imitation, and discipleship; of separation from the world, perfectionism, New Covenantal legalism, fruitage of the Spirit, pietism, suffering obedience, and moral accountability; of social reform, primitivist-mystical-eschatological communitarianism and covenantal-eschatological-martial discipline."[218] Karlstadt's emphasis upon mortification and Schwenckfeld's concern with "the subjective, charismatic-pneumatic organization of the primitive Christian church"[219] must also be emphasized.

---

[217]Regin Prenter, *Spiritus Creator: Luther's Concept of the Holy Spirit*, trans. by John M. Jensen (Philadelphia: Fortress Press, 1953) 206.

[218]George Williams, "Sanctification in the Testimony of Several So-Called Schwärmer," in Asheim, 194-211, 195.

[219]Karl Ecke, *Fortsetzung der Reformation: Kaspar von Schwenckfelds Schau einer apostolischen Reformation* (Blaubeuren-Ulm, 1965) 36f.

We have seen Hoffman's confidence that the justified person can with free will do godly works:

> They are the true dead who have the true salvation and liberation from sin, who are purified of all misdeeds through the blood of Jesus Christ ... all who are dead themselves in the Lord, having routed out and laid aside the old Adam. ... And therefore that sinful seed, being dead, cannot make unrighteousness fruitful; for he who has been born of God has the upper hand and victory, and therefore *no sin can issue*. [220]

The justified, therefore, become ontologically sinless and can no longer sin for they are maintained by a true regeneration. And such perfection, even divinization, through an experiential sanctification was not limited to the persons we have surveyed. Melchior Rinck could rhetorically ask, "What is then that Gospel other than the affirmation of God that to them that *better themselves*, the forgiveness of their sins is promised?" Balthasar Hubmeier substituted *Gerechtmachung* for *Gerechtfertigung*; Hans Denck spoke of being divinized by the invisible wine of God's invisible chalice.[221] A characteristic emphasis throughout these perspectives is the combination of Spirit and Law (especially by use of the Old Testament) in service to sanctification.

In response to this "charismatic" orientation Luther's central question, first expressed in regard to the Strasbourg inquiry about Karlstadt, is "What makes a person a Christian?"

> My sincere counsel and warning is that you be circumspect and hold to the single question, what makes a person a Christian? Do not on any account allow any other question or other art enjoy equal importance. When anyone proposes anything ask him at once, "Friend will this make one a Christian or not?".[222]

Luther's own response is a resounding rejection of *anything* done by a person to ground salvation in himself.[223] Not even faith makes a person a Christian! "Always something is lacking in faith. However long our life, always there is enough to learn in regard to faith."[224] It is worthwhile exploring this point further because while the Reformation charismatics

---

[220]*Van den gevangenen ende vrien wil*, c. 1531. *Bibliotheca Reformatoria Neerlandica* 5 (The Hague, 1909) 151, quoted by Williams, "Sanctification in the Testimony," 199.

[221]Williams, "Sanctification in the Testimony," 203ff.

[222]LW 40, 67.

[223]"It is evident that no external thing has any influence in producing Christian righteousness or freedom. ... " *The Freedom of a Christian*, 1520. LW 31, 344f.

[224]LW 40, 253. On the uncertainty of faith cf. pp. 241, 252, 253, 255, 260.

criticized Luther for relying upon faith alone, Luther criticized them for submerging the gospel in the externals of a quest for sanctification. In the process of developing Luther's understanding of faith we shall begin to understand his positive answer to "What makes a person a Christian?".

FAITH

What makes a person a Christian is the Person, Jesus Christ, who died for the sins of humankind and was raised from death by God for the salvation of humankind. This Jesus Christ is the eternal mediator and savior. On this gospel Luther and his charismatic opponents agree. They disagree on how this is appropriated and what its consequences are.

For Luther, we are related to God through trust in Jesus as Christ.[225] This trust is a personal experience[226] but it may not be accounted for either in terms of our inner life nor our outward behavior.

> So, my brother, cling firmly to the order of God. According to it the putting to death of the old man, wherein we follow the example of Christ, as Peter says (1 Pet. 2:21), does not come first, as this devil (Karlstadt) urges, but comes last. No one can mortify the flesh, bear the cross, and follow the example of Christ before he is a Christian and has Christ through faith in his heart as an eternal treasure. You can't put the old nature to death, as these prophets do, through works, but through the hearing of the gospel. Before all other works and acts you hear the Word of God, through which the Spirit convinces the world of its sin (John 16:8). When we acknowledge our sin, we hear the grace of Christ. In this Word the Spirit comes and gives faith where and to whom he wills. Then you proceed to the mortification and the cross and the works of love. Whoever wants to propose to you another order, you can be sure, is of the devil. Such is the spirit of this Karlstadt.[227]

Faith or trust in God which is the work of the Holy Spirit "when and where he wills" is always "by hearing" (*ex auditu*). As such the Word is always the living Word of address to us. It is a Word which in preaching comes from outside of us (*extra nos*) and proclaims what Christ has done for us (*pro nobis*). Luther's critique of Karlstadt, Müntzer, and others is that they invert this order. "Dr. Karlstadt and his spirits replace the

---

[225]Cf. inter alia, WA 40¹, 366, 24f.

[226]"*sapiente experimentalis*" WA 9, 98, 21; "*experientalis cognitio in Christo,*" WA 3, 230, 10. Cf. Ingolf Dalferth, "Luther on the Experience of Faith," *Heythrop Journal* 21/1 (1980): 50-56.

[227]LW 40, 149. This is also the thrust of Article V of the Augsburg Confession. T. Tappert, *The Book of Concord* (Philadelphia: Muhlenberg Press, 1959) 31; cf. Prenter, *Spiritus Creator*, 257f.

highest with the lowest, the best with the least, the first with the last. Yet he would be considered the greatest spirit of all, he who has devoured the Holy Spirit feathers and all."[228]

> Now when God sends forth his holy gospel he deals with us in a twofold manner, first outwardly, then inwardly. Outwardly he deals with us through the oral word of the gospel and through material signs, that is, baptism and the sacrament of the altar. Inwardly he deals with us through the Holy Spirit, faith, and other gifts. But whatever their measure or order the outward factors should and must procede. The inward experience follows and is effected by the outward. God has determined to give the inward to no one except through the outward. For he wants to give no one the Spirit or faith outside of the outward Word and sign instituted by him, as he says in Luke 16:29, "Let them hear Moses and the prophets." Accordingly Paul can call baptism a "washing of regeneration" wherein God "richly pours out the Holy Spirit" (Titus 3:5). And the oral gospel "is the power of God for salvation to every one who has faith" (Rom. 1:16).[229]

If we may speak about an order of salvation in Luther's theology it is in terms of the Word coming from outside of us through preaching, being heard and believed with the result that the sinner calls upon God and is saved. That this "order" is not created by Luther just to answer the charismatics is seen by his emphasis upon God's "sending" in his early writings.

> For these four points are so interrelated that the one follows upon the other, and the last is the cause and antecedent of all the others, that is, it is impossible for them to hear unless they are preached to; and from this, that it is impossible for them to believe if they do not hear; and then it is impossible for them to call upon God if they do not believe; and finally it is impossible for them to be saved if they do not call upon God. Thus the whole root and origin of salvation lies in God who sends.[230]

Again, in this context, we recall that while preaching is the necessary condition for saving faith, it is not sufficient, for it is the Holy Spirit who works faith in the heart. "As long as I . . . cannot pour faith into people's hearts, I neither am able nor ought to force or compel anyone to believe; for God alone does this, coming to dwell beforehand in the heart. That is why we should leave the word free and not add our work to it: we possess

---

[228]LW 40, 83; also pp. 84, 90, 91, 147f., 178, 184, 187, 221f.

[229]LW 40, 146; also pp. 190ff., 212ff.

[230]Lectures on Romans, 1515-1516. LW 25, 413. Cf. also his earlier notes on Lombard's *Sentences*, WA 9, 92, 28-36; Dalferth, "Luther on the Experience of Faith," 51f. Later Luther will see both the papists and the charismatics as cohorts in the same error; for an example LW 40, 81, 128f., 248.

the *ius verbi,* but not the *executionem.* We have to preach the word, but
the consequences should be left to God alone in his pleasure."[231]

Even these few quotations, which could be greatly multiplied from the
entire corpus of Luther's writing, indicate the theological orientation of
his critique of Karlstadt and the others. Luther certainly is not rejecting
religious experience, not even extraordinary religious experience;[232] he is
rejecting the *order* of salvation which the charismatics proclaim. They
have no call,[233] they invert reality making the Word of God dependent
upon faith,[234] and consequently choose their own means of ascent to God
rather than receive God's descent to them.[235] In every area of Christian
life they change gospel into law. So Luther wrote to the Christians in
Strasbourg:

> Ask your evangelists, my dear sirs and brothers, to turn you away from Luther
> and Karlstadt and direct you always to Christ, but not, as Karlstadt does, only to
> the work of Christ, wherein Christ is held up as an example, which is the least
> important aspect of Christ. . . . But turn to Christ as to a gift of God. . . . For such
> matters these prophets have little sympathy, taste, or understanding. Instead
> they juggle with their "living voice from heaven," their "laying off the mate-
> rial," "sprinkling," "mortification," and similar high-sounding words. . . . They
> make for confused, disturbed, anxious consciences . . . meanwhile Christ is
> forgotten.[236]

Just as Christ is made into a new law so also are the sacraments. Both the
understanding of the Lord's Supper in terms of remembrance and baptism as contingent upon the faith of the believers throw the burden of
proof for salvation back upon the Christian.[237] But faith wants certainty:

---

[231]WA 10³, 15, 6-12. Quoted by Dalferth, "Luther on the Experience of Faith," 56.

[232]For example speaking in tongues is not forbidden so long as there is an interpreter.
LW 40, 142, including the footnote.

[233]LW 40, 111, 113, 222, 383ff.

[234]LW 40, 260ff.

[235]LW 40, 66ff., 83, 117, 124, 149.

[236]LW 40, 70; also pp. 84, 101, 134f. In his lectures on Galatians, 1531, Luther says,
"Therefore there is no difference at all between a papist, a Jew, a Turk, or a sectarian.
Their persons, locations, rituals, religions, works and forms of worship are, of course,
diverse; but they all have the same reason, the same heart, the same opinion and idea. . . .
'If I do this or that, I have a God who is favorably disposed toward me; if I do not, I have a
God who is wrathful.' There is no middle ground between human working and the
knowledge of Christ; if this knowledge is obscured, it does not matter whether you become
a monk or a heathen afterwards." LW 26, 396.

[237]LW 40, 205ff., 239ff.; LW 35, 164, 170ff.

"For faith (as I have often said) does not want some one simply to say or sing thus, but wants a word of God that plainly says: So it is and not otherwise. For faith wants to be no reed that the wind shakes (Mt. 11:7)."[238]

The great danger in the charismatics, as Luther saw it, was that his struggle to proclaim the certainty of salvation against papist works-righteousness would be dissolved into the even more terrifying psychological works-righteousness of introspection and interiorization. This would be an introversion of faith into self-reflection and thus the grounding of faith in oneself rather than the external Word, Christ. "We are baptized; not because we are certain of our faith but because it is the command and will of God. . . .Whoever allows himself to be baptized on the strength of his faith is not only uncertain, but also an idolater who denies Christ. For he trusts in and builds on something of his own. . . ."[239] "Faith may waver and change, but God's Word remains forever."[240] The Christian is *simul iustus et peccator* in his faith as well as his works; therefore he is to look to Christ, not to himself, for certainty. In self-reflection upon faith the Christian confronts himself not as a believer but as a non-believer, or in any case as one who does not know whether he believes. In this existential situation Luther's position is "I do not know whether I believe; but I do know in whom I believe."[241] In other words, although faith is certainly necessary, the Christian is to rely upon God's grace not on his own faith. "There is quite a difference between having faith, on the one hand, and depending on one's faith and making baptism depend on faith, on the other. Whoever allows himself to be baptized on the strength of his faith, is not only uncertain, but also an idolater who denies Christ."[242] The question Luther addresses to Karlstadt and others is that if you begin with the inner word of the Spirit, how do you know you are not finally talking only with yourself? Luther believed that the external or outer mediation of the "inner Word" by Word and sacrament

---

[238]LW 40, 219.

[239]LW 40, 252.

[240]LW 40, 260. We "should be certain that we are in a state of grace on account of Him who is certain." Lectures on Galatians, 1535. LW 26, 378f.; WA 40¹, 577, 5.

[241]Otto Hof, "Luthers Unterscheidung zwischen dem Glauben und der Reflexion auf den Glauben," *Kerygma und Dogma* 18 (1972): 294-324, 323f., also 294ff.

[242]LW 40, 252; WA 26, 164.

must be unconditionally adhered to, otherwise one is thrown back upon oneself. The latter situation was precisely what Luther had experienced in his monastic struggle to find a gracious God. Thus it is not surprising that he viewed Karlstadt, Müntzer, and others in terms of a relapse into a monastic works-righteousness:

> These prophets avoid, run away from, and are silent about the main points of Christian doctrine. For in no place do they teach how we are to become free from our sins, obtain a good conscience, and win a peaceful and joyful heart before God. This is what really counts. . . . But their spirit cannot give quietness or peace, but goes on and teaches special works in which they are to exercise and discipline themselves. They have no idea how a good conscienc can be gained or ought to be constituted.[243]

"Unmediated revelation" and the believed "inner Word" alone undercut for Luther the certainty which came from the "outer Word's" guarantee that it is God who is actually in dialogue with persons.

Luther's fundamental critique of any theology which dissolves the intimate connection between the Spirit and the external means of the Spirit's mediation by Word and sacrament is expressed by the following points in his *Against the Heavenly Prophets* as well as elsewhere:[244]

1. The symbolic interpretation of the Lord's Supper opens the door to a general allegorical interpretation of Scripture. However, there is no binding force to allegorical interpretation for it has no measure beyond the subjective. It rests upon intuition and thus becomes a "spiritual juggling." "The hardened Karlstadtians . . . can neither prove their assertions with Scripture nor wrest them from the text, but produce only their own notions and ideas. . . ." "Brother, the natural meaning of the words (of the biblical text) is queen, transcending all subtle, acute sophistical fancy. From it we may not deviate, unless we are compelled by a clear article of the faith. Otherwise the spiritual jugglers would not leave a single letter in Scripture." "Therefore, interpretations of God's word must be lucid and definite having a firm, sure, and true foundation on which one may confidently rely."[245]

2. If one denies the bodily presence of Christ in the sacrament, then only the believing subject remains, at best "remembering" the historical event of Christ's death. "Christ on the cross and all his suffering and his

[243]LW 40, 222f.; WA 18, 213.

[244]The following four points are indebted to Deppermann, *Melchior Hoffman,* 124.

[245]LW 40, 190; cf. 189; WA 18, 178-79.

death do not avail, even if, as you teach, they are 'acknowledged and meditated upon' with the utmost 'passion, ardor, heartfeltness.' Something else must always be there. What is it? The Word, the Word, the Word. . . . Even if Christ were given for us and crucified a thousand times, it would all be in vain if the Word of God were absent and were not distributed and given to me with the bidding, this is for you, take what is yours."[246]

3.   Spiritualization of Word and sacraments leads in the end to a new works-righteousness with the foci of human interiority and Christ as an example to be imitated. "You should carefully examine Dr. Karlstadt's spirit, noting the way he proceeds, how he would tear us from the Word and lead us toward works. To achieve all this the better, and to make a good impression, he holds before you the works of Christ himself, so that you might be alarmed and think: oh really? Who should not follow Christ?"[247] "Out of the word of Christ he makes a pure commandment and law which accomplishes nothing more than to tell and bid us to remember and acknowledge him. Furthermore he makes this acknowledgment nothing else than a work that we do. . . . "[248]

4.   Ultimately the spiritualization of Word and sacraments leads to rationalization of the Christian faith. Karlstadt "teaches us what Frau Hulda, natural reason, has to say in the matter, just as if we did not know that reason is the devil's prostitute. . . ."[249] "For in this matter of reason Peter Rültz (representative of Karlstadt in his *Dialogus*) boasts very loftily, and here speaks aptly in the manner of the heavenly prophets, namely, as we said, they do not come through the external Word to the spirit but from the spirit they come to the external Word. They hold to the word of Christ in John 12 (John 15:26-27): 'The Spirit of truth will bear witness and you also will be witnesses,' just as if the apostles had received the Spirit without the external Word of Christ. Satiated with the inner witness, Peter Rültz boasts that he receives the external in order to teach and correct others."[250]

---

[246]LW 40, 212f.

[247]LW 40, 134.

[248]LW 40, 206.

[249]LW 40, 174; cf. 192ff.

[250]LW 40, 195.

5. Luther also emphasizes in some of his other writings that the inversion of "outer" to "inner" leads to the ancient heresy of donatism—the validity of the Word and sacraments depends upon the character or in this case spirituality of either the preacher or the recipient. To rest the promise of God upon our faith or that of others is to be "like butter in sunshine."[251] "It is not a fruit of the Spirit to criticize a doctrine by the imperfect life of the teacher."[252] "We are baptized; not because we are certain of our faith but because it is the command and will of God. For even if I were never certain any more of faith, I still am certain of the command of God. . . . In this I cannot err, for God's command cannot deceive. But of my faith he has never said anything to anyone, nor issued an order or command concerning it."[253]

On the other hand Luther does not himself take a donatist position and assume that the charismatic position does not have the Word: "Still we must admit that the enthusiasts have the Scriptures and the Word of God in other doctrines. Whoever hears it from them and believes will be saved, even though they are unholy heretics and blasphemers of Christ. It is not a minor grace that God gives his Word even through evil rogues and the godless. In fact it is in some respects more perilous when he proclaims it through holy than through unholy folk. For the thoughtless are tempted to attach themselves to the holiness of the people rather than to the Word of God."[254]

6. Finally we may note that what Luther sees behind the orientation to the inner Word and the consequent emphasis upon sanctification is a dualistic world view which separates Spirit and matter and thus believes that divine revelation is possible only in the realm of the Spirit. Such a dualism cannot understand the dialectical tension of a theology of Law and Gospel, where the Spirit is mediated by external means to the Christian who is simultaneously sinner and righteous.

To the favorite passage of Karlstadt and others, "The spirit alone gives life: the flesh is of no avail" (John 6:63), Luther opposes his holistic theological anthropology.

---

[251]LW 40, 252.

[252]LW 40, 57. Cf. also On the Councils and the Church, 1539. LW 41, 151, 152.

[253]LW, 40, 252.

[254]LW 40, 251. For similar reflections regarding the papacy cf. LW 40, 231f.

> Flesh and spirit you must not understand as though flesh is only that which has to do with unchastity and spirit is only that which has to do with what is inwardly in the heart. Rather, like Christ in John 3 (6), Paul calls everything "flesh" that is born of the flesh—the whole man, with body and soul, mind and senses—because everything about him longs for the flesh. Thus you should learn to call him "fleshly" too who thinks, teaches, and talks a great deal about lofty spiritual matters, yet does so without grace. . . . On the contrary, you should call him "spiritual" who is occupied with the most external kinds of works. . . .[255]

In this same passage Luther defines living according to the flesh as unbelief, a condition which continues to plague the Christian. Only a godly Christian can make such a confession. "Now it is a marvelous thing that he who is righteous before God and has the Holy Spirit says that he is a sinner. It is right, however; he confesses what he has been and still is."[256] "Thus a Christian man is righteous and a sinner at the same time, holy and profane, an enemy of God and a child of God. None of the sophists will admit this paradox because they do not understand the true meaning of justification. This was why they forced men to go on doing good works until they would not feel any sin at all."[257]

7. This Lutheran dialectical theology which opposes a dualism of spirit and matter had the social consequence of the concept of vocation in the world.

> For the *Schwärmer* the social consequences of their understanding of salvation and the modalities of sanctification ranged from revolution (Müntzer, Münsterites) to withdrawal from the world either in conventicles or communitarian plantations (Mennonites, Hutterites) . . . almost all kinds of *Schwärmer*, from the Zwickau Prophets to the Amish Mennonites, have understood their suffering as an objective confirmation or an ever renewed authentication of their discipleship, assuring them of their being on the right way to sanctification.[258]

In an article on the abiding influence of mysticism in Luther's thought, Oberman states that it is astonishing that Luther did not criticize the *Schwärmer* for their great radicality but rather he reproached them for not being radical enough. They distinguished faith in the heart and Christ in heaven whereas both are involved with each other.

---

[255]Preface to the Epistle of St. Paul to the Romans, 1546 (1522). LW 35, 371f. See also LW 40, 203ff.; 37, 94-96, 99, 236, 249, 288.

[256]LW 36, 355.

[257]Lectures on Galatians, 1535. LW 26, 232f.

[258]Williams, "Sanctification in Testimony," 210. Cf. also George Williams, "German Mysticism in the Polarization of Ethical Behaviour in Luther and the Anabaptists," *MQR* 48 (1974): 275-304.

> Hence the speculation of the sectarians is vain when they imagine that Christ is present in us "spiritually," that is speculatively, but is present really in heaven. Christ and faith must be completely joined. We must simply take our place in heaven; and Christ must be, live and work in us. But He lives and works in us, not speculatively but really, with presence and with powers.[259]

In summary we may say that Luther opposed all orders of salvation which confused justification and sanctification. Any faith "that attributes more to love than to faith . . . (imagines) that God regards and accepts us on account of the love with which we love God and our neighbor after we have already been reconciled. If this is true, then we have no need whatever of Christ."[260] Because Christians do not have perfect fear, love, and trust toward God they are condemned by the law no matter what program of regeneration and sanctification they are involved in fulfilling. "For the true God does not regard or accept us on account of our love, virtue, or newness of life (Rom. 6:4); He does so on account of Christ."[261]

Therefore the church is not a community of the recognizable elect but an institution with earthly means of communicating the gospel. Luther sees nothing but "mischief" arising from those who depend upon only an "inner call of God." "This God condemns through Jeremiah (23:21), who says 'I did not send them, yet they ran. I did not speak to them, yet they prophesied.' "[262] Anyone who "relies on his own spirit and inner feelings for authority" must prove it with miraculous signs.[263]

The church, therefore, is recognized not by its holiness of life but by the "possession of the holy word of God." "Now, wherever you hear or see this word, preached, believed, professed, and lived, do not doubt that the true *ecclesia sancta catholica,* 'a Christian holy people,' must be there, even though their number is very small. . . . And even if there were no other sign than this alone, it would still suffice to prove that a Christian, holy people must exist there, for God's word cannot be without God's people, and conversely, God's people cannot be without God's word."[264]

---

[259]Lectures on Galatians, 1535. LW 26, 357; WA 40¹, 546, 3-8. Cf. Oberman, "Simul Gemitus et Raptus," 44f.

[260]Lectures on Galatians, 1535. LW 26, 398.

[261]Ibid.

[262]LW 40, 222.

[263]LW 40, 113. Cf. also LW 40, 383ff.

[264]On the Councils and the Church, 1539. LW 41, 150.

In our earlier discussion of Luther's theology we proposed the heuristic device of asking where and how fellowship with God occurs. The answers derived from Luther's theological motifs stress that fellowship with God occurs here on earth not in heaven through God's gracious acceptance of the sinner. Thus righteousness *coram Deo* is not an intrinsic capacity or possession of the Christian but a continuous gift. All efforts to usher in the Kingdom of God both politically and spiritually are therefore repudiated as theologies of glory. Christ's kingdom cannot be visibly identified with either remade social orders or "reborn" persons but only with God's Word. The certainty (*certitudo*) of the presence of God is always and only His Word not human works, lifestyles, feelings, or even faith. Thus Luther continually repudiated all attempts by his charismatic opponents to create security (*securitas*) whether it be by spiritually authenticated leadership, lifestyle, or exegesis.

Luther's theology of the cross informed his efforts to take seriously the task of world-building and the maintenance of culture and society with the insight that every culture and social structure is only relative and instrumental for the humanization of persons. This is a faith which can live with the doubt and meaninglessness of cruciform service to neighbor and community because it proceeds *from* God rather than *to* God; it is based on trust rather than directed toward success.

LEGACIES OF THESE CONFLICTS

Luther's first encounters with charismatic phenomena were through the Zwickau prophets, Karlstadt, and Müntzer. On the basis of the positions of these men, Luther created a stereotype which he then found confirmed by the events in Karlstadt's Orlamünde, Müntzer's various activities, and the Peasants' War. "Each of these men did indeed possess many of the characteristics of the false prophet: they lacked a proper call, they boasted of special revelation, they confused the worldly and divine kingdoms, they were legalistic, they were involved in inciting mob action, they were vain, they resisted a fraternal admonition, and so on."[265]

Unfortunately, Luther all too frequently extrapolated these initial experiences and judgments to others who to him seemed to share one or another characteristic with Karlstadt and Müntzer. Thus Luther has been

---

[265]Mark U. Edwards, Jr., *Luther and the False Brethren* (Stanford CA: Stanford University Press, 1975) 201. Cf. also Rupp, *Patterns*, 195.

judged for his rush to judgment against the charismatics of his day which precluded brotherly if not ecumenical dialogue.[266] On the other hand Luther's intervention and protection of Karlstadt in the aftermath of the Peasants' War as well as his generous preface to Karlstadt's *Apology* ought not be forgotten.[267] Rupp's assessment here is worth quoting:

> Luther by no means understood the whole of Karlstadt: but some he did understand. It is easy to read the story as Barge reads it, as though Karlstadt's hopeful and forward-looking lay Puritanism was ruthlessly ironed out only by force. . . . It is easy to point out that the lack of much that was thereby excised was to be a permanent defect of Lutheranism: how defective much of Protestantism has been in the kind of "inward religion" to which Karlstadt's mystical theology has corresponded: how badly Germany has suffered from not having the kind of Puritan freedoms which the English Free Churches have bred, with their emphasis on the power of the congregation and their large place for lay initiative. But it is part of the tragedy that these ideological encounters never happen in a vacuum. . . . Moreover, much of Luther's criticism was deep and penetrating and is still cogent. He knew, as Karlstadt did not, what it means to begin with the bruised conscience which needs peace with God, and how immense is that Christian liberty which comes through living faith in Christ. His reading of the relating of law and Gospel, and of the meaning of law in the Christian life left room for liberties and beauties which might have perished: . . . Bach, and . . . Handel. Those of us who, with Martin Luther and Richard Hooker, are Protestant but not Puritan can still turn gratefully to Luther's profound rationale in seeking to combat the petrifying moralism into which Protestantism so dangerously falls, in defying that sectarianism which imperils the return to Christian unity.[268]

Nevertheless we need to be sensitive to the fact that Luther's theological critique of his charismatic contemporaries is colored with harsh invective and ad hominem arguments which serve no useful purpose in today's ecumenical dialogues.

A constructive contribution to the present, however, is Luther's dialectical relating of doctrine and life which understands doctrine not merely in terms of content but in terms of its function: "Doctrine directs us and shows the way to heaven. . . . We can be saved without love . . . but not without pure doctrine and faith." Doctrine and life are incomparable, not at all on the same level; and therefore the devil's argument "about not offending against love and the harmony among the churches" is spe-

---

[266]Cf. the Preface to Ecke, *Fortsetzung der Reformation,* 8; Steck, *Luther und die Schwärmer,* 60f.

[267]Cf. Edwards, *Luther and the False Brethren,* 77ff.; Rupp, *Patterns,* 148.

[268]Rupp, *Patterns,* 152f.

cious.[269] The function of doctrine is the proclaiming of the forgiveness of sins as unconditional promise. That is why the church stands or falls on the basis of its relation to the doctrine of justification by faith.[270] That is why Luther would sharply differ from the charismatic dissociation of doctrine from life as expressed for example by Dennis Pederson in his Bible lecture at the International Lutheran Renewal Leaders' Conference: "It is not important what I teach but how." Thus Luther's relationship to his charismatic contemporaries is not an incidental chapter in church history but is related to the fundamental apprehension and sense of the Reformation.[271]

At the same time we must not be misled by Luther's vigorous insistence upon the Word and the external means of grace into thinking that these means of grace contain grace in themselves. "When the means of grace is understood as being united metaphysically with the Spirit, the Spirit is understood as being a divine power which by the means of grace is placed at the disposition of man in his efforts to reach God. The difference between spiritualism and antispiritualism is then only the understanding of how to get possession of this divine power."[272] The result is the same whether the watchwords are *Gelassenheit* and *mortificatio* or *opus operatum*. Again, the Spirit is not the means for human ascent to God, but rather God's descent to persons. Thus Luther, even in his conflict with his charismatic opponents consistently retained a theocentric view of the Spirit's sovereignty over the means of grace.

THE LUTHERAN CONFESSIONS

The legacy of the conflicts between Luther and the charismatics became part of the Lutheran heritage through the Lutheran confessional writings. As might be expected the Lutheran Confessions break no new ground on this topic but rather reiterate the major themes already expressed by Luther: the rejection of Donatism;[273] the creation of faith by

---

[269]Lectures on Galatians, 1535. LW 27, 41f.; WA 40², 51f.

[270]Cf. Steck, *Luther und die Schwärmer,* 23f. Eric W. Gritsch and Robert W. Jenson, *Lutheranism. The Theological Movement and Its Confessional Writings* (Philadelphia: Fortress Press, 1976) 42f.; Leif Grane, *Modus loquendi theologicus. Luthers Kampf um die Erneuerung der Theologie (1515-1518)* (Leiden: Brill, 1975).

[271]Steck, *Luther und die Schwärmer,* 5.

[272]Prenter, *Spiritus Creator,* 258.

[273]The Augsburg Confession, 1530. Article VIII, Tappert, *The Book of Concord,* 33.

the Holy Spirit through the external means of Word and sacraments; the rejection of deification and rigorous perfectionism; and the rejection of the necessity of good works for salvation.

The ministry of the Word is to be extolled in opposition to those "who dream that the Holy Spirit does not come through the Word but because of their own preparations. They sit in a dark corner doing and saying nothing, but only waiting for illumination. . . . "[274] It is important to note that the Augsburg Confession, as well as Luther, does not confine the Holy Spirit within the Word and sacraments in any *opera operato* sense. It states that the Word and sacraments are the means through which the Holy Spirit works faith "when and where he pleases, in those who hear the Gospel."[275] "For the unique contribution of the CA's doctrine of the Holy Spirit is the subtle tension and delicate balance between the promise and the freedom of God: God is free to work faith 'when and where he pleases in those who hear the Gospel' (CA 5,2); yet Melanchthon asserts that in faithfulness to the promise, God 'gives the Holy Spirit' through the Word and Sacraments as through means/instruments' (CA 5,2). Therefore prayers that 'implore' rather than formulae that 'bestow' the Holy Spirit seem more appropriately to reflect the careful distinctions and implicit dialectic of the CA."[276] The Formula of Concord, Epitome and Solid Declaration, reiterates this view.[277]

The Confessions also thoroughly reject the ideas of Schwenckfeld[278] including his ideas of perfection and those of others in preparation for receiving the Holy Spirit.[279] It is of interest that the Confessions continue to express Luther's view that the charismatics and the papists are formally similar in their *ordo salutis* of ascent to God.

> We reject and condemn the erroneous and heretical teaching . . . (t)hat our righteousness before God does not depend alone on the sole obedience and merit of Christ but in renewal and in our piety, in which we walk before God. But this piety rests for the greater part on their own peculiar precepts and self-chosen spirituality as on a new kind of monkery.[280]

---

[274]Apology, 1531. Article XIII, Tappert, *The Book of Concord*, 212f.

[275]Article V, Tappert, *The Book of Concord*, 31.

[276]"The Augsburg Confession in the United States," *Currents in Theology and Mission* 7/2 (1980): 85.

[277]Tappert, *The Book of Concord*, 471, 520, 536.

[278]Tappert, *The Book of Concord*, 499f., 635.

[279]Augsburg Confession, Articles V, XII.

[280]Formula of Concord, Tappert, *The Book of Concord*, 633f., also 498.

In the Smalcald Articles (1537) written by Luther, Müntzer and the papacy are equated in their "spiritualism."

> We must hold firmly to the conviction that God gives no one his Spirit or grace except through or with the external Word which comes before. Thus we shall be protected . . . from the spiritualists who boast that they possess the Spirit without and before the Word and who therefore judge, interpret, and twist the Scriptures or spoken Word according to their pleasure. Müntzer did this, and many still do it in our day who wish to distinguish sharply between the letter and the spirit without knowing what they say or teach. The papacy too, is nothing but enthusiasm, for the pope boasts that "all laws are in the shrine of his heart," and he claims that whatever he desires and commands in his churches is spirit and law, even when it is above and contrary to the Scriptures or spoken Word.[281]

The one section of the Lutheran Confessions that might indicate a concession to Karlstadt and others on the necessity for mortification and regeneration, as well as theological legitimation for contemporary Lutheran charismatics,[282] is Article VI, "The Third Function of the Law," of the Formula of Concord.[283] In contrast to Luther's double use of the law (*duplex usus legis*) which we have already discussed above in terms of revealing sin (theological use) and restraining crime and building up the human community (civil use), Melanchthon introduced a triple use of the law (*triplex usus legis*).[284] Here the law is given a third use in moral instruction in the sanctification of the regenerate. Because Luther himself never deviated from his teaching of the double use of the law,[285] this became an issue which the Formula of Concord attempted to resolve. It is

---

[281]Tappert, *The Book of Concord,* 312. Cf. also Ernst Kinder, "Zur Lehre vom Heiligen Geist nach den Lutherischen Bekenntnisschriften," *Fuldaer Hefte* 15 (1964): 7-38, 19ff.

[282]Cf. Theodore R. Jungkuntz, "Response to Dr. Lazareth," in *Confession and Congregation (The Cresset,* Occasional Paper: 3) (Valparaiso IN: Valparaiso University Press, 1978) 7-59, 58.

[283]Tappert, *The Book of Concord,* 563-68.

[284]*Loci Communes,* 1533. *Melanchthon on Christian Doctrine,* ed. and tr. by Clyde Manschreck (New York: Oxford, 1965) 127.

[285]Cf. Werner Elert, "The Third Use of the Law," *The Lutheran World Review* (1949), and *The Christian Ethos* (Philadelphia: Muhlenberg Press, 1957); referred to by William Lazareth, "The Question of the 'Third Use' of the Law," in *Confession and Congregation,* (Valparaiso IN, 1977) 48-56. Cf. also, Wilfried Joest, *Gesetz und Freiheit. Das Problem des Tertius Usus Legis bei Luther und die Neutestamentliche Parainese* (Göttingen: Vandenhoeck & Ruprecht, 1961) 133; Ole Modalsli, *Das Gericht nach den Werken* (Göttingen: Vandenhoeck & Ruprecht, 1963) 167, 191, 214.

also an issue which has continuing theological significance in light of pietistic or pentecostalistic conceptions of progressive regeneration.[286]

While, as Lazareth points out, the material of Article VI "is not always lucid or well organized, its content remains a faithful witness to the holy Scriptures" and to Luther's concern to protect the Christian faith from the continual threats of moralism and legalism.[287]

> Believers, furthermore, require the teaching of the law so that they will not be thrown back on their own holiness and piety and under the pretext of the Holy Spirit's guidance set up a self-elected service of God without his Word and command.

> Believers, furthermore, require the teaching of the law in connection with their good works, because otherwise they can easily imagine that their works and life are perfectly pure and holy. But the law of God prescribes good works for faith in such a way that, as in a mirror, it shows and indicates to them that in this life our good works are imperfect and impure.[288]

Thus, here as elsewhere, the Lutheran Confessions are relevant to any and all claims for growth in sanctifying perfection.

---

[286]Lazareth, "The Question of the 'Third Use,' "48.

[287]Ibid., 53, 52.

[288]Tappert, The Book of Concord, 567.

3

THE "SECOND REFORMATION"— PIETISM

From our point of view Pietism will be understood as a "bridging" movement between Luther and the Lutheran tradition on the one hand and contemporary charismatic movements on the other. An immediate problem in such a conceptualization is, of course, that Pietism itself is part of the Lutheran tradition and continues to exercise influence on contemporary Lutheran churches throughout the world. Nevertheless, while Pietism's role in the continuities of the Lutheran tradition cannot be ignored, neither can Pietism's discontinuity with and criticism of Luther and the Lutheran tradition. Here we may find parallels to, even antecedents in, the sixteenth-century charismatic expressions we have already discussed. This provides another aspect of the "bridging" phenomenon of Pietism between the Reformation and contemporary issues. We shall attempt within the limitations of our study to do justice to all these aspects. At the same time we shall draw attention to those particular aspects of Lutheran Pietism which appear to be striking antecedents or at least parallels to contemporary charismatic concerns. What, for example, is the relationship between Pietism's watchword, "Theologia experimentalis,"[1] and the contemporary claim that "What charismatics

---

[1]Gottfried Arnold, *Theologia experimentalis. Das ist: Geistliche Erfahrungslehre oder Erkenntnis und Erfahrung von den vornehmsten Stücken des lebendigen Christen-*

are bringing forth is not a new statement of doctrine, but a fresh experience of it."?[2]

Clearly, at least at first glance, both movements seem to place praxis above, if not in place of, theory. Yet, as we shall see, the preoccupation with praxis is not without exceedingly important theological ramifications for both Pietism and consequent theology. Thus it is not, in retrospect, surprising that there were sharp conflicts between Pietism and representatives of Orthodox Lutheranism. The intimate relationship between theology and praxis which may be discerned in these struggles may provide perspective on the contemporary tensions between Lutheran and charismatic movements.

While Pietism's orientation about "experience" gives it an unmistakable flavor, it also hinders efforts at definition. Indeed, Pietism as a transconfessional movement is as variegated as the sixteenth-century charismatic movement we have just surveyed. For our purposes we shall limit our discussion to Lutheran Pietism and its major figures, but even within these limitations no attempt will be made at an exhaustive interpretation, although a working definition of Pietism is in order.

While recent study may have different evaluations of Pietism, there is some consensus that the term or concept as well as the movement itself needs further definition and historical study. One recent partisan judgment even claims that Pietism is undoubtedly "One of the least understood movements in the history of Christianity."[3] From the perspective of scholars involved in the fields of religious and social history, the concepts of Pietism appear not only somewhat inconsistent but also dominated by theological interpretations.[4] Thus the many handbooks of church history present Pietism as an epoch within modern Protestantism lasting from about 1657 to 1725. The article in *Religion in Geschichte*

---

thums, 1714. Cf. also, Martin Brecht, "Christentum als Lebensordnung: Die Frömmigkeit des Pietismus," in *Evangelischer Glaube im Wandel der Zeit* (Stuttgart: Steinkopf, 1967) 54-67, 55.

[2]*CRAL*, 34.

[3]F. Ernest Stoeffler, *The Rise of Evangelical Pietism* (Leiden: E. J. Brill, 1971) 1. For a recent and thorough analysis of research cf. Martin Schmidt, "Epochen der Pietismusforschung," in Berg and Dooren, eds., *Pietismus und Reveil* (Leiden: Brill, 1978) 22-79.

[4]Hartmut Lehmann, *Pietismus und Weltliche Ordnung in Württemberg vom 17. bis zum 20. Jahrhundert* (Stuttgart: Kohlhammer, 1969) 14. For a study from the point of view of the sociology of knowledge, cf. Martin Scharfe, *Die Religion des Volkes: Kleine Kultur- und Sozialgeschichte des Pietismus* (Gütersloh: Gerd Mohn, 1980).

und Gegenwart by the well-known scholar of Pietism, Martin Schmidt, is one of the best examples of this approach. Thus we shall quote its opening definition.

> Pietism is the term for the far-reaching movement of the late 17th and early 18th centuries which set for itself the goal of a new Reformation because the first Reformation had become stuck in Old Protestant Orthodoxy, in the institutional and dogmatic. Pietism's watchwords therefore became "life" vs. "doctrine," "Spirit" vs. "Office," "power" vs. "appearance"(2 Tim. 3:5). The Reformation's central concept of faith received the characteristic addition, "living faith," the liveliness being sought in the ethical "fruits of faith," above all love; thereby affecting the social characteristic of Pietism. Christian perfection became the main theme. Therefore it is natural to view the essence of Pietism in its piety. . . . In the place of justification with its correlation of Word of God (as promise)—faith and law—gospel appeared *rebirth*.[5]

Certainly there is good reason for approaching the definition of Pietism from the perspective of theology. After all, its major proponents in Lutheranism were pastors and theologians. The radical forerunner and influence upon Philipp Spener, Christian Hoburg (1606-1675), stated quite starkly that justification is a fiction whereas rebirth is reality,[6] and it was Spener, commonly known as "the father of Pietism," who significantly reoriented theological thinking.[7] Yet at the same time that these theological perspectives are taken seriously, a more inclusive orientation is being advocated by some recent scholars which recognizes the desirability of a flexible definition of Pietism in light of its long historical development and variety of styles. "A definition which does not wish to be abstract and of no consequence for its (Pietism's) historical development may not therefore be static-normative, but rather must be a clear model based upon the historical development of Pietism."[8] Hartmut Lehmann's comparison of these two orientations will serve as a useful summary.[9]

---

[5]Martin Schmidt, "Pietismus," *RGG* 5:370; cf. 370-83. The founding in 1964 of the Historische Kommission zur Erforschung des Pietismus is an indication of the growing scholarly interest in Pietism. This Commission supports the monograph series, Arbeiten zur Geschichte des Pietismus, and the yearbook *Pietismus und Neuzeit*.

[6]Martin Schmidt, *Pietismus* (Stuttgart: Kohlhammer, 1972) 14; "Speners Pia Desideria," in Schmidt, *Wiedergeburt und Neuer Mensch: Gesammelte Studien zur Geschichte des Pietismus* (Witten: Luther-Verlag, 1969) 129-68, 164 (hereafter cited as *WNM*).

[7]*WNM*, "Speners Wiedergeburtslehre," 169-94, 170.

[8]Lehmann, *Pietismus und Weltliche Ordnung in Württemburg,* 14.

[9]Ibid., 14-21.

Three features belong to a narrow definition of Pietism:

1.   An emphasis upon religious edification in small circles (Collegia Pietatis, edification hours, conventicles, private religious meetings) which mostly are regarded as more important than formal worship in the church. Above the doctrine and worship of the church, Pietism valued the community of conscious, rigorous Christians. The church as an institution of salvation and grace and as a comprehensive organization was supplemented, even partly displaced in Pietism by voluntary, local associations of decided believers, those Christians who, as "reborn in the Lord," felt themselves to be superior to the mass of church-Christians, thus dividing the church into two different groups.

2.   Although Pietism is mainly characterized as a movement for religious renewal and intensification, and as an expression of religious individualism, there soon arose a strong "clerical" tradition that everyone who wished to be a Pietist had to recognize. This found expression in terms of the interpretation of both church history and the Bible. In the former, Spener and those seen as his legitimate heirs, including local leaders, became the authoritative source for questions of faith. In the latter, there arose a naive biblicism which regarded the Bible as the source for guidance in all areas of life. The Bible was read from the perspective of the "patriarchs" and "fathers" of Pietism.

3.   At the same time there was also a subjective element in Pietism, a religious individualism, which nevertheless was limited by the important membership in conventicles. It was in these relationships that one could be characterized as a "brother" and accepted as reborn. These relationships among Pietists were strengthened by their consciousness of separation from the "world" and from the "children of the world." The address "brother" characterized the spiritual community of the awakened and transcended geographical limitations. "Although individual pietists sometimes doubted their rebirth, supported by the brothers, they relied unflinchingly upon divine grace and thereby strove to overcome sin by repentance and penance and by a deeply felt conversion and over various stages of personal 'sanctification' to acquire eternal salvation."[10]

A broader definition which allows a greater comprehension of the variable qualities within Pietism may also be summarized in three points:

1.   Pietism arose in many places as an inner churchly reform movement which desired a confirmation of doctrine in practical life. The

---

[10]Ibid., 17.

demand that faith, if it would be genuine, must be proved in this life by good works was not universal and observed at all times. "Although the 'Praxis Pietatis' was one of the most significant achievements produced by Pietism, it did not belong to the essence of historical Pietism."[11]

2. Pietist theology was never a closed system. Within the Pietist tradition particular "patriarchs" and their followers represented various theological teaching in particular aspects and sometimes even conflicting views. This was true even in such central doctrines as the Kingdom of God and chiliasm. Even the religious self-understanding of pietists varied.

3. Similarly the ethical standards and behavior of pietists were not the same in terms of their understanding of "inner worldly asceticism" and frequently rigorous ethics. Certainly luxury and extravagance were rejected by all pietist circles but there is hardly more than a formal similarity in this between a north German noble in the eighteenth century and a Schwabian farmer or laborer in the nineteenth century.

From the perspective of sociology and the sociology of knowledge, Pietism may be viewed as a direction in Protestantism which, while it does not break or separate from the organizational unity of Protestantism, may develop its own supplementary organizations and institutions. These have their own distinct character as a subculture subordinated to a value-cosmos with its own rigid morality. This subculture is defined by its sharp demarcation from the "world," emphasis upon the individual's unmediated relationship to God, and rigorous exegesis of "the Word." Guarantors of the subcultural value-continuity include authorities ("fathers"), a canon of literature (devotional literature), and special meetings (devotional house) which serve the transmission of values. Other various interventions in the psyche and relations of individual members include socialization, "conversion," and sanctioning by "divine" intervention.[12] At the same time we must recognize that Pietist values as much as those of charismatics whether of the sixteenth or twentieth century may be alien to us not because of the religious orientation per se but because they reflect another culture.[13]

---

[11]Ibid., 18.

[12]Scharfe, *Die Religion des Volkes,* 25f.

[13]Ibid., 61. Cf. also Hartmut Lehmann's review of *Pietismus und moderne Welt,* 147-57 in *Pietismus und Neuzeit* (Bielefeld: Luther Verlag, 1975) 148.

It is not our goal to resolve the tensions between the narrow (theological) and broad (sociological, historical) interpretations of Pietism nor to synthesize them in some way. It is enough for our purposes to be aware of the scope of definitions which reflect both the range of contemporary scholarship and the manifold nature of Pietism and its relationships. Our interest in Luther and the Lutheran tradition as resources for understanding and relating to present expressions of charismatic renewal will naturally orient us toward theological interpretations of Pietism.

This, however, does not mean that the concrete social and historical factors involved in the origin and growth of Pietism are to be excluded. On the contrary, just as the historical and social factors of the late medieval crisis provide insight into our understanding of the dynamics and concerns of the Reformation and its renewal movements, so an overview of the post-Reformation crises may contribute perspective to our understanding of Pietism's own initial quest for security and certainty.

It is commonplace to point out that all renewal movements are posited upon an awareness of decline or even loss of that which is to be renewed. Pietism's emphasis upon experienced faith presupposes that the context of Pietism was one of declining or lost religious experience. One could also surmise that the Pietist orientation around rebirth of the individual Christian to a regenerated and sanctified life reflects both the contemporary lifestyle and/or ethical potential proclaimed by the Reformation but not realized.

Following the death of Luther, theological controversies arose within the Lutheran churches over the correct interpretation of Luther's theology and the Confessional writings. This was further exacerbated by the intimate connection between church and state. Because the empire recognized as legitimate only those Lutheran churches which subscribed to the Augsburg Confession (1530), the territories claiming legal recognition had to prove they were Lutheran. Thus there arose territorial bodies of doctrine based upon the Confessions and the writings of Luther and Melanchthon. The dispute between those who claimed to speak for Luther (Gnesio Lutherans) and those who followed Melanchthon (Philippists) precipitated a number of bitter quarrels which did not find resolution until the Formula of Concord (1577) and the comprehensive Book of Concord (1580) which became the standard for Lutheran doctrinal teaching. From this starting point German Lutheran theologians proceeded to give even more complete, systematic elaborations of Reformation doctrine. The oft-quoted example of this is Johann Gerhard's (+1637) *Loci theologici* which appeared from 1610-1622 in nine large volumes. However, this was only one of a line of dogmatics which culminated with David Holazius's (+1713) *Examen theologicum* (1707). This period is known as Protestant Orthodoxy or Protestant Scholasticism both because of its range of topics and its methodology. The doctrinal implications of the Reformation were carefully worked out in highly rationalistic Summae which depended upon the reintroduction of Aristotelian concepts and methods of argumentation frequently cast in polemical mold against Roman Catholic, Reformed, and even other Lutheran teachings. Much has been made—perhaps too much—of the intellectualistic formalism and religious aridity associated with this scholastic method, rationalism, and importation of natural theology. Yet certainly in the understanding of Pietist circles Lutheran Orthodoxy had substituted assent to doctrine for "living faith," tyrannized Christian freedom by scholastic theology, transformed the Bible from the Word of God to a source book for dogmatic systems, and undercut Christian sanctification by labeling it works-righteousness.

Thus as we have already indicated, as a reaction against Lutheran Orthodoxy, Pietism expressed itself in concepts and slogans such as "life versus doctrine," "Holy Spirit versus the office of ministry," and "reality versus the appearance of godliness." The latter slogan indicates the shift of Pietism's attention from the doctrine of justification to regeneration. But the intellectual, dogmatic system of Orthodoxy was not the sole context for the rise of Pietism. The historical, social context was also important. Here we refer to the devastation of Germany during the Thirty Years' War (1618-1648) and the failure of the Reformation in the education and socialization of the laity.

Beginning as the last of the religious wars, the Thirty Years' War soon involved most of the European states in an international political struggle. The policy of using mercenary armies which were maintained by allowing them to live off the land of friend and foe alike wreaked incredible devastation in Germany. Cities were plundered, the countryside ravaged, populations decimated by warfare, plague, and starvation. The destruction and confusion caused by the mercenary armies marching to and fro for decades across Germany not only wrecked the economy but also adversely affected religion and culture. Churches and schools had been burned, many of those still standing were leaderless, and care of the sick and poor was practically nonexistent. In the face of the concomitant spiritual and religious disintegration, it is not surprising that the orthodox theological debates of the universities were of little interest to the people.

The physical, moral, and religious crises created by the Thirty Years' War were further compounded by the Reformation's seeming inability to carry through its goals of educating and socializing the people to its beliefs. A recent study, massively documented with *Schulordnungen, Kirchenordnungen,* Visitation Articles, private correspondence, and tracts, presents a variety of reasons for this failure.[14] The schools had to be supported by municipalities or princes or both and thus came under the pressure to inculcate civic virtues. With the differentiation of schools for the masses and for the elite, education shifted toward training the ruling class of a bourgeois society. The work load of children made attendance at school, catechism, and worship difficult. Popular religion with its superstitions and folklore was never rooted out and was preferred by many to the stern approach of underpaid pastors whose preoccupation with right belief isolated them from the people.

The process of bureaucratization of church and school "dried up the movement's original appeal and channeled it into routinized procedures." The accommodation to the dominant social milieu also "contributed to the erosion of the popular base." "To the extent that the ecclesiastical establishment turned professional and efficient, it isolated itself from the public. As clergymen came to be better trained, more literate, better-spoken, they tended to talk above the heads of their flock."

> As disseminated in sermons, catechisms, tracts, hymns, Bible comments, and housefather books, the Protestant message was pitched to the solid burgher. From his life and work it derived its values and images. Its religious thrust, and its utility in solving problems, instilling confidence and mitigating misfortune was best suited to the stable householder. As for the great multitude of men and women, they could have found little survival value in doctrines whose framers made no attempt to integrate their precepts with the practical needs and aspirations of plain people.[15]

It is in this context, and against this background of the insecurity of war and its concomitant social breakdown, and the gap between Lutheran doctrine and social change that the rise of Pietist renewal movements

---

[14]Gerald Strauss, *Luther's House of Learning. Indoctrination of the Young in the German Reformation* (Baltimore and London: Johns Hopkins University Press, 1978).

[15]Ibid., 305-307.

may be seen. It is, therefore, not surprising that Pietism viewed the Reformation as incomplete and endeavored to fulfill Luther's reformation of doctrine through their reformation of life.

PIETISM'S RELATION TO THE REFORMATION

As a general introductory comment we agree with the claim that whether or not Pietism consciously acknowledged it, there is no Pietism which would be conceivable without Luther.[16] This is recognizable in three Pietist concerns: the Bible, personal faith, and the activity of faith in love. The fundamental biblical texts used in the prolific Pietist publication of Bibles was the Luther text. Furthermore the Pietists continued Luther's emphasis that the exegesis of the Bible is the task which makes theology theology. The Pietist emphasis upon personal "living faith" is a reflection of Luther's "What help is it to you that God is God if he is not God to you?"[17] and his definition of faith in his famous preface to Romans. Finally, Pietist activities in developing education, schools, orphanages, and outer and inner missions are also in line with Luther's exhortations for faith to be active in love, indeed, the indivisibility of faith and love.

Pietism understood itself to be the continuation of the Reformation, indeed a "new Reformation."[18] In speaking of the Reformation as a continuing task, Spener wrote:

> I certainly think that still with the Reformation by no means did everything take place that should have happened and on this I follow its descendants who have been and still are rightly bound to work. And what I lamented elsewhere in the *piis desideriis* that just as the departure from Babel indeed occurred but that the temple and the city still were not built and many evil things had been brought from Babel which still needed to be purified by Ezra, Nehemiah and the prophets inspired by God so also I acknowledge this to be the case with our Reformation which has not come as far as it should but rather has remained, so to speak, at the point of having laid the groundwork for the building. Therefore I certainly desire that not only that the subject may be brought up afresh as it was in Luther's time but that what remains should be made good.[19]

[16]Erwin Mülhaupt, "Die Bedeutung Luthers für den Pietismus," *Luther* 37/1 (1966): 19-33, 21. Cf. also M. Schmidt, *RGG,* 5:372.

[17]Ibid., 23; WA 2, 137, 6.

[18]Philipp Spener, *Pia Desideria* (1676), ed. by Kurt Aland (Berlin: De Gruyter, 1955) 58, 3f. For a discussion of this self-understanding, cf. Schmidt, *WNM,* 306, n.23.

[19]Spener, *Theologische Bedenken* 4 Bde. (Halle, 1701) 3:179f., quoted in Ernst Zeeden, *Martin Luther und die Reformation im Urteil des deutschen Luthertums* 2

The Pietist desire for the completion of the Reformation focused on the ethical fruits of faith. The contemporary degeneration and abuses of the Christian life in Germany were to be rectified by continuing the Reformation beginnings. Of central importance to this Pietist platform was Luther's *Preface to Romans*[20] which the Pietists believed offered exactly what was needed—the equation of faith and rebirth: "Faith, however, is a divine work in us which changes us and makes us to be born anew of God, John 1 (:12-13). It kills the old Adam and makes us altogether different men, in heart and spirit and mind and powers; and it brings with it the Holy Spirit. O it is a living, busy, active, mighty thing, this faith. It is impossible for it not to be doing good works incessantly."[21] Thus Luther is presented by Pietism as a chief witness for rebirth and the ethical verification of faith. The later Pietists—Franck and Arnold, who were concerned for the certainty of salvation—found Luther's statement of faith as a "divine work in us" equally meaningful.

The question, of course, is whether Pietism's emphasis corresponded to Luther's intention. While conceding that this is a difficult question to answer, Martin Schmidt does provide us with some helpful perspectives.[22] Both Luther and Pietism understood faith to be the central organ of the Christian life and grace as the divine activity in the process of salvation. Where they parted ways was in their views of the relationship of faith to its fruits. For Pietism the verification of faith lies in its ethical achievement, in its "fruits." The reborn, the new person, refers to a quality of being, a higher nature, which takes effect and becomes visible. Luther on the contrary focuses on the battle between the old and new man, the conflict expressed in his phrase "simul iustus et peccator." For both Luther and Pietism, rebirth was a process, but while the Pietists directed their attention toward the goal and affirmed the process for its sake, Luther did not. For Luther, victory remains the judgment of God and thus the final, ethical chapters of Romans are as important as the

---

(Freiburg: Herder, 1952) 198f. For Spener's discussion of the exodus from the spiritual Babel cf. *Pia Desideria*, 40, 29-42, 13; 42, 8-13.

[20]Preface to the Epistle of St. Paul to the Romans, 1546 (1522). LW 35, 365ff.; WA, DB 7, 3ff.

[21]Ibid., 370.

[22]"Luthers Vorrede zum Römerbrief im Pietismus," *WNM*, 299-330; for what follows cf. 327ff.

dogmatic ones for they witness both to faith and its incompleteness in the ongoing struggle of daily life.

The dynamic which Pietism set in motion and which engaged their thinking was not that of Luther's dialectics of law and gospel, sin and grace, damnation and faith, but rather the development of faith itself in the new life. Here there is an orientation to the categories of being, harmony, and completion—the manner of thinking which characterizes pre-Reformation and charismatic thinking. The Pietist emphasis upon power as an independent value in the Christian life is a perspective, Schmidt argues, that has its source in pre-Reformation mystical spiritualism. From a structural point of view, Thomas Müntzer appears as a connecting bridge from mysticism, over Luther, to Pietism.[23] For both Müntzer and Pietism there is a distinct interest in the visible working of the Word which is not present in Luther.[24] Pietism's relationship to Reformation spiritualism is even more clearly seen in light of the influence of Caspar Schwenckfeld. In spite of his condemnation by the Formula of Concord, Schwenckfeld continued to have an "underground" influence through the sixteenth and seventeenth centuries through the emphasis upon interiority, perfectionism, oppression of the corporeal as the end of God's way, a theocentrically-dominated primacy of grace, theology of rebirth, self-judgment on the basis of conversion, renunciation of the world as test of the seriousness of conversion, the scorning of mere right belief without inspiring power, the demand for converted clergy, and others.[25]

> Mystical spiritualism goes back to the beginning of the Reformation itself, possibly back into the Middle Ages. . . . Since the Reformation we see it relatively clearly. Immediately next to Luther there appeared men who reproached him for going only half way; in addition to Andreas Bodenstein von Karlstadt and Thomas Müntzer there was above all Caspar Schwenckfeld von Ossig (1489-1561) about whom an entire school formed, and Sebastian Franck

---

[23]Martin Schmidt, "Das Selbstbewusstsein Thomas Müntzers, eine Vorform des Pietismus, und sein Verhältnis zu Luther," *WNM*, 9-23.

[24]Cf. Gerhard Ebeling, "Luther and the Beginning of the Modern Age," in Heiko A. Oberman, ed., *Luther and the Dawn of the Modern Era* (Leiden: Brill, 1974) 14; and M. Schmidt, "Speners Pia Desideria," *WNM*, 132, 159, 161-63.

[25]M. Schmidt, "Speners Wiedergeburtslehre," *WNM*, 170, 185, 191; Emmanuel Hirsch," Schwenckfeld und Luther," in his *Lutherstudien* 2 (Gütersloh: Bertelmann, 1954) 56, 66; I was unable to obtain Heinrich Bornkamm, *Mystik, Spiritualismus und die Anfänge des Pietismus im Luthertum* (1926). Cf. also M. Schmidt, "Teilnahme an der göttlichen Natur," *WNM*, 238-98, especially 239-43.

(1499-1542) who became an historian, later Valentin Weigel (1533-1588) and Jakob Böhme (1575-1624), who likewise gathered secret groups of students and followers. Further to be named here would be Paul Felgenhauer (1593-after 1677), Joachim Betke (1601-1666), Lorenz Grammendorf (ca. 1575-1650) and above all Christian Hoburg (1607-1675), as well as finally Friedrich Breckling (1629-1711), the student of Betke and Hoburg, who substantially assisted Gottfried Arnold in his history of the church and heretics. . . .[26]

That Pietism would develop in tension with the contemporary forms of Lutheran ecclesiology and theology is due, in part at least, to its connection to those Reformation spiritualists against whom Luther directed his most critical and substantive attacks. For example Karlstadt, with his theology of rebirth and sanctification, was a forerunner of Pietism. In this regard there are not only material agreements but actual historical lines of connection which have hardly been explored. In the century of Pietism's origin, the seventeenth, Karlstadt's central writing on *Gelassenheit* (1523) was reprinted as were other of his writings, but not under his name. Karlstadt received a rehabilitation in Pietism by, among others, Gottfried Arnold.[27]

We may summarize and conclude these introductory comments on the relationship of Pietism to the Reformation by saying that from the historical perspective, Pietism believed itself to be the resumption of the Reformation with the goal of recovering primitive Christianity. Materially speaking, Pietism set about to continue the Reformation as the transformation of the world through the transformation of persons. Personal transformation came from rebirth: "Children of God by the new birth." The first Reformation was seen by the Pietists and the Reformation spiritualists as a true beginning, but it had proceeded no further than reforming institutions, at which point it had been laid aside, if not sterilized, by the following Orthodoxy. Now, however, Pietists saw that the original reform had to be completed by a reform of individuals and the recovery of primitive Christianity. The new man was to be formed according to the image of Jesus Christ, and therefore all personal and historical experience was related to the second or third article. Salvation is no longer guaranteed by a dogma such as the Trinity, a doctrine such as

[26]M. Schmidt, "Gottfried Arnold—seine Eigenart, seine Bedeutung, seine Beziehung zu Quedlinburg," *WNM*, 331-41, 332. Cf. also F. E. Stoeffler, *The Rise of Evangelical Pietism*, 200ff.

[27]Ulrich Bubenheimer, "Andreas Rudolff Bodenstein von Karlstadt," in *Andreas Bodenstein von Karlstadt 1480-1541*, ed. by Wolfgang Merklein (Karlstadt, 1980) 40.

justification with its law-gospel differentiation, or institutions such as the preaching office or the sacraments, but rather by a personal, unmediated relationship to the New Testament. Genuine piety, rooted in personal closeness to the Bible, formed a stronger bond than dogma, doctrine, tradition, and church order. Its ecumenical thrust focused on the free coming together of believers drawn to Jesus.[28] The historical and theological aspects of these points may be developed by a review of selected Pietists.

SELECTED PIETISTS

While Philipp Spener is popularly referred to as the "Father of Pietism," it is important to realize that the previous generation as well as he himself was deeply influenced by the rise of Lutheran Pietism generated by Johann Arndt (1555-1621). Personally influenced by the stream of mystical spiritualism referred to above, Arndt wrote the formative classics for Pietism: *True Christianity* (1605) and *The Little Garden of Paradise* (1610). The emphasis in these books is upon conversion, oneness with Christ and a holy life; the central theme is the new life which is a dying to the world and the self and living for God on the highest ethical level. In the introduction to an old edition of Arndt's two major works, the author writes that God saw the ruin of the post-Reformation church and graciously sent help that the evil seed should not overrun everything.

> He granted this through the sending and preparation of Johann Arndt whose importance for this time and the history of the church can be summarized generally in three points:
>
> 1. He powerfully asserted over against the dead faith of the head which left the old man unchanged the voice of James: "Prove to me your faith by your works."
> 2. He clarified anew the mystics and led back to the purity of God's word.
> 3. He sought to put a stop to the ethical decay of his time by serious, edifying preaching of repentance and faith as well as by the introduction of Christian discipline.[29]

Although Arndt professed his continuing subscription to the Augsburg Confession and the Formula of Concord,[30] there were contemporary

---

[28]M. Schmidt, "Der ökumenische Sinn der deutschen Pietismus und seine Auswirkungen in der Bibelverbreitung," *WNM,* 342-56, 355f.

[29]Unfortunately my edition gives no indication of author or date; the title page is as follows: *Johann Arndts Sechs Bücher vom Wahren Christentum nebst dessen Paradies-Gärtlein* (Dreizehnten Abdruck, Stuttgart: J. F. Steinkopf) xvi.

[30]Ibid., 747-48.

Lutheran theologians and pastors who thought that his emphasis upon rebirth, the life of Christ *in nobis,* and continuing sanctification were alien elements within Lutheranism. Among other things Arndt seems to have desired to expand the marks of the church from the Word and sacrament to include "love."

> Word and sacrament are rightly held as marks of the church; however many false Christians clothe themselves with these, they have frequently used Word and sacrament but have not become a hair better. Therefore it is necessary to add also the third mark, namely, love, which is nothing other than the noble life of Christ.[31]

We shall have the opportunity to speak more of Arndt's themes in connection with later Pietists for "The general impact which Arndt's piety had upon his age and upon later generations would be difficult to overestimate."[32] As the eighteenth century theologian Johann Georg Walch said: "He who has not tasted Arndt, has lost his spiritual appetite."[33]

PHILIPP JAKOB SPENER (1635-1705)

Spener was born in the Alsatian town of Rappoltsweiler and grew up in a home whose Lutheran emphasis upon faith had shifted to piety. He found his father's well-worn copy of Arndt's *True Christianity* along with Puritan literature such as Baily's *Praxis Pietatis* in the family library.[34] This context of Arndtian and Puritan piety at home was reinforced by his youthful association with the local countess who stood in a mystical-quietist line of piety. In his university studies in Strasbourg Spener was introduced to Luther's writing by his teacher Konrad Dannhauer. After completing his theological studies in 1659 Spener visited various centers of learning: Basel where he studied Hebrew; Geneva where he learned French and absorbed the experiential piety of the great preacher Labadie; and Tübingen where he read and discussed Grossgebauer's *Voice of a Watchman* which had just appeared in 1661. Returning to Strasbourg he received his doctorate in 1663. By this time he was well-educated in a

---

[31]Ibid., 791.

[32]Stoeffler, *The Rise of Evangelical Pietism,* 211.

[33]Horst Weigelt, *Pietismus-Studien. Der Spener-hallische Pietismus* (Stuttgart: Calwer, 1965) 49.

[34]Ibid., 29.

Lutheranism influenced both by Arndtian pietism and the Reformed tradition of Bucer and Calvin. He was soon called to be senior pastor at Frankfurt am Main (1666). In addition to his preaching and pastoral care he made an immediate impact through his orientation of catechetical instruction as an aid to spiritual life and edification. His next contribution was the development of the so-called *collegia pietatis*. Beginning in 1670 there were gatherings twice a week at Spener's house to discuss the Sunday sermon and edifying literature. After 1675 only the Bible was used. By this means Spener intended "to establish among Christian individuals a holy and close friendship, that each one learns to recognize the Christianity of the others whereby the fire of love is more and more inflamed among us, from which so much passionate desire arises that everyone may be edified at every opportunity and by their example may excite others next to them to heartfelt earnestness."[35] From its beginning, the conventicle was in tension with the church establishment which saw the danger of an *ecclesiola in ecclesia*. Later divisions arising out of the conventicle movement led Spener, after his Frankfurt period, to discontinue it. Nevertheless his introduction of this type of catechetical instruction and the establishing of conventicles was the prelude to the Pietist movement.

The essential beginning of the movement is generally dated from the publication in 1675 of his *Pia Desideria*. Written as a foreword to Arndt's *Postilla*, the "Pious Desires" became the progammatic writing of German Pietism. Spener himself soon recognized its importance and translated it into Latin for international use. The six concrete proposals to be realized for reform of the church are:

1. Expanded reading of the whole Bible not only by pastors who should no longer limit themselves to the pericopes but also by house fathers and in private meetings.

2. Renewed emphasis upon the universal priesthood of believers and their responsibilities. All are called to study the Bible, teach, remove, console, and lead a holy life.

3. Exhortation to move the people from a mere knowledge of doctrine to pious praxis as the expression of living faith. This applies to clergy as well as laity.

---

[35]Spener, *Dreyzehn Theologische Sendschreiben* (1716) 51; quoted by Weigelt, *Pietismus-Studien*, 34.

4. Reduction of theological controversy and confessional polemic and the establishment of true doctrine by repentance and a holy life.

5. Reform of theological studies not only in terms of curriculum by including books such as the *German Theology,* Tauler's sermons, Arndt's *True Christianity,* and Kempis's *Imitation of Christ* but also by instituting *collegia* at academic centers to emphasize Christian life and devotion.

6. Shift preaching from rhetoric to edification. Arndt's *Postil* exemplifies such preaching.[36]

Martin Schmidt emphasizes that the significance of Spener's *Pia Desideria* is not these particular proposals for reform in themselves but the total conception of the writing. The *Pia Desideria* is a theological work in its own right and not just a call for reform. As such, it gave a new orientation to theological thinking in its entirety.[37] Thus this writing warrants our closer consideration.

The kernel of Spener's program revolves about the renewal of the entire person. "Our entire Christianity exists in the inner or new man, whose soul is faith and its effects are the fruits of life."[38] This is the locus for Spener's fundamental opposition between old and new birth, the world and the Spirit of God. The spirit, desire, love, mode, wisdom, splendor, delight, life, and judgment of the world—all stand in unreconcilable opposition to God.[39] Therefore Christianity begins with mortification over against the world. The essential task of the Christian is to preserve himself unstained by the world.[40] This concept of "world" has to do with the concrete temptations and errors of daily life—from ambition, desire for fame, pride in knowledge, greed, drunkenness, passion for games, and brawling. "The opposition between the world and salvation is so deep that it must be overcome by an event sui generis—an event that only knows *one* analogy, birth. This event can have only *one* creator, God himself, who is here actively renewing as the omnipotent Creator."[41]

---

[36]Spener, *Pia Desideria,* 53-81.

[37]Schmidt, *WNM,* 130, 170ff. Cf. also Stoeffler, *The Rise of Evangelical Pietism,* 232.

[38]Spener, *Pia Desideria,* 79, 35-36.

[39]Ibid., 17,4; 68,6; 71,26; 71,27; 71,30; 17,2; 22,14; 12,8; 14,16; 17,6; 72,4; 12,22; 8,2. Schmidt, *WNM,* 135.

[40]Ibid., 39, 19.

[41]Schmidt, *WNM,* 136.

The characteristic of Spener's view of rebirth is its teleological orientation entirely toward the New Man and his growth. Therefore he polemicized against the opinion that faith could be the embodiment of the relationship to God and Christian conduct. Faith is in no way able to carry the entire content of the new being; it requires completion through its fruits, love, or even by the decisive modifier, "living."[42] This "living faith" is never born only of the Scriptures but through the Spirit. The Word of God is certainly the seed that begets the new life but the possibility exists that it may be manipulated and unrealized. Only the inner man values and uses worship and sacrament, prayer, and Scripture study.

This emphasis upon the new man is the point of departure for perfectionism, a hope to be realized in history. As applied to the pastorate this has the ring of donatism, for only the pastor who is a true Christian is able to lead others carefully on the way of the Lord.[43] Applied to theology, this leads to a devaluation of doctrine and an emphasis upon the life of the church and the individual. Applied to ecclesiology, it results in ecumenical openness for unity and is not dependent on doctrinal agreement but upon a Christian lifestyle which cuts across confessional lines. "For the genuine conversion of Catholics, Jews, and heathen stands as the shining goal before the renewed, true evangelical church. Genuine piety, genuine life according to the will of Jesus leads from itself to union."[44]

The essential emphasis of the *Pia Desideria* is its historicization in consideration of primitive Christianity. The desire to again take up its outer life-form and thereby master its inner form is a theme which runs through the history of the church from ancient monasticism through the Reformation spiritualists and Anabaptists to the modern charismatic movement. But it is Spener who first clearly expresses the hidden tendency of all these movements, that the reality of the primitive Christian period guarantees its accessibility for the present. This does not abolish the concept of the canon but certainly affects it deeply for it gives every period of church history the possibility to be normative. Dogmatic theology is leveled by an historical approach that presents the Bible as the

---

[42]Cf. Spener, *Pia Desideria*, 17,21; 35,9; 61,14; 66,33; 78,33; 79,1; 79,36; 18,1; 28,9; 61,11; 28,21.

[43]Spener, *Pia Desideria*, 67, 5-10.

[44]Schmidt, *WNM*, 149; Spener, *Pia Desideria*, 43,35; 44,17; 45,6.

testimony of the historical life of the early church rather than the record of the address of God. This would appear to be a step toward Enlightenment de-dogmatization except for the decisive motivation of asserting that the power of the Holy Spirit is just as effective today as it was in primitive Christianity. "For truly it is certainly the Holy Spirit who prior to this effected everything in such first Christians, who is given to us by God and who daily is neither powerless nor slow to accomplish the work of sanctification in us."[45] A naturalization as much as a spiritualization follows from this; the result is a transformation of "nature" by "rebirth." The ease by which one can be changed into the other is what Dilthey and Troeltsch saw as the connection between Reformation Anabaptism (Spiritualism) and the modern spirit. This is also the framework for Ritschl's question whether the summons to the *collegia pietatis* does not atomize the church, the *ecclesia* being reduced to the *ecclesiola*. However, the basis for the observed decline of churchly consciousness is without doubt, according to Schmidt, the reorientation to the rebirth of the individual and as a consequence the shift from corporate consciousness of worship to private edification.[46]

Behind the renewal of the individual is the power of God. It is noteworthy that the Pauline verse, "The Kingdom of God exists not in words but in power" (1 Cor. 1:20), is encountered repeatedly in prominent situations, that the primitive Christian characterization of Jesus' preaching by the word "powerful" (Mt. 7:29) is transferred directly as a demand upon the contemporary preaching of the church, that the ideal of Pauline theology can be expressed by nothing better than by the condemnation of its modern caricature with the words "those powerless phantasies."[47]

> In the call by God, in the certainty of his promise which finds its fulfilment in his time, lies the basis for the comprehension of the church's will to renewal, but also the danger for the result. However unrecognizable, the theocentric feature in the concept of the church is threatened by an anthropocentric trait more strongly than the doctrine of rebirth; logically everything comes out of the first three petitions of the Lord's Prayer, but in an unbiblical and non-Reformation short circuit the advancement of piety is equated with the "advancement of the

---

[45]Spener, *Pia Desideria,* 52, 7-10.

[46]Schmidt, *WNM,* 149-50.

[47]For Pietist use of the term "power" and its synonyms, cf. August Langen, *Der Wortschatz des deutschen Pietismus* (Tübingen: Niemeyer [1954], 1968).

Kingdom of God." The entire Pia Desideria can be understood as a concrete interpretation of these petitions for Spener's time.[48]

This anthropocentric reorientation of theology is exemplified by the doctrine of rebirth with its shift from the *Christus pro nobis* to the realization of the *Christus in nobis*. Christian Hoburg (1607-1675), who eventually left the Lutheran ministry to become a Mennonite preacher, gave this sharp expression in his formula, "Justification is fiction, rebirth is fact." Hoburg's relationship to mystical spiritualism, Osiander, Schwenckfeld, and Müntzer has been discussed by Martin Schmidt.[49] Spener's relationship to the spiritualist tradition is illuminated by his relationship to Hoburg which extends as far as language usage.[50] On the crucial issue of the understanding of the relationship of the Word of God to the Spirit, Spener does not go as far as Hoburg. Nevertheless Spener reckons with the possibility of their separation. We have pointed out earlier that for Luther the Word and the Spirit are united indivisibly, but Spener subordinates Luther's *fides ex auditu* by his suspicion that the Word may not be effective without the *additional* power of the Holy Spirit.

> Therefore we should devote ourselves diligently as all the divine means of Word and sacraments have to do with the inner man. It is indeed not enough that we hear the Word with the external ear but rather we must permit it to penetrate also into our hearts so that we ourselves hear the Holy Spirit speaking. This is his sealing and power of the Word with its living movement and feeling trust. Also, it is not enough that we are baptized but rather that our inner man wherein we with the help of Christ take on baptism must cling to it and show testimony of it in our external life. It is not enough to have received externally the Lord's Supper but rather that our inner man by such holy food must be increased.[51]

Luther's deep distrust of the person as having fallen, a point he expressed in his doctrines of the two realms and original sin, was not shared by Spener. Nor did Spener share Luther's rejection of all forms of perfectionism. Contrary to Luther but similar to the Reformation spiritualists, Spener valued primitive Christianity as a historical possibility for the future. Spener prepared the way for an optimistic view of history. "He

---

[48]Schmidt, *WNM*, 153.

[49]Cf. *WNM*, 51-111, 162ff., 249f.

[50]Ibid., 164f. Cf. also Stoeffler, *The Rise of Evangelical Pietism*, 230f.

[51]Spener, *Pia Desideria*, 80, 11-23.

serves—in spite of his retention of the apocalyptic nomenclature for Babel—the de-eschatologizing of Christian hope and the reduction of the Gospel to Christian ethics."[52]

With the publication of Spener's reform program in the *Pia Desideria* there arose a storm of controversies around him. His suggestion to use the *collegia pietatis* as the means for implementing reform of the church triggered Orthodox opposition. Charges of enthusiasm and separation were leveled against Spener so that in 1677 he defended both the *collegia* and his *Pia Desideria* by two tracts, *The Spiritual Priesthood* and *A Letter to a Foreign Theologian Zealous for Christ.* The former used the doctrine of the priesthood of believers to support the *collegia* and the latter defended that against attacks on a broad front. These, plus the rapid spread of pietism from city to city, further enlarged the controversy. Although he had instituted many reforms in Frankfurt regarding church discipline, catechetics, and confirmation, the growing controversy there was a factor which led him to accept the call in 1686 to become chief court chaplain to the Saxon Elector in Dresden. With great hopes he set about to reform the immorality he saw all about him. The result was increasing isolation in the court and the opposition of the theology faculty of Leipzig. Thus in 1691 he accepted a call to St. Nicholas in Berlin. Here he was able to exercise influence in personnel decisions and gave a number of important positions to Pietists as well as forming the new University of Halle into a pietist center. Even in Berlin the charges of enthusiasm and separation continued to give him difficulty, for throughout his life he was never able to take a clear and decisive position regarding enthusiastic Pietism. He continually tried to make mystical spiritualism fruitful for the church.[53] His last years were quieter as A. H. Francke took over the leadership of the Pietist movement.

AUGUST HERMANN FRANCKE (1663-1727)

Next to Spener, Francke is the second man of Lutheran Pietism. Indeed, more so than Spener, it was Francke who determined Pietism.

From his youth, Francke excelled in languages and in 1684 he went to Leipzig to teach Hebrew. His interest in biblical languages drew him into an association with some young theologians, the *collegium philobibli-*

---

[52]Schmidt, *WNM*, 168.

[53]Weigelt, *Pietismus-Studien*, 43-44.

cum. His first acquaintance with Spener occurred in the context of Spener's answer to the group's inquiry about Bible study. Soon afterward, Francke had an unexpected experience which changed his life. In need of funds and seeking to expand his biblical knowledge, he began work as an exegete for the Superintendent Caspar Hermann Sandhagen. Required to preach on John 20:31 he wished to present the distinction between a true living faith and an imagined faith built on authority and custom. His reflections on this drove him to examine his own inner condition, the truth of God, and the reliability of the Bible. In the midst of the deep existential crisis and imploring prayers consequential to this reflection, he felt himself to be reborn. He had personally experienced the central point of all Pietist thinking and aspiration—rebirth. He fell to his knees and thanked God as he never had before in his life. "Everything was decided; now for the first time he began to be a real, convinced, resolute, selfless and clear-sighted Christian." Naturally he described his experience in terms of Luther's description of faith in the Preface to Romans.[54] From this point Francke entered into a close personal and spiritual relationship with Spener. This relationship was instrumental in Francke's move to Halle in 1691 where he soon became professor of Oriental languages and then (1698) professor of theology. During his growth, he had begun the "Francke Institutions" which became world famous and characterized Halle as a center for education and charity based on Christian principles: school for the poor (1695), common school, orphanage, teacher training school (1696), and high school (1697). These institutions gave concrete expression to the essential Pietist goal: the changing of the world through the changing of persons.[55]

Francke's genius was to embrace this goal of a world ruled by the will of God and shape it by educational, organizational, and technical principles. The following six points summarize his plan:

1. A plan is necessary. At the same time, however, it is granted that one may not become a slave to the plans. A model is necessary (the education establishments in Gotha and in the Netherlands for the orphanage), but one must be able to free oneself from the models.

---

[54]Martin Schmidt, *Pietismus,* 64. Weigelt, *Pietismus-Studien,* 61ff. K. Aland, "Bermerkungen zu August Hermann Francke und seinem Bekehrungserlebnis," in *Kirchengeschichtliche Entwürfe* (Gütersloh: Gütersloher Verlagshaus, 1960) 543-67, 547ff.

[55]M. Schmidt, *Pietismus,* 76.

2. An individual cannot work alone. One must be united and coordinated with others. The director must furnish tasks and engender independent, joyous responsibility.

3. The school is the model of life just as the child is the model of the adult. In his preaching Francke characteristically took the theme "the blessed orphan-condition (*Waisenstand*) of the child of God." Education is particularly the model of life insofar as in it knowledge and action are united like faith and love in Christianity. Action is the verification of knowledge as love is the verification of faith.

4. Time must be highly esteemed for it is only given once. Therefore one must develop the consciousness for the passing moment in oneself and the students.

5. Small things must be esteemed. Therefore realities belong in an effective, life-approximating school. Francke himself acquired English and Italian in his youth, and later French. He regulated exactly the structure of the days, the instruction, clothes, and food. He had a sense for concrete realities; for example distinguishing the education of the sons of nobility from those of the middle class because the life-tasks of the two estates were different. Thus he praised Christian wisdom not just in general but applied it concretely.

6. With all the attention and care directed to the small and daily things, one should nevertheless not lose sight of the whole.[56]

> Francke founded or promoted with these six fundamental principles all the Christian works, the outer mission, the inner mission as care and education of the poor and sick, the distribution of Bibles, diaspora service especially in southern and eastern Europe, ecumenical exchange especially in England and Sweden, and service to prisoners. The expression "seminarium" hotbed (Pflanzstätte—place for growing plants) is exactly right. The church was understood as the universal tree-nursery and plant-garden for the new, God-obedient humanity.[57]

It was Francke who, more than Spener, gave Pietism its profile. This took place mainly through the creation of institutions such as the Halle orphanage. From this point, Pietism was not solely dependent upon persons. "Francke was through and through an educator. As is well known, nothing works so strongly and profoundly in education as the example.

---

[56]Martin Schmidt, "A. H. Francke's Stellung in der pietistischen Bewegung," in *WNM*, 195-211, 207-208.

[57]Ibid., 208.

He himself was the best model for everything that he desired and undertook. . . . "[58]

Francke's theological contribution to Pietism—to modern Protestantism for that matter—can only be discussed in the framework of his own displacement of dogmatics by Christian praxis. In terms of his own experience and theology he once again pushed the Bible to the center of life. His biblical studies set about to improve the traditional Luther text in order to throw into bold relief the Bible's essential authority as the book of life, as an ethical imperative. Francke's own conversion experience in which he went through radical doubt about the authority of not only the Bible, but also of Christian tradition and the reality of God himself, came about not by the traditional means of authority but rather the modern means of experience. Therefore God and the validity of Christian statements about God, humankind, and the world could no longer be demonstrated dogmatically by external authority with its systematic relationships but rather by experience. Thus conversion accounts as well as the astonishing increase of orphanages were for Francke the credible refutations of atheism. Everything that he thought and did was directed forward to a task and a goal—ultimately Christian perfection.[59]

Thus "true" faith means that sin is not allowed to rule. The move away from Luther's understanding of faith is indicated by Franck's opposition to weak faith and strong faith. Francke did not understand Luther's straightforward view that faith simply takes God's promise as true and honors it simply because it does not believe God to be a liar. Rather, faith is treated in terms of its quality and accomplishment. Weak faith is no longer the characteristic condition of persons in history but a condition to be overcome. Luther's favorite expression that "where there is no temptation, there is the greatest temptation"[60] is nowhere in Francke. For example, the Lord's Supper rests upon the proleptic view of the future accomplishments of the disciples rather than the forgiveness of sins. Here again we see Pietism's interest in "power," for the Lord's Supper is a means to increase the believer's power and aid the growth of the inner man. Here, too, the modern anthropocentric element in Pietism comes to the fore in the relation between the humanity and exemplary faith of

---

[58]Schmidt, *Pietismus*, 82.

[59]Schmidt, *WNM*, 210.

[60]WA 3, 420, 16; 3, 433, 2; 5, 170, 25; 15, 456, 30.

Jesus and the ethical activity of the believers. The *theologia experimentalis*—thematically expressed by Gottfried Arnold—finds its programmatic expression over against the Reformation in which the believer is directed to the divine promise rather than thrown back upon himself for analysis of his process of salvation.[61]

GOTTFRIED ARNOLD (1666-1714)

Next to the Pietism developing from and around Spener, Francke, and Halle which maintained connection with the territorial churches, there arose a more radical Pietism of a mystical-enthusiastic type that advocated separation from the established churches and combined with all sorts of sectarian streams. One of the most original and interesting persons associated with these developments was Gottfried Arnold. "This theologian—and he belongs without doubt to the leading theologians of Pietism—fundamentally formulated and comprehensively proved historically the definite programme of modern times: 'Christianity without the church—Christianity against the church'—Christianity as a personal and thoroughly private decision, Christianity as an atmosphere which permeates the surroundings."[62]

Born in Annaberg, Silesia, Arnold studied at Wittenberg University where from the beginning he was offended by Lutheran Orthodoxy. He was, however, an excellent student, especially of ancient Christianity. After acquiring his doctorate he was uncertain what to do and went to Dresden where he came under the influence of Spener. Through Spener he acquired a teaching post in Quedlinburg where he came into contact with a radical group of mystical-spiritualists. He was a professor of history at Giessen University for one year (1697-1698), a post he relinquished in protest against the theological position of the university. He then returned to Quedlinburg. Following his marriage in 1701 he shook off his most radical tendencies and made his peace with the church which he then served through a variety of pastorates, his life ending while a superintendent in Perleburg. In spite of his short life he produced an extraordinary body of literature.

Arnold's importance for his time and his influence upon later generations may be seen in his most significant studies of the history of the

---

[61]Cf. Schmidt, *WNM*, 232-37.

[62]Martin Schmidt, "Gottfried Arnold—seine Eigenart, seine Bedeutung, seine Beziehung zu Quedlinburg," *WNM*, 331-41, 331.

church: "Die Erste Liebe Der Gemeinen Jesu Christi, Das Ist Wahre Abbildung Der Ersten Christen Nach Ihren Lebendigen Glauben Und Heiligen Leben" (1696) and "Unpartheyische Kirchen—und Ketzer-Historie" (1699-1700). In these works the church, its official representatives, and decisions always appear in his historical interpretation as the perverters and suppressors of genuine piety. He defended the heretics and the misunderstood. They should be taken most seriously and their writings studied without bias in order that their true significance be recognized.

Arnold was barely into his thirties when, with the help of some others, especially the mystical-spiritualist Friedrich Breckling (1629-1711), he published his comprehensive "Impartial History of the Church and Heresy." This incredible history of the church begins with the New Testament and proceeds to 1688. Its 1729 edition, excluding index, comprises over 2,700 pages of small print![63] In its opposition to all manifestations of orthodoxy, this is hardly an "impartial" history. However, the title should be understood not in terms of "impartial" but as "unconfessional, trans-confessional."[64] Mystical spiritualism's sharp criticism of the formation of all churches characterized and rejected all of them as "religious factions." These external structures (*Mauerkirchen*) were rejected in comparison to the inner church of the heart composed of truly believing persons. To the mystical spiritualists it was not just the "Papist" church which was Babel but the Protestant churches as well. The Thirty Years' War was seen as God's judgment upon the churches' false trust in worldly power to establish Christianity as well as a judgment upon the false, external Christianity of appearances, of culture and institution. It is this kind of "impartial" education in church history that Arnold proclaimed as "historical truth."

Of all the Pietists, Arnold had the closest and most thorough relationship with mystical spiritualism. He advocated without forbearance the principle that participation in worship and the Lord's Supper was service to idols if it lacked adequate inner attitude and, above all, a change of the entire life. In his "Erklärung vom gemeinen Sectenwesen Kirchen- und Abendmahl-gehen" (1700) he utilized the criticism of the Old Testament

---

[63]Arnold, *Unparteiische Kirchen—und Ketzerhistorie vom Anfang des Neuen Testaments bis auf das Jahr Christi 1688.* Photographic reprint, 2 vols. (Hildesheim: George Olms, 1967).

[64]Schmidt, *Pietismus,* 85.

prophets and Jesus himself to condemn church services. The very first martyr, Stephen, was stoned to death merely because he expressed the biblical proclamation that "the Most High does not dwell in churches made by hands." Here Arnold appears to be a "Karlstadt redivivus" excoriating all forms of externality in the church.

One of Arnold's major contributions to Pietism was that the "proof" for Christianity was not theoretical or dogmatic but rather was based upon experience and was therefore *historical*. Certainly Spener and Francke were already oriented toward this perspective with their respective emphases upon primitive Christianity as the historical proof for the attainability of Christian perfection and the important role of the individual. Arnold proceeded from these views to emphasize the thoroughly historical character of Christianity. The Bible was presented not as a collection of views and doctrines but rather as a report of events and facts, as a description of persons and community made living by their activity. He placed historical reality over against logical-theoretical arguments. Knowledge—historical science—was the handmaiden to truth. The truth was always historical truth. This was expressed in his methodology where the older reception of truth from authority is overcome by the insistence upon reading the sources and forming one's own judgment.

The importance of Arnold consists in his closeness to mystical spiritualism and in the admission of historical science into faith's consciousness. Both elements foreshadow the modern period. However, Arnold's one-sidedness was expressed in a principle of individualism and in his kind of historical science. The significance of community, of the church, was obscure if not hidden to him. Insofar as he speaks positively of the church it is of a group of individuals, a gathering together of reborn persons. Thus in his first work, "Die erste Liebe der Gemeinen Jesus Christi" (1696), he placed against the contemporary churches the fact that the first Christians met in homes rather than the temple.

His other one-sidedness is the "partiality" or bias of his historical work. His program, of course, was that science would bring forth historical truth. The great turning point in the history of Christianity for Arnold was patronage of the church by Constantine and the cessation of persecution; this is Christianity's downfall. From this point on modesty, openness, and freedom are displaced by pride, hypocrisy, greed, involvement in worldly affairs and offices, oppression of conscience, and tyranny.[65] He

---

[65]Cf. Arnold, *Unparteiische Kirchen—und Ketzerhistorie*, 1:4:3:152f.; also 144ff. Cf.

understood his historical work to be in service to the reform of life by the rebirth of the individual. History was to serve the inner elevation by devotional consideration of the past.

Without doubt Arnold's significance for church history resides in his radical perspectives of 1693-1702. We shall attempt to summarize his major writings of this period and then conclude with brief observations on the long final period of his activity within the church.[66]

Rebirth is the central theme in both the *Abbildung* and the *Ketzerhistorie*. In the former it is the Archimedian point by which the entire institution of the fallen church is to be revolutionized. In the latter, it is the criterion by which the entire history of the church is to be judged.

As "Archimedian point," rebirth is concerned not with the church as institution but with the individual. The clear subordination of institution to the individual Christian is expressed by the ordering of the *Abbildung:* conversion, worship that focuses on the action of the servants of God, and the relationship of the Christians to one another and then to the world. Throughout the book, rebirth is anthropologically considered as the essential turning point of the individual and his subsequent conversion and illumination, all of which determine his future life. Methodologically Arnold developed two lines from this center: toward God (love to God, formation in God's image, union with God) and toward the world (active faith, conduct according to God's Word, sin, fruits of true Christianity).

Characteristic of Arnold's work is that he begins not with the gospel but with the description of conversion. "The beginning of being a Christian is 'the true conversion to a true basis of the true effective Christianity.' "[67] The Holy Spirit effects knowledge of our depravity which our blind nature is unable to know. Through the knowledge of sin conversion shall lead to a turning to God. This effective repentance turns away from the prior sinful activity and is only possible in a faith which finds Christ through the Holy Spirit in the Word and through him, the Father. Certainty is sought in God alone; the Spirit must give witness to their spirit that they are children of God. The result is a holy life, conversion of

---

Jürgen Büchsel, *Gottfried Arnold. Sein Verständnis von Kirche und Wiedergeburt* (Witten: Luther Verlag, 1970) 43ff., 87-88.

[66]Unless otherwise indicated the following section is heavily dependent upon Büchsel's study, *Gottfried Arnold.*

[67]Büchsel, *Gottfried Arnold,* 47; *Abbildung,* 1:1,1:1.

the will, expansion of the kingdom of God, and preaching God's gospel to the entire world.

Since Arnold continually emphasized the significance of the Holy Spirit in conversion, he can speak of the first step to being a Christian as the beginning of illumination. While he emphasizes conversion as a human act, illumination is a passive process. Christ is the mediator between God and persons. No one can know God unless God himself opens that person's heart. The heart must receive the Word. The Word is the Word of Christ; it is his law. In a formulation reminiscent of Karlstadt, Arnold writes: "Therefore the promise of the Lord must be fulfilled in the faithful, that he will write his law in their hearts."[68] Every true Christian must receive the Word in his soul. This means the indwelling Word which is Christ, not merely the external letter. One can hear the external Word without surrendering his own will, but the knowledge which makes one holy is only heard by a pure soul. This is acquired by turning away from the world and oneself.

By the Spirit, the soul can be elevated to God. The soul's change of direction toward God is rebirth. Without the Spirit the soul can do nothing pleasing to God; it is dead. By the Spirit, one receives not only a new alignment but something like a super-earthly quality. The goal is finally community with God. The person is renewed in the image of God. The completion or perfection of this process is union with God. The emergence of the living structure of rebirth takes place through two related aims: (1) God must be received in the innerness of the person. God became man therefore we are able to receive him and recover again the image of God; (2) This new becoming of the person must be expressed even in his behavior. The new person can be measured in his effective faith, by his fruits, by his conduct in the world. "These are the two main themes which run through Arnold's entire work."[69]

These themes become the criteria for Arnold's description and evaluation of the church. The personal elements are placed above the institutional. The church is understood to be a community of individuals, the reborn, and not an institution. Thus hierarchy and community are in opposition, and from the viewpoint of a church which rests upon the

---

[68]Büchsel, *Gottfried Arnold*, 48; *Abbildung*, 1:3,5:20. Fulfillment of the commandments is possible for the reborn. Büchsel, *Gottfried Arnold*, 54.

[69]Büchsel, *Gottfried Arnold*, 52.

equality of its participants in rebirth, hierarchy is rejected. Christians manifest their brotherly community in that they call each other brothers and sisters. The strong bond of brotherhood, just as rebirth, is created and maintained by the Holy Spirit. The church is where there is true faith. Whoever is not in Christ cannot really belong to the community.

> The church as visible, true church stands and falls therefore with the earnestness of the Christian existence of its members. Thus if rebirth is the foundation, then the church must continually prove itself to be the church by keeping itself pure from hypocrites and sinners. The criterion of rebirth is effective also for the church at this point: just as rebirth expresses itself by a holy life, so the church is recognizable therein as the community of the reborn, that one finds in it a holy and God-pleasing life (III, 1, 16; p. 344).[70]

Arnold also applies his second criteria of rebirth to the church: interiority. Just as the kingdom of God dwells within the individual so it dwells within the community. External means have only external consequences therefore he opposes any compulsion regarding Christian existence. The freedom of the Spirit opposes binding Christians to any institution. "The Christian is related directly to God because the church does not mediate rebirth, but rather is first formed by the reborn."[71]

Here is where the conflict between visible and invisible churches arises. Arnold decides without hesitation for the invisible church which is the only true church since the rise of the hierarchy. The suffering of Christians now is no longer by the unchristian state but by the unchristian church. Thus suffering remains the sign of the true church and Arnold opposes the suffering church to the powerful state church.

Arnold also understands the sacraments in light of the centrality of rebirth. Baptism is the sign of conversion and rebirth by which anyone who becomes a Christian is taken into the community. The introduction of infant baptism tends in the direction of *opera operato*. The Lord's Supper is the repeated recollection of rebirth, the place where the believer must be able to positively answer the question whether his life and confession are in harmony. Therefore the Lord's Supper also serves as the manifestation of the community of believers.

Church discipline is related both to this understanding of the Lord's Supper and the conception of an invisible church without compulsion. From the former perspective wherein the community depends upon the

---

[70]Ibid., 58.

[71]Ibid., 59.

Christianity of its members which is measured by the individual's expression of rebirth by works of love, hypocrites and public sinners cannot be united with true Christians. However, the latter perspective raises an insoluble problem for Arnold—rejecting the compulsion he demands. He attempts to resolve this with the presupposition that one can always see who is the true Christian by the unqualified correspondence between interiority and good works. Church discipline then is an act of the community of the reborn against those who do not take seriously being a Christian. Supposedly this is only possible in a community of the reborn because only this community does not take compulsion for granted.

For our purposes it is not necessary to sketch Arnold's final development.[72] The events in his life which turn out to be "breaks" in his biography do not cause any changes in his theological views. They were, rather, the expression of his theology and the consequences of a maxim which ruled his life and thought, namely, that faith and life are inseparably bound together. The active faith which also effects its understanding is the characteristic of a true Christian. The motivating force of Arnold's activity resides in this basic insight.[73]

PIETIST MOTIFS

Arndt, Spener, Francke, and Arnold were of fundamental significance for the development and leadership of Lutheran Pietism. Our brief sketches of their work provide us with both a basis upon which we may present a more systematic summary of Pietist motifs and a hedge against the temptation to develop an anachronistic systematic theology of Pietism. It would, of course, be desirable to supplement the above sketches with the contributions of others such as Zinzendorf, Bengel, and Oetinger as well as movements such as Württemberg Pietism and the Awakening. This is not necessary for our purposes and also is precluded by lack of space. In what follows we shall attempt to present an overview of the Pietist motifs of rebirth, sanctification, and the church.[74]

---

[72]Büchsel, *Gottfried Arnold,* provides a summary on 195-204.

[73]Ibid., 195.

[74]Surveys are readily available in encyclopedia articles and handbooks such as *RGG, The Encyclopedia of the Lutheran Church* and *Die Kirche in Ihrer Geschichte* (Band 4, Lieferung O: Martin Schmidt, *Pietismus*; and Lieferung R: Erich Beyreuther, *Die Erweckungsbewegung*). For more specialized studies cf. Hartmut Lehmann, *Pietismus und weltliche Ordnung in Württemberg;* H. Weigelt, *Pietismus-Studien,* etc.

REBIRTH

The central motif for Pietism is rebirth. Unlike Orthodoxy which viewed rebirth as only one element within the *ordo salutis*, Pietism understood rebirth as comprising the entire process of salvation.[75] Thus Spener wrote that rebirth is the necessary substance (or cause—Materie) of our Christianity, "... it is the basis of all remaining sanctification or the spring from which all good things must necessarily flow which are from us or done by us. Therefore he among us who correctly understands this (rebirth), assuredly also rightly understands his entire Christianity."[76]

Classic expressions of the motif of rebirth may be found in Theophil Großgebauer's *Treuer Untericht von der Wiedergeburt* (1661), Spener's comprehensive collection of sermons, Johanna Eleanora Peterson's *Notwendigkeit der neuen Creatur* (1699), Gottfried Arnold's *Kirchen- und Ketzerhistorie* (1699), his *Wahren Abbildung des inwendigen Christentums* (1709), his pastoral theology *Die geistliche Gestalt eines evangelischen Lehrers* (1704), as well as his *Lehren der Gläubigen* (1700), Johann Reitzen's *Historie der Wiedergeborenen* (1724), Christian Gerber's *Historie der Wiedergeborenen in Sachsen* (1724), A. H. Francke's *Katechismuspredigten* (1726), and in Christoph Oetinger's *Abriss der evangelischen Ordnung zur Wiedergeburt* (1735). As we have already seen, Büchsel claims that rebirth forms the center of Arnold's anthropology.[77] Further references to Zinzendorf and Oetinger may be found in the recent essay by Klaus Peter Blaser.[78]

To posit rebirth as the central motif of Pietism is not to gloss over its various interpretations both among Pietists themselves and between contemporary scholars of Pietism. Since there is no present consensus on the interpretation of this motif we shall simply present the major perspectives. It is not our task to resolve or synthesize what remains controversial in contemporary scholarship. It is of interest, however, that both major lines of research contribute to our search for historical

---

[75]Schmidt claims that the understanding of rebirth as the "Urbegriff" for the entire process is rooted in pre- and Reformation spiritualism. *WNM*, 184, 24.

[76]"Der hochwichtige Articul von der Wiedergeburt" 1715, 2d ed., 1. Quoted by Schmidt, *WNM*, 172.

[77]Schmidt, *WNM*, 24; Büchsel, *Gottfried Arnold*, 57.

[78]"Pia desideria dogmatica," in *Der Pietismus in Gestalten und Wirkungen,* ed. by Bornkamm, Heyer, and Schindler (AGP 14) (Bielefeld: Luther-Verlag, 1975) 98-119.

antecedents and understanding of contemporary charismatic movements. On the one hand there is the position of Emanuel Hirsch that Spener and the churchly pietism which derived from him must be understood from the tradition of the Lutheran Orthodox perspective of justification. On the other hand is the presently influential interpretation of Martin Schmidt that the motif of rebirth in Spener and others displaced and took the place of justification.[79] Since we have relied extensively upon Schmidt's interpretation which includes the argument that Pietism is influenced by mystical spiritualism including such Reformation spiritualists as Karlstadt, Müntzer, and Schwenckfeld we shall begin with Schmidt's views.

Schmidt's interpretation that rebirth is the center of Spener's theology and that all other theological motifs are grouped around it runs throughout Schmidt's extensive studies but is most carefully established textually in his essay, "Speners Wiedergeburtslehre."[80] Here he sees the Pietist point of departure in its sharp demarcation from justification. Even if it makes a strong appeal to justification, it converts it to its own use; justification becomes a moment in the all-encompassing motif of rebirth. In his great sermon collection (*Der hochwichtige Articul von der Wiedergeburt*) Spener discusses the necessity of rebirth. This includes the sinful corruption of the person and the nobility (noble birth) of the reborn. God is the creator, the Word and baptism the means; the preacher is the mediating person for rebirth. Rebirth itself exists in the ignition of faith, in justification as adoption, in the creation of the new person. The reborn is described by their code of duties as well as their spontaneous characteristics. God's dealing with the reborn is set forth in terms of their care, their chastisement, but also their good qualities, their righteousness, their freedom from the law, God's presence in their heart, their eternal inheritance, their inertia in the estate of being God's children. Finally there is the repetition of rebirth for those who have fallen out of this estate. It actually amounts to a continual renewal and self-examination. Here justification is certainly only one, indeed a passing moment, in the whole process.[81]

---

[79]For a critical discussion of Schmidt's interpretation cf. Johannes Wallman, "Wiedergeburt und Erneuerung bei Philipp Jakob Spener: Ein Diskussionsbeitrag," in Lindt and Deppermann, eds., *Pietismus und Neuzeit* (Jahrbücher zur Geschichte des Pietismus, 3) (Bielefeld: Luther-Verlag, 1977) 7-31.

[80]*WNM*, 169-94, cf. 171ff.

[81]Ibid., 173, n. 14.

The centrality of rebirth to Pietism is linked to the perception of the corruption of the world and persons. God and sin are mutually exclusive and thus the opposition between the sphere of the sinful world and the sphere of salvation extends so deep that it can be overcome only by an event sui generis. The only feasible analogy for such a sui generis event is birth. The author of this event is God himself, actively renewing the fallen creation. In the face of this miracle of God's approach and nearness to man, Spener returned to using the linguistic treasure of mysticism for the secret intercourse of God with man. As a consequence he appropriated as descriptions for the divine nature not God's historical activity but rather his eternal essence, not God's act but rather God's being. However, this orientation, tied to the sphere of the mystery of God, necessarily ended in the rational: he succumbed to the consequence of his logical principle of the final identity between God and the reborn person. The salvation process becomes a rational construction because the paradoxical fact that God loves the *sinner* works against the logical claim that God can know and recognize only that which is like him.[82] This perspective that participation in the divine nature is possible only by identity reflects the mystical spiritualist tradition which incorporated platonic and aristotelian principles: the platonic schema of the original image and its likeness, and the aristotelian principle that like is known by like. A further consequence is that love becomes the key to understanding the divine nature and under the impact of the principle of identity is understood as eros rather than agape.[83]

Thus rebirth is the initiation by the Holy Spirit of the process whereby the new creature grows in faith and likeness toward God.

> Just as Christ has a divine nature because begotten by the Father he is essentially God, so he has made us participate in another kind of divine nature, II Peter 1:4. There a kind of divinity has been effected in us by rebirth, and will continue to develop by renewal: thereby we are indeed not gods but nevertheless God's children and his image, becoming not the original image of his essence but nevertheless an image of his holiness. The Lord through his divine power causes this image to increase more and more in us until we shall become like him, when we shall see him as he is, I John 3:2.[84]

---

[82] *WNM*, 271 with references in note 121.

[83] *WNM*, 135, 186, 269ff.; Anders Nygren, *Agape and Eros* (Philadelphia: Westminster, 1953) in Kurt Aland, ed., *Pietismus und Bibel* (Witten: Luther-Verlag, 1980) 54 (hereafter PuB).

[84] *WNM*, 270; for numerous other citations cf. 269-71.

The development of our rebirth through the *praxis pietatis* will be discussed below under the heading of sanctification.

An alternative interpretation of Spener and Pietism is that the central concern is not rebirth per se but rather the process of renewal. Here we may recall the predilection of charismatic groups to speak of "charismatic renewal."

Lutheran theology up to Pietism used the concept of rebirth in various senses. The Formula of Concord, without sanctioning a particular interpretation, has a threefold usage of the term rebirth: (1) the totality of justification (forgiveness of sins) and the consequent sanctification; (2) only justification (Melanchthon in the Augsburg Confession); and (3) only the sanctification and renewal which follows justification (Luther's major perspective). Lutheran Orthodoxy added the further understanding of rebirth as the gift of faith. Cognizant of these usages, Spener developed a complex concept of rebirth which included the ignition of faith, justification, and the creation of the new person. He distinguished between rebirth and renewal, and placed the striving for perfection in the sphere of renewal not in that of rebirth. Thus J. G. Walch's charge that Pietists are fanatics because of their mixture of rebirth and renewal to the detriment of justification does not apply to Spener.[85] In this sense rebirth is understood as the act of God which creates new life; it is a forensic act. Renewal is the sphere in which the reborn person cooperates with God in an ongoing process. Rebirth and renewal are analogous, respectively, to being awakened from death and the healing of sickness. Thus, a reform program such as that of the *Pia Desideria* diagnosed the corrupted state of the church as a sickness and prescribed the means for its healing and improvement as being through renewal, not in the article of rebirth. From this point of view the main desire is not rebirth but renewal—the process of growth in faith and the striving for perfection. The latter are rooted in rebirth and belong to the doctrine of renewal.[86]

RENEWAL AND SANCTIFICATION

The central concern of the reform program of Pietism involved the renewal of the whole person. "Rebirth does not bring the person imme-

---

[85]Johann George Walch, *Historische und Theologische Einleitung in die Religions-Streitigkeiten der Evangelisch-Lutherischen Kirche* (1733) 2:749-50. Cf. Wallmann, "Wiedergeburt und Erneuerung bei Philipp Jakob Spener," 25.

diately to perfection. It is rather the beginning of the salvation process upon which renewal of the spiritual life must follow. In the rebirth God has lodged in the person a spark of the spiritual life which in the renewal shall be fanned into a flame."[87]

The concept of renewal itself is ambiguous or, better, polyvalent. Renewal is the creation of the new person both ethically and ontologically. It is the perfection of the divine image received in rebirth that includes growth in ethical virtue and union with God. The concern of classical Pietism for ethical verification of faith and therefore a growing sanctification is related to the concern for certainty of salvation. The teleological orientation toward the "new man" leads fundamentally toward perfectionism. Negatively renewal is seen as the overcoming and destruction of sin which ranges from the progressive weakening of the old man to the killing of the old Adam. Positively, it is the participation in the divine nature. The new life may be understood as a fine synergism; a growth process rooted in rebirth; a progessive activity directed by the Holy Spirit.[88] In this process the law serves both as a scourge against the old man and a norm for the new life.[89] In short, God's eschatological promise must become a contemporary reality. The Reformation's theocentric and eschatological orientation becomes anthropocentric and historical. Thus Schmidt summarizes the essence of Pietism with the formula: to change the world by changing man.[90] The means for this renewal is the Word of God.

THE WORD OF GOD AND THE CHURCH

From its first programmatic expression in Spener's *Pia Desideria,* Pietism's fundamental proposal for reform of the church was to bring the Word of God more fully among the people.

> That one should be intent upon bringing forth the Word of God more richly (or fully) among us. We know that by nature we have nothing good in us and that if anything shall be in us it must be worked in us by God. The Word is the powerful

---

[86]Cf. Wallmann, "Wiedergeburt und Erneuerung bei Philipp Jakob Spener," 22-29; Erhard Peschke, *Bekehrung und Reform: Ansatz und Wurzeln der Theologie August Hermann Franckes* (AGP 15) (Bielefeld: Luther-Verlag, 1977) 98-109.

[87]Peschke, *Bekehrung und Reform,* 105.

[88]*WNM,* 176ff.

[89]Peschke, *Bekerung und Reform,* 108.

[90]*WNM,* 133, 281, 255.

means to this end by which faith in the gospel must be ignited. . . . Indeed the more richly the Word is dwelling among us the more we are believing and accomplishing the fruits of faith.[91]

Spener and the Pietists understood this desire to be clearly the continuation of Luther's Reformation.[92] The programmatic call was for biblical theology in place of scholastic theology as the means for growth in renewal. Following rebirth one must hear and read the Bible and make its teaching fruitful for life. Knowledge of biblical languages as well as meditation upon the Bible serve the goal of "translating" its message from the head to the heart. There was a predilection for the New Testament and an emphasis upon its literal sense as the book of life.[93]

Pietism's identification of the Bible with the Word of God had the double effect of loosening Luther's bond between Scripture and the Holy Spirit and of historicizing and psychologizing the Scripture. The purpose of the Bible was understood in terms of personal edification and guidance to the validation of rebirth. This subjective orientation is reflected in Francke's hermeneutical schema of distinguishing the kernel from the husk. This distinction is an exegetical possibility only for the reborn. Certainly the unregenerate may ascertain the correct message but he is unable to appropriate it spiritually. Only the enlightenment by the Holy Spirit makes possible the distinction between the true and false sense of the Scripture. The goal of this hermeneutic is the praxis pietatis, the Christ in us.[94]

> While according to the Lutheran understanding of Scripture, Word and Spirit form a concrete unity, and the close cooperation of both is expressly emphasized; the husk-kernel concept has its origin in spiritualistic conceptions which emphasize the difference of opposition between Word and Spirit. The view that the believer comprehends the inner spiritual kernel whereas the unbeliever only the outer material husk belongs to the basic religious perception of spiritualistic thinkers.[95]

---

[91]Spener, *Pia Desideria,* 53, 31ff. Cf. Martin Schmidt, "Philipp Jakob Spener und die Bibel," in PuB, 9-58.

[92]Cf. Spener, *Pia Desideria,* 57, 9ff.; 58, 3ff.

[93]PuB, 58; Peschke, *Bekehrung und Reform,* 108; *WNM,* 355-56; Erich Beyreuther, *Der geschichtliche Auftrag des Pietismus in der Gegenwart* (Stuttgart: Calwer Verlag, 1963) 12-15.

[94]Erhard Peschke, "August Hermann Francke und die Bibel," in PuB, 59-88; 66, 84.

[95]Ibid., 70.

Nevertheless biblical instruction even in terms of its "outer" forms played an important role in daily life and consequently stimulated intensive biblical study both academically and practically. Through the Halle school and the person of Johann Albrecht Bengel, Pietism contributed serious studies on the history, grammar, and languages of the Bible. Their concern was not limited to hermeneutics but extended to philology and the development of new translations from critically examined Greek texts of the New Testament.[96]

One of the great biblicists of Pietism was Bengel (1687-1752) who exerted a profound influence upon Württemberg Pietism. Known especially for his textual studies which led to a Greek Testament (1734) and his influential biblical annotations, *Gnomon Novi Testamenti* (1742), he emphasized total application of the person to the text and the total application of the text to the person ("Te totum applica ad textum; rem totam applica ad te"). Thus the encounter with Scripture as well as that of the experience of God forms a circle. "Faith believes the authority of Scripture and the reality of God, and experience confirms faith."[97]

But how is the reality of God, the certainty of the experience of God, mediated? The first answer which appeared to Bengel was present in his youthful experience in Stuttgart. This was the enthusiastic mysticism of radical Pietism which posited the immediate union of the soul with God. The other answer was the customary one given by the church: Word and sacrament as the means of grace. Neither in itself was satisfactory to Bengel, but behind both he saw the old Word of the Bible. The Bible then is the medium in which God spoke directly to him, to the inner recesses of his heart. As contradictory as it may appear, Bengel experienced mysticism's unmediated encounter with God in the Word of Scripture. The Scripture is the place where God is directly accessible, where the Father personally speaks. It is clear that in some important points Bengel remains on the soil of spiritualism. The emphasis upon the directness of the God-relationship means that in an essential sense the Scripture is no longer a medium. Only those having the gift of the Spirit have this experience with the Scripture. The careful and pious reader of the Scripture is therefore compared to the cultivated field which is ready to

---

[96]Cf. Emanuel Hirsch, *Geschichte der neuen evangelischen Theologie* 2 (Gütersloh: Mohn, 1960) 177-86.

[97]Martin Brecht, "Johann Albrecht Bengel und der schwäbische Biblizismus," in PuB, 193-218, 194.

receive the seed. This perspective, however, made it difficult for Bengel to make understandable the individual's various relationships to the words of the Bible. It was difficult to clarify whether the reception of the Word of God is prepared by the Spirit or whether the Word brings the Spirit with it. Certainly, however, a new type of Pietist piety arose with this emphasis on the direct relationship of the heart to the Word of Scripture. This biblicist piety is more adequate and substantive in its relationship to Scripture but it nevertheless also remains indebted to the orientation of radical mystical Pietism.

On the positive side, the equivalence of Scripture and Word made possible a uniquely intense connection with the Word. Exegesis, prayer, and meditation merge with one another. The entire Bible is seen as itself—the content of faith. There arises a "higher philology" where grammar is pursued by the heart and all of existence. This, however, is also the source of Bengel's major exegetical error—his interpretation of the book of Revelation. "Bengel no longer saw to what extent the treasure is given to us in earthen vessels. . . . For his realism depended upon particular mystical-enthusiastic presuppositions, upon the accessibility of the heavenly world, upon the nearness of divine things and upon the discernible end of history."[98] Thus Bengel's biblicistic thought structure was no less problematic than the Orthodox orientation to the Bible. He sought to comprehend the Scriptures as a coherent whole, as a chronological history of salvation structure which is not only a source for preaching but a pattern for an ethical-social system. This is the source for the great nineteenth-century Pietist movements which attempted to build pure and holy communities.[99]

This brings us back to our introductory comments where we indicated that the intention of Pietism, historically speaking, was to recover primitive Christianity. Materially, this meant the transformation of the world and the church by the transformation of individuals through rebirth and renewal. The primitive church was idealized and historicized in the sense of being attainable in the present. These marks of Pietist ecclesiology are evident in Spener and Francke as well as Zinzendorf, and Arnold's entire church historical work is in service to this goal. Primitive Christianity was

---

[98]Ibid., 196-97.

[99]Martin Brecht, "Christentum als Lebensordnung. Die Frömmigkeit des Pietismus," in *Evangelischer Glaube im Wandel der Zeit* (Stuttgart: Steinkopf Verlag, 1967) 54, 67, 66.

a historical reality and therefore it may once again be realized in history. It is a theme which is sharpened in the nineteenth century by Søren Kierkegaard's emphasis upon "contemporaneity with Jesus." On this basis the New Testament became the essential writing for both the individual and the church; institutional expressions of the faith are displaced by the personal, unmediated relationship to the New Testament. Genuine piety rooted in personal closeness to the Bible formed a stronger bond than dogma, doctrine, tradition, and church order. The ecumenical implication of this orientation resided in the view that unity was not guaranteed by the activity of the churches in their sructured offices of Word and sacrament but rather as the free coming together on the basis of believers drawn to Jesus.[100]

The reform of the church begins with the piety of the new man. This includes the pastor as well as the layperson, the only difference being that the latter does privately what the pastor does publicly. This emphasis upon the church as the community of the reborn has the following consequences. The image of the church as the body of Christ received a shift in accent from emphasis upon the head to emphasis upon the members. The judgment of the truth of the church is related now to its life rather than the purity of its doctrine. Thus there is a Donatist echo in the view that only the pastor who is a true Christian may lead others.[101] In the course of Pietism's development the Reformation's emphasis upon the priesthood of the baptized will shift toward that of the priesthood of believers. The reciprocal love of its members rather than Word and sacrament becomes the mark of the church.[102] Because the church is examined expressly in its structure and its detriments are located in the members themselves rather than in their relationship to their head, Spener does not reach a dogmatic perspective but rather remains in historical analysis. That the church is the body of *Christ* disappears behind the fact that it is a *body* suffering from disease. Its earthly life condition is taken to be more important that its heavenly nourishment, the Word and sacraments. The ecumenical orientation of Pietism focused

---

[100]Cf. *WNM*, 355-56; cf. 133ff.; and M. Schmidt, "Das Frühchristentum in der evangelisch-lutherischen Überlieferung vom 18.-20. Jahrhundert, insbesondere in Deutschland," in *Oecumenica* (1971/72) 88-110.

[101]Spener, *Pia Desideria*, 67, 5ff.; *WNM*, 143.

[102]Ibid., 28, 9f.; 61, 3; *WNM*, 145.

on its doctrine and praxis of piety signifies an extensive dedogmatization and confessional indifference. But for the emphasis upon the present power of the Holy Spirit this would appear to be a decisive step toward the Enlightenment. The shift from corporate worship toward private edification, however, is not the result of autonomous reason but individual rebirth and renewal.[103]

THE EFFECTS AND CONTRIBUTIONS OF PIETISM

Pietism's dissolution of Orthodoxy's confessional consciousness is directly related to its own self-understanding as an international and interconfessional movement. Thus Pietism was a decisive preparation for the modern, ecumenical movement. In the understanding of its best representatives, Pietism was a "second Reformation" leading the church out of confessional rigidity toward a brotherhood of the reborn. Church-dividing dogma and ecclesial-confessional traditions were displaced by a strong new community consciousness formed by the reborn individuals' consciousness of a personal relationship to God and brotherhood with those of similar experiences.[104]

In its ecclesiology, Pietism exerted strong influence upon hymnody and preaching. Once again the doctrinal was displaced by the personal and exhortatory. The image of the pastor shifted from that of minister of the Word of God to that of the personally accountable witness and example of the spiritual life, of "godliness." The sermon was supplemented by small-group discussion and study of the Bible. The interest in exemplary living led to increased attention to biographical and autobiographical stories of outstanding and reborn Christians. The consequences of this interest were both intensive work on the Bible in terms of exegesis, annotated editions, revisions, and translations, and historical and biographical studies.

Pietism's concern for studying and meditating on the Bible found its practical locus in the famous *collegia pietatis*, later known as "Stunde." The hours devoted to discussion of Scripture and religious experience provided small group support for the strengthening and edification of

---

[103]Cf. *WNM*, 149ff.

[104]Cf. Andreas Lindt, "Pietismus und Ökumene," in *Pietismus und Moderne Welt* (AGP 12) (Witten: Luther-Verlag, 1974) 138-60.

individuals. This concern of Pietism for the individual was certainly one of its strengths but it was also one of its weaknesses. The conventicle posed the possibility of creating two classes of Christians: the normal "church-goers" and the "better" Christians of the "ecclesiola in ecclesia." On the one hand there was the established church (the Volks- and Staatkirche) that distributed the Lord's Supper to the unworthy and related church discipline to its own concerns. On the other hand there was the conventicle, the gathering together of the holy community not only as a church within the church but even on occasion as separate from the "Babel" of the established church. Although this was certainly not the desire of Spener who had hoped to reform the church through it, the conventicle posed the danger of appearing to be a place of escape from the church for devout Christians.

Nevertheless the importance of these conventicles and Stunde cannot be overestimated. They were determinative of life and piety, even influencing the choice of marriage partners. Because the leadership of the experienced, older brethren was charismatic and spiritual, great inner riches were developed. On the other hand these small groups could be characterized by a narrow and strict spirit that generated conflict. Nevertheless Pietism offered a spiritual home to many and the possibility to realize an earnest Christian existence.[105]

This emphasis upon the individual's praxis pietatis enriched dogmatics through the focus upon love, perfection, and sin as concrete phenomena. While standing against ethical laxity, Pietism ran into the dangers of an unchristian narrowness and indifference if not antagonism toward the world. The world was to be changed by changing the hearts of individuals. This was the motivating force for Pietism's great caritative works. But in spite of its orphanages, hospitals, educational contributions, and its inner and foreign missions, Pietism's concern for the individual precluded development of a *social* ethic.

Pietism's achievement was to recall attention to the element of personal decision in faith and to remind the church that it is a community bound together by faith and fellowship. It linked both of these concerns to the necessity and possibility of emulating original Christianity.

---

[105]Cf. Brecht, "Christentum als Lebensordnung," 58-60.

CONTINUITIES AND DISCONTINUITIES WITH THE REFORMATION

We have already referred to the fact that the leading representatives of Pietism understood themselves not only as heirs of the Reformation but also leaders of its renewal into a "second Reformation." Luther's "Preface to Romans" was of particular importance in this regard, for it appeared to offer exactly what Pietism believed necessary—the equation between faith and rebirth. Luther's affirmations that "Faith is not the human notion and dream that some people call faith," and "Faith, however, is a divine work in us which changes us and makes us to be born anew to God," are perhaps the most extensively quoted statements made by Luther in Pietism.[106] Here Luther is presented as the chief witness for rebirth and the opponent of all reform movements that remain merely external without fundamentally changing the heart. The latter, of course, refers to the decay of faith brought about by Orthodoxy's intellectualizing, which therefore necessitates a "second Reformation."

To what extent was Pietism's self-professed understanding to be a "second Reformation" faithful to Luther? This is a difficult question to answer. The following attempt to provide a systematic overview may be seen by some as too simple but it has the value of relating directly to Luther's theological motifs already presented. We shall first discuss Pietism's continuity or agreement with Luther and then turn to discontinuities.

CONTINUITIES

In addressing theological and religious attention directly to the Bible, Pietism represented one of Luther's central concerns. Francke was not alone in emphasizing the point that genuine theology is biblical theology. We are already familiar with Pietism's extensive work on biblical languages, translations, and exegesis as well as the use of Bible study among the laity.

Because, according to Francke, the Word of the Bible is not a dead letter but the concrete historical means of grace which communicates the Spirit, the Holy Scriptures are the only means of conversion. Faith is kindled in the heart and strengthened by the Word.

---

[106]Cf. Martin Schmidt, "Luthers Vorrede zum Römerbrief in Pietismus," *WNM*, 299-330, 316. Luther, "Preface to the Epistle of St. Paul to the Romans" (1546), LW 35, 365-80, 370; WA, DB 7, 3-27. Cf. also Peschke, *Bekehrung und Reform*, 137.

In opposition to the intellectualist system of Orthodoxy, Francke emphasized personal application of the biblical truths of faith and existential relationship to the facts of salvation. This rejection of an "opus operatum" view of the Word is similar to the young Luther's emphasis upon personal faith and the right hearing and use of the Word and sacraments.

There is also in Francke a radical consideration of the person in his totality. There is no neutral sphere between good and evil. The natural unregenerated person in his totality is separated from God and blind to spiritual things. This in turn necessitates a total conversion of the whole person. The poles of the salvation process therefore are not sickness and healing but rather death and rebirth. It is by the cross and mortification that we attain rebirth and resurrection. The life of a child of God is a life under the cross. "The Cross is the mark of the Christian. Behind this concept, which meets us also in a modified form in mysticism, is recognizable Luther's view of the hidden God, who works in opposition, against reason and by breaking, by the way of the Cross, draws his own to himself."[107]

In agreement with Luther, Francke emphasizes repeatedly that our salvation is effected by God's grace alone—neither before, during, nor after conversion do our works have an influence upon our justification. At the same time, faith and love are inseparable even though they are distinguished. Here, too, Luther's "Preface to Romans" that emphasizes faith as "a living, busy, active, mighty thing" is called upon by Francke and others.

DISCONTINUITIES

Lutheran Orthodoxy did not acknowledge the validity of Pietism's calling upon Luther for support of their renewal movement. Rather than relive these older polemics, we may refer to contemporary scholars who point to the difference between Luther and Pietism.

In the Pietist emphasis upon the Bible there is at best a spiritualist coloring and shift of accent. The central weight falls not upon the Word of God but rather upon the work of the Holy Spirit. At worst, the Word and the Holy Spirit are separated. For Luther, Word and Spirit are united indivisibly with one another. The Spirit is bound to the Word; the Word

---

[107]Peschke, *Bekehrung und Reform*, 140.

contains the Spirit. Thus Luther's emphasis upon *fides ex auditu,* faith by hearing the Word. There is a tendency in Pietism to downgrade external hearing and to see the Word as mere clothing that may be shed for the Spirit.[108]

As a consequence, radical doubt is to be overcome in Pietism, not by hearing the Word of God as an address of promise (the authority of the Word) but by experientially verified faith. Thus it is Pietism which introduces the usage of modifiers for the term faith: weak faith, dead faith, living faith, powerful faith, etc. Luther's straightforward position that faith simply takes God's promise as true and honors it in that it does not take God to be a liar[109] is displaced by discussions about the quality of faith and its accomplishments. The charismatic movement is also marked by the passion for "more" faith, "more" power, etc.[110]

This orientation allows the development of a hermeneutic of the Bible as the pattern for life. In the final analysis Pietists viewed Scripture as the confirmation and legitimation of their own experience.[111] The idea of an order of God that has as its goal personal conversion displaces justification as the midpoint of Pietist theology. At this point there is a shift from Luther's emphasis on *pro nobis* and, thereby, the loss of Luther's dialectic of *simul justus et peccator.* Pietism emphasized the visible formation of the renewed person who had been verified by the ethical fruits of faith. Rebirth thus signifies a higher nature and quality of being. Luther, on the contrary, remains with an ongoing battle between the old and new man which is never transformed into a visible victory on earth. Victory always remains the judgment of God, not the possibility of the Christian. The dynamic of Pietism was not Luther's dialectic of law and gospel, sin and grace, damnation and faith, but rather the development of the power of faith in renewal and good works.[112]

Pietism's displacement of justification[113] by rebirth denotes a shift

---

[108]*WNM,* 164.

[109]Dictata, 1513-1516.WA 4, 287, 5; 360, 8; De Captivitata Babylonica, 1520, WA 6, 516, 42; 517, 33; Das Magnificant, 1520-1521. WA 7, 593, 26; De Servo Arbitrio, 1525. WA 18, 619, 6 and 22.

[110]Cf. *WNM,* 232-34; also Frederick D. Bruner, *A Theology of the Holy Spirit* (Grand Rapids MI: Eerdmans, 1970) 128-29.

[111]M. Schmidt, "Der Pietismus und das moderne Denken," in *PuMW,* 9-74, 40.

[112]Peschke, *Bekehrung und Reform,* 142; *WNM,* 327ff., 159, 173, 238-98.

[113]On the Pietist understanding of justification cf. Hirsch, *Geschichte der neuen*

from Luther's theocentric orientation to an anthropocentric orientation. This comes into sharper focus when we recall our earlier dialogical mode of expressing Luther's theology in terms of God's *descent* to the sinner as opposed to the medieval and Reformation spiritualists' motif of the sinner's *ascent* to God. To Luther the gospel is radical good news because it is God's promise to accept the *sinner*. God descends to the person who is unlike Himself. The Aristotelian theorem is turned inside out—unlike is known by unlike. We have already referred to Spener's discussion of rebirth in just the opposite terms. God loves the sinner but because like may be known by like, it is necessary for the sinner to be reborn.[114] As harsh as it sounds, this seems to be a classic case of what is thrown out of the front door (by Luther) returning through the back door (by Pietism).

It is this motif of ascent toward God through rebirth and renewal that explains the synergistic expressions within Pietism. Persons cooperate in the process of salvation. Using Francke's terminology, Peschke describes this synergism as obedience to God's prevenient grace and cooperation with it.

> Such expressions, supplemented by anthropological-psychological ways of thinking, by the demand to constantly examine the process in one's own soul and to reflect upon oneself, as well as by contemplation upon "divine compassion" and the beginning of the divine work of salvation in men, have effected a modification of Luther's leading concepts.[115]

Indeed, we may argue that here we have not merely a modification of Luther's central position but rather a reversal of it—the person is thrown back upon himself and his experience of faith for his certainty of salvation. This is fundamentally the voluntaristic position of Erasmus that Luther so forcefully countered in *De servo arbitio*. Whenever, no matter to what extent, the burden of proof for salvation rests upon the believers, the only options are pride or the despair of uncertainty, for the person is really being asked to overcome himself. It is of interest that Schmidt sees a line of development here from Francke to Nietzsche. Unlike Luther who guides weak believers toward the unconditional truth of God's Word and the invariability of God's promise, Francke refers them back to their

---

evangelischen Theologie, 2:138-51, 155-61, 233-49, 288-94; Ritschl, Geschichte und Probleme (Gütersloh: Mohr, 1977); Weigelt, *Pietismus-Studien,* 105-18; and Gerhard Müller, *Die Rechtfertigungslehre,* 77-83.

[114]*WNM,* 186, 271.

[115]Peschke, *Bekehrung und Reform,* 142f.

faith.[116] From a modern perspective the catechetical sermons of the great Halle pietists appear related to contemporary existential theology.

> Here as there man stands in the midpoint; the humanity of Jesus, so that also the exemplary or original faith of Jesus receives deciding significance, the ethically acting and self-responsible man, who practically takes up the eschatological future of Jesus, the beloved and again the exercising of love in neighborliness of man—these are the decisive categories. Therein is grounded the essential modernity of Pietism. Its central anthropological orientation creates something new, also over against the Reformation in which man is not thrown back upon himself and therefore does not essentially analyse the process of salvation, but rather is bound to the divine Word of promise.[117]

The question of the modernity of Pietism echoes Troeltsch's evaluation of the continuity of Reformation Spiritualism and Anabaptism with the modern spirit. This is of interest to us because of the recent effort of Davis to see the early Anabaptists in terms of a charismatic renewal movement. At the same time, however, this critique of Pietism's anthropocentrism also gives credence to Ritschl's evaluation of Pietism in terms of an individualism which intensified the religious eroticism of medieval *Brautmystik* and the asceticism of medieval monasticism.[118] This common link of medieval and modern was already intimated by Luther when he equated the papacy with the enthusiasts in the Smalcald Articles.[119]

A further indication of Pietism's anthropological-psychological orientation and thereby its discontinuity with Luther is its concern to be able to give concrete declarations concerning the time, place, and circumstances of conversion. This is an interest that may well be continued in the charismatic movement's concern for the gift of tongues. This general demand for a temporal establishment of conversion is alien to Luther.

Pietism departs from Luther in its understanding of the relationship of faith and works. We have repeatedly referred to Spener, Francke, and other leading Pietists who regard works as the verification of faith or at least a sign of faith. The ethical fruits of faith thus become indications of a

---

[116]*WNM*, 233f.

[117]*WNM*, 237.

[118]Cf. Troeltsch, *Social Teachings of the Christian Churches, Protestantisches Christentum und die Kirche der Neuzeit* in *Die Kultur der Gegenwart* 1/4 (1906): 408. Cf. also *PuMW*, 138f.

[119]Cf. T. Tappert, *The Book of Concord* (Philadelphia: Muhlenberg Press, 1959) 312-14.

person's degree of growth in faith and the quality of his existence in grace. Luther is not concerned for such goal-determined inferences. Although Luther can express the view that works are signs of faith, his major perspective is that our standing in justification cannot be determined by the form of our sanctification.[120]

The Pietist position in regard to the world is also a deviation from Luther. Francke, for example, demanded that the children of God refrain from all worldly pleasures. The world posed the danger of unleashing a person's desires and thus leading him to become a slave to sin under the pretext of an alleged freedom. In the battle against sin, every opportunity for sin must be fled. Great significance for the development of sin is ascribed to earthly-sensual reality, especially human corporality.[121]"The pietistic indifference and occasional antagonism toward the created world paved the way for an almost *total* secularization of the natural (physical-ness, work, recreation, love of nature, nationalism, state, economical questions; cf. the frequent controversies between church musicians and pietists)."[122]

Finally, Francke and Pietism in general distinguished themselves from Luther in the understanding of the church. The Lutheran conception that Word and sacraments alone are the constitutive elements of the church is regarded as insufficient. While for Luther the true church remains hidden from the eyes of men, Francke's "kernel-community," while remaining within the Lutheran church, may be distinguished from other Christians by perceptible, examinable signs of particular piety. In this way the concept of the church approaches that of an ideal, independent community of saints. In the striving for perfection, Pietism reduced ecclesiology as well as theology to a form of Christian ethics.[123]

Pietism arose in the social context of the insecurity and uncertainty of the aftermath of the Thirty Years' War and the apparent impotence of Orthodoxy to respond to the critical social and religious issues of the day. Luther was an important figure to the Pietists, many of whom knew

---

[120]Peschke, *Bekehrung und Reform*, 143. Cf. W. Joest, *Gesetz und Freiheit. Das Problem des tertius usus legis bei Luther und die neutestamentliche Parainese* (1961 3d. ed.) 213 n.244.

[121]Peschke, *Bekehrung und Reform*, 144.

[122]"Pietism," *Encyclopedia of the Lutheran Church*, p. 1905.

[123]Cf. *WNM*, 168.

firsthand much of his writing, but the Pietist leaders either ignored or did not know his famous polemical works, especially those directed against their "forerunners," the enthusiasts. It would be interesting to know how Arndt, Spener, Francke, and their contemporaries would have responded to Luther's treatise, "Against the Heavenly Prophets." Would they have understood themselves also to be on the receiving end of Luther's critique of Karlstadt and Müntzer? Certainly their concerns for rebirth of the individual Christian and renewal of the church bore remarkable similarities. What is even more remarkable is that Pietism did not separate from the church. It raised critical questions of the received Lutheran tradition and in turn was rigorously questioned by the Orthodox exponents of the tradition. Nevertheless, Pietism remained as a renewal movement— some would claim the most significant movement since the Reformation—within the Lutheran churches. It remains to be seen to what extent contemporary charismatic movements within the Lutheran churches share the concerns and orientations of the Reformation renewal movements and later Pietism, but we may hope that contemporary renewal movements will share Pietism's place within the Lutheran tradition rather than rejecting the Reformation as many did in the sixteenth century.

4

"THE THIRD REFORMATION"— CHARISMATIC MOVEMENTS

At the outset we wish to state clearly that the expression "third Reformation" is not intended polemically.[1] Rather we wish to express by this phrase the Lutheran charismatic concern to continue and revitalize the Reformation. It may be of interest to note that charismatics themselves use equivalent expressions such as "the new Reformation." Dr. Paul Toaspern, a leader of charismatic renewal in the German Democratic Republic, stated in a recent lecture that "the Holy Spirit helps us to a second Reformation."[2] We have already referred to Larry Christenson's claim that "What charismatics are bringing forth is not a new statement of doctrine, but a fresh experience of it."

---

[1] The earliest use of this phrase of which we are aware carried polemical overtones in its reference to the intention of the *Schwärmer* to complete the Reformation. Cf. Martin Bucer, "Grund und Ursach," in *Martin Bucers Deutsche Schriften* ed. by R. Stupperich (Gütersloh: Mohn, 1960) 1:258, 35. The earlier Pentecostal interpretation of the Reformation, however, saw the Reformation as the release of a small stream of grace that had been dammed up by the contemporary churches of the Reformation. Cf. Walter Hollenweger, *Enthusiastisches Christentum. Die Pfingstbewegung in Geschichte und Gegenwart* (Zürich, Zwingli Vl., 1969) 465f. For other references to the charismatic movement as a "new Reformation" cf. Victor Pfitzner, *Led by the Spirit* (Adelaide: Lutheran Publishing House, 1976) 9; and *PPP*, 2:177.

[2] Bible lecture given at the International Lutheran Renewal Leaders' Conference, Helsinki, 18 August 1981.

The above expression appears to echo the concerns we have already noted in the "charismatic movements" of the sixteenth century and in Pietism. There, too, the concerns focused on both prophetic protest and the goal of renewing a church perceived to have "missed the mark." Contemporary charismatic renewal movements are saying that "the churches need renewal."[3] There is an emptiness in the life of the churches which is reflected in the lives of its members. An educated ministry lacks the "warmth and conviction of personal dedication" and lives remain unchanged while the hunger for God goes unsatisfied. Where is the presence, the power, and the praise of God? The credibility of the church rests upon the changed lives of its people, thus only the praise-filled experience of God's presence and power is the answer to today's experience of insecurity and uncertainty. The depersonalization of contemporary life in the midst of materialism and secularism disposes persons to search for a personal experience of reality. In this context charismatic renewal speaks not of having something new but of *becoming* and *being* a new person. Through the rebirth and renewal of persons comes the renewal of community without which the church is inoperative and evangelism ineffective.

> Those in the Lutheran renewal in the United States think they are doing more than just theorizing about the structure of Christian community. In the context of radically committed relationships, they are shaping their understanding of authority, submission, headship, responsibility, obedience, and freedom. Committed relationships in community belong to Christian hermeneutics.[4]

These committed relationships are taking the form of covenant communities which transcend denominational boundaries. As such the charismatic renewal is ecumenical with a common experience overtaking and passing the years of ecumenical discussions by the churches. Like Pietism, the charismatic movement understands itself to be an interconfessional and international movement. Also, like Pietism, there arises within the renewal an anti-institutional element. In his Bible lectures at the recent International Lutheran Renewal Leaders' Conference, Dr. Dennis Pederson stated: "I have declared unilateral disarmament regarding ecumenical relationships; I am one with everyone who believes." And, "Doctrine is not life, theology is not life, organization is not life; all these are but the

---

[3]The following brief sketch is dependent upon Kilian McDonnell's introductory essay in *PPP*, 1:xix-lxix.

[4]Ibid., xlvii.

conclusions of men concerning things which are not clear in Scripture....
There is a better way, to be in the place where we know what is on the
heart of God."⁵ According to Kilian McDonnell, " . . .there is, in some
expressions of the renewal, a despair of institutional Christianity with a
consequent move to vaporise the church. If one has Jesus and the Bible,
does one really need the church?"⁶ In social as well as ecclesial questions
the renewal of the individual is believed to be the necessary presupposition for the renewal of the community.

The parallels of charismatic renewal with the earlier renewal movements previously discussed are striking. Indeed, in his essay McDonnell
states that "The history of the charismatic renewal is in some sense
rooted in Methodism," which in turn has direct ties to Lutheran Pietism.⁷
This observation of similar concerns and similar forms of expressing
them—not an unusual occurrence in surveying the history of the
church—may well relate to the inner forces of parallel contexts. However, the connections between renewal movements are not limited to
similar responses to analogous historical contexts. There are also specific
links as is illustrated by the influential Norwegian church leader Ole
Hallesby. Hallesby's theology developed out of Lutheran Pietism and the
"Erfahrungstheologie" of the "Erlangen school." He was a prominent
leader in the Church of Norway until his death in 1961. Of interest to us is
Engelsviken's claim that " . . . Hallesby has been instrumental in prepar-

---

⁵Helsinki, Finland, 20 and 21 August 1981.

⁶*PPP*, 1:li.

⁷Ibid., lvi-lvii. Cf. Martin Schmidt, *John Wesley*, 2 vols. (Zürich: Gotthelf-Verlag,
1953-1966), 1:271-73; 2:59-60, 255-59, 273f., 407. Cf. also Arnold Bittlinger, *Papst und
Pfingstler. Der römisch katholischpfingstliche Dialog und seine ökumenische Relevanz*
(Frankfurt am Main: Lang, 1978), 173ff., and the section "Das Erbe des deutschen
Pietismus," in Heribert Mühlen, *Die Erneuerung des christlichen Glaubens* (Münich:
Don Boxo Verlag, 1974) 251-57. The thesis of Vinson Synan's *The Holiness-Pentecostal
Movement in the United States* (Grand Rapids: Eerdmans, 1971) is "that the historical
and doctrinal lineage of American pentecostalism is to be found in the Wesleyan tradition." More specifically: "The basic premises of the (Pentecostal) movement's theology
were constructed by John Wesley in the eighteenth century. As a product of Methodism,
the holiness-pentecostal movement traces its lineage through the Wesleys to Anglica-
nism and from thence to Roman Catholicism. . . . The basic pentecostal theological
position might be described as Arminian, perfectionistic, premillennial, and charismatic."
8, 217.

ing the ground for the Charismatic Movement in Norway and even for a theology of the Charismatic experience based on Lutheran tradition."[8]

The church's loss of credibility and, worse, plausibility reflects a crisis of the modern world not unlike those faced after the late medieval period and the post-Thirty Years' War in Europe. The modern world, in the sense of Troeltsch's description of the West as determined by the Enlightenment, has been in a context of crisis since the end of World War I. Optimistic beliefs in culture, reason, human autonomy, idealism, and progress have been severely eroded if not destroyed. This has been occurring at the very same time that the Enlightenment methodology and critique of religion have finally arrived in theology with their relativization of history and the Word. We need not belabor the obvious characteristics of our time: enormous insecurity of every type, fears of the future, breakdown of traditional values, plurality of competing world views, norms and definitions of reality, loss of power by individuals and nations, and individual isolation and dehumanization. "Charismatic renewal shows signs of having a particular impact in places of sharp *political conflict* and/or *constant tension,* where present insecurity and danger provide a definite incentive for seeking the face of God in repentance and humility."[9] Some would argue that our present age of anxiety is, in part at least, the fallout of Hiroshima and Nagasaki. The anxiety stimulated by awareness of our unprecedented possibility to end the human species has been internalized and has caused considerable spiritual concern. "At one level we have discussed God as our 'ultimate concern' and 'ground of being,' and we have considered being 'honest to God,' the 'death of God,' and the new promise of the 'secular city,' in a 'world come of age.' These discussions have been popular media events. While they may be exhilarating to some, they have been confusing to many others and not satisfying spiritually."[10]

---

[8]Tormod Engelsviken, *The Gift of the Spirit. An Analysis and Evaluation of the* Charismatic Movement from a Lutheran Perspective (Unpublished dissertation, Aquinas Institute, School of Theology, Dubuque IA, 1981) 135.

[9]Peter Hocken, "A Survey of the Worldwide Charismatic Movement," in A. Bittlinger, ed., *The Church is Charismatic: The World Council of Churches and the Charismatic Renewal* (Geneva: WCC, 1981) 119.

[10]James H. Smylie, "Testing the Spirits in the American Context. Great Awakenings, Pentacostalism, and the Charismatic Movement," *Interpretation* 33/1 (1979): 41. Following the completion of my study I was referred to a recent popular study that makes a similar analysis of the contemporary context of anxiety and loss of confidence in science

One of the ironies of church history is that Pietism, the renewal movement in response to an earlier crisis, contributed to the development of the present plausibility crisis. Pietism not only succumbed to the Enlightenment, it provided the transition to it.

As a matter of fact many inner lines of connection lead from Pietism to the Enlightenment. First of all, Pietism undermined faith in the effectiveness of ecclesial institutions: next to baptism appeared conversion; the Lord's Supper became the communal celebration of the awakened; ecclesial confessional praxis could no longer persist before the pressure toward personal experience of the forgiveness of sins; the office of the ministry did not support the pastor but rather the ethical-religious personality (of the pastor supported) the office; the idea of the Theologia practica led to the depreciation of the symbols; a basic mystical disposition prepared the way for the relativizing of dogma; the pressure for holiness was a step toward the ethicizing of religion. Further, the teaching of the inner light prepared the way for the religion of reason.[11]

Pietism administered a severe shock to Protestantism by its subjectivizing of church and dogma. With the displacement of objective dogma by subjective experience as the criterion for religious legitimacy, the groundwork was laid both for the "psychologization" of the Christian faith and the relativization of its content since one person's experience may differ from another's.[12] All of which leads to uncertainty about faith or what most recently has been called "the heretical imperative." Confronted by a plurality of competing world views the individual is compelled to choose. Subjective certainty depends upon cohesive social support for the choice made.[13] It is no wonder then that today there is a growth market in yoga, the occult, spiritism, and religious and psychological self-help books which have the typical theme that God or the "reality" of your choice is best approached through self-analysis. The *reality* which

---

and technology as a context conducive to the rise of charismatic movements. Cf. Jeremy Rifkin and Ted Howard, *The Emerging Order: God in the Age of Scarcity* (New York: G. P. Putnam's Sons, 1979), especially ch. 10: "The Charismatics: A New Liberating Force?" Cf. also Roger Mehl, "Approche sociologique des mouvements charismatiques," *Bulletin de la Société du Protestantisme Francais* (1974): 555-73.

[11]Hans Leube, *Orthodoxie und Pietismus. Gesammelte Studien* (AGP 13) (Bielefeld: Luther Verlag, 1975) 122-23.

[12]Cf. Peter Berger, *The Social Reality of Religion* (London: Faber and Faber, 1967) 157. Berger claims that Pietism and Rationalism have shown considerable affinity to the point where they merge in psychologism. On Pietism's relation to psychology cf. also "Pietismus" in *RGG*, 5:370ff.

[13]Cf. Peter Berger, *The Heretical Imperative: Contemporary Possibilities of Religious Affirmation* (New York: Doubleday, 1979).

matters most is inside yourself! The modern context then is radically anthropocentric and throws individuals back upon themselves. This helps to explain the appeal of the charismatic movement as a form of group support for intense individual experience.[14] As a preliminary question we must wonder, in light of the consequences of Pietism, whether personal experience is a sufficiently firm authority.

This brief explanation of the crisis context for charismatic renewal movements is not to be taken as an effort to "explain them away." Indeed, it is important to note that many social scientists are revising the theories that Pentecostal and charismatic movements may simply be explained by social and economic deprivation theories.

> This is not to suggest that deprivation is totally unrelated to the rise and growth of movements. Poverty, marginal existence, the lack of prestige, power, status, and the opportunity to participate in decisions affecting their own lives may well constitute a favorable climate for the rise of crises movements. They facilitate their rise but they are not causative in the determinative sense.[15]

In terms of social science, a constant such as real or imagined deprivation cannot be used to explain a variable such as the rise of charismatic movements. In other words, everyone experiences some form of deprivation but not everyone becomes a charismatic.[16]

---

[14]The appeal and growth of Fundamentalism and the evangelical movements are alternative expressions of a search for authority and support in a relative and pluralistic world. Cf. Richard Quebedeaux, *The New Charismatics* (New York: Doubleday and Co., 1976) 25ff.; Walther von Loewenich, "Das christliche Menschenbild in Umbruch der Moderne," in *Der Pietismus in Gestalten und Wirkungen* (Bielefeld: Luther Verlag, 1975) 326-42, 327-28; Erling Jorstad, *Bold in the Spirit, Lutheran Charismatic Renewal in America Today* (Minneapolis: Augsburg Publishing House, 1974) 22ff.

[15]Kilian McDonnell, *Charismatic Renewal and the Churches* (New York: Seabury Press, 1976) 34.

[16]Cf. Hollenweger's review of R. Anderson, *Vision of the Disinherited*, in *Theological Renewal* 14 (1980): 38-40. William J. Samarin agrees with Hollenweger; cf. his "Religious Goals of a Neo-Pentecostal Group in a Non-Pentecostal Church," in Russel Spittler, ed., *Perspectives on the New Pentecostalism* (Grand Rapids: Baker, 1976) 134-49, 147f. Anderson's argument is that while charismatics do not have the material deprivation of early Pentecostals ". . . they may suffer a real or imagined deprivation of respect and prestige. I would hazard the hypothesis that status deprivation and an anti-rationalist, anti-bureaucratic—anti-modern—temper has combined to predispose most of the recruits to the neo-Pentecostal movement. Pentecostals, old and new, have typically testified that before their conversion to Pentecostalism they felt empty and hungry for God or for something they could not articulate. In short, they felt deprived." *Vision of the Disinherited: The Making of American Pentecostalism* (New York and Oxford: Oxford University Press, 1979) 229.

The theories in question are related to the efforts by Max Weber and Ernst Troeltsch to distinguish types of religious groups—the famous church-sect typology.[17] Although later scholars used the church-sect theory to explain the causes and conditions for the rise of certain groups, the theory itself essentially maintained that new religious movements: (1) begin with a sect-like character; (2) are break-offs from church-type bodies; (3) are rooted in economic deprivation; and (4) generally develop into churches. Because the rise of classical Pentecostalism in the United States during the early part of this century correlated very well with the main elements of the church-sect theory, sociologists have developed their thinking concerning the origin and development of religious groups from the church-sect theory orientation.

The more important theories which focus on the social factors behind and in new religious groupings are summarized by McDonnell under the headings social disorganization, economic deprivation, social deprivation, ethical deprivation, and psychological maladjustment. McDonnell's summary is so useful we wish to quote it at length.

The Social Disorganization Theory.

Movements arise when the times are out of joint, when one culture has contact (sometimes violent contact) with another and culture shock manifests itself, when family structures are disrupted, when rapid social change calls into question the old alignments and the old values, when there is migration from one milieu to another (from a rural setting to the city), when there are extreme distresses, deportations, detribalizations, and catastrophes. Movements arise in these circumstances because they provide instruments for organizing life in meaningful patterns and give purpose to the newly constructed system of relationships.

The Deprivation Theories.

1. Economic deprivation: persons who live a marginal existence because of poverty turn to movements to compensate for the harsh realities. . . .
2. Social deprivation: some individuals feel that they do not share the rewards of society in the same manner as do others. These rewards are such things as prestige, power, status, the opportunity to participate fully in the life of public institutions. . . . Having been deprived on a basis which is frequently unjust, those deprived tend to form or join movements to redress the wrong.
3. Ethical deprivation: if a person feels that the dominant values of society no longer provide a meaningful framework within which he can find meaning and purpose for his life, if these dominant values do not provide the tools for organizing one's life in a manner that has purpose and pattern, then such a

---

[17]The following is a summary of McDonnell's chapter "Disorganization and Deprivation: Movements and Their Causes," in ibid., 17-40. The chapter critically reviews contemporary sociological studies of the Pentecostal charismatic movements.

person will look around for an alternative. Such persons are the raw material of movements. Movements provide a structure of meaning, a universe of purpose, and present one with ideals.

Psychological Maladjustment Theory.

Certain persons are psychological cripples. They do not fall within the rather ample limits of normality. Because of the predispositions of their deviant, usually neurotic, personality profile, they are attracted to certain kinds of activities or certain types of enthusiastic groups.[18]

It may be noted here that the social disorganization and deprivation theories describe the contextual conditions sketched for the rise of renewal movements in the Reformation and Pietism.

The most recent research, generally, has reconsidered the validity of these theories, recognizing their inadequacies, limited usefulness, and historical relativity. Social theories "do not point to necessary conditions nor to causes but to favorable conditions and to facilitating factors."[19] Specific positive results of recent social scientific inquiry into Pentecostal-charismatic groups emphasize the importance of personal recruitment, especially along lines of preexisting relationships; and the remarkable social-cultural heterogeneity within the movements. However, the theory of relative deprivation, especially in relation to power, continues to be investigated.

Here deprivation and ideology touch at the point of power. Those whose occupational status is less have less power, as occupation is more indicative of power than education or wealth. In the Pentecostal ideology "the baptism in the Spirit" is specifically an act of empowerment. There is a whole "power vocabulary" in Pentecostalism, in large part borrowed from the Scriptures: "You will receive power when the Holy Spirit comes on you" (Acts 1:8). This power is directed toward the effective witnessing to the gospel and therefore to recruiting. "And you will be my witnesses not only in Jerusalem but throughout Judea and Samaria, and indeed to the ends of the World" (Acts 1:8). The relationship between relative deprivation in reference to power and the power vocabulary of the Pentecostal-charismatic ideology is still not clearly established and needs further scientific investigation.[20]

It is of interest, however, to recall that contemporary independent historical-theological researches of the Reformation Radicals and Pietism have also pointed to the centrality of a "power vocabulary."[21]

---

[18]Ibid., 20-21.

[19]Ibid., 39.

[20]Ibid., 36.

[21]Cf. *WNM*, 9-23, 328, 150-53, 162.

In conclusion, McDonnell points out that social theories should be used critically rather than casually discarded in the face of changing social situations. Because social theories are empirically grounded in observation they are not universally valid ideas but rather rooted in history and geography. "The test of a social theory of movements is not its universal applicability, but its adequacy within a limited framework."[22] Once again, we are directed toward historical analysis and description. In the next section we turn to this task in terms of a historical-descriptive analysis of the rise and development of charismatic renewal movements within the Lutheran churches in general and discussion of a few case studies in more depth. Following this section we shall attempt to describe the theological motifs dominant in these movements.

LUTHERAN CHARISMATIC RENEWAL MOVEMENTS: HISTORY

It is now a commonplace to date the rise of the Pentecostal churches by the remarkable Azusa Street revival in 1906 in Los Angeles. Our thesis is that contemporary neo-Pentecostal and charismatic renewal movements have lines of continuity in the sense of leitmotivs reaching back to the Reformation and Pietism. The more immediate antecedents of the Pentecostal churches include the holiness movements rooted in Methodism and the later foreshortening of the personal achievement of perfection from a lifelong process of struggle to the character of an event. Since the story of the twentieth-century growth of Pentecostal churches is readily available we need not review it here.[23] It is sufficient for our purposes to point to the groundwork laid in the 1950s by the *Full Gospel*

---

[22]McDonnell, *Charismatic Renewal and the Churches*, 40. Cf. also Francoise van der Mensbrugghe, *Les Mouvements de Renouveau charismatique. Retour de l'Espirit? Retour de Dionysos?* Unpublished dissertation (Faculté Autonome de Théologie, Université de Genève, 1978) 18ff.

[23]A beginning point for those interested in pursuing this story is Walter Hollenweger, *Enthusiastisches Christentum*, and Hollenweger, ed., *Die Pfingstkirchen: Selbstdarstellungen, Dokumente, Kommentare* (Stuttgart: Evangelisches Verlagswerk, 1971). Cf. also Nils Bloch-Hoell, *The Pentecostal Movement: Its Origin, Development and Distinctive Character* (London and New York: Allen and Unwin/Humanities Press, 1964). The Wesleyan and other roots of the Pentecostal movement are examined in Vinson Synan, *The Holiness-Pentecostal Movement in the United States* (Grand Rapids: Eerdmans, 1971) and Synan, ed., *Aspects of Pentecostal-Charismatic Origins* (Plainsfield NJ: Logos International, 1975). Richard Quebedeaux, *The New Charismatics*, also includes a useful appendix on recent "Scholarly Investigations."

Business Men's Voice and local and regional chapter meetings which provided opportunity for non-Pentecostal clergy and laity to become acquainted with Pentecostals. The Pentecostal movement was further "dignified" by the widespread positive impact of Du Plessis. During much of the 1950s he participated in the ecumenical movements as a Pentecostal "observer." "By the 1950's, some mainline church leaders had even come to regard Pentecostalism as a 'Third Force' in world Christianity—with Protestantism and Catholicism—and Du Plessis himself can be credited with the growth and spread of that attitude during the decade."[24]

Thus the 1950s were a period of preparation for the neo-Pentecostal and charismatic renewal that appeared in the historical denominations in the 1960s. The original focus for this development was St. Mark's Episcopal Church in Van Nuys, California. In 1959 two nominal Episcopalians, John and Joan Baker, received the baptism of the Holy Spirit through the witness of Pentecostal friends. Their priest, Frank Maguire, was startled by their sudden and vigorous involvement in the life and work of their parish. Maguire, seeking collegial and pastoral advice, turned to his friend and colleague, Dennis Bennett, rector of St. Mark's. Bennett met the Bakers and himself soon received the baptism of the Holy Spirit (November 1959). Although Bennett's ministry was positively affected by this experience, the rapid spread of the Pentecostal experience among the diocese laity caused a division in the parish. The crisis which followed prompted Bennett to resign as rector. Some months later he was appointed to St. Luke's Episcopal Church in Seattle, Washington, beginning his ministry to a dramatically revived church.[25] The story received widespread publicity in both *Time* and *Newsweek*. "By 1963, it was estimated that 200 Episcopalians in the Los Angeles diocese were speaking in tongues, and six out of 225 congregations of the American Lutheran Church in California had been affected by the glossolalia phenomenon."[26] One of the first Lutheran pastors to arise as a prominent

---

[24]Quebedeaux, *The New Charismatics*, 54; cf. also Rex Davis, *Locusts and Wild Honey: The Charismatic Renewal and the Ecumenical Movement* (Geneva: WCC, 1978) 26ff.; Jorstad, *Bold in the Spirit*, 21ff.

[25]Quebedeaux, *The New Charismatics*, 54; cf. Bennett's own account of his charismatic experience and its affects, *Nine O'Clock in the Morning* (Plainfield NJ: Logos International, 1970).

[26]Quebedeaux, *The New Charismatics*, 57-58.

spokesperson for the renewal was Larry Christenson of Trinity Lutheran Church, San Pedro, California. All forms of private and public media picked up the revival-renewal as a hot topic made newsworthy by the participation of the milddle-class members of the historic demoninations. "Four years after its inception, Neo-Pentecostalism was a clearly recognizable religious movement—affecting both clergy and laity, students and professionals, men and women, in the Episcopal Church and almost all the mainline Protestant denominations in the United States." Soon neo-Pentecostalism was also a movement within Roman Catholicism.[27] By the late 1960s the charismatic renewal was spreading widely among the Lutheran churches not only in North America but throughout the world.

For a variety of reasons it is difficult to provide a thorough and accurate description of the extent and growth of the charismatic movement within the Lutheran churches. This is partly due to the nature of the movement itself. Charismatic renewal within the Lutheran churches is still in process and varies according to cultural contexts. It is important to realize that we are discussing a movement occurring *within* the Lutheran churches and that, therefore, apart from its visible leadership among clergy, professors, and laity, it is almost impossible to estimate the numbers of laity involved. Only in some national churches, namely in the USA, have initial research findings been compiled, and only recently has the Lutheran World Federation (LWF) begun to solicit information on the charismatic renewal from its member churches. As we mentioned at the beginning, this study itself derives from the proposal at the Evian Assembly of the LWF (1970) to initiate a dialogue between Lutherans and Pentecostals. Furthermore, neo-Pentecostal and charismatic renewal movements are based on shared experience rather than printed and defined doctrine and separate institutions and organizations.[28] Because of these reasons we shall focus our attention upon the churches where the movement has developed its expressions in forms most easily accessible to our type of literary research. This should not be interpreted as a

---

[27]Ibid., 59; 63ff.

[28]Cf. W. Hollenweger, "Charismatische und pfingstlerische Bewegungen als Frage an die Kirchen heute," in M. Lienhard and H. Meyer, eds., *Wiederentdeckung des Heiligen Geistes* (Frankfurt: Lembeck, 1974) 53-76, 64. The significance of this for theological method is discussed by Hollenweger in "Flowers and Songs. A Mexican Contribution to Theological Hermeneutics," *International Review of Mission* 60/238 (1971): 232-44.

minimizing of the "presence, power and praise" of charismatic renewal in other Lutheran churches but rather an indication of the limits of our research. It is simply not possible for this study to undertake a participant-observer approach on a sufficiently broad scale to be useful. We shall, however, conclude by utilizing the results of surveys as a means of presenting a general description.

THE UNITED STATES OF AMERICA

In 1976 a leading charismatic, Lutheran theologian reflecting upon the past decade wrote, "A movement that among Lutherans has survived ten years of toleration at best and harassment at worst and yet continues to grow both in size and in maturity, is a movement which must be reckoned with. Its challenge must be heard even while it too must allow itself to be challenged."[29] The following is a brief chronological description of that challenge and response as it developed from 1960 to the present in the American Lutheran churches.

In contrast to the relative "peace and prosperity" experienced by Americans (mostly white!) in the 1950s, the 1960s was a decade of unnerving and accelerating confusion and crisis in every sector of life from international politics to race relations to personal mores. Kilian McDonnell has claimed that the cultural responses to and in the 1960s had a formal similarity to Pentecostal culture and that, therefore, "it is little wonder that Pentecostalism is enjoying a new popularity."

> It is in terms of pre-literary, oral Pentecostal culture that part of the ecumenical significance of the movement can be found. Pentecostalism has moved into the historic Protestant Churches since the early 1960's. Contemporary culture is oral and non-literary, as seen in the hippy movement, sensitivity sessions, T-groups, drug culture, communes. These movements belong to a post-literary culture which is experience-oriented, unstructured, spontaneous, inward, almost atomistic in its concern for the now at the expense of history, pursuing illumination, dominated by a sense of presence, sure that somewhere there is ultimate worth. To a greater or lesser degree the movements represent a turning back to recapture the original unstructured experience of the meaning of life.[30]

---

[29]Theodore R. Jungkuntz, "Charismatic Worship: Challenge or Challenged?" *Response* 16/1 & 2 (1976): 4-10, 4.

[30]Kilian McDonnell, "Pentecostal Culture: Protestant and Catholic," *One in Christ* 7/4 (1971): 310-18, 315. Cf. also Sydney E. Ahlstrom, *A Religious History of the American People* (New Haven: Yale University Press, 1972) chs. 61 & 63.

At the same time that the moral hypocrisy of the nation and the social conservatism of the churches were being exposed and criticized in pulpits and classrooms of the historic denominations, theologians were writing about the "death of God," "a new morality," and pronouncing that the parish church is obsolete. The laity, however, continued to cling to inherited beliefs while yearning for religious meaning. It is within this framework that the charismatic movement became increasingly attractive to Lutherans. "No membership list of believers can be drawn up, but the movement among Lutherans grew so strong that by 1963 it could no longer be regarded as a temporary, glamorous fad. By then lay persons, pastors and seminary students had received the charismatic gifts."[31] Emphasizing the power and reality of the Holy Spirit in personal life, there arose an uncommon focus among Lutherans: speaking in tongues, prophecy, and healing.[32]

The American Lutheran Church (ALC) was the first major Lutheran body in the USA to confront charismatic renewal. In retrospect it is clear that no one was prepared for this and that everyone was preoccupied with the issue of speaking in tongues. Clearly the initial introduction of charismatic renewal was divisive in the congregations.[33] The ALC appointed a commission including one charismatic pastor to prepare a study which was to be submitted to its General Convention. The committee included pastors, seminary professors, a psychiatrist, and a clinical psychologist. A ten-day field study of four congregations was part of the data for the study report. A study of glossolalia was submitted to the General Convention in 1962. The final report, including the field study was approved for release by the Church Council in 1963. One of the four introductory statements "stressed that glossolalia is not normative for salvation. Neither is it normative for the Christian's growth in grace. The fruits of the Spirit do not necessarily accompany the gifts of the Spirit (cf.

---

[31]Jorstad, *Bold in the Spirit*, 24-25.

[32]For accounts of individual experiences cf. Larry Christenson, *CRAL*, ch. 2; Don Matzat, *Serving the Renewal. The Stories of the Men of Lutheran Charismatic Renewal Services* (Flushing NY: Bread of Life Publication, 1978); and Jorstad, *Bold in the Spirit*, chs. 3-5. The 1962 Lutheran Church in America (LCA) study document, "Anointing and Healing," antedates the charismatic movement among Lutherans but addresses some of the issues. Cf. McDonnell, *PPP*, 1:21-55.

[33]Jorstad, *Bold in the Spirit*, 25; "A Report on Glossolalia," American Lutheran Church, USA (1963) in *PPP*, 1:55-63, 58.

1 Cor. 13:1-3)." The report suggests recognition of the deepening of spiritual life by "a variety of spiritual experiences"; shared responsibility by the total congregation for its integrity; avoidance of self-righteousness; legitimacy of a ministry of intercessory prayer; value of fellowship groups; opportunities for noncharismatic Bible or prayer groups; danger of exclusive emphasis upon glossolalia; respect for others; and a warning against the promotion and exploitation of speaking in tongues. Such observed promotional activities in "some congregations of the American Lutheran Church" are "deplored and to be avoided." The theological and exegetical suggestions are directed against the introduction of the "cultural baggage and the exegetical tradition of classical Pentecostalism."[34]

The controversy continued within the ALC and spread to the student body of Luther Seminary. Increasing requests to the Church Council for guidance led to the adoption in 1964 of "A Statement with Regard to Speaking in Tongues." This statement reiterates the Lutheran teaching that "the Holy Spirit is given in baptism"; warns against the tendency "to confuse glossolalia with the fullness of the Spirit and to give it the status of a permanent possession." "In the presence of potential blessing there is also potential danger and the possibility of much confusion." From the perspective of the New Testament, tongues are marginal but love is central as the fruit of the Holy Spirit. "Therefore the American Lutheran Church asks of its pastors and congregations: (1) that there be neither promotion nor practice of speaking in tongues at meetings in the congregation or at meetings where congregations are acting together; (2) that there be no instruction in the technique or the practice of speaking in tongues; (3) that those who profess to have the gift reserve its use for their devotional life."[35]

This clear position of the ALC did not silence the growing debate about the meaning of "baptism with the Holy Spirit" which now became further compounded by the introduction of healings. Denominational pressure led to some pastoral resignations and in 1965 another statement appeared: "Christian Faith and the Ministry of Healing."[36] By this time

---

[34]*PPP*, 1:58-63. Cf. also Jorstad, *Bold in the Spirit*, 26-29; and McDonnell, *Charismatic Renewal and the Churches*, 44.

[35]*PPP*, 1:108-11.

[36]Cf. Jorstad, *Bold in the Spirit*, 31ff. The statement is printed in *PPP*, 1:112-31.

the movement was present in the other two major Lutheran bodies in the USA: the Lutheran Church in America (LCA) and the Lutheran Church-Missouri Synod (LC-MS).

The first gathering of LC-MS charismatic pastors was held in 1968, although the charismatic movement had entered the Synod in the early 1950s. Forty-four pastors in the Synod claimed to have received the baptism of the Holy Spirit; by 1971 the number was estimated to be over two hundred. In 1968 the Commission on Theology and Church Relations was requested by the president of the Synod to begin a study of the charismatic movement with special reference to baptism in the Holy Spirit. The next year the synodical convention directed the commission to "make a comprehensive study of the charismatic movement with special emphasis on its exegetical aspects and theological implications." The result was the 1972 statement: "The Charismatic Movement and Lutheran Theology."[37] The Roman Catholic scholar of the charismatic movement, McDonnell, comments:

> Given the very strong doctrinal and confessional stance of this church, the 1972 statement . . . represents a balanced, calm, though essentially negative evaluation of the charismatic renewal. No sweeping statements were made as to the belief systems of persons involved in the renewal.

The three-part statement (1) "presents general background information on the history of the movement, its sociological and psychological dimensions, and characteristic theological views of Lutheran charismatics; (2) an analysis of relevant Biblical data; and (3) evaluation and recommendations from the perspective of Lutheran theology."[38]

By this time the charismatic renewal had become a significant minority movement among Lutherans. The first documentable evidence of its extent was gathered by the Youth Research Center in Minneapolis and presented in *A Study of Generations.*[39] In 1973, the number of charismatic Lutheran clergy in the LC-MS was estimated to be three hundred; less than two hundred in the LCA.[40] To these charismatics it became evident that charismatic renewal among Lutherans had reached the point

---

[37]*PPP*, 1:321-63.

[38]Ibid., 321, 323.

[39]Ed. by Merton Stommen, et. al. (Minneapolis: Augsburg Publishing House, 1972).

[40]*Christianity Today*, 31 August 1973, as quoted by E. Jorstad, "A Movement for Our Time," *Event Magazine* (Nov.-Dec. 1973): 18.

of requiring some sort of structure. Important regional organizations providing leadership resources and communications included "Lutheran Charismatic Renewal" of Valparaiso, Indiana, and Lutheran Charisciples of Portland, Oregon. On the national level the first "International Lutheran Conference on the Holy Spirit" met in Minneapolis, 8-12 August 1972. "No official sanction by any denomination was sought or offered."

> The format, which has been continued by later Lutheran charismatic conferences, included morning sessions with prayer, a songfest, and a Bible study. Then participants broke into smaller workshops for instruction and discussion, and at times, ministry on topics of special interest to charismatics: an introduction to the movement, congregational renewal, Christian family relations, miracles and discernment, tongues, the occult, and spiritual warfare. A prayer-and-praise session was planned for 4 p.m. daily. For the evening program a well-known charismatic speaker presented a major address. In 1972 . . . only one (out of six speakers) was Lutheran.[41]

These conferences have continued annually with ever-increasing attendance.

Beginning in the fall of 1973 the various charismatic Lutheran groups and ministries began to plan closer cooperation. This resulted in the formation of Lutheran Charismatic Renewal Services (LCRS) and a "National Leaders' Conference" that met at the Word of God community in Ann Arbor, Michigan in February 1974. The latter met again in 1975. It is of interest to note that the Word of God community is an ecumenical charismatic community with Roman Catholic origins.

Larry Christenson describes the threefold function of the LCRS in terms of primarily providing help and resources for Lutheran charismatics through conferences, tapes, information and literature, and assistance to local leaders. Examples of information include the "Lutheran Charismatic Renewal Newsletter," and listings of prayer meetings around the country where Lutheran charismatics are welcome called the "Directory of Lutheran Charismatic Prayer Meetings." "Secondly, LCRS serves as a necessary point-of-contact between church officials and the renewal. . . . A third task of the LCRS is to relate to those individuals and groups who are outside the structure, and to represent their concerns to the church."[42]

---

[41]Jorstad, *Bold in the Spirit*, 93ff., 36; cf. also 79ff. Jorstad says at least 8,000 people attended some of the sessions; Christenson, one of the leaders, claims more than 10,000 (*CRAL*, 135). Cf. also Gunars Ansons, "The Charismatics and their Churches: Report on Two Conferences," *Dialog* 15/2 (1976): 142-44.

[42]Christenson, *CRAL*, 138f.

The National Leaders' Conference made progress in coordinating the movement on local, regional, and national levels, as well as planning programs. More important, the conference began to deal seriously with the gap between the renewal experiences of the participants and confessional Lutheran theology. Again, it is of interest to note the Catholic contribution to this awareness. Larry Christenson refers to the challenge from Steve Clark and Ralph Martin, leaders in the Catholic Charismatic Renewal, to get a clearer grasp of Lutheran identity. Fr. McDonnell told the group "the Lutheran charismatic renewal will remain on the periphery of the church if it does not become Lutheran. . . . A renewal which is basically revivalist and classical Pentecostal can never be integrated into the Lutheran church. . . ."[43] It is perhaps significant that the name "charismatic" has recently been dropped from conference titles.

In the following years this challenge to relate the charismatic renewal in the Lutheran churches to Lutheran confessional theology has been taken quite seriously. We shall have the opportunity to explore this further in a later section but we shall mention here the work of Theodore Jungkuntz, a LC-MS professor of theology at Valparaiso University, Valparaiso, Indiana. As part of his efforts he published *A Lutheran Charismatic Catechism* (1979)[44] "in order that Lutherans might be simply and accurately informed regarding what Holy Scripture and the Lutheran Confessions teach relative to certain questions arising out of what has recently come to be known as the 'charismatic renewal of the Church.' " More recently, in 1980, the International Lutheran Center for Church Renewal was established in St. Paul, Minnesota with the express purpose being "to provide theological and doctrinal definition and interpretation of the charismatic renewal within historic Lutheran traditions and to give voice and shape to the apostolic, prophetic and intercessory task of renewal."[45]

Nevertheless, at the same time that charismatic Lutheran leadership was becoming more sensitive to the need to relate their experience to Lutheran theology and to create a strategy for renewal, there was growing

---

[43]Ibid., 9; Jorstad, *Bold in the Spirit*, 99; McDonnell, "The Relationship of the Charismatic Renewal to the Established Denominations," *Dialog* 13/3 (1974): 223-29.

[44]Flushing NY: Bread of Life Ministries, p.1.

[45]Morris G. C. Vaagenes, Jr., "Editorial," *LRI* 1/1 (1980): 3; cf. also 16. This new quarterly journal has an international editorial board. Cf. also, W. D. Peterson, "Moving Toward a Renewal Strategy," *LRI* 1/2 (1980): 20-21.

concern among noncharismatic Lutheran leadership to gain understanding of the renewal and to provide guidance for congregations and church-wide agencies confronted by the renewal. In 1972 the Indiana-Kentucky Synod of the LCA requested the LCA "to take note of the recent rapid rise of Pentecostalism in our congregations and communities and because divisiveness and confusion are caused thereby among our people to provide guidance to our congregations in understanding and dealing with this phenomenon."[46] The LCA statement, "The Charismatic Movement in the Lutheran Church in America. A Pastoral Perspective," was published in 1974.[47] At the same time, "A Study-Report on the Charismatic Renewal Movement" by Roger Nostbakken of the Lutheran Theological Seminary, Saskatchewan, was distributed to the Evangelical Lutheran Church of Canada. The LCA statement recognized the contribution that the charismatic movement can make to the quality of life in the LCA but also expressed concern that the charismatic Lutherans not be bound by Pentecostal theology. Certainly, "A narrow concept of the activity of the Holy Spirit is unacceptable and open to all Luther's criticism of the Enthusiasts."[48] "The most important contribution for pastors and theologians is helping charismatics understand their experience in harmony with the Scriptures and the confessional position of the Lutheran church. *Not enough has been done in this area.*"[49] While the LCA statement found "no cause for Lutheran pastors or people to suggest either explicitly or implicitly that one cannot be charismatic and remain a Lutheran in good standing," a prominent spokesperson for charismatic renewal had a difficult struggle to achieve tenure at one of the LCA seminaries.[50]

Tensions also have continued in the LC-MS. In 1975 Concordia Theological Seminary, Springfield, issued a "Policy Statement Regarding the Neo-Pentecostal Movement" that criticized what the faculty regarded as the non-Scriptural and non-Lutheran character of the movement. Students ascertained to be Neo-Pentecostal are ineligible for the program

---

[46]Minutes, Sixth Biennial Convention of the Lutheran Church in America (1972) 52-53.

[47]*PPP*, 1:547-67.

[48]Ibid., 564.

[49]Ibid., 551. My emphasis.

[50]The case concerns Dr. Mark Hillmer, professor of Old Testament at Northwestern Lutheran Theological Seminary, St. Paul. Cf. the news note in *LCRN* 1/7 (June 1975): 3.

leading to certification for a call to ministry although they may enter the Master of Divinity program.[51] The Synod itself soon thereafter (1977) supplemented its 1972 document by a statement including detailed guidelines for congregations and pastors titled "The Lutheran Church and the Charismatic Movement." These guidelines include the express statement that "Persons who propagate Neo-Pentecostal doctrine in Lutheran congregations often divide the church and thereby give offense to their flocks. Therefore they must take seriously the possibility of coming under church discipline."[52] Theodore Jungkuntz responded to the statement by claiming that it was inspired by a spirit of "fear of the re-emergence of spiritualistic, Anabaptist 'Schwärmerei'" and burdened by an inadequate understanding of what Lutheran Charismatic Renewal is all about.[53] The 1979 LC-MS convention reaffirmed its former position and statements.[54] A month later the Synod's position was reiterated by its president, J. A. O. Preus, in the greeting he was invited to give to the Eighth International Lutheran Conference on the Holy Spirit.[55]

In concluding our description of the charismatic renewal within the Lutheran churches in the USA we wish to draw special attention to the work of the Division of Theological Studies of the Lutheran Council in the USA. LCUSA is a cooperative national agency of the ALC, LCA, LC-MS, and Association of Evangelical Lutheran churches. Under LCUSA auspices, four national conferences were organized between 1974 and 1976. Each involved twenty to twenty-five pastors and theology professors including four who were charismatic Lutherans. The papers commissioned for these meetings are printed in *The Holy Spirit in the Life of the Church*. Of particular interest are Sections 2 and 3 in Appendix A. The former, "Concerns the Charismatic Movement Among Lutherans: Addresses to the Lutheran Church," asks whether the Lutheran heritage has room for the following spiritual horizons of charismatics:

---

[51]McDonnell, *Charismatic Renewal and the Churches*, 64.

[52]*PPP*, 2:307-24, 321. Cf. also the Synod's Resolution 3-10 A, "To Clarify the Synods' Position Regarding Charismatic Teaching," 1977 Convention Proceedings, pp. 131f.

[53]"A Response," *The Cresset*. Occasional Paper: 2 (1977), 11pp.

[54]Cf. 1979 Convention Proceedings, Resolution 3-10, p. 121.

[55]The address is printed in *The Lutheran Witness* (September 1979) 290-91. There were an estimated 15,000 participants. The decline in attendance from the prior year's 22,000 was attributed by the chairman to the energy crisis. Cf. *The Lutheran* (5 September 1979) 18.

> The experience and exercise of the charismata described by Paul in 1 Corinthians 12: 4-10. A deepened appreciation and use of prayer. "The possibility of an experience of God ('baptism in the Spirit') which makes one's Christian heritage (baptism) come alive in new modalities of Christian growth (sanctification)."
>
> "A greater love of the Bible and its message."
>
> "An awareness of dimension described biblically as 'principalities and powers.'"

The latter section, "Concerns Addressed to Lutheran Charismatics," requests clarification on the relationship of charismatic experience to justification, charismatic use of Scripture, relationship of charismatic gifts to congregational and personal renewal, and ecumenical experience of the church. The section concludes with the concern "that the renewal will become so integrated into the total life of the church that it will be neither an isolated segment nor a cause of painful divisions."[56]

An overall impression of the development of the charismatic movement within the Lutheran churches in the USA should not overlook the personal pain it has caused to various clergy and laity as well as incidents of congregational division, especially in its early years. Nevertheless, the movement has been characterized by a strong desire to remain and work within the churches. The leadership of both the charismatic movement and the churches has exhibited growing sensitivity, discretion, willingness to listen, and acceptance of the possibility and necessity of understanding the charismatic experience in a manner consonant with the Scriptures and Lutheran theology. Although a major critical and constructive work on the latter concern has not yet appeared, it may be hoped that the improved climate will facilitate it. However, we cannot ignore also the movement's ambivalence toward institutional structures. On the one hand it speaks frequently of confrontation and possible departure from the church. On the other hand it is itself busily creating parallel (para?) ecclesial-type structures.

THE GERMAN DEMOCRATIC REPUBLIC

Because of the intensive and extensive work of the Theological Studies Department of the Bund der Evangelischen Kirchen in der DDR, the charismatic movement in the German Democratic Republic is easier

---

[56]Paul D. Opsahl, ed., *The Holy Spirit in the Life of the Church: From Biblical Times to the Present* (Minneapolis: Augsburg Publishing House, 1978) 232, 245.

to document than in other countries, namely the USA. From 1977 to 1979 the Theological Studies Department developed and published a series of documents that: (1) provide bibliographical and documentary information; (2) report on a consultation consisting of representatives from various areas of the life of the church, one-third of whom represented the charismatic movements; (3) provide a descriptive presentation of the movement; and (4) offer a careful theological evaluation of the movement.[57]

The historical development of the charismatic movement in the DDR has pre-war roots in the Blumhardt tradition of healing and the meeting of pastors from Saxony with representatives of the Oxford Movement. By 1960 the major center had formed. Under Pastor Bernhard Jansa, the Julius Schniewindhaus near Magdeburg became an ecumenical center for divine healing; and Slate (Pastor Paehl), Bräunsdorf (Pastor Küttner), and Großhartmannsdorf (Pastor Richter) became centers for spiritual awakenings. The second stage of development from about 1960-1970 was characterized by the building up of communities around the various centers. Growing "discovery" of the value of the Lutheran Confessions and liturgical worship accompanied an evangelization campaign which won over entire parishes with their pastors. Under the leadership of Richter, the "Christusdienst" developed which by the mid-1970s included ninety pastors and their congregations of the Evangelical Lutheran Church. Their annual meetings emphasize ministry and the strengthening of parishes rather than theological work. The

---

[57]Available from Theologisches Studienabteilung beim Bund der Evangelischen Kirchen in der DDR, 104 Berlin, Auguststrasse 80.

"Charisma und Heiligen Geist," Beiträge D4 (1977) 32pp; "Nachträge zu D1-D4," Beiträge D7 (1978); "Dokumente zur charismatischen Bewegung" (1978) 37pp.

"Das Wirken des Heiligen Geistes und die Wirklichkeit der Kirche," Beiträge A2 (1978) 65pp. This report on the consultation held in Wittenberg, 16-20 April 1978, includes the preparatory material, reports of the working groups and lectures. The main lecture by Christoph Hinz, Gnadau, presents an intensive introduction and discussion of the contemporary discussion of pneumatological questions.

"Charismatische Bewegung in der DDR," Beiträge A3 (1978) 94pp. A partial English translation of this document is in *PPP*, 2:453-83. This report is based upon the research of a committee of six theologians and a sociologist who conducted forty in-depth interviews with leaders and visited fifty groups. They also examined the materials used by the groups. A short summary of the report is printed in *Zeichen der Zeit* 6 (1979): 218-26: "In und Neben der Kirche," by Christof Ziemer. A very brief report of this study in English by Erwin Prange, "The Charismatic Movement in East Germany," is in *LRI* 1/2 (1980): 16-18.

members pledged themselves to regular participation in church services and celebration of communion, furtherance of community life, daily Bible study and prayer, thrift, and regular pastoral encounter. The emphasis upon frequent communion arose from Richter's experience in his previous parish in Schneeberg in the Erzgebirge. To face the occult powers that haunted his house, he and his wife celebrated communion daily. When transferred to Großhartmannsdorf where the people normally communed only twice a year, he introduced weekly communion for the parish. A prayer group, the Philip's Fellowship, formed there in 1966. A similar group, the St. John's Fellowship, was already formed there. It was at these two centers during this period that the first experience of the gift of tongues appeared. Other influences during this period of development included contacts with West German evangelical communities such as the Brothers of the Common Life, the Evangelical Sisters of Mary (Darmstadt), the Brotherhood of Christ (Selbitz), the Brotherhood of Jesus (Gnadenthal), and visits by Larry Christenson and Steve Lightle from the USA.

The third stage of development was the emergence of the charismatic movement among the youth from about 1970-1975. This was foreshadowed, it seems, by three major retreats: Buckow, 1968; Schiewindhaus, 1968/1969; and Großhartmannsdorf, 1972/1973. Direct contact with representatives of classical Pentecostalism was influential in emphasizing particular charismatic experiences such as baptism in the Spirit and glossolalia. The "Jesus-People" movement also contributed to the charismatic outbreak among the youth. A 1974 report to the LWF emphasizes that the widespread charismatic movement among the youth in the DDR "did not originate through the churches and has little to do with them. . . . There were no founders—it just happened."[58]

The contemporary situation since about 1975 is characterized by a certain stabilization of the circles and centers and a subsiding of the movement's more spontaneous expressions. A closer cooperation among the groups and a working out of the theological implications of their experiences is occurring. Numerous applicants for the formation programs run by the churches have come out of the youth movement.

---

[58]Christoph Michael Haufe, "The Renewal of the Church in Crisis Situations and the Work of the Holy Spirit," mimeograph report to LWF Department of Studies Staff Seminar, Geneva, 15-19 December 1974, p.6.

The social and cultural context of the charismatic movement in East Germany has parallels to that described for the USA. There is the sensitivity to the modern crises of the breakdown of social structures affecting the family, village, and community. There is the reaction against the modern elevation of rationality and functionalism which displaces personal relationships and leaves emotional needs unfulfilled thereby creating a "one-dimensional" person. The relativity of contemporary secular values and a scientific world view has corroded the certainty of traditional perspectives and judgments.

Furthermore, the churches' involvements in ecumenism and social ethics, not to mention biblical criticism and contemporary theological developments such as the theology of revolution, only seem to mirror the rationality, distance, and secularism of the world as well as neglect of the dimension of personal renewal.

> In the area of social organization rationality and functionality are valued as the fundamental values. The so-called wave of nostalgia shows nevertheless that many people have a yearning for functionally superfluous decoration and ornamentation, for forms of life and conventions which have been considered antiquated by the advance of the scientific-technical revolution. This means that a potential of unfulfilled emotional wishes and yearning is present which cannot be covered by rational thought and functional order. The charismatic movement meets such needs: here biblical stories are emotionally recalled, prayers are formulated in baroque language and worship services are opulently celebrated. Historical distance is no longer experienced: what is essential to people is always the same.[59]

The characteristics of the various groups have much in common although there are variations in accents between them as well as in the course of their development. There is strong interest in the renewal of the churches that is experienced as both the present, direct work of God, and the goal to be striven for and realized. Particular spiritual experiences are valued as visible signs of God's will for renewal. The basic experience—which appears to proceed from inner crisis sharpened by encounter with the movement—has the character of a radical transformation. In the understanding of the movement, this basic experience unites the conscious, personal decision for a life with Jesus with the experience of being filled with the Holy Spirit. "Elements of the pietistic concept of conversion as well as Pentecostal baptism in the Spirit

---

[59]"Kirche und charismatische Erneuerung," Bund der Evangelischem Kirchen DDR, 5.

are certainly recognizable in the union of decision and experience of the Spirit."[60]

The most conspicuous signs of the renewal movement are the experiences with particular charismata known from the primitive church as characterized in the Pauline lists in Romans 12 and 1 Corinthians 12. Healing, prophecy, and glossolalia are understood as manifestations of the Holy Spirit in the lives of the individual and community. The hallmarks of the Spirit-filled life are the overcoming of the old life of sin and the growth in the new life of the Spirit. The goal is a concrete realization of a changed life. "The growth of basic experiences and their evolution into the process of spiritual growth calls for a complete faith orientation of the whole man. There is no neutral area of the natural or the human. The decision is either for Christ or for evil. Ethical norms have to be brought in line with the commandments of the Bible. Clearly, the accent is on norms (for example, purity in sexual ethics). Norms cannot be accommodated in a false way to the spirit of our age."[61]

Oriented toward practice, the acquiring of salvation, the concern of the movement is to mediate experience. Thus "up to now the charismatic movement has not developed any distinct, independent theology." However, certain theological shifts of accent are recognizable within the development of the movement. The piety which was initially more strongly oriented to the Second Article now emphasizes more strongly the pneumatological relations through the influences of the Pentecostal and charismatic movements. There is a partial recognition of the danger of granting autonomy to experience and thereby overvaluing it. It is emphasized that these experiences be referred back to objective givers of salvation such as baptism and the Christ event. The charismatic movement, however, has reservations in regard to contemporary theology and knowledge, claiming that scientific exegesis hinders immediate access to the Bible and the contemporary normative understanding of the world leaves no room for the experience of God.[62]

The Theological Studies Department report referred to above ("Charismatische Bewegungen in der DDR") gives such a succinct summary that we wish to quote it at length for our conclusion.[63]

---

[60]Ziemer, "In und Neben der Kirche," 221. Cf. also *PPP*, 2:463.

[61]*PPP*, 2:466.

[62]Ziemer, "In und Neben der Kirche," 222f. Cf. *PPP*, 2:478ff.: "Kirche und charismatische Erneuerung," 5f., 14-19.

As far as its relationship to the church is concerned, the charismatic movement is at pains to see itself as a movement within the church. . . . (T)he charismatics underscore their rejection of a merely individualistic understanding of salvation and stress rather a stronger orientation to the community.

However, there is also a clearly evident tension between the charismatic movement as a movement and the church. As a movement it is a permanent and clearly articulated calling into question of the leading trends in theology and church, of all institutional safeguards, and of the canonical establishment of structures and offices. The tension becomes apparent when the movement sets up its own activities within the church and seeks to pursue them in light of its own uniquely formulated objectives.

It is constantly emphasized that in this process no estrangement from the church is envisioned. Whether this in fact can be avoided will depend on the one hand, whether the churches are willing and in a position to be receptive to the renewal objectives of this movement, and, on the other hand, whether the charismatic movement is ready to face questions emanating from theology and the church, and whether it can overcome its inherently spiritual exclusiveness.

There is undoubtedly a specific orientation which is characteristic of the situation in our country. Thus, for example, it is typical for our situation that the involvement of our youth took place precisely within the charismatic movement whereas in other countries . . . young people have found an abundance of different forms of religious expression. . . . Since a religious renewal in our context can only take place within the church, there is also a greater pluralism within the movement in our country than elsewhere. To that extent association with the church, something which is consciously sought and emphasized, is a necessity proceeding from our particular situation.

Another specific characteristic of the movement in the DDR is the largely critical attitude adopted with respect to the (classical) pentecostal churches and their theology. . . . This attitude is typical since it manifests clearly the great efforts toward integration with the churches. . . . Theologically speaking, therefore, the charismatic movement in the DDR manifests a certain union of charismatic and evangelical elements.

Finally, the question must be asked whether and in what manner the social situation in the DDR finds its resonance in the movement. A conscious response to the challenges which this situation puts on church and Christian does not exist. The concentration on spiritual questions in the narrow sense manifests rather an alternative concept which contrasts with the strong emphasis on the social responsibility of the church.

RESPONSES OF OTHER LUTHERAN CHURCHES TO CHARISMATIC RENEWAL

Unfortunately the documentation of the responses of most of the Lutheran churches is not nearly as complete or accessible as that concern-

---

[63]We are using the English translation in *PPP*, 2:482-83.

ing the USA and the DDR. In what follows we shall survey available materials on the other Lutheran churches, proceeding by country. The main resource for this survey is constituted by responses of member churches to questions sent out by the General Secretary of the Lutheran World Federation in March 1975.[64] Supplementary materials will be used wherever possible. It should not be assumed that lack of a response to the LWF inquiry indicates an absence of the charismatic movement in that particular church. The following statement by Walter Hollenweger refers to the "Third World":

> There is no reliable overview of the charismatic renewal in the Third World. Generally speaking we know that it is strong in Brazil, Mexico, Trinidad, Argentina, Indonesia, Korea and South Africa. As to its strength in other countries, opinions vary. Problems of establishing the extent and character of the charismatic renewal are almost insurmountable, firstly because the scene is changing all the time, secondly because there is no accepted definition of the charismatic renewal, and thirdly because it is almost impossible to get accurate statistics and descriptions.[65]

Africa. In Ethiopia the beginning of the charismatic movement in the mid-1960s goes back to two small Pentecostal missions, one Finnish and one Swedish, that were particularly influential with high school and university students. Pentecostal doctrine was promulgated through the distribution of Pentecostal literature and the popular summer Bible courses offered by these missions. The Finnish Mission Chapel in Addis Ababa attracted a considerable number of well-educated men. The visit by the Kenya evangelist, Omacha Chacha, who had been teaching the Bible course at the Swedish Mission in Awasa, led to "baptism in the Holy Spirit" of a number of young people.

The growth and enthusiasm of the movement created strains with the missionaries, especially over the question of who should preach at public

---

[64] The letter dated 20 March 1975 poses four questions:
"a) Which charismatic and evangelical groups exist in the area of your church?
b) Since when have these groups existed and how large are they?
c) What influence do they have?
d) Are there tendencies to separate these groups out of your Church? If so why? Which possibilities do you see to work against such tendencies of separation?"
For descriptions by charismatics themselves cf. "Renewal Around the World," *LRI* 1/1 (1980): 18-20.

[65] Hollenweger, "Roots and Fruits of the Charismatic Renewal in the Third World," 11. For a major study of South India cf. Werner Hoerschelmann, *Christliche Gurus. Darstellung von Selbstverständnis und Funktion indigenen Christseins durch unabhängige, charismatische geführte Gruppen in Südindien* (Frankfurt a.M.: Peter Lang, 1977).

services. A large group consequently left the chapel and formed the Full Gospel Church in Addis Ababa. By 1973 the Full Gospel Church was reputed to have 25,000 members and was the channel for the mainstream of the charismatic movement. The church's application for recognition by the Ministry of the Interior was not granted.

"From the beginning some of our Churches' leaders have been aware of this new spiritual force. In 1967 the Reverend Ezra Gebre Medhin and other leaders of the Addis Ababa Congregations of the ECMY (Evangelical Church Mekane Yesus) began a dialogue with leaders of the charismatic movement, and through this openness in attitude in the early days of the movement, the ECMY has probably been saved from any major split on the issue."[66] Especially in those places where the charismatic movement has been welcomed, it has been possible for ECMY charismatics to remain effective members of the church. Issues that have caused tension relate to questions concerning liturgy and order in the church, association with Pentecostal culture, and conflict between older church members and charismatically influenced youth. The strong evangelization efforts by the charismatics and neo-Pentecostals have also caused concern, especially through their influence in prayer groups. "The worship in prayer groups placed great importance on freedom. Sometimes strongly emotional, the meetings consisted of preaching testimonies, tongues, prophecy, visions and healing. All-night prayer meetings were held which 'could be described as unorganized and even disorderly.' "[67]

By 1976 the leadership of the ECMY felt that an official statement was necessary. In August of that year a consultation was held which involved forty persons, representing every level of the church. Divided into three groups, the consultation issued three reports which together constituted the final document. The first part reviewed the person and work of the Holy Spirit in the Bible. The second part presented church statements on the charismatic issue from the ALC and LCA in the USA, the Methodist Church in Britain, the Church of Scotland, and the United Presbyterian Church in the USA. The conclusion to part two states: "We have seen how other churches reacted towards the charismatic movement. They were open to it, allowed it to develop within their churches

---

[66]"The Evangelical Church Mekane Yesus and the Charismatic Movement," Report to LWF, 10 May 1975, typescript, p.3.

[67]"Introduction" by McDonnell to "The Work of the Holy Spirit," statement by the ECMY, 1976, *PPP*, 2:150-82, 151.

and regarded it as a blessing from God. Therefore we recommend the ECMY to be open to it, see it as a blessing and guide it according to the Word of God."[68]

The final part of the statement recommends "Practical Solutions for the Difficulties within the ECMY." It recognizes in the charismatic renewal movement the revival for which the congregations have long prayed. The form of the revival, however, with its emphasis upon prayer and gifts of the Holy Spirit, speaking in tongues, healing, exorcism, and free and informal worship "tends to break down established ways of worship." The resulting conflict should be distinguished as "necessary" and "unnecessary." The former is that between God and Satan. The latter includes issues of authority, doctrine, and worship, and arise from sin and disorder in the community. The authority conflict which is largely aligned by generations is to be overcome through growth of mutual respect and understanding built upon widespread mutual Bible study. Unnecessary conflict over doctrine has arisen through ignorance of ECMY teaching.

> We accept with appreciation the insistence by leading representatives of the Revival Movement that they will abide by the ECMY constitution and the Lutheran Confession.
>
> We would underline the necessity for teaching of the ECMY doctrine to all church members. . . .
>
> Seeing that some people tend to base their doctrine on personal experience rather than the Word of God, it is important that our church members learn to understand that the Holy Scripture is the supreme authority for our faith.

Regarding freedom within worship the report appeals to Article 7 of the Augsburg Confession: "It is not necessary that human traditions or rites or ceremonies instituted by man should everywhere be the same." It is recommended that glossolalia be restricted from meetings where there is no interpretation but otherwise welcomed and encouraged. Finally, the ECMY believes "that the Revival Movement can be of great blessing to the Church if it is handled in the right way."[69]

The Reverend Tormod Engelsviken has written an extensive documentary on the Pentecostal movement in Ethiopia titled, *Molo Wongel: A Documentary Report on the Life and History of the Independent Pentecostal Movement in Ethiopia 1960-1975.* Engelsviken was a mis-

---

[68]Ibid., 178.

[69]Ibid., 180f.

sionary to Ethiopia for the Norwegian Lutheran Mission from 1971-1973 and taught theology at the Mekane Yesus Seminary in Addis Ababa. His report is based on his personal knowledge of persons and events in Ethiopia as well as his study of the relevant literature. Reverend Engelsviken graciously sent me a photocopy of his as-yet-unpublished manuscript, but because it arrived after the completion of my study, it is not incorporated here.

South Africa. The Evangelical Lutheran Church in South Africa, South Eastern Region, reported that only occasionally do persons speak in tongues.

Australia. Although there was no official response to the LWF request for information, the presence of the charismatic renewal among Lutherans is indicated by the recent book, *Led by the Spirit,* by Victor Pfitzner. Pfitzner, who is a lecturer in New Testament theology at the Luther Seminary, North Adelaide, developed parts of his book from lectures he was invited to give to various groups in the Lutheran Church of Australia including its Fourth General Convention in 1972. "Both these past papers and the present study were requested in view of the challenge, and often confusion, caused by the charismatic or neo-Pentecostal movement within the major denominations, including the Lutheran Church." Written from a confessional Lutheran perspective the book critiques charismatic ideas that "experience substantiates the truth and reality of faith."[70]

Papua New Guinea. At present it is still difficult to determine with much accuracy the size and vitality of the charismatic movement among the Lutheran churches. A recent report[71] refers to four groups of worship. Their origin appears to be related to both external stimulation and internal problems. Young people who have attended education institutions on the coast have returned with extreme versions of Pentecostalism. The local contexts seem to be most receptive to this if the local church life is weak and persons have not been able to assume the normal authority roles of their culture. Thus the charismatic movement appeals to people who are seeking "other means to remain firm in their faith."

---

[70]Pfitzner, *Led by the Spirit,* 5, 21. Cf. *PPP* for statements from the Anglican, Methodist, Presbyterian, and Roman Catholic churches.

[71]14 April 1980. Personal letter from the Church Resource Development Office of the Gutnius Lutheran Church, Papua New Guinea.

"In those areas where there is strong leadership, whether that is by a pastor or lay Christians, and where the pure Word of God is continually shared with the people, we seem to have no problem with a charismatic type movement."

So far the charismatics within the Gutnius Lutheran Church have stressed that they are and want to remain Lutherans. Some tensions, though, have arisen over substitution of free worship patterns of witnessing and testimonies for the Lutheran liturgy and questioning of infant baptism.

EUROPE—Czechoslovakia. The report from the Evangelical Church of Silesia refers to an evangelical lay movement of a pietistic character whose goals are evangelization and renewal within the church. Yet, it is stated that this movement has hardly any charismatic elements.[72]

Denmark. The 1975 Danish report to the LWF points out that in recent years there has been a growing charismatic movement in Denmark which remains unorganized as such but is centered around certain pastors and laymen. The intention of the movement is renewal within the various churches; thus there is not a tendency to form separate charismatic churches. Yet, the firsthand experience of the Danish charismatic pastor and leader, Svend Boysen, presents a different picture. At the International Lutheran Renewal Leaders' Conference he described sharp conflicts within local congregations and persecution of charismatics by other parishioners. Boysen himself expressed concern about damage to persons through the charismatic movement and asked what should be done about this. There was no response from the consultation. Recent news releases from Denmark have pointed out official ecclesiastical concern over clergy who are conducting exorcisms.[73]

Finland. The Finnish report to the LWF is from the Research Institute of the Lutheran Church. It states that there is little information about charismatic movements in Finland. "In any case their significance in Finland is rather meager."[74] The reason for this may be the strong and

---

[72]For the statement of the Czech Brethren cf. *PPP*, 2:521-30.

[73]Cf. Svend Boysen, "Testimony: 'I will Build,' " *LRI* 1/2 (1980): 19f., and Boysen, *Kristenheden Karismatisk Opbrud* (1980) "Exorcism in Denmark," *Church News from Denmark*, September 1981.

[74]Cover letter by Juoko Sihvo, director of the Research Institute of the Lutheran Church, 5 May 1975.

widespread influence of Pietism in Finland which without the typical charismatic phenomena (for example, glossolalia) fulfill the desire for renewal present in the country. "In Finland one of the most conspicuous developments in the sphere of religion over the last decade has been the rapid expansion of the New Pietist Revival." The goals of the revival movement echo those we have seen in the charismatic movements in other countries: the satisfaction of personal emotional, religious needs and the renewal of the church. The interesting element in the Finnish situation is that there have been decades of collaboration between church and revival movements to the extent that the latter has been institution- alized. The New Pietist Revival thrives most successfully in those places where the people are most alienated from the local congregation. "The Revival movements are thus apparently compensating for the failure of the Evangelical Lutheran congregations as such to function as religious frames of reference for their members." Furthermore, the revival move- ments also offer a powerful sense of mutual solidarity in the face of contemporary feelings of insecurity and social alienation.[75]

A personal account from a Lutheran charismatic pastor emphasizes that all over Finland "there are signs of revitalization and a rise in mission interest." The renewal has been nurtured within the church. "We called the movement within the Lutheran Church 'Renewal of the Spirit in the Church.' This emphasized that we were working within the Evangelical Lutheran Church and avoided the term 'charismatic.'" Pastor Pennanen, himself influenced by Dennis Bennett's testimony, *Nine O'Clock in the Morning*, as well as the Finnish renewal movements stimulated by the Pentecostal preacher, Niils Yli-Vainio, and the Swedish Lutheran charismatic, Ulla-Christina Sjoman, says: "The benediction of the rain of the Holy Spirit has watered the dry ground."[76] The Finnish Lutheran Church has not taken an official stand on the charismatic movement, but a research project on it under the direction of Dr. Harri

---

[75]Juoko Sihvo, "Expanding Revival Movements and Their Circumstances in Finland," paper presented to the International Conferences for the Sociology of Religion, the Hague, 1973.

[76]Erkki Pennanen, "Charismatic Renewal in Finland," *LRI* 2/1 (1981): 18-20. Cf. also the unpublished papers and reports by Harri Heino (Kirkon tutmkimuslaitos, 33101 Tampere 10, Finland): "The Charismatic Movement in the Finnish Lutheran Church," "Charismatic Renewal and New Religious Movements in Finland," and "Development Trends in the Charismatic Renewal."

Heino is jointly supported by the Church Research Institute and the faculty of theology in the University of Helsinki.

France. The charismatic movement is represented by ecumenical prayer groups in the Paris region, Montbéliard and in Alsace. There are no separatist tendencies but rather a deepening of faith and greater ecumenical understanding. The author of the report, who is himself personally engaged in the charismatic movement, sees in it great hope for the churches. At the same time he expressed concern that the emphasis upon personal religious experience, which is understandable in light of the French Protestant disposition toward social and political activism, might lead to a forgetfulness of Christian action.

It may be noted that plans are being made for an international charismatic meeting to be held in Strasbourg in 1982.

Germany. In West Germany most of the evangelical and charismatic groups are critical of the churches and their ecumenical activities but they are not separatistic. In Bavaria, communities such as the sisterhood of the "Casteller Rings" (Schwanberg bei Kitzingen) or the "Christbruder-schaft" (Selbitz) like the brotherhood of the "Common Life" and of "the Cross" are partially rooted in Pietism. In turn, they appear as forerunners of the charismatic renewal. Of particular importance is the ecumenical study center Schloß Craheim, which until recently was directed by Pastor Arnold Bittlinger, an international leader. in the charismatic renewal. Craheim may be seen as a type of European center for the theological penetration of the charismatic movement.

The rejection of the Pentecostal movement in the so-called "Berlin Declaration" of 1909 has been overcome in a series of conversations between representatives from the charismatic renewal movements within the churches. Since 1975 there have been seven of these meetings that have emphasized recognition of common goals.[77]

In comparison to other countries the charismatic movement plays an insignificant role; however, its important contribution is that it is well-versed in modern theology. As a renewal movement it is thought to be compatible with Lutheranism.

The concern to locate charismatic renewal in the center of life of the church was evident in 1963 in the "Mülheim Theses on Community and

---

[77]Cf. *Evangelische Information*, 36/79, pp.11f.

Charism." Though they did not constitute an official document, Arnold Bittlinger, who participated in this meeting which centered on the calling of the lay person, sought to have them regarded as representing the position of the three united churches of Germany. "The accent was not on a special charismatic experience, nor on a special movement, but on the charism as constitutive of the normal life of the church and the Christian life."[78] This effort to incorporate charismatic renewal into the church so that it does not become trans- or extra-parochial was also emphasized in the "Würzburg Theses" of 1976:

> The charismatic renewal puts in question a Church to which people belong as a matter of custom, which is characterized by the passivity and indifference of most of its members. Nevertheless, the charismatic renewal is at the heart of the Church and within the continuity of its teaching tradition. It looks for dialogue with all theological trends which contribute to the renewal of the church.
>
> Its goal is the charismatically-renewed Church, which would render a special charismatic movement superfluous.[79]

In the same year the Conference of Bishops of the United Evangelical Lutheran Church in Germany issued a similar document that recognized a hopeful sign in the charismatic renewal of God's claim upon the total person.[80] In 1979 the Evangelical Church in Germany continued the thrust of the Mülheim and Würzburg Theses by emphasizing the integration of the charismatic dimension into the total fabric of Christian and church life. It emphasized a trinitarian theological orientation, sensitivity to theological implications, and openness to the ecumenical potential of the charismatic renewal.[81]

Holland. The report of the LWF from the Evangelical Lutheran Church in the Netherlands states that while there are large numbers of well-established charismatic movements in the Netherlands, their influence

---

[78]*PPP*, 1:104-108, 104.

[79]"Theological Guidelines for the Charismatic Congregational Renewal in Protestant Churches," *PPP*, 2:147-50, 150.

[80]"Renewal in the Holy Spirit," 1976, *PPP*, 2:268-70.

[81]"Evangelical Spirituality," 1979, *PPP*, 2:486-89. For further information cf. Wolfram Kopfermann, ed. *Charismatische Gemeinde—Erneuerung. Eine Zwischenbilanz*, Koordinierungsausschuss für Charismatische Gemeindeerneuerung in der evangelischen Kirche (Hamburg, 1981).

varies according to parish context. The strongest influence by the charismatics is upon the youth.[82]

Norway. The Church of Norway Council on Foreign Relations has prepared two reports on the charismatic movement in Norway. The first (1975) was in response to the LWF questionnaire and the second (1979) was in response to a request for information by the World Council of Churches in relation to their planned consultation on the significance of the charismatic renewal for the churches.

The first report states "that charismatic movements have a certain influence within the Church of Norway, but this influence is not organized in a way that gives it a say on church policies and theology. The movements take part in ordinary congregational life and do their work there." The report briefly describes three movements: (1) "Youth with a Mission," an interdenominational charismatic group which tries to work with and in the churches. Established in the early 1970s it is clearly charismatic stressing extraordinary gifts of grace. It scarcely has any Lutheran characteristics." (2) An older, loosely organized charismatic group which arose in the 1960s in connection with the work of the Full Gospel Businessmen's Fellowship International. The members of the groups are linked through a periodical "Dypere Liv" (Deeper Life). This group has gained some influence within the Church of Norway; for example, some students at the Free Theological Faculty are connected with it and have weekly meetings. There is interest here in relating to Lutheran theology and working within the church. They stress the gifts of grace, glossolalia, healing, and exorcism. (3) Finally, there is a Pentecostal movement, the Valley of Saron, with a nationwide reputation led by Aril Edvardsen. It is congregationally organized. Its large summer meetings west of Kristiansand attract thousands of people including pastors and laity from the Church of Norway.

The 1979 report states that there has been a considerable growth of the charismatic movement in Norway since 1970. The movement is also within the Lutheran Church. In addition to the description given above, two other expressions of the charismatic movement are presented: "The Seminar Circle" and "Agape." The former "rests on a solid Lutheran foundation and is essentially guided by ministers of the Church of Nor-

---

[82]For an extensive Dutch statement cf. that of the Gereformeerde Kerken, "The Work of the Holy Spirit in the Community," *PPP*, 1:147-207.

way and by other people employed by the Church." It has arranged a series of so-called Holy Spirit Seminars to discuss the Holy Spirit and His work. The "Agape" movement is centered in the Seamen's Church in Oslo with connections to the Full Gospel Businessmen's Fellowship International. Theologically speaking, this is a more complex group.

The charismatic movements have in common the emphasis upon tongues, prophecy, healing, and intercession with imposition of hands. Those that emphasize baptism in the Spirit emphasize sanctification and exorcism. The Lutheran charismatics reject a special baptism by the Spirit apart from baptism. The latter work toward deepening the revival movement and they attach great importance to evangelizing and mission. While there is the preaching and practicing of healing, the Bishops' Conference in 1978 strongly warned against exorcism, a practice that appears to be continuing.[83]

The major concern about charismatic movements from the perspectives of the Church of Norway is related to the theological problems and congregational tensions arising from the prominent place given to experience. "Many people consider exactly the emotional experience as the means by which God first and foremost communicates. As a consequence, one often looks for the experience, and considers the gift of tongues as a manifestation of the Holy Spirit having administered the gift of grace."[84] Furthermore, charismatic expression creates anxiety among noncharismatics.

In spite of the problems which have arisen, the Church of Norway has recognized positive elements and impulses in the charismatic renewal movement including revitalized evangelization, Bible study, and worship. "It would be fateful if the Christian church officially would exclude itself from a revival movement like the charismatic—particularly at a time when the entire Christianity is filled with a burning desire for a new spiritual fullness."[85] Thus the Church of Norway's Bishops recently

---

[83]Cf. "Bishop Attacks Exorcism," *Church of Norway News* 2/81 (2 April 1981): 14f.; "Evil Spirits Exist Today, Bishop Lislerud says," *Church of Norway News* 3/81 (7 July 1981): 3f.

[84]"Factors for the Perception of the Charismatic Movement in Norway," 1979 report to WCC, typescript p.3.

[85]Ibid., 4.

stated: "In assessing the charismatic movement, our attitude should be that of an attemptive openness."[86]

Tormod Engelsviken's dissertation provides an in-depth description and analysis of the charismatic movement in Norway. He investigated five denominationally related theologies of charismatic experience: (1) the Pentecostal, Aril Edvardsen, who identifies openly with the international charismatic movement; (2) Ole Hallesby, long-time professor of systematic theology at the Free Faculty in Oslo; (3) the Agape Foundation led by the Lutheran pastor, Hans-Jacob Frøen, assisted by Steinar Remetun; (4) students at the Free Faculty of Theology, Oslo; and (5) the Holy Spirit Seminars sponsored by a rather loosely knit group of church leaders.[87]

(1) Aril Edvardsen. As the Church of Norway report indicates, Edvardsen attracts tens of thousands of participants to his summer conferences, more than half of whom claim to belong to the Church of Norway. Although he is a classical Pentecostal, he understands himself to be a representative of the international charismatic movement. "He has largely been able to set the agenda for the theological debate among Christian leaders concerning the Charismatic Movement. This has forced Charismatics and non-Charismatics alike to take a definite position in relation to Aril Edvardsen and his ministry and theology."[88]

His restorationist ecclesiology is central to his charismatic theology. He sees the Reformation as a reversal of the post-Constantinian decline of the church, and therefore posits that those denominations which stem from the Reformation revive or restore some aspect of Christian truth. As such they are preparations for the Pentecostal culmination of renewal and final restoration in our own day. The tragedy is that denominational doctrines have impeded the final unity of the church. The charismatic experience now, however, is the sufficient basis for full ecumenical fellowship. Edvardsen unites doctrine, methodology, and experience through his emphasis upon baptism in the Holy Spirit which is a conscious experience of the power of the Holy Spirit evidenced by glossolalia. The purpose of this is power for mission. There are two classes of

---

[86]*Church of Norway News* 9/80 (17 December 1980): 6.

[87]The following brief descriptions are summarized from the extensive sections on these five charismatic expressions in Turmod Engelsviken, *The Gift of the Spirit*, 76-266.

[88]Ibid., 77-78.

Christians distinguished by the presence or absence of Spirit-baptism. The method for reception of Spirit-baptism is doctrinal appropriation (baptism in the Spirit), forgiveness of sins, and personal surrender to the Spirit which includes prayer, laying on of hands, and speaking in tongues. Faith is the person's natural capability to be actively obedient to God's Word and thereby "achieving or receiving all the benefits of salvation."[89]

(2) Ole Hallesby. As one of Norway's most influential modern church leaders, Hallesby was primarily effective as a preacher and teacher. Considered a "theologian of experience," he placed the doctrine of the Holy Spirit at the center of his theology. His focus on pneumatology is of special interest because he developed this before the rise of the charismatic movement but in reference to the Holiness and Pentecostal movements of the twentieth century. As a Pietist and theologian of experience, "Hallesby takes as his theological point of departure the spiritual self-consciousness of the regenerated man."[90] "Hallesby *shares* with the Holiness/Pentecostal Movements of his time (and with the Charismatic Movement today) the *basic assumption* that the baptism and the fullness of the Spirit are to be understood in terms of *conscious experience* with several observable consequences in the lives of individual Christians and the ministry of the church." He himself had a charismatic experience.[91] Hallesby developed an elaborate *ordo salutis* which need not be reviewed in detail here. "Faith (conversion) and justification are *preconditions* for the Spirit's indwelling. Moreover, regeneration, assurance and sanctification are the *results* or *consequences*. The effects of the gift of the Spirit are experientially verifiable. Yet they are based exclusively on the objective reality of Christ's redemptive work in history and God's justification of the believing sinner."[92] Although Hallesby criticized the Pentecostals for dividing Christians into two classes with reference to Spirit-baptism, he himself moves in the same direction. His description of the experience of baptism in the Spirit, growth in sanctification related to the experience of the fullness of the Spirit is paralleled by features of the charismatic experience.[93]

---

[89]Ibid., 133.

[90]Ibid., 138, cf. also 161ff.

[91]Ibid., 162, 138 n. 188.

[92]Ibid., 163.

[93]Cf. Ibid., 167.

(3) The Agape Foundation. The charismatic movement in Norway is now dated to a 1970 meeting sponsored by the Full Gospel Businessmen's Fellowship International. One of the Lutheran pastors there was Hans-Jacob Frøen. "Frøen has for the last ten years been the uncontested spiritual leader of the most radical wing of the Charismatic Movement within the Lutheran Church in Norway."[94] The purpose of the Agape Foundation led by Frøen is to revive the spiritual gifts in the congregations—to promote charismatic renewal. Although the foundation serves within a Lutheran context, it is biased against confessional theology which it regards as uncorrected by the Scriptures. "It is a basic assumption on Frøen's part that it is impossible to adhere fully to the Bible and the Lutheran Confessions at the same time."[95] Engelsviken notes that Frøen regards Larry Christenson to be in agreement.[96]

Baptism in the Holy Spirit is understood as a free gift of grace but there are also conditions for its reception. First, there must be a right understanding of baptism in the Holy Spirit. Here there is an emphasis on correct doctrine as understood by Frøen and the Agape Foundation. Second, the experience must be longed for to the extent of abandoning personal prestige and pride. Third, sin which is an impediment to receiving the experience must be confessed. Fourth and finally, the decisive step is to seek the experience through prayer and laying on of hands.[97]

> Although the Agape Foundation defines its own theological position as Lutheran, it nevertheless acknowledges the tension and conflict that exist between Confessional Lutheran theology and its own theological views. The formal principle of *sola scriptum* is contrasted with the material contents of the Lutheran understanding of the doctrine of the Spirit. In fact, the Agape Foundation calls for a "sacrifice" or "correction" of Lutheran doctrine in certain important respects.[98]

These "corrections" include a hermeneutics of personal revelation; separation of regeneration and baptism in the Spirit as is related to an ideal of three separate experiences of the Spirit (birth of the Spirit = new life; baptism in the Spirit = power; fullness of the Spirit = sanctification); the

---

[94]Ibid., 169.

[95]Ibid., 171.

[96]Ibid., n. 283.

[97]Ibid., 181-83.

[98]Ibid., 189.

quasisacramental character of the laying on of hands; miraculous confirmations of the gospel; tongues as the specific gift of baptism in the Spirit; and a dualistic anthropology.

(4) Free Faculty of Theology Students. These persons take a more critical stance in regard to the international charismatic movement; and they desire to interpret their charismatic experiences within the framework of Lutheran confessional theology. They maintain that "the spirit may manifest himself *directly* to *Christians* who exist within the reality of the Spirit."[99] Their concern is that Lutheran theology not restrict the Spirit's freedom by too tight a connection to Word and sacraments.

(5) The Holy Spirit Seminars. These are organized by six to seven leaders from various positions within the Church of Norway who have received the support of several bishops. "The most influential Charismatic theology in terms of popular impact within the Church of Norway has been the theology represented by the so-called 'Holy Spirit Seminars.' "[100] There is more sensitivity both to Lutheran theology and developing a theological interpretation of the charismatic experience in conjunction with Lutheran doctrine. The major theological spokesperson is Lutheran theologian and pastor Oddvar Søvik.

SOUTH AMERICA—Argentina. The 1975 report to the LWF by the Iglesia Evangelica Luterana Unida refers to the strong fundamentalist and Pentecostalist churches and movements in Argentina but claims that apart from some lay involvement there is no charismatic movement within the Lutheran church.

---

[99]Ibid., 223.

[100]Ibid., 246. Cf. also *Den Hellige and I Kirkens Liv*, ed. by Tormod Engelsviken, Ove Hanssen, Kjell Sannes (Oslo: Luther Forlag, 1981).

5

LUTHERAN CHARISMATIC THEOLOGY

Is there a Lutheran charismatic theology? Or, a charismatic Lutheran theology? Or, does the charismatic renewal movement within the Lutheran churches share to such an extent the orientations of the sixteenth century and later Pietist renewal movements that concern with praxis displaces theological reflection and formulation? The great scholar of Anabaptism, Robert Friedmann, claims that the Anabaptists not only were unconcerned with theology, they regarded it as a stumbling block to discipleship. "To talk about the theology of Anabaptism seems like talking about squaring the circle. Apparently there is none, and all discussions along this line seem to miss the point."[1] We have already seen how Pietism echoed in its own way this sixteenth-century rejection of a separation of faith and life which they regarded as concomitant with the development of systematic theology. Religious renewal movements have a tendency to regard discursive thinking on religious questions as a substitute for living out God's commandments and as being directly related to lack of spiritual immediacy. Furthermore, there is an immediacy to renewal movements that displaces ongoing theological reflection in favor of witnessing to present experience. The experience of faith is

---

[1]Robert Friedmann, *The Theology of Anabaptism* (Scottdale PA: Herald Press, 1973) 17.

more important than doctrinal formulations of it. This is a conviction that transcends denominational boundaries. Thus Christenson's statement, "What charismatics are bringing forth is not a new statement of doctrine, but a fresh experience of it,"[2] is paralleled by the Roman Catholic statements of Edward O'Connor and Kevin Ranaghan: "The Pentecostal Movement (in the Roman Catholic Church) is not characterized by a new doctrine on the Holy Spirit, but by the fact that the traditional doctrines have come to life with new freshness and vigor."[3] And, "It is this existential, concrete, handing on of a living faith experience which gives rich and lasting meaning to persons in the world, which contemporary theology, both right and left, must recognize as the de facto reality of the pentecostal movement."[4]

This does not mean that charismatic renewal movements do not have theological perspectives and emphases. It does mean that by and large the theology of charismatic renewal movements either remains implicit or is unconsciously borrowed from the immediate Pentecostal background out of which neo-Pentecostal and charismatic renewal movements arose. Insofar as charismatic theology is implicit it poses difficult problems for anyone who wishes to describe and analyze it. Thus the sources like those of the sixteenth century and Pietist parallels consist largely of testimonies, witnessings, biographies, and autobiographies of persons in the movement. Furthermore, unlike an institutionalized church, a religious movement does not have easily defined structural and ideological boundaries.[5] It is only within about the last five years that charismatics themselves have consciously begun work on relating their experience to Lutheran theology and tradition. This development, as we have seen, is

---

[2]*CRAL*, 34-35.

[3]Edward O'Connor, *The Pentecostal Movement in the Catholic Church* (Notre Dame IN: Ave Maria Press, 1971) 241.

[4]Kevin and Dorothy Ranaghan, *Catholic Pentecostals* (New York: Paulist Press, 1969) 262.

[5]Friedmann, *Theology of Anabaptism*, 96: "Anabaptist writings were never scholarly structured or otherwise discursive but always of a confessional or testimonial nature." Cf. Quebedeaux, *The New Charismatics* (New York: Doubleday and Co., 1976) 208f. Cf. also P. S. Brewster, ed., *Pentecostal Doctrine* (Gloucestershire, England: Grenehurst Press, 1976) 4: "But by its very nature, the Pentecostal revival has kept its best and most articulate leaders so active in proclaiming the truth verbally that too few of them have found the time to write their message."

particularly forceful in America, Scandinavia, and both Germanies. Nevertheless,

> It is a fundamental sociological principle that the leadership of a voluntary association can only be so far out of line with the expectations of its constituency before that leadership is questioned.[6]

If there is any validity to the above "sociological principle," then the desire for charismatic Lutheran leaders to critically relate their experience to Lutheran theology and the Confessions indicates widespread concern to foster renewal both *within* the Lutheran churches and *in dialogue* with the Lutheran tradition. That this is indeed the case may be seen not only in the theological work of individual charismatic Lutheran theologians but also in the development of strategy and structures for renewal on an international level.

Before beginning a description and analysis of charismatic Lutheran theology some words of caution are in order. We are dependent mainly upon the writings of the leadership of the renewal, but this leadership is varied in cultural and theological background. At the same time, however, we note that the writings most accessible to us are from the Western and Northern hemispheres. While a thorough analysis of the context of charismatic theology is beyond the scope of our study, we need to bear in mind that some emphases and nuances may reflect non-charismatic factors. For example, the American free church and voluntarist congregational setting provides a different context for Lutheran theology than the state church context of, perhaps, Germany. Furthermore, it may make a difference whether the charismatic theologian is operating out of the more conservative, confessionally oriented LC-MS or the contemporary academic theology of West Germany. There is also the variation in fundamental religious concerns that affect all theologians. For example, it has been said that while Luther's basic question was "How do I get a gracious God?," the contemporary Christian in secularist cultures is asking "How do I get a gracious neighbor?" Anyone who has had the opportunity to observe or participate in charismatic services and gatherings can testify to the pervasive feeling of mutual acceptance most evident in the group's willingness to listen to the visions, prophecies, and confessions of individual members no matter how banal they may appear

---

[6]Jeffrey Hadden, *The Gathering Storm in the Churches* (Garden City NY: Doubleday, 1969) 258-59; quoted by Quebedeaux, *The New Charismatics*, 209.

to an outsider. If we take seriously the reports of initial charismatic experiences there may be another variation on this theme, "How do I find a deep experience of joy?" This is not to suggest that the gospel does not apply to all contexts but to remind ourselves that its formulation reflects the experience of the human situation.

That the charismatic renewal arises out of specific religious experience is a commonplace, yet it deserves analysis because it is the hermeneutic if not the source itself for charismatic theological reflection. How may the charismatic hunger for God and for knowledge of His presence be described? Kilian McDonnell suggests that there is hardly one word that better describes the renewal movement than "presence." "The categories for expressing the content of this experience are most commonly presence, power, praise, and of these presence is the most primary."[7]

In what follows we shall attempt to let charismatic Lutheran theologians speak for themselves.

The Presence of God—Baptism with the Holy Spirit. The charismatic point of departure for theological reflection is not justification but rather baptism in the Holy Spirit.

> This accent on the person of the Holy Spirit is linked to the *experience* of receiving or being filled with His *presence*. Precisely because He is a person, He must be received. The effectual *presence* of the Holy Spirit cannot be assumed simply because a person agrees to correct doctrine. It is possible to hold the doctrine on the Holy Spirit, yet not *experience His presence and power*. The doctrine must find expression in *personal experience*. This is a fundamental perception of the charismatic renewal.[8]

Acquaintance with charismatics and an overview of charismatic literature reveals that their focal point for the experience of God's presence and power and the concomitant issue of praise is baptism in the Holy Spirit. All the historical accounts point to the "outburst of tongues" as the genesis for neo-Pentecostal and charismatic renewal movements. As Hollenweger points out, the baptism of the Holy Spirit is "generally but

---

[7]*PPP*, 1:xxii; and his essay "Die charismatische Bewegung in der katholischen Kirche," in M. Lienhard and H. Meyer, eds., *Wiederentdeckung des Heiligen Geistes* (Frankfurt: Lembeck, 1974) 28. For supportive charismatic autobiographical testimony cf. *CRAL*, ch. 2, and Heribert Mühlen, ed., *Erfahrung mit dem Heiligen Geist* (Mainz: Grünewald V1., 1979); and others.

[8]*CRAL*, 35; my emphasis.

not always identified with speaking in tongues."[9] Already a number of questions arise: What is "baptism in the Holy Spirit?" How is it related to the sacrament of baptism? Is the gift of tongues necessarily connected with Spirit baptism?

Recent works by Lutheran charismatics attempt to sort out these questions and respond to them. Obviously when these questions are addressed to charismatics by non-charismatics they take on a polemical edge. Thus Lutheran charismatics have taken up an apologetic task which may help to explain the omission of various theological motifs in light of their concern to respond to specific questions.

In the beginning of the charismatic renewal during the early 1960s, Lutheran as well as other charismatics depended upon classical Pentecostalism as a framework for understanding and expressing their new experience. This imported two basic Pentecostal perspectives that by the next decade were recognized as sources of major tension with the Lutheran tradition. One was fundamentalism, which we shall have an opportunity to discuss later. The second was a two- or three-stage schema for receiving the Holy Spirit that was in opposition to the Lutheran understanding of baptism as a sacrament and that separated the reception of the Holy Spirit from baptism. A recent Pentecostal essay on their doctrine of baptism in the Holy Spirit states:

> A careful reading of the Acts of the Apostles indicates that salvation, baptism by immersion in water and the baptism in the Holy Spirit are separate and distinct experiences. Salvation, the new birth, comes when we repent of our sin and receive Christ by faith as Saviour and Lord (Ephesians 2:1-10). Baptism is the outward, public confession of the inward experience that has already taken place. The baptism in the Holy Spirit is that great act of Jesus Christ in enduring [*sic*] a Christian with the galvanic power from on high, that energy-full endowment of the Holy Spirit.
>
> We avow that speaking with other tongues, that is in languages never learned by the speakers, is the Bible evidence of receiving the baptism of the Holy Spirit.[10]

---

[9]Quoted by Quebedeaux, *The New Charismatics,* 128.

[10]T. W. Walker, "The Baptism in the Holy Spirit" in Brewster, *Pentecostal Doctrine,* 27f., 34. Cf. also Walter Hollenweger, *Enthusiastisches Christentum Die Pfingstbewegung in Geschichte und Gegenwart* (Zurich: Zwingli V1, 1969) 372ff.; Quebedeaux, *The New Charismatics,* 128ff.; Christenson, *CRAL,* 36ff.; Hollenweger, "Charismatische und pfingstlerische Bewegungen als Frage an die Kirchen heute," in Lienhard and Meyer, *Wiederentdeckung des Heiligen Geistes,* 53-76, 55f.

It was not long before Lutheran charismatic leaders began to realize that by utilizing Pentecostal categories to express their experience to fellow Lutherans who were not charismatics, they were indeed speaking in a "strange tongue" in more ways than one. Of those alert to this problem, one of the most consistent and cogent has been the Roman Catholic scholar of charismatic movements, Fr. Kilian McDonnell. In 1972 he wrote: "I know a Lutheran charismatic who is no longer theologically identifiable as a Lutheran. He has borrowed from the classical Pentecostals in the areas of their greatest weakness: exegesis and systematic theology. . . . But if the Lutheran charismatic is to be of service to those who need a theology of the charismatic spirituality within a Lutheran framework it will not do to take over uncritically the Wesleyan or the classical pentecostal categories. The Lutheran neo-Pentecostals must set the charismatic spirituality within the authentic Lutheran theological tradition."[11] That this concern extends beyond a few leaders is evident in responses from participants at two Lutheran charismatic conferences (1975) to the question of the needs of the Lutheran charismatic movement. It needs ". . . to shed some of the classical Pentecostal trappings and allow the Spirit to move more freely in our midst; . . . to relate charismatic experience to the categories of Lutheran theological expression; . . . to train its leaders, especially in relating charismatic experience to sacramental theology; and . . . to divorce itself from both legalism and fundamentalism."[12]

In response to this concern, Lutheran charismatic theologians have begun to move away from the classical Pentecostal view of conversion followed by baptism in the Holy Spirit towards an "organic view" of the work of the Spirit that, Christenson argues, is more related to the Lutheran tradition. This organic view ". . . understands the kind of experience which people are having in the charismatic renewal as a manifestation of Christian growth. . . . It marks a progression in one's life as a Christian, not an event by which one becomes a Christian."

On the other hand, however, the distinctive experiential expectation of the Wesleyan-Holiness-Pentecostal tradition remains a vital part of the charismatic renewal. A distinct experience of personal renewal in the Holy Spirit

---

[11]"Baptism in the Holy Spirit as an Ecumenical Problem," in McDonnell and Bittlinger, *The Baptism in the Holy Spirit As An Ecumenical Problem* (Notre Dame IN: Charismatic Renewal Services, Inc., 1972) 31f. Cf. also *ST*, 99.

[12]"Lutherans Poll Attitudes on Charismatic Renewal," *LCRN* 1/5 (April 1975): 4.

continues to be a normal occurrence in the renewal. And while there is no doctrine of speaking in tongues as the "initial evidence of baptism with the Holy Spirit," nevertheless the experience of tongues as well as other spiritual gifts, is expected and is in fact widespread.[13]

Appealing to Luther's Large Catechism, Christenson goes on to affirm that the Holy Spirit is "inseparably linked with the Word and with Christ." The latter are the norms for interpreting and evaluating the experience of the Holy Spirit. Furthermore, the bestowal of the Holy Spirit in the sacrament of baptism is not a one-time event but an ongoing work. Here Christenson refers again to Luther's statement that the drowning of sin is a lifelong process of "spiritual baptism."[14]

Faith, baptism, and the manifestation of the Spirit are normally inseparable. "Repentance, baptism, forgiveness of sins, faith, the reception of the Spirit—in whatever order or manner they may be experienced—are a unity." The gift of the manifestation of the Spirit may be distinct from baptism, occurring before, with, or after it. Thus mechanistic views to coerce the Spirit are rejected, but "when baptism does not lead to the manifestation of the Spirit, steps should be taken to rectify the matter."[15]

Christenson sets out to clarify the renewal's usage of the phrase "baptism with the Holy Spirit" by distinguishing theological statement from the description of experience. In the former sense it is clear that every Christian has been "baptized with the Spirit" through Christian baptism. "The term, however, is also used in an experiential sense. When used in this way it refers to the event or process by which the power of the Holy Spirit is released in a fresh way. In this sense baptism with the Holy Spirit is the Spirit being actualized or coming to more conscious manifestation, in one's life." At the same time Christenson claims that while the phrase itself may entail some difficulties that might be overcome by more varied terminology, charismatic renewal is not tied to any particular theology of baptism. Although Christenson claims that questions about baptism in relation to charismatic renewal are the result of the ecumenical nature of the renewal and not the experience itself,[16] the first part of

---

[13]*ST*, 38.

[14]Ibid., 40 (LW 35, 30-31).

[15]Ibid., 43f.

[16]Ibid., 51-54.

Engelsviken's study calls this into question. "Although the Lutheran interpreters of the Charismatic experience take pains to avoid the charge of dividing Christians into groups or classes with regard to their experience of the Spirit, it seems to be inherent in *any* theology that views the Charismatic experience as a desirable goal for *all* Christians. . . . Whether the fullness of the Spirit is understood as a gradual process or an instantaneous event, or whether the Charismatic experience is reputable or not, may make a difference with regard to the possibility of *observing* the distinctions between Christians, but does not change the fundamental reality of two (or more) classes of Christians."[17]

The extent to which Christenson has taken seriously the concern to relate his charismatic experience to the Lutheran tradition is evident by comparing his 1976 book, *The Charismatic Renewal Among Lutherans*, which we have extensively quoted above, with his 1968 book, *Speaking in Tongues*. Aside from the almost self-conscious references in the former to *Lutheran* theologians (but rarely to Luther!) as compared to his earlier references to Pentecostal leaders, the earlier book appears to be much more influenced by Pentecostal theology. There is a hesitancy to discuss the theology of baptism with the Holy Spirit although he insists that there is a sound biblical one. ". . . (T)he baptism with the Holy Spirit is not a theology to be discussed and analysed. It is an experience one enters into." However, some clues for this theology soon emerge: "Water baptism is a rite or sacrament administered by the Church, on the authority of Christ." "Baptism with the Holy Spirit is administered by Jesus himself."[18] The reason why the distinction is made here between Church and Holy Spirit, Christ and Jesus is not clarified.

The baptism with the Holy Spirit is described in the 1968 book by means of the acrostic "PILOT": its purpose and result is Power; it is Instantaneous, occurring at a definite moment in time; it is a distinctive Link in the divine chain which binds us to Christ; it is Objective in its outward manifestation, which is speaking in Tongues. "This is as far as we can go theologically. We can discern the pattern of the baptism with the Holy Spirit in the Book of Acts, and see the part which speaking in tongues plays in it. But we cannot set this down as a rigid doctrine or

---

[17]Tormod Engelsviken, *The Gift of the Spirit. An Analysis and Evaluation of the Charismatic Movement from a Lutheran Theological Perspective.* Unpublished dissertation. (Aquinas Institute School of Theology, Dubuque IA, 1981) 260.

[18]*ST*, 40f.

formula. Scripture itself shows us that the pattern allows for considerable flexibility."[19]

While Christenson disavows theological reflection or development in favor of praxis, there are definite theological implications in his "practical consideration." The purpose of baptism with the Spirit and its objective manifestation in speaking in tongues is to recapture the power of the early church. "We in the modern Church have unquestionably *lost* something . . . very little of the modern Church could bear comparison with the spiritual drive, the genuine fellowship, and the gay unconquerable courage of the Young Church."[20] Baptism with the Spirit enabled the early church to give powerful witness to Jesus. This same baptism with the Spirit is the *prerequisite* to being a witness today. In his section titled "Prerequisite: You Must Receive the Holy Spirit," Christenson compares our relationship to God with a courtroom setting. In the process he strongly implies an Anselmian theory of the atonement, gives a legal framework for witnessing, entails a particular hermeneutical approach, and breaks Luther's dialectic of the Christian being sinner and righteous at the *same time*. We shall have the opportunity to return to these issues later; our purpose at the moment is only to observe that the charismatic emphasis upon baptism with the Spirit and its relation to practice has definite implications for theology. Theology and praxis are inseparable.[21]

Theodore Jungkuntz (LC-MS) has discussed baptism with the Spirit in numerous essays and tracts. Unlike Christenson, he definitely sets out to relate charismatic experience to Lutheran theology. Like Christenson, Jungkuntz relates baptism with the Spirit "organically" to water baptism:

> Baptism in the Holy Spirit is understood not as an event "beyond" sacramental baptism in the sense of "separate from," but as an event "within" sacramental baptism and yet an event to be "distinguished" from its initial expression with water. Such a view in no way diminishes the significance of sacramental baptism, but merely speaks of the manner by which, according to God's promise, the benefits of sacramental baptism might be more fully released and manifested in the life of the believers.[22]

---

[19]*ST*, 45-54.

[20]*ST*, 58f.

[21]Cf. *ST*, 62-70. In spite of Christenson's avowal in both books that experience is not normative, an apparent suspicion of theological reflection repeatedly surfaces.

[22]Theodore Jungkuntz, "A Response," *The Cresset,* Occasional Paper 2 (1977), 4.

Jungkuntz sees no biblical or confessional reason why the Lutheran emphasis upon the "sacramental nature" of baptism should not be united with the Pentecostal emphasis upon the "manifestation nature" of baptism. At the same time he insists that:

> Any experience designated "Baptism in the Spirit" which called into question the bestowal of the Holy Spirit through sacramental baptism, even when administered to an infant, could not be harmonized with Holy Scripture and the Lutheran Confessions and would be tantamount to selling one's birthright for a mess of pottage.[23]

To illustrate his conviction that charismatic renewal may be related to a sound sacramental theology, Jungkuntz makes an analogy between Word, baptism, and the charismatic manifestations with engagement, marriage, and intercourse. The faithful response to the proclamation of the Word is like an engagement which is then publicly ratified by baptism ("marriage"). The consummation of marriage in sexual intercourse is ". . . comparable to the way in which faith-intimacy with Jesus produces the experience of being filled with the Holy Spirit and the consequent conception of charismatic gifts."[24] Jungkuntz may not want to overemphasize this analogy (although he uses it elsewhere[25]) but the question arises whether Christians without charismatic gifts are like marriage without sexual intercourse. It is of interest that in his *Catechism* he also implies sexual intimacy as a paradigm for the close relationship of sacramental baptism and Jesus' baptism in the Holy Spirit by quoting Jesus' reference to man and woman becoming one flesh.[26] Since our present interest is the Lutheran charismatic understanding of baptism with the Holy Spirit we may defer until later a discussion of the implication that non-charismatics are unconsummated and the hermeneutics of biblical support.

We have looked at the perspectives on baptism with the Holy Spirit of two American Lutheran charismatic theologians. We shall supplement this by reviewing a short essay on the subject by the West German

---

[23]Theodore Jungkuntz, "Charismatic Worship: Challenge or Challenged?" *Response* 16/1&2 (1976):7, 5.

[24]Theodore Jungkuntz, "Testing the Spirit of the Charismatic Renewal," *Lutheran Charismatic Renewal Newsletter* 1/7 (June 1975): 3.

[25]Theodore Jungkuntz, "A Response to Scott H. Hendrix's 'Charismatic Renewal. . . .' " *Currents in Theology and Mission* 5/1 (1978): 55.

[26]Theodore Jungkuntz, *A Lutheran Charismatic Catechism*, 5.

Lutheran charismatic, Arnold Bittlinger.[27] Bittlinger, presently a consultant on charismatic renewal to the World Council of Churches, also relates baptism in the Spirit to sacramental baptism. The charismatic experience is potentially given in baptism and must be actualized in the life of the baptized. "The essence of a charismatic experience is the experience of encountering Jesus Christ as the Head of His Body, which is the Church . . ., who gave gifts and ministries to men."[28] The primary charisma is the gift of eternal life in which all the other charismata have their basis.

Bittlinger forcefully rejects the view that there is a second stage for Christians, the so-called "spirit baptism."

> Since Pentecost, there is only one baptism: the baptism by water and Spirit. It is impossible to separate these two elements. By water and Spirit we are bound inwardly and outwardly to the Body of Christ. . . . We cannot divide the Body of Christ between the inward and the outward. We cannot distinguish between the "visible" and the "invisible" church. . . . Therefore: Every Christian is baptized in water and in Spirit—otherwise he is not a "Christian" in the full sense of the word. Actualizing the charismatic aspect of baptism is not an act of receiving, but of releasing the Spirit who is already dwelling in the Christian.[29]

We have reviewed three Lutheran charismatics on the subject of baptism in the Holy Spirit. We shall follow the same procedure in discussing other motifs important to our understanding of Lutheran charismatic theology. There are obviously other Lutheran charismatic theologians upon which we could draw, but the three we have chosen are not only recognized leaders by the charismatics but also have expressly applied themselves to the task of relating their charismatic experience to Lutheran theology. A final, but not insignificant, point is that their writings are readily accessible. We are aware of the question of possible distortion by heavy dependence upon the leading and best known charismatic theologians; for example, how representative are they of popular charismatic piety? We hope to provide a more complete account when comparing the renewal and Lutheran tradition.

Charismata. An element which runs throughout the charismatic renewal movements, indeed the source of their notoriety, is common witness to

---

[27]Arnold Bittlinger, "Baptized in Water and in Spirit—Aspects of Christian Initiation," in McDonnell and Bittlinger, *The Baptism in the Holy Spirit as an Ecumenical Problem*, 1-26.

[28]Ibid., 14.

[29]Ibid., 20.

the return of the charismata. The gifts listed in 1 Corinthians 12:9ff. and Romans 12:6ff. accompany baptism with the Holy Spirit. "One thing is constant in Scripture, and it is most important: It is never merely *assumed* that a person has been baptized with the Holy Spirit. When he has been baptized with the Holy Spirit the person *knows* it. *It is a definite experience.*"[30]

Within the charismatic renewal this "definite experience" is uniquely expressed by glossolalia—speaking in tongues. Christenson says that of the nine charismata listed by Paul in 1 Corinthians, the only gift without precedence in the Old Testament and the Gospels is speaking in tongues. "Historically, speaking in tongues is uniquely related to the work of the Holy Spirit in and with the Christian Church. It is apparently a gift which He reserved for the Church." Its significance is derived from the baptism with the Holy Spirit.[31]

In an early essay, Christenson describes the gift of tongues and discusses its theological and practical aspects.[32] He argues that Scripture does not speak against tongues but against its misuse, and that therefore the remedy for misuse is not non-use but correct use. Tongues, correctly understood and used, is not primarily a means for preaching the gospel but a sign that God abides in the midst of his faithful. It is a sign of the reception of the Holy Spirit, but is not to be developed into a doctrine which posits that its absence means the absence of the Holy Spirit. Furthermore, its highly personal nature precludes a normative description. In its various forms, speaking in tongues is a nonlearned expression of praise and prayer that edifies the believer. Thus its primary locus is in personal devotions.

Christenson discusses the theological aspects in terms of Lutheran and biblical doctrine. The Lutheran Confessions established no special teaching on this subject. "Speaking in tongues is a subordinate aspect of faith and its exercise; the Lutheran church had no occasion to set forth a special doctrine concerning it." Nevertheless, the teaching is in Scripture. Since Lutheran doctrine is based upon the Bible and the Bible certainly speaks of tongues, we can be certain that this is not a new doctrine in the

---

[30]*ST*, 38; author's emphasis.

[31]*ST*, 30, 32.

[32]Larry Christenson, *Die Gabe des Zungenredens in der Lutherischen Kirche* (Marburg an der Lahn: Edel, 1963).

Lutheran church. Thus, Christenson argues, not the doctrine but the experience is new.[33] This is a theme which runs throughout his writings and parallels the apologetic thrust of theologians throughout the history of the church; to wit, we are not innovators.

In reviewing the biblical teaching about tongues, Christenson makes the following observations: (1) Speaking in tongues is the gift of the Holy Spirit. It was a common experience in the early church. (2) Although the Bible uses varied terminology for speaking in tongues, it is essentially the gift of the Holy Spirit to speak a language never before learned. It is not in itself or the speaker "ecstatic"; the speaker has the same possibilities for self-control as in his mother tongue. (3) Tongues is a form of prayer. (4) It is primarily for personal devotion. (5) It is not necessary for salvation. (6) Speaking in tongues was not limited to the early church. On this latter point he refers to Luther's reference to Mark 16:17f. that these signs are valid for all Christians and if anyone is a Christian he, in faith, shall also have the power to do these signs.[34]

Under "practical aspects," Christenson calls for understanding and pastoral direction for both charismatic and non-charismatic. The two extremes of misuse and non-use must be avoided so that the gift of tongues may be a blessing not only for the speakers but for the enrichment of the body of Christ.

Speaking in tongues is not the only gift that the charismatic renewal practices. Christenson notes that "The charismatic renewal has emphasized some gifts more than others, notably the catalogue given in 1 Corinthians 12:8-10. Charismatics need to be on guard lest this emphasis become a permanent stance."[35] Nevertheless, the renewal serves an important purpose in reminding the church of some of the more neglected gifts. This category includes healing, prophecy, vision, and revelation, as well as speaking in tongues. Tongues express the praise of God; healing exhibits the power of God. The reason the contemporary church lacks the power of early Christianity is that we attempt to get or receive the spiritual realm with the help of our human wisdom and reason. We have pulled the revelation of God down to the level of human

---

[33]Ibid., 18f.

[34]Ibid., 22. Christenson gives no reference but Luther's "Sermon am Auffahrttage" (29 May 1522) seems to be the source; cf. WA 10, 3:144, 13ff.

[35]*CRAL*, 76.

possibilities, to the level of human questions, doubts, and speculations.[36] "Healing was never meant to be an option in the Christian Church— something that's all right for those who like to go off on special tangents. The ministry of healing is part of the gospel, and therefore it is an obligation." "Though human reason cannot encompass its working, a simple believer can obediently bring the sick to the Lord—and they will experience God's healing power."[37]

The presence of God is confirmed and reinforced through prophecy, vision, and revelation that are "a wholesome complement to the emphasis upon purely rational processes and conclusion." Beneficial use of these gifts may be further developed through instruction and as an example Christenson includes the "Principles of Spiritual Perception" which was developed in his own congregation.[38]

We may expect much of Christenson's charismatic Lutheran theology to be similarly expressed by other Lutheran charismatic theologians. Jungkuntz can find "no compelling reason why prophetic gifts might not be released today as well as in New Testament times."[39] In fact, ". . . the person who is sacramentally united with Jesus ought prayerfully to expect Jesus to manifest in his 'sheep' any of the boundless and surprising range of gifts to be used in the worship of God and the ministry to Christ's Body (1 Cor. 12:1-13, 27-31; 14:1-5), and in the giving of a powerful witness to the world (Acts 1:4-5,8)." Charismatic gifts are not merely options, "they are necessary manifestations simply because of God's command and promise, and active openness to them is our proper response."[40]

It is not surprising given the LC-MS training and orientation of Jungkuntz that he consistently and painstakingly seeks to relate the Lutheran charismatic renewal to Luther and the Lutheran Confessions. His erudition in this regard is evident in all his writings. For example, the charismatic expectation for the charismata is related to the rite of confir-

---

[36]Christenson, *Der Dienst der Krankenheilung in der Kirche—Möglichkeit oder Verpflichtung?* (Marburg an der Lahn: Edel, 1964) 15.

[37]*CRAL*, 98f., 104.

[38]*CRAL*, 105, 107-11.

[39]Theodore Jungkuntz, "The Canon, The Charismata, and the Cross," *The Cresset* (September 1979): 25-29, 27.

[40]Jungkuntz, "A Response," 9, 11.

mation.[41] The charismatic expectation of the miraculous is in accord with the evangelical, incarnational emphasis of the Lutheran Reformation. It is the secularization process stemming from the Enlightenment and Industrial Revolution that has clouded this expectation and led to a powerless, Pentecostal-less Christianity. "Miraculous manifestations are to flow forth from a oneness with God. They are not the result of a human manipulation of God. . . . Our oneness with the Father is given only in Jesus as we through baptismal faith abide in him. As we exercise this faith by yielding to Jesus' 'baptism in the Holy Spirit' . . . and thus allow Jesus to bring us into that overflowing communion with the Father . . . the miraculous will also become more and more manifest in us and through us."[42]

The most extensive and sophisticated biblical and theological discussion of the charismata is the work of Arnold Bittlinger who is regarded by McDonnell as "perhaps the most competent theologian within the charismatic movement."[43] In his study on speaking in tongues Bittlinger calls for a demythologizing of glossolalia in terms of both its supernatural aura and the Pentecostalist mythos associated with it.

> Speaking in tongues is not mystical submerging of the self, unintelligible stammering, compulsive speaking; it is not bound to some kind of emotional outburst; but rather *it is a completely "normal" speaking in a language which the speaker has not previously learned and which he himself also does not understand*. . . . The one speaking has complete control over his speech, he can not only begin or cease at any time, but he can also speak loud or soft, slow or fast.[44]

Bittlinger gives numerous cases to substantiate the argument that speaking in tongues is actually the gift of an unlearned, actual language. The popular description of glossolalia in terms of ecstasy and enthusiasm is misleading. However, if these terms are used in their root sense—as denoting stepping out of the egocentrically determined sphere of life into the divine sphere—then all charismata are ecstatic and enthusiastic.

---

[41]Cf. Jungkuntz, *A Lutheran Charismatic Catechism*, 6ff.; and "Pray the Lord of the Harvest," *LCRN* 5/8 (August 1979).

[42]Theodore Jungkuntz, "A 'How To Do It' Manual on Miracles," *LCRN*, Pastoral Edition, n.d.

[43]"Introduction" to Bittlinger, *Gifts and Ministries* (London: Hodder and Stoughton, 1974). For a bibliography of Bittlinger's works cf. his *Papst und Pfingstler*, 244-46.

[44]Arnold Bittlinger, *Glossolalia: Wert und Problematik des Sprachenredens* (Schloß Craheim: Kühne Verlag, 1969³) 47, cf. also 11. My emphasis.

Nevertheless, terms like "mysticism" are less than useful unless expressly interpreted.

The function of tongues in personal devotion, the Pauline sense of tongues as a means for self-edification, is interpreted in the sense of a therapeutic experience. Yet, Bittlinger states that there is not a direct correlation between tongues and having or not having the Holy Spirit. Those who have received the gift of tongues have it as a power for service to themselves, the church, and the kingdom of God on earth.[45] The understanding of the charismata in terms of service is further developed in Bittlinger's other writings.[46] Briefly defined, "a charism is a gratuitous manifestation of the Holy Spirit, working in and through, but going beyond, the believer's natural ability for the common good of the people of God."[47] Without love, the charismata are worthless.[48]

Justification. The beginning point for theological and religious discussion regarding charismatic renewal is obviously and quite naturally baptism with the Holy Spirit and the consequent expression of the charismata. Since religious experience is the traditional neuralgic point for Lutheran theology, it is only natural for Lutheran theological discussions also to begin with these subjects. But what about the central doctrine of the Lutheran tradition: justification by grace alone? We have already referred to the apologetic purpose and situational character that typifies much of the literature of Lutheran charismatics. If we bear this in mind we should not be surprised that a cursory review of their literature does not find many chapters devoted to the subject of justification; after all, their major concern is not that of writing a systematic theology. Once more, we also recall Christenson's point that the fundamental perception of the charismatic renewal is the experience of doctrine, not statements about it. Thus, where we are unable to find specific expositions of the doctrine of justification, we shall deduce the Lutheran charismatic position from their writings. This process also will be used in the discussion of other doctrines where necessary.

---

[45]Ibid., 26f., 54-58.

[46]For example, Bittlinger, *Gifts and Ministries*, and *Im Kraftfeld des Heiligen Geistes* (Marburg an der Lahn: Edel, 1971[4]) and essays in *Die Bedeutung der Gnadengaben für die Gemeinde Jesu Christi* (Marburg an der Lahn: Edel, 1964).

[47]Bittlinger, *Gifts and Ministries*, 20.

[48]Cf. Bittlinger, *Im Kraftfeld des Heiligen Geistes*, 90ff.

A reading of Larry Christenson's major writings nowhere reveals a discussion of the theological motif of justification aside from a brief rejection of self-justification in connection with a reflection about the parable of the good Samaritan. This is, in spite of the caveats mentioned above, remarkable in light of Christenson's self-conscious efforts to relate charismatic renewal to Lutheran life and thought. Yet there are in these writings clues to his understanding of justification. These clues are in his emphasis upon the priority of God's activity in empowering the Christian to live more effectively and fruitfully as a witness to the gospel. However, Christenson tends to communicate double messages. At the same time that he emphasizes the priority of God's action—baptism with the Holy Spirit is not "my own decision"—there is the expression of the gospel in terms of a lifestyle to be imitated rather than the gift of God's forgiveness and love. When he says the gospel lifestyle is a human impossibility, he nevertheless speaks of the gospel not in traditional Lutheran terms as the forgiveness of sins but as "a quality and style of life."[49] His concern is with sanctification not justification. The seeking for fullness of the Holy Spirit ". . . is not with a view to becoming a Christian, but to receiving power to live the Christian life more effectively and fruitfully. . . ."[50] The one clear reference to forgiveness and acquittal of sins is in his courtroom analogy of the Christian's call to be a witness to Christ's substitutionary atonement.[51] The overriding concern for sanctification dissolves the dialectical tension of such classic Lutheran motifs as the Christian being simultaneously sinner and righteous, and living under both law and gospel. I have found only one oblique reference to the *simul* theme: "Every Christian who is a witness also finds himself, at times, in the role of the Accused.[52] There is also no development or utilization of the classic Lutheran law-gospel dialectic which is related to Luther's understanding of justification. Our purpose at this point is not to begin a critique of Christenson's theological position but rather to illustrate that his orientation is such that he does not explicitly articulate a theological position on the doctrine of justification.

---

[49]Cf. the works already cited. The reference to self-justification is in his *SAJS*, 88; the quotation, 96.

[50]*CRAL*, 48.

[51]*ST*, 68. Cf. also his passing reference to the Christus Victor motif in *SAJS*, 41.

[52]*ST*, 66.

Jungkuntz, however, explicitly refers to justification by quoting the Formula of Concord statement on the centrality of justification by faith to which Lutheran charismatics "wish in more than a merely formal sense to be faithful."[53] Although Jungkuntz too is concerned with sanctification, he wants to overcome charges of synergism by distinguishing justification and sanctification.

> Any talk about "conditions" (for baptism in the Holy Spirit) must be preceded by talk about the distinction between justification and sanctification. . . . In the Lutheran Confessions justification is a "condition" for the logically subsequent sanctification of the believers through the Holy Spirit, but it is a "condition" which no human being can fulfil. It is a "condition" which God himself fulfils in us when through the Gospel in Word and sacraments his Holy Spirit works justifying faith within us. . . . Whereas in the miracle of his justification a person is involved in a manner which can be described as "purely passive" (FC SD III, 8-11—Tappert, 540-41), in the miracle of his sanctification a person is involved in a manner which the Confessions can designate as being a kind of "cooperation. . . ." (FC SD II, 65-66—Tappert, 534).[54]

Throughout his writings Jungkuntz strives to maintain an emphasis upon justification in its confessional expression and in relation to the motif of the theology of the cross and a Confessional Christology.[55] On the latter point, he warns charismatics against being misled into an adoptionist Christology that presents Jesus as the example we are to follow.[56]

In turning to the writings of Bittlinger after those of Christenson and Jungkuntz there is the distinct awareness that Bittlinger does not appear to feel their pressure to "prove" that "Lutheran" and "charismatic" are not mutually exclusive. This may, of course, only reflect personal differences but it is probably also related to national church contexts. While the North American context has tended to place charismatic Lutherans on the defensive, Bittlinger was for some time supported by the church in

---

[53]Jungkuntz,"A Response," 9; cf. T. Tappert, The Book of Concord (Philadelphia: Muhlenberg Press, 1959) FC SD III, 6; p.540. Cf. also Jungkuntz, A Lutheran Charismatic Cathechism, para. 61, p.15.

[54]Theodore Jungkuntz, "Conditions?" LCRN 4/6 (June 1978): 1. Cf. also, Jungkuntz, "Epicurianism and Sanctification: The Bondage and the Freedom of the Will," LCRN, Pastoral Edition, n.d. (1979?), and "Charismatic Worship: Challenge or Challenged?" 5-6.

[55]Cf. for example, Theodore Jungkuntz, "Secularization Theology, Charismatic Renewal, and Luther's Theology of the Cross," Concordia Theological Monthly 42/1 (1971): 5-24.

[56]Jungkuntz,"A 'How To Do It' Manual on Miracles," 1.

ecumenical, charismatic work as director of the Ecumenical Academy at the "Lebenszentrum für die Einheit der Christen Schloß Craheim." Thus while his writings reflect an evangelical, Lutheran theological orientation, they are not at all characterized by self-conscious appeals to Luther, the Lutheran Confessions, and Lutheran theologians. His apologetic endeavors focus on clarifying and interpreting the charismatic renewal rather than arguing its compatibility with Lutheran tradition. Because his work is more exegetical than doctrinal we do not easily find sections explicitly devoted to particular theological motifs such as justification and Christology.

In his *Gifts and Ministries* which includes chapters from some of his other books (for example, *Im Kraftfeld des Heiligen Geistes*) he echoes Luther when he describes salvation in terms of being freed to be human. "To be a slave of Christ means to be independent of everything that would induce us to be inconsistent with the will of Jesus. It does not mean, however, to be under a forced lordship to Christ. We have been freed to our essential humanity, to our real function, by Christ."[57] In general, as indicated by the titles of his books, Bittlinger is concerned to exegete the biblical passages concerning the charismata and their relationship to discipleship and ministry. This, in turn, calls our attention to a theme which we have encountered throughout our survey of charismatic Lutheran literature: sanctification.

Sanctification. When we discussed Luther's theology earlier, we noted that its orientation was toward a theology of testament in distinction from a theology of covenant. Charismatic Lutheran theology tends to have the opposite orientation; it is a covenant-type theology. While not explicitly spelled out, this orientation is expressed through the charismatic emphasis upon baptism with (or in) the Holy Spirit and the consequent growth in regeneration or sanctification. The many early critical responses by non-charismatics to the charismatic emphasis upon personal sanctification have somewhat tempered the charismatic expressions of regenerated life in the Spirit but not changed its perspective. Christenson notes this when he says, "The initial emphasis on personal spiritual awakening indicated that the charismatic movement has a clear-cut affinity for evangelical theology. Some aspects of the movement,

---

[57]Bittlinger, *Gifts and Ministries*, 111; cf. also 18.

such as the 'Jesus People,' have even been dubbed a revival of fundamentalist Christianity (with a touch of frontier revivalism)."[58]

A primary means to personal sanctification is speaking in tongues. The results may range from assurance of salvation to cessation of smoking. "The edification which one experiences through the exercise of speaking in tongues is on a highly individual basis. Your own program of sanctification is tailor-made by the Holy Spirit according to your individual need, and according to the place He is preparing you for in the Body of Christ."[59] Prayer for "fullness or release of the Holy Spirit in one's life" is a seeking for "power to live the Christian life more effectively and fruitfully."[60]

The more effective and fruitful life is a life patterned upon Jesus which not only gives guidance in the details of life but also separates one from the world. " 'He's (Jesus) just a part of everything we do. The whole family life revolves around Him—where He wants us to go on vacation, what He wants us to give to the Church, what He thinks about Jerry switching from paper route to football. Just everything. It's wonderful.' "[61] Separation from the world is the recognition of the impending destruction of the world and that discipleship to Jesus means commitment to spiritual warfare. This is related not only to individual sanctification but also to social ethics and will be further discussed below.[62]

Renewal is what the charismatic movement understands itself to be about. As we have already seen, the term "renewal" not only appears frequently in the charismatic Lutheran literature but also is incorporated in the title of their journals. Jungkuntz interprets "authentic spiritual renewal in the church" in light of the first of Luther's Ninety-Five Theses—the entire life of believers is to be one of repentance.[63] The Christian is to grow in the manifestation of the sanctification given by his baptismal faith until it is completed in his own death and resurrection. Speaking in tongues is an optional rather than necessary expression of

---

[58]*SAJS*, 13.

[59]*ST*, 78-79.

[60]*CRAL*, 48.

[61]*ST*, 59.

[62]Cf. *SAJS*, 70ff.

[63]Jungkuntz, "A Response," 3.

sanctification "in the sense that not every Christian manifests the same gifts. But the option should lie more with God than with man."

> The Reformers' answer (to the question of whether good works are necessary or optional) might also serve as a pattern for responding to the question of the relationship of the charismatic gifts to sanctification: they are never optional but neither are they as independent entities necessary for sanctification which occurs only by faith. They are necessary for the empirical expression of sanctification only because of and in keeping with God's command and promise.[64]

Thus the Christian should pray for the charismatic gifts and cooperate in the Spirit-wrought manifestation of sanctification in our lives. Mortal sins, those sins that "rule in those areas of our life over which we are by God's Spirit able to have control," cannot coexist with manifestations of the Holy Spirit. Appealing to the Formula of Concord, Jungkuntz concludes that there are conditions "which stand as prerequisites for the on-going baptism or filling with the Holy Spirit (Eph. 5:18), but these 'conditions' are not to be met as 'works of the law' but as fruit of the 'hearing with faith' (Gal. 3:1-5)."[65] It is in this context that Jungkuntz advocates the "third use of the law" which he argues is a dimension of charismatic renewal and the Lutheran Confessions.[66]

Bittlinger presents a more nuanced view when, in discussing the statement that God is love, he says,

> Love never demands more than it gives. Love does not expect perfection from imperfect beings, but it educates them (Jungkuntz's third use of the law). The total life of the Christian is growth. That is why God loves imperfect people. To grow means nothing other than to let oneself be loved by God, for God's love transforms. If someone wants to exert himself in bringing about his own perfection, he does not need God's love and consequently he does not experience it either. God remains "severe" for him.[67]

There is concurrence among the above Lutheran charismatic writers that tongues and the charismata serve not only to edify the individual but also to build up the body of Christ, the church. Under the subject of charismatic Lutheran ecclesiology, we shall also include their understanding of Word and sacraments.

---

[64]Ibid., 10, cf. also 11.

[65]Jungkuntz, "Conditions?" 1f. Cf. also, "Epicurism and Sanctification: The Bondage and the Freedom of the Will," *LCRN*, Pastoral Edition, n.d. (1979?).

[66]Theodore Jungkuntz, "Response to Dr. Lazareth," *The Cresset*. Occasional Paper 3 (1978) 57-59. Cf. also his "Ethics in a Relativizing Society," 13, 15.

[67]Bittlinger, *Gifts and Ministries*, 119. Cf. also *Glossolalia*, 26-27, 55-56.

Ecclesiology. In conformity with Article VII of the Augsburg Confessions, Lutherans have traditionally identified the church as "the assembly of all believers among whom the Gospel is preached in its purity and the holy sacraments are administered according to the Gospel." In charismatic literature there appears to be a third "mark" of the church alongside Word and sacraments. This is church discipline. Christenson rhetorically asks whether the Lutheran church is being challenged to remember her task of "continual self-reformation." It is worth quoting Christenson at length on this topic.

> The habits and practices of the church are brought under scrutiny by any renewal movement. Is the church ready to receive this kind of scrutiny from the charismatic movement?
>
> In the charismatic movement a fairly widespread emphasis on order and authority has emerged. . . . Charismatics see personal experience and behaviour as subject to structures of authority.
>
> This has come about through a serious examination of family and church order. Generally speaking, hierarchical as opposed to egalitarian or democratic models have prevailed. Charismatics speak easily and without embarrassment of father-led families, elder-led communities.
>
> Charismatics are doing more than theorizing about the structure of Christian community. They are putting their insights to hard tests of practice. They are shaping their understanding of words like "authority," "headship," "responsibility," "obedience," and "freedom" in the context of radically committed relationships.[68]

Motivated by love, the charismata are manifested within the Christian community as specific forms of ministry. The favorite image here is that of a body with different members each functioning for the purpose and goal of the body as a whole. The charismata are, therefore, "appointed ministries (which are to) be desired, sought after, prayed for, and received *in the congregations.* The Body of Christ, in its local expression, is weakened and crippled to the extent that any one of these ministries becomes atrophied. Conversely, the Body functions in power and with truly spiritual results to the extent that all of these ministries are brought into coordinated action." When this occurs the Christian community develops a lifestyle that attracts others. "Over the long run, the greatest service which the church can perform in and for the world is to *be* that house-hold of faith which, by its example, demonstrates a better way of life."[69]

---

[68]*CRAL*, 133.

[69]*ST*, 124, cf. 110-24; *SAJS*, 83f.

We have referred above to Jungkuntz's advocacy of the third use of the law. However, apart from an oblique reference to the connection of church discipline to the visibility of the church,[70] I have not found that he develops this into a mark of the church. Nor have I found this dimension specifically discussed in the writings of Bittlinger. The charismatic emphasis upon sanctification, though, is not without import on its ecclesiology and we shall have the opportunity to return to this when we discuss the popular expressions of Lutheran charismatic renewal.

In discussing baptism in the Holy Spirit, we have touched on the traditional Lutheran understanding of Word and sacrament. Now we have the opportunity to explore further the charismatic Lutheran view of these traditional marks of the church.

Sensitive to the fears that the charismatic movement may be a modern-day echo of the sixteenth-century enthusiasts' separation of Word and Spirit, Christenson says:

> The enthusiasts were ready to set Scripture aside in favor of their own revelations. This finds no parallel in the charismatic renewal, where the Bible functions as the fountain, rule and norm for faith and life. If anything, charismatics may be criticized for a too-literalistic reading of the Bible. But there is no voice in the renewal proposing that Scripture be set to the side in favor of direct (or further) revelations of the Spirit. Charismatics would agree wholeheartedly with Luther that the Spirit has tied himself to the external Word.[71]

Nevertheless, charismatic renewal seeks to recover for the church its heritage of "prophecy, vision, and spontaneous revelation," the purpose of which is to further our obedience to God and our experience of God's power.[72] Engelsviken corroborates this when he discusses the charismatic perspective that Scripture is not merely an authoritative norm for Christian doctrine but provides examples and patterns for Christian praxis. It is primarily in the area of practice that the gap is seen between the primitive church and today's church. This in turn motivates the restorationist motif in charismatic theology.

> Closely associated with the awareness of the gap between the richness of the operation of the Spirit in the theory and practice of the normative Scriptures and in today's church, is the *motif of a needed restoration or reformation.* Biblical doctrine and biblical experience of the various aspects of the Spirit's

---

[70]Theodore Jungkuntz, "Incarnational and/or Spiritual," *LCRN* 3/10 (October 1977): 2.

[71]*CRAL*, 112.

[72]Ibid., 106, 104.

work should be restored in the church today. This motif is a basic incentive in the Charismatic Movement shared by all our authors.[73]

The suspicion of "enthusiasm" regarding charismatic renewal probably arises from the denigration of theological studies, especially historical criticism, which runs through much of the renewal literature. One could suggest, along with Christenson, that this reflects "literalism" rather than renewal. Yet the question, in the context of the whole movement, remains and is illustrated by the claim that "The charismatic renewal has recalled her church to more spontaneous modes of revelation, a wholesome complement to the emphasis on purely rational processes and conclusions."[74] At best there is the implication that the experience of speaking in tongues is verification of the Word.[75] The difficulty here is not only that of elevating experience over promise but also the fact that tongues is not a uniquely Christian phenomena.[76]

Jungkuntz is less ambiguous on this issue when he argues that religious experience (or Spirit-baptism) "must be an event *following* faith rather than establishing it." It is not experience but rather God's word of promise that is the basis for faith. This Word of God comes to the person from outside him and therefore the experience of Spirit-baptism derives its content and meaning from God's Word.[77] Engelsviken's analysis of the charismatic movement in Norway basically agrees with the position of Jungkuntz. God's action in Christian initiation or in the "gospel of ministry" is emphasized. However, persons themselves are actively encouraged to seek the charismatic experience. Expectation and faith are created by preaching and reception of the fullness of the Spirit is prepared by confession of sin. "The actual seeking of the experience takes place in *specific prayer* for the Holy Spirit and in *communal intercession* with laying on of hands. Although nothing is asserted with regard to any specific gift as evidence of the fullness of the Spirit for ministry, it is

---

[73]Engelsviken, *The Gift of the Spirit*, 254.

[74]*CRAL*, 105.

[75]*ST*, 77.

[76]Cf. for example, David Christie-Murray, *Voices from the Gods: Speaking with Tongues* (London: Routledge and Kegan Paul, 1978) 4, 13. Jungkuntz expresses a similar view, cf. "A Response to Scott H. Hendrix's 'Charismatic Renewal' " 56-57.

[77]Jungkuntz, "Secularization Theology, Charismatic Renewal, and Luther's Theology of the Cross," 13, 20, 18, 21. Cf. also *A Lutheran Charismatic Catechism*, 10.

expected that the experience that follows should be conscious and have tangible, observable results. An experiential result of the prayer for the Spirit is expected which easily may be construed as evidence of the Spirit."[78]

In the writings of Bittlinger there is little or no direct treatment of the problematic of the Word-Spirit relationship. Still, many of his writings are concerned with exegesis of biblical texts in light of charismatic experience and these studies manifest exegetical skill and awareness of contemporary biblical scholarship. He makes clear that teaching as a charisma is the manifesting of the Spirit and not one's own wisdom. In terms of content, teaching encompasses the entire area of dogmatics and ethics, that is, everything concerning Christian belief and life. "That teaching is a gift of the Spirit means that it can never be rigidly fixed in dogma but rather is given new for every situation. The Spirit is dynamic and does not allow himself to be kept in any manner, not even in a textbook of dogmatics or ethics."[79]

In terms of a charismatic theology of sacraments, the sensitive issue for non-charismatic Lutherans is, of course, the sacrament of baptism. We have already discussed this above and noted that for the selected charismatic Lutheran theologians we are discussing, there is a sensitivity to the problems inherent in importing classical Pentecostal terminology into charismatic Lutheran theology. Insofar as phrases such as "Baptism in the Spirit," "Spirit-baptism," are used there is the concern that baptism as sacrament has been replaced or displaced by subjective religious experience. It is fair to say that Christenson, Jungkuntz, and Bittlinger hold to the Lutheran tradition of infant baptism as a sacrament. Again, as we have also noted earlier, the main orientation of charismatic Lutheran theology is experiential rather than doctrinal. "There is a sound biblical theology for the baptism with the Holy Spirit. But the baptism with the Holy Spirit is not a theology to be discussed and analysed. It is an experience one enters into."[80]

Jungkuntz agrees that "baptism in the Holy Spirit" is not an event " 'beyond' sacramental baptism in the sense of 'separate from,' but as an event 'within' sacramental baptism and yet an event to be 'distinguished'

---

[78]Engelsviken, *The Gift of the Spirit*, 257.

[79]Bittlinger, *Im Kraftfeld des Heiligen Geistes*, 122.

[80]*ST*, 40. Cf. also, *CRAL*, 47.

from its initial expression with water." In other words, baptism in the Holy Spirit is the release of the benefits of sacramental baptism.[81] Bittlinger emphasizes the same point: "What God has given in baptism must be *actualized* in the life of the individual."[82]

What is interesting is the linking of the sacrament of baptism with confirmation. This is most clearly set forth by Jungkuntz. He claims that the rite of confirmation has degenerated in many Lutheran congregations to the point that it contributes "toward making 'void the word of God' (Matt. 15:1-9)." He then argues that ". . . both Holy Scripture and the Lutheran Confessions urge upon us a 'confirmation' which consists not in an ecclesiastical rite as such but in the continuing release of the 'gifts' and 'fruit' of the Holy Spirit in one's own personal experience. . . ." "Lutherans especially are ripe for a 'confirmation' of this sort. They are already 'children of God,' but few of them see themselves as bold 'soldiers of Christ.' Looked at in terms of the four great festivals of the Church— Christmas, Good Friday/Easter, Ascension, and Pentecost—they do fairly well as sacramentally appropriating the historical realities signalled by the first three festivals. . . . But how have Lutherans related to Pentecost? . . . By their general failure to 'thirst' for the release of the Holy Spirit in their lives . . ., they have all but refused to respond to the call to enlist in God's army. . . ."[83]

The historical-theological and ecumenical implications of this development lie in the similarities of the charismatic relationship of baptism and confirmation to Roman Catholic doctrines and also to the Wesleyan holiness tradition which in turn may have some roots in Müntzer.[84] The following words may be applicable, *mutatis mutandis,* to charismatic Lutheran theology:

> This similarity between the Roman Catholic doctrines of baptism and confirmation and the Wesleyan doctrines of conversion and entire sanctification has gone largely unnoticed. Yet it can be enlightening to those in the Wesleyan tradition to examine the common elements in their otherwise rather divergent

---

[81]Jungkuntz, "A Response," 4.

[82]Bittlinger, "Baptized in Water and in Spirit," 11.

[83]Jungkuntz, "Pray the Lord of the Harvest," *LCRN* 5/8 (1979): 1f. Cf. also Bittlinger, "Baptized in Water and in Spirit," 15, and *CRAL*, 48ff.

[84]Cf. Lawrence W. Wood, *Pentecostal Grace* (Wilmore KY: Asbury Publishing Co., 1980) especially ch. 7: "The Wesleyan Doctrine of Christian Perfection as a Reinterpretation of the Roman Catholic and Anglican Rite of Confirmation," and Rupp, *Patterns of Reformation* (Philadelphia: Fortress Press, 1969) 271-72.

traditions, especially since such a study could enhance one's own understanding of the meaning of the baptism with the Spirit in the light of a more comprehensive doctrine of the Church as an organism. . . .[85]

Since the Lutheran charismatic renewal in general has not developed particular perspectives on the Eucharist, we may conclude this section on ecclesiology with a discussion of their view of office and ministry. The literature we have been reviewing exhibits a juxtaposition of universality and particularity or, in more traditional terms, the priesthood of all believers and an ecclesial hierarchy. In this respect it seems to parallel Pietism.

On the one hand, all three authors emphasize that the charismata are gifts equally available to all Christians. "*Who* is to receive the Holy Spirit? Every single believer! The Holy Spirit is not a special gift for a small group of privileged Christians. He is for every single believer." At the same time, reception of the Holy Spirit is a prerequisite to being a witness. The gifts of the charismata are gifts for ministry in the Body of Christ. Thus each member is to contribute "his unique ministry toward the upbuilding and work of the Body."[86]

On the other hand, charismatic Lutherans are strongly minister- and leader-oriented. "Charismatics see personal experience and behaviour as subject to structures of authority. This has come about through a serious examination of family and church order."[87] This is reflected in the charismatic position regarding the role of women. The Genesis description of the husband-wife relationship is ". . . paradigmatic for a headship pattern which Scripture with consistency and catholicity extends to men-women relationships in the entire community—not that all women are automatically to be subordinate to all men, but that every woman is to be subordinate to some man, be he her husband, her father, or some

---

[85]Wood, *Pentecostal Grace*, 241. Cf. also Jungkuntz, "Secularization Theology, Charismatic Renewal, and Luther's Theology of the Cross," 16f.; *A Lutheran Charismatic Catechism*, 6ff.

[86]*ST*, 63, 62, 123. Insofar as reception of the Holy Spirit is an addition to salvation it could appear that this is a return of donatism.

[87]*CRAL*, 133f. Cf. also Jorstad, *Bold in the Spirit: Lutheran Charismatic Renewal in America Today* (Minneapolis: Augsburg Publishing House, 1974) 55; and Christenson, *The Christian Family* (Minneapolis: Bethany Fellowship, 1971); Larry and Nordis Christenson, *The Christian Couple.*

surrogate such as her elder or pastor."[88] Although I am not aware of Bittlinger's position regarding women, his views on authority and ministry are similar to those of Christenson and Jungkuntz.

Social Ethics. There is a growing awareness among the leadership of the charismatic renewal that revitalized faith has social as well as personal implications. "While the charismatic movement has underscored the central importance of the personal in Christianity, it has more lately also been moved by a concern for the social."[89] So far the only direct literary expression of this is Larry Christenson's small book, *Social Action Jesus Style*. Because this is a sustained effort to relate charismatic renewal to the development of a Christian social ethic, we shall review the book at length.

From Christenson's point of view charismatic renewal brings not merely a new dimension but a fundamental reorientation to social action. This is set forth by analyzing the problem of the contemporary church's orientation to social action and then the presentation of the solution from the charismatic perspective.

The problem is that the contemporary non-charismatic church echoes the world; it is bound to the status quo and thereby is a kind of culture-religion. This status quo is "shaped by the political and social doctrine of liberalism."

> Even a cursory reading of religious publications reveals a distinct tendency on the part of church officialdom to parrot the pronouncements and programs of the liberal status quo, the secular establishment. . . .
>
> A charismatic approach to social action seeks to remain free of entanglement with a secular status quo, whether conservative or liberal. It recognizes the sovereignty of the Spirit. . . .[90]

The common thread running through contemporary social concern "is summed up in the central dogma of contemporary social theology: *We must change the Structures of Society.*" Because "a great many Christians today do not believe in or reckon upon the genuine guidance of the Holy

---

[88]Jungkuntz, "The Question of the Ordination of Women," *The Cresset*, special issue of 1978-1979 (December-January) 2. Cf. also Jungkuntz, "Ethics in a Relativizing Society," *Confession and Congregation*, 14; and Quebedeaux, *The New Charismatics*, 109f.

[89]*SAJS*, 13f.

[90]*SAJS*, 30-32.

Spirit" they are limited "to a narrow list of issues, dictated by the secular establishment" and therefore are insensitive "to those concerns which the Lord Himself sets before His Church."[91]

The solution is disentanglement from the status quo, recognition of the world's bondage to Satan and conformity to the "battle strategy" of the New Testament. This battle strategy has three themes: "Spiritual Warfare," "Separation from the World," and "The Household of Faith." We shall describe each theme in order. Since our enemy is the world and Satan, "a charismatic approach to social issues must look beyond the immediate or seemingly obvious solution to a problem. . . . This means dealing not only with the need that meets our eye, but also with the enemy whom we do not see with our eyes—dealing with him by using 'the weapons of our warfare.' " These weapons are those listed by Paul in Ephesians 6:10-18 and the charismata. When the real enemy, that is, Satan not injustice, is recognized, "an emphasis on *spiritual gifts* gains added significance. Such gifts as wisdom, knowledge, healing, miracle, and discernment of the spirits hold out the potential for dealing with problems in a way that goes beyond traditional social activism. Why settle merely for political or economic action if divine power is available for dealing with a problem?"

> The ways of the world and of Satan seem attractively logical. They approach the problem of injustice and suffering head on, with sound moral imperatives. But they conveniently avoid any reference to the real cause which lies behind the injustice and suffering. The power of the Evil One. And the law has ever been his ally.

It is in this context that we are to imitate Jesus and follow in his steps.[92] Engelsviken affirms this when he says, "For all the theologies of the Charismatic experience the ministry of Jesus in the power of the Spirit represents an *ideal*, a *pattern* and a challenge. Jesus exhibits in his life the possibilities of a Spirit-filled life. He is an example to *follow*."[93] This was further emphasized by the lectures given at the International Lutheran Renewal Leaders' Conference.

To follow Jesus is to separate from the world. "In order to help the world *in the way that Jesus wants the world to be helped*, the church must maintain a certain aloofness from the world."

---

[91]*SAJS*, 39, 36, 34.

[92]*SAJS*, 31, 51, 39f., 68f., 53, 67, 59ff.

[93]Engelsviken, *The Gift of the Spirit*, 262.

> To expend great efforts at reforming or improving the structures of society would be like Noah leaving the building of the ark to help some of his neighbours put in the spring planting—a poor stewardship of one's time.

"The Achilles heel of modern social theology" is its concern for human material and social needs, and its fundamental error of involvement with one's fellowman—*Mitmenschlichkeit*.[94]

The charismatic understanding of separation from the world resembles that of the sixteenth-century Anabaptists. "The church calls people to be delivered from slavery to the world-system, and to enter the freedom and security of a new community, God's people, the church. The church, as a separated community, is meant to be God's example in and to the world—a people who have heard of the destruction which is to come, and have believed in the Savior who has been offered."[95]

This separated community is the household of faith. Its lifestyle is meant to attract those outside it. But in order to attract others, the church must direct its attention inward not outward. Its primary ministry is to its members in order to create an attractive climate "for the acceptance of the Gospel." "A ministry of social action to the world will always remain a coordinate task of the church. Over the long run the greatest service which the church can perform in and for the world is to *be* that household of faith which, by its example, demonstrates a better way of life."[96]

For the charismatic renewal this demonstration of a better way of life is central to its approach to social action.

> If an encounter does not permit of an evangelistic thrust, it must be questioned. This is a control principle necessitated by the priority we assign to evangelism. If we cannot sound the evangelistic note relatively toward the beginning of the operation, then we had better recheck our signals.

The charismatic movement orientates people "not toward a cause, but toward community." Here, in its concern for the renewal of society by means of renewal of the individual, there seems to be a marked echo of both the Anabaptist and Pietist conceptions of Christian responsibility.

> A charismatic approach to social action also looks for the renewal of society. But it does not expect this to come about simply through reforming the structures.

---

[94]*SAJS*, 70, 72, 75, 74.

[95]*SAJS*, 76.

[96]*SAJS*, 83f., 99-100.

New structures by themselves tend to exchange one set of problems for another.
. . . More than new structures, the world needs new people.[97]

Christenson has provided the most comprehensive reflection on the charismatic renewal and social ethics. Following our previous pattern we shall now look at this theme in the writings of Jungkuntz and then Bittlinger. We have already referred to Jungkuntz's argument for the legitimacy of the third use of the law in Lutheran theology. While his emphasis upon the law as instruction in sanctification is certainly controversial within Lutheran perspectives, it at least does not surrender the law to Satan as Christenson infers. Jungkuntz directs his argument against what he sees as the relativizing antinomianism in contemporary culture. The law and order of creation express the immutable will of God. In his essay, "Ethics in a Relativizing Society," he applies this orientation to the contemporary issues of women's liberation and gay liberation.

God's revelation in creation is testimony to the functional (not ontological) subordination of women to men. "The basic biological fact in the relationship between husband and wife is that the husband sends and his wife receives. And that a male should be successfully raped by a female is quite unthinkable. The penis represents the male's natural role of sending and directing within the male-female relationship; the vagina represents the female's natural role of submitting and receiving within the relationship." The exploitation of either party by tyranny (male) or rebellion (female) mocks God and contributes to the chaos of contemporary family life. Denial of the immutable role-relationship between the sexes by women's liberation is only a step away from denying it in regard to homosexuality as well.[98]

A review of many of Jungkuntz's other writings does not indicate a specific concern for social ethics. Once again, we may remind ourselves that like many charismatic theologians Jungkuntz wants to respond to the critiques directed to charismatic experience and therefore has not yet directed his attention to the implications of charismatic renewal for social ethics. Thus it is not an attempt to argue from silence but rather a descriptive statement when we say that Jungkuntz's expressed ethical concerns revolve around personal sanctification and discipleship. The same description may be given of Bittlinger's writings, although there is

---

[97]*SAJS*, 86, 105.

[98]Jungkuntz, "Ethics in a Relativizing Society," 14-15.

more explicit discussion of the charismata in terms of upbuilding the Christian community and service to others.

Up to this point we have limited our discussion of Lutheran charismatic theology to the writings of Christenson, Jungkuntz, and Bittlinger. Without doubt these men are among the leading theologians of the charismatic renewal movement. We have concentrated upon these leading Lutheran charismatics because we want to exercise caution in comparing the charismatic renewal and Lutheran tradition so that we are not comparing one movement at its worst with another at its best. But what about more popular or occasional expressions by charismatic Lutherans? We conclude this section on charismatic Lutheran theology by surveying a small portion of the immense literature that has grown out of the Lutheran participation in charismatic renewal.

Since much of this literature is more in the form of testimonial than theological reflection, the experiential aspect is always in the forefront. What is immediately striking is the similarity of the description of this experience by charismatics to the expressions used in the sixteenth-century and Pietist renewal movements. For lack of a good descriptive term, one may call this an "adverbial Christianity" or "Christianity with a plus." Faith becomes "living faith," "sacramental baptism is supplemented by baptism with the Spirit, etc." " 'I have always been happy in my faith. I have always loved my Lord from my heart. But now it's so all "more so." ' " Frequently this "faith with a plus" experience is seen in contrast to a previous life of "dead faith." Pastors frequently describe this in terms of being "burned out." For example, " 'How could a man think he was passing out the bread of life every Sunday and still remain so utterly hungry himself? I was empty, and I knew it.' "[99] "I was like a fountain gone dry." "In my days of spiritual leanness I used to plead with God to have mercy upon me. . . . But when the Holy Spirit flooded my soul with love, I felt it."[100] These examples could be multiplied many times over but

---

[99]LC-MS pastors, quoted by Jorstad, *Bold in the Spirit*, 42, 46. A charismatic leader from Norway: ". . . this is not a case of more than Jesus, but more of Jesus"; Hans J. Frøen, "What is the Baptism in the Holy Spirit?" in Norris Wogen, ed., *Jesus, Where Are You Taking Us?* Messages from the First International Lutheran Conference on the Holy Spirit (Carol Stream IL: Creation House, 1973) 113, 132, 128.

[100]Rodney Lensch, *My Personal Pentecost* (Kirkwood MO: Impact Books, 1972) 4, 20. The author resigned from the LC-MS ministry and began his own renewal ministry. For an ALC military chaplain's experience see William G. Olson, *The Charismatic Church* (Minneapolis: Bethany Fellowship, 1974).

it is not necessary to belabor the point that theological analysis of these testimonials will be limited mainly to induction. The difficulty is that, as Fr. McDonnell puts it, "there is in circulation within the renewal along-side of good material a sea of charismatic-Pentecostal literature which is enthusiastic theological fluff."[101] Example: "Wonder Bread Builds Strong Bodies Seven Ways." In this essay the acrostic RED FISH is constructed from "seven slices of bread out of a loaf of Wonder Bread to build an appetizing sandwich which a lost world needs."

Repentance	=	the joy of the Lord in the forgiveness of sins.
Electricity	=	praise and worship of God.
Discipleship	=	they loved not their lives to the end.
Fellowship	=	how they loved one another.
Internal Combustion Engine	=	the power of Jesus Christ through the Holy Ghost, to build up the Body of Christ.
Submission to Authority	=	submitting to one another.
Humble Service	=	serving one another in love.

We have pictured each of the above truths as a slice in a delicious seven-sliced sandwich. The Church is becoming the "Bread" for the world. As Head of the Church, Christ Jesus truly is the "Wonder Bread" building a strong Body seven ways.[102]

The forms of expression are much closer to American Pentecostalism than traditional Lutheran formulations and tend to raise the question of which theology they communicate. It is for this reason that our analysis of Lutheran charismatic theology has focused on the writings of leaders who are self-consciously concerned about the theological implications of charismatic renewal. Not surprisingly our three charismatic theologians vary in terms of their orientation in ways which probably reflect their backgrounds and roles. Christenson as a highly involved international

---

[101]Kilian McDonnell, "Towards a Critique of the Churches and the Charismatic Renewal," *One in Christ* 16/4 (1980): 329-37, 337.

[102]By Delbert Rossin (a LC-MS pastor) in *LCRN* 1/5 (1975). Other examples: "the door principle" in Donald Pfotenhauer, "The Shepherd, the Door and the Sheep," *LCRN* 1/3 (1975); "the baseball diamond test" with Jesus on home plate in Jungkuntz, "Testing the Spirit of the Charismatic Renewal," *LCRN* 1/7 (1975).

leader[103] as well as parish pastor has a more apologetic orientation; Jungkuntz, a professor of theology nourished on LC-MS confessionalism, is concerned to relate charismatic renewal to Lutheran confessional theology; and Bittlinger, now a consultant to the WCC on charismatic renewal, takes an exegetical approach in many of his writings. One should not expect any more theological uniformity among charismatic theologians than non-charismatic theologians. Certainly there is consensus on the centrality of baptism in the Spirit and the charismata, but individual expression of these and related concerns varies from person to person. The major difficulty, as we have repeatedly pointed out, in describing Lutheran charismatic theology is that theology is not the primary concern of the leaders of the renewal. This experiential over theological orientation in itself raises questions to and for the Lutheran tradition. We are now ready to explore more systematically comparisons and contrasts between charismatic renewal and Lutheran tradition.

CHARISMATIC MOVEMENTS AND LUTHERAN TRADITION: COMPARISONS AND CONTRASTS

The charismatic movement within the Lutheran churches has yet to develop any distinct, independent theology. This is a consequence of their essentially practical orientation which places experience over doctrine.[104] As we have seen, charismatic renewal, like Pietism, values the testimonial over systematic theology. In its best sense there is an evocation of Luther's emphasis upon the priority of the preached Word and the recognition that faith comes by hearing. There may also be present in this charismatic orientation a groping for an alternative theological method to the traditional literary forms. Walter Hollenweger suggests that this "oral theology" has ecumenical and intercultural significance.

> Western Christianity and Judaism are religions of the book. We are introduced to our tradition by reading records of the past. It is strange for us to learn that

---

[103]"Recently, four US leaders have been released into broadened ministries. Pastors Larry Christenson, Don Pfotenhauer, Morris Vaagenes and Delbert Rossin have been granted full or partial release from parish responsibilities by their respective churches to fulfill apostolic roles in the development of renewal leadership." *Lutheran Renewal International* 1/2 (1980): 20.

[104]Cf. Ziemer, "In und neben der Kirche. Charismatisch Bewegung der DDR,"*Zeichen der Zeit* 6 (1979): 222; and "Kirche und charismatische Erneuerung," 14.

there are other ways of recording and passing on the values of the past. Yet there are such other ways. . . . In these pre-literate or post-literate cultures (Hollenweger refers to African independent churches, American black churches, Latin American Pentecostal churches) the medium of communication is, just as in biblical times, not the definition but the description, not the statement but the story, not the doctrine but the testimony, not the book but the parable, not a systematic theology but a song, not the treatise but the television program, not the articulation of concepts but the celebration of banquets.[105]

This is very discomfiting to theologians tied to a literary media. At best we assume such oral theology is de facto inferior to our academic standards. At worst we impugn an alternative theological method with ignorance and heretical theology.[106] There may also be some unrecognized anxiety among the established theologians that charismatic renewal will make them superfluous. The form of theologizing carried out in descriptive categories such as stories, visions, and testimonies "makes it independent of Western experts, skills and capital." Furthermore, oral theology "is available to the whole community, as long as the community stays together. Not everybody knows everything, but in principle everybody has access to the whole tradition, which is exactly the function of a modern communication system, only in the case of an oral culture it functions without electronic gadgets."[107]

As frustrating as it may be to an outsider who wishes to have a clear presentation of the systematic theology of charismatic renewal, the concentration upon experience and its stories may indicate a fruitful development in theological method. However, at the same time, the displacement of theology by experience may also indicate a deep-seated anger at and rejection of ecclesial and academic theologies. Again and again, even in the best representatives of the Lutheran charismatic renewal, one encounters suspicion and angry rejection of traditional theology. Without the charismata it is charged that preaching degener-

---

[105]Walter Hollenweger, "Roots and Fruits of the Charismatic Renewal in the Third World," *Theological Renewal* 14 (1980): 13.

[106]At the same time it is important to retain critical awareness of self-serving factors and heretical orientations in spurious forms of "oral theology" as for example the "electronic church" phenomenon in the West. As Mark Sills states, "The real problem is one not of content but of application. The 'electronic church' is a heretical movement and a danger to biblical Christianity because it denies the essentiality of the organized church." "The Docetic Church," *The Christian Century* (21 January 1981): 37-38, 37.

[107]Hollenweger, "Roots and Fruits," 16.

ates into worldy wisdom, lifeless creeds and dogmas, dead ritual, and tradition.[108] The blessing of tongues is that it "bypasses the mind." The Norwegian Lutheran charismatic, Hans J. Frøen, addressed the First International Lutheran Conference on the Holy Spirit and exhorted the audience to lay aside the doctrine and prejudice that obscures the biblical testimony to the charismata: "But we have read it (the Bible) through Lutheran eyeglasses. Let us get rid of all these eyeglasses...." Theologians, he continued, may be expected to be obstinate and set in their ideas. Furthermore both liberal and non-liberal theologians do not take the Bible seriously as God's Word because they do not understand the (charismatic) teaching about the Holy Spirit.[109] As McDonnell points out, "There is in the renewal a suspicion of theology, theological schools and theologians. With remarkable ease theologians are judged to be persons of little faith."[110]

In all of this there are parallels to the kind of repressed anger that surfaced in the sixteenth century in Karlstadt, Müntzer, and others who accused Luther as well as the establishment of withholding the living Word of God from the people. Although these earlier expressions were far more vehement and colorful than the suspicions and charges of contemporary charismatics, the import is the same: theologians have submitted the dead letter for the living Spirit.

This brings us again to the central thesis of our study: the present phenomenon of charismatic renewal is neither unique in terms of the history of the Lutheran churches nor a fundamental theological departure from prior expressions of renewal. Lutheran charismatics have a divided mind on this thesis. For some the movement is fresh and different, for others it is a restoration of the experience of the early church, for still others it is both. Christenson exemplifies this third position. For him the charismatic movement is the ongoing revelation and supernatural manifestation of the Holy Spirit. This is biblical and "marked the origins of Christianity."

---

[108]ST, 73; cf. also CRAL, 94-95; SAJS, 47ff., 50ff., 74f., 96, 105.

[109]Norris Wogen, ed., Jesus, Where Are You Taking Us?, 115, 129, 209, 215. Cf. also William Olson, The Charismatic Church, 26; Erwin Prange, "A Time for Healing," LCRN 1/4 (1975): 2; and Ziemer, "In und neben der Kirche," 223.

[110]McDonnell, "Towards a Critique of the Churches and the Charismatic Renewal," 337.

Any genuine move of the Spirit surely will underscore basic truths of the faith, as part of its total proclamation. It can be helpful to note similarities between the charismatic renewal and other movements in the church, either past or present. But we do not understand or explain a fresh movement of the Spirit simply by pasting a familiar label on it. We must look beyond the similarities. We must also discover that which is different.[111]

Similar perspectives are evident in the *Lutheran Charismatic Renewal Newsletter* and the new journal of the International Lutheran Center for Church Renewal, *Lutheran Renewal International*. What is of interest in the many articles in these two major publications of the Lutheran charismatic movement is the use of the term "restoration."[112] Restoration is the term that is frequently used to describe various renewal movements in the history of the church, especially Anabaptism.[113] It is also the heuristic term used by Scott Hendrix in his critique of charismatic renewal. This position is strongly rejected by Jungkuntz who emphasizes that the renewal is not to be understood as restoration of the New Testament church but rather as "revitalization, refreshment, and modernization of the church."[114] Bittlinger, whose writings do not share Jungkuntz's desire to legitimatize charismatic renewal by the Lutheran Confessions and free it from suspicions of *Schwärmerei*, refers to the renewal as both a "rising up of the primitive Christian experience of the Spirit" and its development.

The cry we hear in many ecclesiastical quarters, "Back to the early church!" is understandable. Even so, it seems to me that it is also possible to view church history positively. I believe that nothing of that which bore the germ of developmental possibility in the original church has been lost. Indeed, I believe

---

[111]*SAJS*, 13; cf. *ST*, 18, and *CRAL*, 113.

[112]See for example, Donald Pfotenhauer, "Pressing the Tests of Leadership," *LCRN* Pastoral Edition, n.d., 2ff., and W. D. Pederson's editorial in *LRI* 1/3 (1980): 4.

[113]The terms "restoration" and "restitution" have been used in historical studies to designate renewal movements in general and the sixteenth century Anabaptists in particular. Cf. for example Hans J. Hillebrand, "Anabaptism and History," *MQR* 45 (1971): 107-22; Franklin H. Littel, "In Response to Hans Hillebrand," *MQR* 45 (1971): 377-80; J. H. Yoder, "Anabaptism and History. 'Restitution' and the Possibility of Renewal," in Hans-Jürgen Goertz, ed., *Umstrittenes Täufertum 1525-1975* (Göttingen: Vandenhoeck & Ruprecht, 1975) 244-58; and the collection of articles in the *Journal of the American Academy of Religion* 44 (1976): 7-86.

[114]Hendrix, "Charismatic Renewal, Old Wine in New Skins," *Currents in Theology and Mission* 4/3 (1977):158-66; Jungkuntz, "A Response to Scott H. Hendrix's," 54.

the opposite—much of what was still undeveloped at that time has matured
during the course of church history.[115]

Here restoration and development appear complementary. It is of interest to note the similarity of titles between Bittlinger's "Die charismatische Erneuerung der Kirchen: Aufbruch urchristlichen Geisterfahrung," and that of an earlier charismatic Lutheran, Karl Ecke, *Durchbruch des Urchristentums*.

Regardless of where one stands in the interpretive spectrum between understanding charismatic renewal as the restoration of primitive Christianity and the repristination of historical enthusiasms, Christenson's point should be well taken: understanding is not aided merely by the application of familiar labels. Nevertheless, both within and without the charismatic renewal, persons have pointed to its similarities and/or relationships with earlier renewal movements. It is understandable that Lutheran charismatics who have repeatedly emphasized their desire to remain within the Lutheran churches and work for their renewal are concerned that identifying them with sixteenth-century and Pietist renewal movements may lead to misunderstanding if not the discrediting of their present concerns. Nevertheless the similarities appear too strong to be simply dismissed with the claim that the charismatic movement is introducing a new and fresh element of renewal in the churches. To ignore previous conflicts between renewal movements and Lutheran theology will not make the present latent and actual conflicts disappear. Rather, only a clarification of the perennial neuralgic points of conflict will serve to prepare an agenda for serious theological dialogue. McDonnell addressed this issue well when he stated:

> The renewal wishes that the church take seriously and evaluate positively the individual experience of Christians in the renewal. But how seriously do those in the renewal relate to the total experience of the Church? How positively do they evaluate that experience? Is what the Spirit is doing today so totally unrelated to what the Spirit has done in the past, in the total life of the church, and the theology which grew out of it, that this experience has nothing to say to the renewal today?[116]

---

[115]A. Bittlinger, "Die charismatische Erneuerung der Kirche: Aufbruch urchristlichen Erfahrung," in Claus Heitmann & Heribert Mühlen, eds., *Erfahrung und Theologie des Heiligen Geistes* (Hamburg/München: Rauhen/Kösel, 1974) 19-35; Bittlinger, *Gifts and Ministries*, 115.

[116]McDonnell, "Towards a Critique of the Churches and Charismatic Renewal," 335f.

In what follows we shall compare and contrast contemporary Lutheran charismatic theology to both the earlier renewal movements and the Lutheran tradition formed by Luther and the Confessions. Up to this point we have attempted to let leaders of the charismatic movement speak for themselves. Now we shall attempt to critically evaluate the Lutheran charismatic movement with the conviction that only a critical approach will facilitate the dialogical confrontation necessary for the integrity of both the charismatic movement and the church. In taking this position we are in agreement with the most recent report of the Theological Studies Department of the DDR, "Kirche und charismatische Erneuerung," that mere toleration of the charismatic movement is the first step toward its isolation. Both our review of the historical conflicts between renewal movements and the Lutheran tradition as well as present tensions between the charismatic renewal and the Lutheran churches would indicate that efforts to avoid serious and critical dialogue would result either in tensions increasing to the breaking point or sterility. The claims of truth of the charismatic renewal must be taken seriously and that means critically.

Proposals to integrate the charismatic renewal movement into the churches which arise out of anxiety over confrontation, regardless of which side commends them, are prone to suppressing honest theological exchange. The renunciation of critical distance is detrimental to both sides: for the renewal this would level differences and repress the contributions it believes it can make to the community; for the churches this would be a failure to appreciate the character of the renewal. If the churches prematurely agree that the concerns of the charismatic renewal are also its concerns and that even essential differences are not all that serious as to preclude integration, the renewal may well be co-opted. When specific concerns are absorbed they may be neutralized or domesticated.

Marginalization of the movement by either side is equally unacceptable. The most promising possibility is "dialogical plurality." "This model proceeds from the ecclesiological, biblically founded conviction that there must be space in the sphere of every church for a responsible plurality of theological convictions and Christian lifestyle which in the scope of the comprehensive ecclesial community have their particular representatives and can form subsidiary groups and communities."[117] We

---

[117]H. Meyer, "Transkonfessionnelle Bewegungen—Hoffnung oder Gefahr?" *Beiheft*

understand our contribution to the possibility of "dialogical plurality" to be a critical examination of the implicit and explicit theology of Lutheran charismatic renewal movements. To quote again from the recent DDR report: "We need patient theological discussion and dialogue which should be conducted in a tough but fair (*hart aber fair*) manner with each other. No theme should be taboo in this dialogue."[118]

LUTHERAN CHARISMATIC THEOLOGY: A CRITIQUE

It may be apparent by now that glossolalia or speaking in tongues has not been a central concern of our discussion. The reason for this is because in itself glossolalia is not an issue for the Lutheran tradition. The Lutheran Confessions are not concerned with this phenomena and Luther himself does not give it or the other charismata much attention. The interesting point about Luther's reference to speaking in tongues in relation to his controversy with Karlstadt is that they take different positions than one might expect. Karlstadt is against speaking in tongues whereas Luther finds it permissible when accompanied by interpretation. Although Luther understands 1 Corinthians 14 in terms of speaking foreign languages (an interpretation also held by some contemporary charismatics), his point is still well taken:

> For St. Paul writes of the office of preaching in the congregation, to which it is to listen and to learn from it, when he says: Whoever comes forward, and wants to read, teach, or preach, and yet speaks with tongues, that is, speaks Latin instead of German, or some unknown language, he is to be silent and preach to himself alone. For no one can hear it or understand it, and no one can get any benefit from it. Or if he should speak in tongues, he ought, in addition, put what he says in German, or interpret it in one way or another, so that the congregation may understand him. Thus St. Paul is not as stubborn in forbidding speaking with tongues as this sin-spirit (Karlstadt) is, but says it is not to be forbidden when along with it interpretation takes place.[119]

---

zur Ökumenischen Rundschau 32 (1978): 55f.; and Gassmann and Meyer, eds., *Neue transkonfessionelle Bewegungen* (Frankfurt: Lembeck, 1976) 42.

[118]Ibid., 70.

[119]"Against the Heavenly Prophets," 1525; LW 40, 142. I do not know if Luther was aware of the occasional manifestations of glossolalia among some Anabaptists. Cf. G. H. Williams and Edith Waldvogel, "A History of Speaking in Tongues and Related Gifts," in Michael P. Hamilton, ed., *The Charismatic Movement* (Grand Rapids MI: Eerdmans, 1975) 61-113, 73; and Peter F. Jensen, "Calvin, Charismatics and Miracles," *The Evangelical Quarterly* 51/3 (1979): 131-44.

Researchers on Pentecostalism and the charismatic movement generally are in agreement that speaking in tongues is not the issue.[120] Thus once again, we wish to emphasize that from the standpoint of Lutheran theology the theological critique of charismatic renewal is not concerned with glossolalia but rather with the charismatic understanding of the gospel.

Speaking in tongues in particular and religious experience in general become an issue when these phenomena are used to legitimate a particular theological position, or to create security (*securitas*) as a substitute, or supplement for the certainty (*certitudo*) of the gospel. A great deal of charismatic literature reflects and at times advocates an understanding of the charismata as the evidence for such security. When this is the case the whole of charismatic theology is affected and regardless of whether traditional Lutheran doctrinal formulae are used or not, the shift in motif creates a theology antithetical to that of Luther and the Confessions.

This displacement of certainty by security is such a fundamental issue—though its temptation is by no means unique to charismatic theology—that it warrants discussion before proceeding to particular theological motifs. Numerous commentators as well as charismatics themselves have expressed the yearning for security in an age of relativism and cynicism that is reflected by the charismatic movements. It is humanly understandable but theologically detrimental when charismata such as tongues, prophesy, and healing are given special priority as signs of apostolic legitimation. These signs are interpreted as evidence that those who receive them stand unmistakably in the succession of the apostles. This desire to create a plausibility structure, "certainty through experience," rewrites the Johannine prologue to be: "In the beginning was experience."

Luther's sharp distinction between certainty and security in which he related certainty to faith includes the awareness of the constant temptation to displace certainty by security, meaning to understand faith as a possession which guarantees life rather than a relationship of trusting God. From the outside, the charismatic movement appears to place its emphasis upon needing experience in order to understand faith as a possession. Certainty is not based upon convincing and doubt-free expe-

---

[120]Cf. K. McDonnell, *Charismatic Renewal and the Churches* (New York: Seabury Press, 1976) 1, 11; Krister Stendahl, "The New Testament Evidence," in M. P. Hamilton, *The Charismatic Movement*, 49-59, 58.

riences but rather upon the confidence (Heb. 11:1; 2 Cor. 5:7) that God does not lie. For security, trust is good but control is better. The temptation to search for the confirmation of faith in personal experiences rather than the Word of God constitutes the quest for security. This is not to minimize the significance of experiences for faith but to understand them to be signs and references, not the basis for the certainty of faith itself. The moment of truth for certainty of faith is when it is confronted by contrary experiences. Thus Paul's distinction between transient experiences such as tongues, prophecy, and knowledge, and the foundations of faith, hope, and love (1 Cor. 13:8ff.) is crucial.

There are Lutheran charismatic theologians who are sensitive to this charge of creating a theology of glory. Thus there is within the charismatic renewal an emphasis upon discipleship which seeks realization in praxis. But again, to those outside the movement, this praxis appears to be not so much living out of certainty than an attempt to spiritually secure life. The charismatic discipleship which sets out the empty life of sin and then fills it with the Holy Spirit appears to be a self-chosen discipleship; an imitation piety closely linked to a community of the like-minded. As we shall argue, this seems to be much closer to Karlstadt's theme of *Gelassenheit* than to Luther's *theologia crucis*.[121] Bearing in mind this general critique of charismatic theology we can now turn to specific theological points.

Justification.

> The Bible speaks of God's saving work in Christ in a variety of ways. Lutherans comprehend this variety in terms of "justification by faith" (Augsburg Confessions; Apology 4:2, 3; Formula of Concord, Solid Declaration, 3:6). "Nothing in this article can be given up or compromised" [for] "on this article rests all that we teach and practice" (Smalcald Articles 2:1,5f.). Thus Lutheran theologians are instructed to affirm and present this article clearly in every age. Here the church tests its witness, doctrine, life and work. Where it is believed and confessed, Lutherans are also free and open to variety, and even prize it as an expression of the true freedom of the gospel which the article on justification affirms.[122]

---

[121]*Kirche und charismatische Erneuerung,* Beiträge A, 1, 4, 15ff., 30ff., Paul D. Opsahl, ed., *The Holy Spirit in the Life of the Church,* 238; Stendahl, "The New Testament Evidence," in Hamilton, *The Charismatic Movement,* 50; J. I. Packer, "Theological Reflections on the Charismatic Movement," *The Churchman* 94/1 & 2 (1980): 7-25, 103-26, 103ff.; and "The Charismatic Movement in the German Democratic Republic," *PPP,* 2:642ff.

[122]Opsahl, *The Holy Spirit in the Life of the Church,* 237f., also in *PPP,* 2:445.

The question to be directed to Lutheran charismatic theology is whether its interpretations of justification by faith remain within the parameters of the Lutheran tradition. Is the fundamental question with which the charismatic approaches the gospel so different from that of Luther and the Confessions that it leads to a markedly different doctrine of justification? We have reviewed in the first section how the Lutheran doctrine of justification is rooted in the problem of the anxious and terrified conscience. The primary question for charismatic theology does not seem to be that of the forgiveness of sins but rather that of power to lead a new life. Certainly these questions are not mutually exclusive but there is a marked difference in accent. For charismatic theology the primary understanding of justification is liberation and empowerment. This charismatic orientation toward power as well as the presence of God leads to a striving for more experiences and more faith. Baptism in the Spirit gives "more of Jesus."[123] In a manner reminiscent of the renewal movements in the sixteenth century and in Pietism there is the penchant to qualify faith, baptism, and the Christian life by adjectives such as "living" and "Spirit-filled." In theological terms we would say charismatics are more interested in sanctification than justification. Furthermore, this interest is colored by achieving security in faith by a praxis pietatis. In psychological terms we would say that the charismatic desire to remain on the mountaintop of spiritual experience disposes them toward a false guilt. "Understandably, those who have had strong and beautiful experiences like to have them continue. If that experience eventually does not come quite as freshly and as strongly as it once did, then comes the temptation to 'help the Spirit' a little—that is, to cheat. Which creates feelings of guilt."[124]

The report by the Theological Study Department of the Association of Evangelical Churches in the DDR outlines three particular consequences of the charismatic understanding of salvation:[125] (1) Salvation is capable of being experienced—it is "experience-able." This means that the person's fundamental conversion may be described because salvation incarnates and exhibits itself in a change in life. God is thus tangibly

---

[123]Frøen, "What is the Baptism in the Holy Spirit?" in Wogen, *Jesus, Where Are You Taking Us?*, 128.

[124]Stendahl, "The New Testament Evidence," 57.

[125]Cf. *Kirche und Charismatische Erneuerung*, 24.

comprehensible. The report adds that this understanding is remarkably close to the materialistic assumption of the contemporary world-view and accounts for the fascination which proceeds from such piety. Salvation is presented not in doctrinal terms but as an "experience-able" (*erfahrbar*) fact. (2) Salvation can be confirmed; it is ascertainable (*feststellbar*). God and his activity of salvation can be reasoned to from the experience of salvation. He who has the Spirit believes he may know how and where the Spirit works. The materialization of the gift of salvation in experiences passes over to the objectifying of experiences in the conception of salvation. One knows exactly how to speak of God and evil, man and the world, redemption and eschatology. This process is also characterized by a direct identification of contemporary evidence by biblical statements. (3) Salvation is "establish-able" (*herstellbar*). The person who has gained his Christian orientation in a fundamental conversion experience binds Christian existence precisely to this fundamental experience and leads others to it. Knowledge of the way of salvation makes possible goal-directed leadership of others. The fundamental problematic is that salvation is understood in terms of the expression of a particular spiritual praxis, and this praxis is not sufficiently distinguished from that salvation which issues from God. The eschatological reservation that we live by faith, not by sight, is forgotten. The charismatic movement is permanently in danger of foreclosing the ultimate by its desire to realize it in the penultimate.

It is of interest that the above critique is independently confirmed by an American theologian, himself a charismatic. Richard Jensen became a charismatic in 1963 while teaching in Ethiopia. After a decade of participation in the charismatic movement Jensen published his theological reflections on his experience. Beginning with a critical analysis of Pentecostal theology Jensen proceeds to a theological critique of the charismatic movement's theology. The message which comes through the former is that while salvation is declared to be by grace alone there are added conditions that obscure this gospel. There is a striving for *more* than is required.

> By meeting the conditions, by doing the *more* than is required, we can move from the realm of Christ to the realm of the Spirit. We can move from sin to holiness. We can move from justification to sanctification, from first faith to total faith, from water baptism to Spirit baptism. One is not called to live by grace alone but is called specifically to live *beyond* the need for grace alone. We are called to live out of our own strength rather than out of the strength of God's gospel. Speaking in tongues in this system almost becomes a sign that we have

moved beyond Christ and his grace for sinners to a higher and more advanced state.[126]

This means that the complementary picturing of justification and sanctification is split into stages correlated to the second and third persons of the Trinity. That is, justification is seen as the work of Christ and sanctification as the work of the Spirit. The emphasis upon holiness and sanctification as experientially legitimated by baptism in the Spirit and tongues shifts the burden of proof from God to the person.

> If holiness (sanctification) is our work for God then we are caught up in the endless cycle of *more*. To become holy always requires more of us: more faith, more good works, more obedience, more everything. Until we receive the initial evidence of our holiness, speaking in tongues, we must live under a cloud of guilt over our lack of spiritual achievement. When we do receive the evidence of our holiness we are tempted to be proud of our achievement. Guilt and pride engulf us when holiness is seen as our work for God.[127]

Jensen goes on to argue that the charismatic movement shares a view of the charismata similar to that which Paul condemned among the Corinthians: "the heresy that claims that Christians live by sight."

> In many instances the neo-Pentecostal movement is filled not with doubting Thomases but with *believing* Thomases. They have turned the story of Thomas around. Thomas wouldn't believe unless he saw. Many today claim that *we will see if we believe*. For Thomas, sight brought faith. For many today, faith brings sight.[128]

Faith. The claim that charismatic theology substitutes sight for faith brings us back to our opening comments regarding certainty and security. "In the Lutheran understanding of experience, so vividly portrayed in Luther himself, all experience, including the experience of faith itself, is ambiguous, and certainty cannot be achieved on the basis of experience alone. Lutherans therefore contrast 'the certainty' of faith based on God's faithfulness of his promise with 'security' based on faith itself."[129] When tongues displaces faith in God's promise as the means of assurance and certainty of salvation, the charismatic movement clearly departs from Lutheran theology.[130] The charismatic equation of tongues with trans-

---

[126]Richard A. Jensen, *Touched By the Spirit. One Man's Struggle to Understand his Experience of the Holy Spirit* (Minneapolis: Augsburg, 1975), 115.

[127]Ibid., 118.

[128]Ibid., 142, 130.

[129]Opsahl, *The Holy Spirit in the Life of the Church*, 238.

[130]Cf. *ST*, 77f.

cendence reflects their urge to eliminate the ambiguity that is part and parcel of all aspects of human existence including the religious. Thus for the charismatic "transcendence cannot remain a matter of mere faith or probability, but must be marked and signaled by the comparative degree, by a something more, an unequivocally identifiable 'plus' calculated to drive a wedge between the sacred and the profane, between what is of God and what is of this earth. . . . In our time, the urge to get free of the ambiguity has come to reflect itself in the re-emergence of glossolalia, now as then the occasion for the re-entry of pagan dualism in Christian thought."[131]

The charismatic emphasis upon *special* faith—not merely the faith which is saving but that which "moves mountains"[132]—excludes Luther's awareness of the ambiguity of experience and burdens the Christian with the implicit demand for *more* faith.[133] This is a guilt-inducing problematic for if the mountain is not moved, if the healing does not occur, if tongues do not break forth, may it then be assumed that our faith is weak and insufficient? Thus Rodney Lensch, now a contributing editor to *Lutheran Renewal International*, writes: "Because I knew I lacked the secret to an abundant, overcoming Christian life I was quite willing to consider anew and afresh any Scripture and if necessary to rearrange my Lutheran doctrine accordingly. I simply wanted to know the whole truth from God's Word." Lensch goes on to testify to the success of his new faith: "The truth of the matter is that my income has been larger since I have walked strictly by faith."[134] In contrast, in the Lutheran tradition faith is faith which comes by hearing not by experiences, even successful ones, which put the burden of proof upon the person. Once again faith is hope, not a possession.

Luther's understanding of faith as confidence and trust in God's promise may be described in relational terms. Charismatic understandings of faith have a decidedly ontological orientation. The question is no longer trust in God's word but the quality of the existing faith. Here again

[131]Roy A. Harrisville, "Speaking in Tongues—Proof of Transcendence?" *Dialog* 13/1 (1974): 11-18, 17f.

[132]Cf. for example, Bittlinger, *Im Kraftfeld des Heiligen Geistes*, 49f.

[133]Frøen, "What is the Baptism in the Holy Spirit?", 128: " 'This is not a case of more than Jesus, but more of Jesus.' And this more of Jesus is what we receive in a baptism of the Holy Spirit."

[134]Rodney Lensch, *My Personal Pentecost* (Kirkwood MO: Impact Books, 1972) 12, 25f., 33f.

the similarity to Pietism and the sixteenth-century renewal appears both in their ontological orientation and their tendency to qualify faith in terms of its life and works.

The charismatic Lutheran departure from Luther's understanding of faith may be explained in a variety of ways. For example, the emphasis upon experience to the point of an uncritical positivism of the facticity of experience is rooted in the charismatic protest against the modern self-understanding which elevates reason and undermines transcendence. Theologically, however, the reason for the charismatic understanding of faith is the separation of Word and Spirit. This accounts for the testimonies that speak of faith in relation to the Bible and then the more complete faith that comes with the Holy Spirit. It is not unusual for this to be related as a reception of the Holy Spirit in a crisis-experience after faith. Parenthetically, it is interesting to observe that the charismatic movement mainly is addressed to those within, not outside, the churches. But the prominence of crisis-experiences as the occasion for receiving the Holy Spirit reminds us again of the closeness of experiential faith orientations to existentialist theology. Ironically, the charismatic rejection of liberal theology bears formal similarity to that which is rejected. Decision leads to change: "In that moment when you say yes to Jesus Christ and let Him come into your heart, He'll change you."[135]

> The charismatic movement stands before the question whether it is conscious of the danger which lies in the formation of its own plausibility sphere, insofar as on the one hand common foundations are abandoned and bridges of understanding are broken, and on the other hand new structures are built up which to the church and (even less) to the world appear hardly communicable and thereby place this testimony itself as well as its community in question.[136]

The charismatic desire for an unmediated experience of God which tends to reduce theology to a Spirit-inspired decision for or against Christ, presents faith in terms of a possession rather than Luther's trust that God does not lie. For Luther the message of salvation does not transfigure or glorify persons and the world but rather reveals them in their true reality. The experience of God under the aspect of immediacy turns out to be surprise over the misery of the world. This is the recognition of the true

---

[135]Frøen, "God Hath Set Some First Apostles," in Wogen, *Jesus Where Are You Taking Us?*, 216.

[136]*Kirche und charismatische Erneuerung*, 62.

crisis and at the same time the true dynamic of all experience of God—the cross and resurrection of Christ.

> The nearness of God is experienced in the face of God's distance, salvation in the face of its absence. But the fundamental experience with which the person responds to this message is faith, the trust in the promised nearness of God in the face of contradictory reality. This experience is fundamental not only because it is the end which marks the insurmountable limit of all experience—there is experience of God only in the mode of anticipation of not having—but also as the beginning which states the encouragement that the message of salvation participates in experience in the midst of the world.[137]

Word and Spirit. The personal danger of the charismatic movement whether in the sixteenth or the twentieth century is to mistake experience of the self and the world for the experience of God. Thus Luther emphasized that faith comes by hearing the Word not by one's experiences. It is in this light that we turn to a discussion of Lutheran charismatic hermeneutics.

The interpretation of Scripture has always been a crucial concern for theology and therefore also a major source of tension and conflict. The Reformation sola scriptura is a hermeneutic that stands over tradition, ecclesial authority, reason, and experience for the determination of the meaning of Scripture. Thus Luther stated, "I want Scripture alone to rule and not to be interpreted according to my spirit or anyone else's, but to be understood on its own terms (*per se ipsam*) and in its own spirit."[138] Religious experience as a guide to the interpretation of Scripture is excluded by Luther as we have already seen in his emphasis upon "the Word, the Word, the Word" over against the enthusiasts' claim to enlightenment by the Holy Spirit. "We must beware of the enthusiasts who boast that they possess the Spirit before and without the Word, and then sit in judgment on Scripture and the spoken word, turning and twisting it as they please. . . ."[139] In other words the imposition of preconceived ideas upon Scripture, including those rooted in religious experience, is strongly rejected. Scripture is to be allowed to speak for itself. From this perspective the charismatic movement presents three problems: a selective exegesis and interpretation based upon contemporary charismatic experience, a separation of Word and Spirit, and perva-

---

[137]Ibid., 28.

[138]WA 7, 98f.

[139]WA 50, 245.

sive fundamentalism. These problems are intertwined but we shall try to treat them separately.

We have repeatedly called attention to the charismatic emphasis upon experience. In the words of Larry Christenson, "The charismatic renewal has recalled the church to more spontaneous modes of revelation, a wholesome complement to the emphasis on purely rational processes and conclusions." Both theoretically and practically the renewal movement is characterized by a rejection of critical biblical studies that are viewed, at best, as a hindrance to a deepening of the knowledge of God. Thus in discussing the prohibition of eating the fruit borne by the tree of knowledge of good and evil, Christenson distinguishes truth in the natural realm from truth in the spiritual realm. The former is open to scientific investigation but the latter is closed to reason. "But the truth from these two realms comes to man in two different ways: from the natural realm by way of reason, from the spiritual realm by way of revelation."[140] One of the DDR reports speaks directly to this, although there is no indication that the authors were aware of Christenson's position.

> According to an old saying, the first sip from the cup (of knowledge) separated us from the knowledge of God, but at the bottom of the cup God waits for those who seek him. The advocates of the charismatic movement are like people who foreseeing the separation from God will not drink from the cup at all. And they feel confirmed in this attitude because they think they have found another unmediated way to God. But is not the cup of knowledge our fate after having eaten from the tree of knowledge?[141]

As we have observed, the renewal movements' rejection of reason in relation to religious experience is partly at least a protest against modern understandings of the world and reality. This is, however, a problematic stance when the struggle against modern reason as normative shifts to the position that reason is irrelevant for faith. This would be a twofold withdrawal from the struggle to understand reality. First, it removes charismatic experience from the possibility of being questioned by others and rejects the inquiries of modern reason as fundamentally irrelevant. Second, it screens out other experiences such as secular experience, alternative Christian experience, and experiences of being abandoned by

---

[140]*CRAL*, 105, 101.

[141]*Kirche und charismatische Erneuerung*, 17.

God. At the same time it withdraws into its own experience which becomes decisive in the struggle regarding reality.

If the unequivocalness of the experience of God is won at this price then the charismatic movement succumbs to an uncritical positivism which relates the facticity of its own experience to the biblical testimony. This takes place when contemporary experiences such as glossolalia and healings are seen as confirmations of comparable experiences in the early Christian community. At the same time on the strength of a presupposed inspiration of Scripture the biblical experiences are used to verify contemporary experiences. Contemporary experience is thus confirmed as experience of God since it is identical with biblical experience. The basis for this circular identification is the presupposed work of the Holy Spirit which also gives the experience unquestionable authority.

This identification of contemporary and biblical experience raises important problems regarding the movement's understanding of Scripture. The use of contemporary experience for access to biblical testimony leads to a selective use of Scripture. For example, 1 Corinthians 12-14 is emphasized while texts critical of spiritual experience, such as 2 Corinthians 12, are hardly considered. Furthermore, when the identification of contemporary and biblical experience takes place, theological reflection is already performed. If the relationship with experience is to be theologically responsible then it is not enough to coordinate one experience with another. It is necessary to clarify contemporary experience in relation to the total witness of Scripture.[142]

It is precisely the kind of charismatic exegesis that "involves a gratuitous modelling of first-century experience on the charismatics' own"[143] which separates Word and Spirit. This is, of course, an extremely sensitive point for Lutheran charismatics. Christenson argues:

> The enthusiasts were ready to set Scripture aside in favor of their own revelations. This finds no parallel in the charismatic renewal, where the Bible functions as the fountain, rule, and norm for faith and life. If anything, charis-

---

[142]While the form of this analysis is largely drawn from the DDR report, ibid., 17ff., there is a remarkable consensus along these same lines by various scholars of the charismatic movement. Cf. for example, McDonnell, "Towards a Critique of the Churches and Charismatic Renewal," 336ff., J. I. Packer, "Theological Reflections," 14, 17, 103-108; Donald Bloesch, "The Charismatic Revival: A Theological Critique," *Religion in Life* 35 (1966): 377.

[143]Packer, "Theological Reflections," 108. For an illustration of this by a leading charismatic theologian cf. *ST*, 91f.

matics may be criticized for a too-literalistic reading of the Bible. But there is no voice in the renewal proposing that Scripture be set to the side in favor of direct (or further) revelations of the Spirit. Charismatics would agree wholeheartedly with Luther that the Spirit has tied himself to the external Word.[144]

Nevertheless, the charismatic movements' desire for unmediated access to God, aptly characterized in the DDR report by the phrase "In the beginning is experience," often finds an independent expression in praxis. The dominating aspect of charismatic piety is direction by the Holy Spirit. This not only limits charismatic experience to the central experiences such as conversion, prayer, and charismata but also overlooks the mediatedness of these experiences. "An utterance in tongues . . . bypasses the mind and flows directly to God in a stream of Spirit-prompted prayer, praise, and thanksgiving."[145] But if the mediation of all experience of God is not taken seriously, there is a tendency toward a docetic Christology and a docetic pneumatology. It should not be forgotten that we have the treasure of the gospel only in earthen vessels. The experience of God in and under the conditions of worldly reality corresponds to the incarnation. The Reformation criterion for knowledge of God in the midst of experience is the Word of God which itself has the character of "mediated immediacy" (God's Word in human mouths). The danger of the charismatic movement is that of isolating the experience of the Spirit.

Finally, there is in the charismatic movement a pervasive fundamentalism. By this is meant a strong rejection of historical-critical biblical studies and methodology as well as a biblical literalism which precludes dialogue with modern thought. We have already referred to Christenson's split between reason and revelation. Reports from churches frequently refer to tensions when charismatic theological students are exposed to the historical-critical method. "Within the renewal there is a deep suspicion that the historical-critical method is vitiated in its suppositions and procedures. Because, as the saying goes, it does not arise from faith and does not lead to faith, this method has nothing at all to say to the renewal."[146]

Thus in a lecture to the First International Lutheran Conference on the Holy Spirit, Hans Frøen stated:

---

[144]*ST*, 112.

[145]*ST*, 73. Cf. also Bittlinger, *Glossolalia*, 56: tongues in direct speech to God.

[146]McDonnell, "Towards a Critique of the Churches and Charismatic Renewal," 336.

There are many liberal theologians who cut away part of the Word of God until these parts are not reliable and cannot be believed in. On the other hand there are many other theologians who, though they are not liberal, are guilty of the same thing in practice. They may not cut away part of the Bible in theory and in word, but their actions show that they have already dismissed many passages and parts of God's Word. In principle there is no difference between these two groups. They tell us that the Bible must be understood differently today, that many things in the Bible belong to the past, and so on. But I believe that God meant what He said for all times. I've always believed in God's Word. I believe in the Bible straight through, from cover to cover, and my deep desire is that the Word of God will take over more and more in my life.[147]

The seriousness of this orientation for both theological work and intra- and extramural ecumenism has been strongly expressed by a leading Roman Catholic biblical scholar, George MacRae.

In the decade of the eighties and beyond, the crucial alignment of Christians will no longer be Protestant and Orthodox vs. Catholic, or if you prefer Protestant vs. Catholic and Orthodox, but rather liberal—in the sense of accepting critical methods and their consequences—vs. fundamentalist, across any and all denominational lines. Ecumenism as it is currently practiced is confined to the former.[148]

Excursus: Luther and Lutheran Charismatics on Selected Biblical Texts.
Lutheran charismatics have been concerned to distance themselves from the criticisms Luther leveled against the theology and exegesis of the enthusiasts. Thus it may be instructive to compare the treatment of selected biblical passages by Luther and representatives of the renewal movement. We shall begin with the Pentecost story in Acts 2, both because of its central significance to the charismatic movement as being the text for arguing that tongues is the evidence for Spirit-baptism and because some leading charismatics such as Bittlinger understand tongues to be true languages. Acts 2 is distinctive in relation to other New Testament references in that the glossolalia in Acts is intelligible, not in need of interpretation as is the case in the Pauline texts. Acts 2 is also unique in that it is the only account of Pentecost.[149] The other major text

---

[147]Frøen, "God Hath Set Some First Apostles," 209. The fundamentalist orientation of the charismatic renewal movements is in continuity with the older pentecostal churches' orientation to the Bible. Cf. Hollenweger, *Enthusiastisches Christentum*, 323ff.

[148]George MacRae, "Reflections on Ecumenism," *Harvard Divinity Bulletin* 11/1 (1980): 11-13, 13. Cf. also the DDR report, 8.

[149]Stendahl, "The New Testament Evidence," 53f. For these reasons which Stendahl understands to be part of the Lucan theology "... it becomes rather precarious—to say the

that is central to charismatic self-understanding and the view of tongues as a gift is 1 Corinthians 12.

Before proceeding with the comparison of the interpretations of Luther and Lutheran charismatics, we may recall that Lutheran charismatics generally understand Luther's attitude to be open to the charismatic experience. Luther's well-known explanation of the Third Article in his Small Catechism ("But the Holy Spirit has called me through the Gospel, enlightened me with his gifts and sanctified and preserved me in the true faith. . . ."), among other references, serves as support for their concerns.

Students of the charismatic renewal have characterized the renewal as restorationist because it has made "the essence of the disciples' experience on Pentecost day, as described in Acts 2, and of the Corinthian experience as described in 1 Corinthians 12-14, into norms, ideals and goals for Christians now."[150] The Spirit-baptism therefore is distinct from conversion and provides the power for witness and service previously lacking. Thus, again, we note the tendency to qualify the noun "Christian" by "reborn."[151] Speaking in tongues is the outward evidence of this event. The implication, sometimes explicitly stated, is that noncharismatic Christians lack something vital ("rebirth"?) and are incomplete.

> If the book of Acts bears witness to normative Christian experience—and it indubitably does—then by every Biblical standard of measurement contemporary church-life is subnormal.[152]

Christenson implies as much when he says, "The baptism with the Holy Spirit, with the manifestation of speaking in tongues, was for *all* believers (Acts 2:4; 10:44-46; 19:6)."[153] Does it mean that one's faith is deficient if one does not speak in tongues? A variation on this theme is expressed by Frøen:

> Today there are many who confuse the spiritual rebirth and the baptism in the Holy Spirit. These are two separate manifestations of the working of the Holy

---

least—to base our understanding of the actual phenomenon of glossolalia on the account in Acts 2."

[150]Packer, "Theological Reflections," 104.

[151]Cf. for example, Bittlinger, *Gifts and Ministries*, 21.

[152]Howard Ervin, *These Are Not Drunken, As Ye Suppose* (Plainfield NJ: Logos International, 1968) 225f. Quoted by Quebedeaux, *The New Charismatics*, 127; cf. also Quebedeaux, 123, 130.

[153]*ST*, 129.

Spirit. I want to underline this: *rebirth and the baptism in the Holy Spirit are two different and separate manifestations of the Holy Spirit.*[154]

A more careful exegetical and theological analysis of Acts by the Lutheran charismatic Richard Jensen rejects the above implications and positions. There are not two baptisms for Christians and Acts 2 cannot legitimately be interpreted from a restorationist perspective. The disciples occupied a unique place and our experiences are not like theirs. "It is dangerous to use a biblical phrase like 'baptism in the Spirit' to refer to experiences and realities which that phrase was never meant to include."[155]

What did Luther say about these texts? Although Luther did not lecture on Acts, he did preach frequently on the Pentecost text. This latter material, consisting of thirty-five sermons preached over the course of his career (1520-1545), has been analyzed by Walther von Loewenich.[156]

As might be expected, Luther understood Pentecost within the framework of his theology. The Christian Pentecost thus stands as the antitype of the giving of the Law on Sinai. The Jewish and Christian Pentecosts express the different character of the old and new covenants. The new Pentecost is for those whose heart is terrified by the Law and its essential miracle is the new courage (*Mut*; *Geist*) which inspired the apostles. Thus Luther's sermons continually dwell on the question of the relationship of Spirit to Law. He emphasizes that the first work of the Spirit is to magnify sin (*amplificare peccata*, WA 29, 383, 12f.). Thereby the Holy Spirit destroys all human self-righteousness and leads to repentance rather than works and merit. Furthermore the Spirit gives courage which frees persons from the fear of men, death, and hell, and leads one out of the alternatives of presumption and despair.

Thus theologically, Luther sees no place in Acts 2 for the claim of evidence of the work of the Holy Spirit through tongues. Indeed, in magnifying sin, the Holy Spirit, from Luther's perspective, is acting quite differently than from charismatic perspectives. Exegetically, Luther does not consider that the miracle of language at Pentecost could have been

---

[154]Frøen,"What is the Baptism in the Holy Spirit?" in Wogen, *Jesus, Where Are You Taking Us?*, 117.

[155]Jensen, *Touched by the Spirit*, 38; cf. 36ff., 106ff., 119ff.

[156]Walther von Loewenich, "Luthers Auslegung der Pfingstgeschichte," in *Vierhundertfünfzig Jahre lutherische Reformation 1517-1967. Festschrift für Franz Lau* (Göttingen: Vandenhoeck & Ruprecht, 1967) 181-90.

glossolalia. The point for Luther is that the languages have a sign-character. For Luther it is no accident that the new covenant and the church began with a language miracle because language is the specifically human organ which distinguishes persons from other animals. Thus the reign of Christ is characterized by the living speech of the apostles, not the stone tablets of Moses; it is a rule of the gospel, not the law. The Holy Spirit writes upon the heart not upon stone, thereby giving persons a new mind.

The Spirit of God is called the Holy Spirit because he sanctifies us, that is why, Luther says, Christians in the Bible are called "saints." This does not mean Christians should be falsely honored because the holiness given by the Spirit does not consist in visible, external things but rather in the forgiveness of sins. This new reality of forgiveness is always in the midst of the old realities which is why the Holy Spirit is called "comforter": "In medio terrore consolatur" (WA 27, 153, 10). The miraculous thing about a Christian is that he is simultaneously in heaven and hell; he has Satan and the Holy Spirit at the same time (WA 27, 153, 4f.). This "simul" takes none of the reality out of life; it must not merely be believed against all experience; it can also be experienced and felt.

The Holy Spirit comes by the Word which is heard and which is Jesus Christ (WA 27, 153, 14.). Thus Spirit, Word, and Christ belong together. The Holy Spirit is active where the Word is purely preached even if by an impious preacher (WA 41, 605, 30). The central point in the church then is not imitation or restoration of the early church, as the monks and Anabaptists think, but rather it is the preaching office (WA 46, 432, 10). The Word then is always the essential outer sign for the presence of the Holy Spirit. While the Holy Spirit appeared "visibiliter" on Pentecost, he has since then been "occulte" in the world (WA 20, 394, 12-14).

It is well known that Luther skeptically opposed visions, dreams, and ecstatic appearances. The "theology of the Word" hesitates to grant them a revelatory character. But Joel's prophecy in Acts 2:17-21 pressed Luther on this issue. Luther responded that not all visions and dreams are worth faith. The means to judge them is the analogy of faith which asks about their agreement with the Word and faith (WA 29, 376, 10-12, 15, 30; 41, 269, 25; 15, 609, 7). The criterion exists in directing the person toward Christ and is concerned with the "res spirituales" not the "res temporales." In other words, household management and rule of the state, despite claims to the contrary by some charismatics, are to be learned elsewhere—by reason.

Finally, Luther emphasized that Pentecost was the festival of the beginning of the church. It shows that the origin of Christianity is a divine not a human work because it is endowed by the "vilest member" of the body—the tongue (WA 34¹, 461, 13-15), meaning that the church is a preaching realm. Thus the church and the cross belong together. The church's beginnings are foolish and weak for they consist of preaching the crucified Christ. This beginning means that throughout its life the church must remain under the cross (WA 29, 380, 7f.). Its privilege is the forgiveness of sins; this is what distinguishes it from all worldly kingdoms.

When we turn to the other important text for contemporary charismatics, 2 Corinthians 12:1ff., we are disappointed by Luther's minimal treatment. Luther gave no lectures on this text and only preached a few sermons on it. In general his comments on the variety of gifts are limited to extolling the office of Word and sacraments and the priority of God's Word. We know that we have a living, speaking God who gives us his certain Word. "We know how he is disposed toward us and what we are to expect from him. Namely, that we by faith in Christ have the forgiveness of sins and are his beloved children. As signs of this we have his baptism and sacrament, office and gifts of the Holy Spirit whereby he works in our hearts. We know that our works and life in this same faith in Christ pleases him, and that he will hear and help us when we call and cry to him in our need and weakness."[157]

In reference to Paul's statement that no one can call Jesus Lord except by the influence of the Holy Spirit, Luther again places this in the context of the office of preaching. Even if the person preaching does not personally have the Holy Spirit, his pointing to Jesus as Lord is nevertheless the work of the Holy Spirit for it is his office without mediation. This applies to the honest and upright preacher as well as to hypocrites.[158]

Furthermore, extraordinary gifts are not an indication that one has the true faith which is the forgiveness of sins and grace in Christ. As Christ points out in Matthew 7:22 even a hypocrite and false saint can do wonders.

> At the last day there will be many who will say to me, "Lord, Lord, have we not prophesied in your name? Have we not cast out the devil in your name? Have

---

[157]Sermon, 1535. WA 22, 170-87; 175, 6, 14. Cf. also, WA 41, 401, 4ff.

[158]WA 22, 179, 14-22.

we not done many deeds in your name?" etc. For it is true that such gifts and deeds certainly have occurred in the name of Jesus and that they will be given to none except the church of Christ. Nevertheless not all persons who have such gifts are righteous but can indeed be false Christians. For such things are given to the church not by the persons but rather by the Holy Spirit in order that those in the office and in relation to the church do many and great things which do not profit them but rather others.[159]

Although the offices and gifts are God's alone he nevertheless accomplishes his purposes through human hands and mouths.[160]

Luther understands Paul's discussion of the spiritual gifts as being particularly applicable to the ministry and leadership of the church because of the dissension and problems which arise where the Word of God and the spiritual gifts are present. This is due to the tendency toward self-chosen works and pride over obedience to what God has ordained. Paul creates an uproar (*wirfft ein knutel inter canes*) when he discusses the spiritual gifts because Satan plants dissension over them by instigating persons to strive for more than God allots them. "Everyone imagines himself to be master of everything. And what is not given nor possible for him, he desires to do. This is a plague that adheres to the Christian church. Hence sects and mobs arise, each damning the other saying: "You do not have the Holy Spirit, I do."[161] Luther, here as elsewhere, never tires of emphasizing that only that which is ordained by God has validity. We can trust what God has instituted and commanded—baptism, absolution, and preaching the gospel—but self-chosen paths to holiness are no defense against the devil.[162]

It is striking that beyond this theological discussion of the varieties of gifts listed in 1 Corinthians 12 Luther does not explicate any of them. However, as we have already noted, he does say he understands glossolalia as the ability to translate, a gift which he claims to have.[163] Nevertheless gifts and offices do not make one a better Christian than others, but are a means to serve others.[164]

---

[159]WA 22, 182, 38-183, 10. Cf. also WA 41, 655, 5ff.

[160]WA 22, 186, 22-25.

[161]Sermon, 13 August 1531 Cf. WA 41, 391, 1ff. WA 34 II, 98, 4-10.

[162]WA 22, 186, 16ff.-187, 20.

[163]WA 15, 609, 7-8.

[164]Cf. WA 22, 184, 11-23; 41, 396, 25-397, 25; 400.

It would seem that Luther's failure to explicitly discuss the spiritual gifts as well as his critical theological reflection upon their misuse in the history of the church—he is fond of quoting the proverb that where man builds a temple to God, the devil builds a chapel next door[165]—has probably discouraged Lutheran charismatics from looking for support in Luther. The one text which Lutheran charismatics have pointed to for support of speaking in tongues is in Luther's sermon on Mark 16:14-20.[166] Of particular interest are Luther's comments on Mark 16:17, 18: "Faith will bring with it these miracles: believers will cast out devils in my name and speak in strange tongues; if they handle snakes or drink any deadly poison, they will come to no harm; and the sick on whom they lay their hands will recover (NEB)."

Christenson writes: "Martin Luther, commenting on Mark 16:17, 18, says, 'These signs (including speaking in new tongues) should be interpreted as applying to *every individual Christian*. When a person is a Christian, he has faith, and he shall also have the power to do these signs.' "[167] Further,

> Martin Luther, commenting on Mark 16:17,18, said, "The signs here spoken of (including that of speaking in tongues), are to be used *according to need*. When the need arises, and the Gospel is hard pressed, then we must definitely do these signs, before we allow the Gospel to be maligned and knocked down."

> I believe that we are in such a time as Luther alluded to. The Scripture gives us every reason to believe that in such a time the Lord will give added power, yes, added gifts—to help His Church meet the challenge. Not only speaking in tongues, but *every* gift mentioned in Scripture is for our day. It is not for us to question the value of these gifts. The fact that they are gifts from Christ is reason enough to desire them earnestly.[168]

Although Frøen does not refer to Luther in regard to Mark 16:17, 18, his comments on this passage are instructive.

> In the Bible it says, "These signs will accompany those who have believed." We read this in Mark 16:17.

---

[165]Cf. WA 41, 391.

[166]29 May 1522, WA 10 III, 133-47.

[167]*ST*, 94. Christenson's emphasis.

[168]*ST*, 133f. Christenson's emphases. In neither case does Christenson give the reference to Luther's works. Cf. also his *Die Gabe des Zungenredens in der lutherischen Kirche*, 29. Jungkuntz also refers to this Luther text but does not give it the weight Christenson does. Jungkuntz, "Secularization Theology, Charismatic Renewal, and Luther's Theology of the Cross," 17.

Was that meant for just the first ten years, or for the first hundred years, or for the past two hundred years? No! It says in my Bible: "These signs will accompany those who have believed." Are we believers?

I've seen these things happen, except this with the serpents; I haven't tried that.

Are we believers? Are these signs following us? When I first took notice of these verses several years ago I said to the Lord, "But dear Lord, this is just not what happens today. There is clearly nothing wrong with your Word, Lord, therefore there must be something wrong with me, with us, with my church."[169]

For a fruitful comparison of Christenson's view with that of Luther it is necessary to quote in full the Luther text from which Christenson draws some lines. After reflecting briefly upon whether Christians should do all the signs listed in Mark 16:17,18, Luther cautions against forcing the text and then reviews various possible interpretations. We begin the text at the same point that Christenson does.

Likewise in regard to individuals, if these words (Mk. 16:17, 18) may not be directed to the community but rather to everyone in particular then this would be the meaning: If a Christian is he who has faith he shall have power to do these accompanying signs and they shall be a consequence (of faith). As St. John says, "He who believes in me shall do these signs and even greater ones" [John 14:12]. For a Christian has the same power with Christ, is one cake (with him)[170] and relates with him to all of life. The Lord has also given him power [Mt. 10:8] against the impure spirits, that they will be cast out and all who are sick made healthy. Thus it is also written in the Psalms [91:13], "You shall step upon the basilisk and shall trample under foot the lion and the dragon." We also read that at that time it has happened. When there was a patriarch in the desert he came upon a serpent, took it by both hands and tore it apart, he is not concerned but says: "Oh what a fine thing it is to have a pure and innocent conscience." Therefore, where a Christian person is there is still the power to do such signs if it is necessary. However, no one should presume to do these (signs) if it is not necessary or demanded. For the disciples themselves have not always and everywhere used (these signs), but rather declared the Word of God alone and confirmed it by miraculous signs as it stands in the text "sermonem confirmante sequentibus signio, and they went forth and preached in all places and their words were confirmed by the signs which followed" (Mk. 16:20). However since the gospel now has spread and become known through all the world, it is not necessary to do signs as in the period of the apostles. But if need requires it and the gospel is threatened and oppressed then we truly must be obliged thereto and must also do signs before we allow the gospel to be abused and suppressed. However I hope it will not be necessary and will not reach that state that I should speak with a new tongue. But it is not necessary since you indeed are able to comprehend and understand me. However if God sends me

---

[169]In Wogen, *Jesus Where Are You Taking Us?* 208.

[170]WA 10 III, 145, 11. Alternative texts give "one church" or "of his church." The parentheses are by translator, the brackets refer to text itself.

there where they do not comprehend then he is able to bestow on me their tongue and language whereby I would be able to be understood. Concerning this no one shall understand himself to do miraculous signs without overwhelming need for we read about the children of the patriarchs that they now and then brought home in their coats heaps of snakes which greatly upset their parents. Therefore the parents punished them because they had tempted God without need. Thus we read of many signs which the faithful have done. It came to pass that a patriarch by chance came upon a basilisk and besought him (God), saying "O Lord, I or this worm must die" [for the basilisk kills by the sight of its face alone], thereupon the basilisk split asunder and burst. But this same appropriate venture may be doing signs without need. I do not know what I should say to this. Some exorcise the devil, but that I know to be dangerous. The devil indeed allows himself to be expelled but should he not be serious but only confirming the person in his error then I would certainly not believe him. We have many examples of this from our own time. . . .[171]

We have quoted this text at length because it reveals a quite different meaning than that given by Christenson. Where Christenson states that Luther assigns the signs including speaking in tongues to every Christian, Luther himself gives this a conditional interpretation. Furthermore, here as elsewhere Luther understands "tongues" as languages and the interpretation of tongues as the skill to translate languages. Not only does this text leave no doubt on this point, but it is also confirmed by frequent references in other writings in regard to 1 Corinthians 12, 1 Corinthians 14, Ephesians 4, and Romans 12. Languages, especially the biblical languages, are crucial to the task of preaching the gospel and interpreting the Scriptures but the gift of languages is not given to everyone. This is a consistent position throughout Luther's career.[172]

In light of Luther's own eschatological and apocalyptic understanding of his time, it is interesting that he does not share Christenson's conviction that we live in a time which needs signs. Luther is cautious about tempting God. Another interesting point in relation to this is Luther's view that signs were for the apostolic period but are really no longer necessary. This view is given by other references he makes to Mark 16:17, 18:

Then the eyes of the blind shall be opened. . . . This is taken literally with reference to the miracles of Christ and the church, as we read in the last chapter of Mark (Mk. 16:17, 18), signs that were necessary to confirm the new Word,

---

171WA 10 III, 145, 6-146, 21.

172Cf. *Answer to . . . Emser*, 1521, LW 39, 181; *Concerning Rebaptism*, 1528, LW 40, 250; *To the Councilmen of Germany*, 1524, LW 45, 363; *Against the Roman Papacy*, 1545, LW 41, 358.

signs that were added to the glory of the church, signs that are not done physically in the last time of the church, now that Christ is no longer weak. They were necessary then as witness to the Jews, who ought to have recognized the church of God.[173]

Christenson claims every gift mentioned in Scripture is for our day. Luther would demur on this. First of all not even all the apostles did all these signs. Secondly, some gifts such as exorcism Luther regarded as dangerous. But is Christenson seriously suggesting that contemporary Christians take up snake handling and drinking poison? Luther certainly cannot be accused of not taking the Bible seriously, but on these points he preferred to allegorize serpents and poison to the lies of false preaching.[174] Christenson says it is not for us to question the value of these gifts but he really cannot use Luther to support this claim either. Finally, for Luther, the Word does not need any "added power" such as speaking in tongues to meet the challenge of the times.

Certainly Luther could extol the outpouring of the Holy Spirit and urge all to get drunk with it but this is focused on the Word of forgiveness, not speaking in tongues or other gifts. Also it is important to notice Luther's awareness of the ambiguity which is always present with the human exercise of signs and gifts.

"Among the Christians there have been many who had five charismatic gifts (*Gnadengaben*). Some were able to do miracles, and yet this served the devil." The gifts themselves are capable of use and misuse, and the law of the danger of having them is utterly clear: "The more beautiful the gifts, and the greater the honor they are paid, the more they tend toward sectarianism. He who has them thinks he understands Scripture and does not allow anyone else a valid place next to him." . . . We do live in the ambiguity of this world into which the incarnate Word has come, taking on the humble forms of our existence. For Luther, the down-to-earth character of the Spirit's gifts, their humanness and their ambiguity, is not a threat to their transcendence but that necessary precondition for their helpfulness to us for whose sake they are all given.[175]

This happened in the early days of the martyrs. But it is also necessary today for the whole church and for us too, to be made drunk with the Holy Spirit and not to fear the pope and the ragings of all the tyrants and devils. For it is the voice and the glory of the churches that we have been bound to the vine in order that we may be made drunk with the Holy Spirit. Christ has called us and has tied us with a most pleasing bond to His vineyards, that is, to His spiritual gifts, with

---

[173]*Lectures on Isaiah*, 1527f.; LW 16, 302; cf. also *The Babylonian Captivity of the Church*, 1520, LW 36, 121.

[174]Cf. his Epiphany sermon of 1522, LW 52, 249.

[175]Karlfried Froelich in Opsahl, *The Holy Spirit in the Life of the Church*, 154f.

which he fills us, so that we fear none of all the things that can harm us. Would that we truly understood and impressed on our hearts the divine promises, namely, that our sins have been forgiven us, that death and the devil have been conquered, and that hell has been destroyed, as this is gloriously proclaimed in Ps. 91:13: "You will tread on the lion and the adder, the young lion and the serpent you will trample underfoot!" He who firmly believes this imbibes these promises, feeds most pleasantly on these vines, and is lord over death.[176]

Lutheran charismatics may wish to criticize Luther's exegesis but they will find little support in it for their own interpretation of the spiritual gifts.

Anthropology. We come now to one of the most critical areas or topics of theology: anthropology. The question of who and what is humankind is a critical topic for theology because it is a fundamental determining element in the conception and explication of salvation. To whom is the good news of salvation addressed? From what is this person redeemed? To what is the redeemed person called? At some time or other most persons have had the experience of being in conversations when answers are given to questions that have not been asked. Such non sequiturs are more or less embarrassing depending upon the company. Charismatic literature is striking in its concentration upon answers with little or no sustained formulation and reflection upon the questions. This is at first surprising unless the charismatic renewal movements share the anthropological presuppositions of our times and therefore assume that analysis is unnecessary. We shall argue later that this is indeed the case; that charismatic theology is not only far less distinctive than it claims but that it also shares the modern presuppositions and content which it elsewhere attacks. Thus the charismatic understanding of the person is not all that different formally from the modern secularist context: humankind is self-perfectible. If this seems to be put too strongly then we may paraphrase it by saying that the potential for self-realization lies within the person awaiting the various processes for actualization which are popular in our day. One looks in vain in charismatic literature for the type of anthropological analysis expressed by Luther. For Luther the person is so curved in upon the self that interiority—whether or not it is introspective in its experience and feeling—is a quicksand of deceit which can lead only to pride or despair. It is because of Luther's experience that he never tired of emphasizing that salvation is not a process of interior self-

---

[176]*Lectures on Genesis*, 1545. LW 8, 251.

development but a gift which comes from outside the person (*pro nobis, extra nos*).

Richard Jensen who as a professor of theology brought critical analysis to his own charismatic experience provides a similar critique. "In my mind it is highly problematic for people to seek to understand spiritual experiences, including the experiences associated with neo-Pentecostalism, with reference to human interiority."[177] Jensen then goes on to discuss two authors who have had a strong influence upon the charismatic movement, Morton Kelsey and Watchman Nee. We might note at this point what Christenson, for example, says of Kelsey's *Encounter with God*: This book "provides a philosophical and theological framework for better understanding the renewal. Its essential value is that of providing an intellectual framework or rationale for many of the experiences which people are having, such as prophesy, vision, healing, tongues, etc. Scholarly and well-researched. Worthwhile reading for pastors and teachers."[178] The importance of Kelsey and Nee was evident also at the recent leaders' conference in Helsinki.

It is worth summarizing Jensen's analysis and critique not only because of its intrinsic value but because his relationship to and participation in the Lutheran charismatic renewal was diminished as a result of the book which he had written in the hope of providing a bridge between mainline Lutherans and the Lutheran charismatic renewal.[179] In terms of theological anthropology the issue as presented by Kelsey and Nee is a dualism which spiritualizes the person in a legalistic direction.

> Kelsey and Nee tend to understand the battle between Spirit and flesh (body/ physical/matter) to be a struggle between man's interior spiritual self and his exterior physical self. The inner self is in direct communication with God and seeks to bring the outer self (soul and body in Nee) under control. Sin is not understood as that which effects our whole being. Sin effects only the bodily/ physical part of man. By tuning in to the interior reality of our lives we can bring the exterior reality of life under control as well. We shall no longer be carnal, fleshly Christians but spiritual Christians.[180]

---

[177]Jensen, *Touched by the Spirit*, 90.

[178]*CRAL*, 149. Christenson also recommends the "Many helpful insights on developing the life of personal holiness" in Nee's book, *The Normal Christian Life*; cf. 146. Bittlinger also quotes from Nee and Kelsey.

[179]Private correspondence. Letter from Richard Jensen, 9 February 1981. For what follows see Jensen, *Touched by the Spirit*, 98-104.

[180]Jensen, *Touched by the Spirit*, 101. The dualistic orientation in charismatic thought is not limited to anthropology but extends to the world. Cf. the DDR report, 25.

Kelsey provides "twelve rules" and Nee lists "seven steps" for training our souls to be open to our inner spiritual world. "But as soon as one adds twelve rules or seven steps to our relationship with God and his Spirit it becomes quite clear that grace is not *alone*. Both Kelsey and Nee are really talking about grace *plus*. It is grace *plus* human openness. It is grace *plus* obedience to the rules and steps. It is grace *plus* man's plunge within and into himself."[181] The characteristic emphasis throughout charismatic literature upon the person being open to the Holy Spirit and living in expectation of the Spirit's gifts is a mark of charismatic anthropology rather than pneumatology. From the perspective of the Reformation persons are not "open" by themselves, but are sinners whose openness to God is blocked by sin and evil. If the human problem is being closed in upon the self then exhortation to be open can at best only create sufficient guilt to which the gospel of forgiveness may be addressed. At worst, of course, this exhortation, or application of the law, creates despair. Again we are reminded that the charismatic emphasis is not so much on the forgiveness of sins as it is on empowerment.

However, it is precisely *within* himself that man is a sinner. The spirit/flesh opposition is not a dualistic anthropology but two different ways of life. Living according to the Spirit is living in obedience to God whereas living according to the flesh is living in rebellious opposition to God. This biblical view sees the person in his or her totality and uses the terms Spirit and flesh to designate personal orientation. Dualistic anthropologies oppose the Spirit and flesh as references to the inner and outer man. A result of this dualistic anthropology is the separation of sanctification from justification and defining the former "in terms of advanced spiritual experience." "As we follow the rules and get in touch with our spiritual 'within,' spiritual experiences result. Such experiences, speaking in tongues for example, are then interpreted as qualitative signs of a deep walk with the inner spirit. Spiritual experiences are easily identified as the signs of *our* (note the 'our') sanctification, growth and maturity." The results are pride and divisiveness.[182] Thus Jensen says:

---

[181]Ibid., 99.

[182]Ibid., 102f. Packer, "Theological Reflections," 119, says, "Two questions needing to be pressed are whether, along with a sense of worship and of love, the charismatic movement also fosters a realistic sense of sin, and whether its euphoric ethos does not tend to encourage naive pride among its supporters, rather than humility."

It is my contention that the tendency to equate human inwardness with the Christian understanding of the "spiritual" as it is done by Morton Kelsey and Watchman Nee is unbiblical and that it provides a dangerous groundwork for the understanding and interpretation of the work of the Spirit and spiritual gifts.[183]

As we have seen from Luther's critique of the renewal movements of his own day, Luther would agree with Jensen.

The charismatic may respond that the call to openness comes not from within the person but rather from the Holy Spirit and therefore one may expect such a stance to be fulfilled. The theological consequences of this, however, continue to be a conception of the person as a being who is an open vessel toward God, as one whose essence is disposable toward God. The consequences are a collapse of the dialectical tension in theological anthropology between the person as imago Dei and sinner. In Luther's terminology this is the collapse of the person as *simul iustus et peccator* into the person as *partim iustus, partim peccator* for whom sin is being displaced by righteousness. This is a theology of progressive sanctification which introduces a third use of the Law in place of the dialectic of Law and Gospel and emphasizes the growth of the individual over the community. These criticisms which may seem abstract within a discussion of theological anthropology are more readily seen in their consequences for Christian ethics.

Ethics. With a major exception there is little sustained reflection within the Lutheran charismatic movement on the subject of Christian ethics. This is not particularly surprising in light of both the charismatic suspicion of theology and the primary concern to sensitize the larger church to the charismata which in turn are highly personal. In regard to the latter point we are reminded of the emphasis upon personal edification as a prime value in glossolalia. The exception referred to above is Larry Christenson's *Social Action Jesus Style*. This title more accurately indicates the content as "imitatio piety" than the title of the first edition, *A Charismatic Approach to Social Action* (1974). The volume exemplifies the social-ethical consequences of the charismatic anthropology sketched above.

The anthropological dualism we noted above is carried over and expanded in the sphere of social ethics. This is accomplished by defining

---

[183]Ibid., 98.

and delimiting social action or ethics to spiritual warfare directed by the specially revealed will of God.

> When we understand "the World" as Jesus and the Apostles did, their apparent disinterest in society begins to make sense. The world, as they saw it, was a world at war. Nothing to do with the little skirmishes which the Roman legions engaged in periodically. Cosmic war. *Spiritual* war. Light against darkness. Good against evil. Christ against Satan. Events in the visible realm were but symptoms of a titanic struggle going on in the "heavenly places" of the invisible realm.[184]

Once the problems of ethics are relieved of ambiguity and ambivalence by presenting them in terms of a cosmic dualism, the obvious approach to social ethics is that of securing divine power, "... power not merely to deal with visible symptoms of evil, but power to bring down the very strongholds of evil."

> It is against the background of this kind of understanding that an emphasis on *spiritual gifts* gains added significance. Such gifts as wisdom, knowledge, healing, miracle, discernment of spirits hold out the potential for dealing with problems in a way that goes beyond traditional social activism. Why settle for political or economic action, if divine power is available for dealing with a problem?
>
> Spiritual warfare, spiritual strategy, spiritual weapons, spiritual victors— issuing in concrete, visible results.[185]

This orientation is formally similar to that of Luther's contemporary, Thomas Müntzer. The goal of Christian ethics is no longer service to the neighbor but rather the establishment of the Kingdom of God with its victory over evil. Not only does Christenson confuse law and gospel but he verges on Manichaeism when he relates the world and Law to Satan: "The ways of the world and of Satan seem attractively logical. They approach the problem of injustice and suffering head on, with sound moral imperatives. But they conveniently avoid any reference to the real cause which lies behind the injustice and suffering: The power of the Evil One. And the law has ever been his ally." Regardless of Christenson's disclaimers here and in his other writings it is difficult to avoid the conclusion that Christenson's understanding of ethics is through and through triumphalistic. It is, in Christenson's terms, a "battle strategy" for the "*total* solution." "While modern social theologians would opt for a

---

[184]*SAJS*, 51. Author's emphasis.
[185]*SAJS*, 53f. Author's emphasis.

measure of improvement in men's immediate circumstances, Jesus and the Apostles envisioned nothing less than their total deliverance from the dominion of evil."[186] In light of our earlier discussion of Müntzer and Hoffman, this orientation has a familiarly disturbing ring to it.

There is no place in Christenson's analysis and program for Luther's emphasis upon the distinction between law and gospel as the hermeneutic for social action. Indeed, charismatic social action specifically renounces the tools and means provided by reason and creation for serving the neighbor. The social arena in which Christian and non-Christian alike may serve others through the law is labeled "secular humanism" and rejected in favor of special revelation. "It is not the goodness or necessity of a work which determines whether we can enter into it, but whether it is the *specific will of God for us to do it at this time.*" Luther's awareness and concern for changing the social structures of his day for the benefit of persons, a concern which is once again coming to the fore in social ethics, is rejected by Christenson as a capitulation to the world.[187] It is of interest that there is a singular lack of reference in Christenson's book to Matthew 25:31-46 which says nothing about spiritual powers, warfare, or separation from the world but rather divides the sheep from the goats on the basis of material aid to the hungry, thirsty, naked, and imprisoned. On the other hand, Christenson does use the verses traditionally used to rationalize non-involvement in social issues such as Mark 14: 7-9 and Luke 18:24.

> Jesus' apparent lack of concern for human poverty has often been remarked. Perhaps He was not intimidated by it, being poor Himself. Some of His sayings seem almost to exalt poverty as a surer way into the kingdom. When some of his followers criticized Mary for expending a whole jar of perfumed ointment on Him, rather than giving the money to the poor, Jesus retorted, "You always have the poor with you. . . ."[188]

---

[186]*SAJS*, 67, 51, 69.

[187]*SAJS*, 37ff., 35; 75f., 92f., 105. Christenson is not alone on this among charismatics; cf. Francoise Mensbrugghe, *Les Mouvements de Renouveau Charismatique. Retour de l'Esprit? Retour de Dionysos?* Dissertation (Faculté Autonome de Théologie, Université de Gèneve, 1978) 23ff., on Luther's concern for structural change; cf. C. Lindberg, "There Should Be No Beggars Among Christians: Karlstadt, Luther, and the Origins of Protestant Poor Relief," *Church History* 46/3 (1977): 313-34; "Through a Glass Darkly. A History of the Church's Vision of the Poor and Poverty," *The Ecumenical Review* 33/1 (1981): 37-52; and "La théologie et l'assistance publique, le cas d'Ypres (1525-1531)," *Revue d'Histoire et de Philosophie Religieuses* 61/1 (1981): 23-36.

[188]*SAJS*, 49f.

Lest there be any doubt of an implied other worldliness, Christenson states it explicitly: "We would suggest three reference points, three themes, which help delineate the shape of New Testament thought in regard to the church's role in society: (1) 'Spiritual Warfare'; (2)'Separation from the World'; and (3) 'The Household of Faith.'" The world is to be saved by the example of the church which withdraws from the world and attracts others to it by its new life. What this finally means is that social ethics are reduced to a tool of evangelism. "If an encounter does not permit of an evangelistic thrust, it must be questioned." For the church to be both the light of the world and evangelistic it must first of all serve its own. "Social action is something which the world should first and foremost see taking place *within* the households of faith. Word-sharing is something which the world should essentially encounter as *coming out* from the household of faith." As we have already noted, there is a strong parallel to Pietism in this program of charismatic social action. "More than new structures, the world needs new *people*."[189] This not only ignores the continuity of the reality of sin in the justified (the Christian as *simul iustus et peccator*) but also, ironically, reflects the cultural context's tribalistic concern for the like-minded. The sanctification of the individual rationalized as a model for others is the priority of charismatic social action. Christenson emphasized this theme at the recent leaders' conference in Helsinki. There he stated that God cannot gather people into a church which is still filled with sin and immorality. Charismatic confrontation of the church on moral issues such as homosexuality, divorce, and adultery is on God's agenda. Christenson further claimed that the 1981 International Lutheran Conference on the Holy Spirit (Minneapolis) manifested the strongest emphasis yet on holiness.

This egocentric ethical orientation is rationalized by arguing that material well-being does not necessarily bring happiness or an improved quality of life. "The Achilles heel of modern social theology," argues Christenson, "is its preponderant emphasis upon man's material and social needs. For when we look at sectors of society which have achieved material and social status, we do not see a particularly appealing picture. They, too, are plagued with turmoil, distress, and dissolution." Christenson goes on to illustrate his point by a constructed dialogue which if seen elsewhere could only be interpreted as a crude caricature of first world racism and imperialism:

---

[189]*SAJS*, 40, 86, 83, 105.

A well-to-do couple went vacationing for two weeks in Mexico. Afterwards, at a party in their home, they were showing slides and telling about their trip.

"You can't imagine the poverty," commented the wife. "It's indescribable. And yet the people seem so *happy*."

Someone offered the opinion that perhaps there would be some way of helping them.

"Yes," said one of the men wryly, "then they could become rich and miserable, like us."[190]

This appears to be nothing more than a clever reversal of the "haves"/"have-nots" relationship which justifies the continuation of the status quo. Until there is evidence to the contrary it is difficult not to apply a recent black theological critique of Pentecostalism to the charismatic movement as well. "The truth of the matter is that rigid class interests lie behind Pentecostal self-definition and expression. These interests reflect the supposed superiority of whites over blacks, of the 'haves' over the 'have-nots,' of the First and Second Worlds over the Third World, and of capitalism over social community."

> It is not by chance that those who consider themselves the "haves" spiritually are the same ones who are the "haves" economically. The whole religious schema reflected in the Pentecostal experience, as a higher level of spirituality, is but a manifestation of the cultural penchant for individual competition which is inherent in Euro-American societies. . . . Bruner's remarks on the "Pentecostal passion for 'more' " might well be reinterpreted in a sociological and economic way with startling conclusions.[191]

Thus social action or ethics from this perspective is an integral part of the charismatic goal to protect what one has, to intensify churchly life, and to protect it from secularizing and rationalizing tendencies. Personal catharsis corresponds to a general tendency to flee the world.

> The renewal's concentration upon the individual and the congregation leads to a problematic narrowing of the horizon of the expectation of salvation. The intensified personal expectation of salvation corresponds to a deficit in the hope of salvation for the world. The world thereby falls all too easily under the verdict of the last judgment. What Christian life in the world as the realm of the penultimate means remains empty. This dualism hinders the necessary discussion (with the world) so that the real challenges of contemporary life hardly come into view. The plausibility of charismatic piety is bought with a problematic loss of openness to the world.[192]

---

[190]*SAJS*, 75f.

[191]James S. Tinney, "Exclusivist Tendencies in Pentecostal Self-Definition: A Critique from Black Theology," *Journal of Religious Thought* 36/1 (1979): 32-49. 45f.

[192]DDR report, 2, 6-7, 25.

This criticism of the renewal's relation to the world in almost exclusively judgmental terms is also voiced by Kilian McDonnell who warns of the sectarian implications in self-separation from the profane tasks of society. "(S)uch secular tasks as feeding the hungry, liberating the oppressed, restoring justice are integral and constitutive of evangelization. Are we going to trivialize evangelization by restricting it to the evangelization of souls?. . . (T)here is in the renewal a vision of the Christian task which is foreshortened and too exclusively interiorized. A more positive attitude towards the world is needed and a willingness to evaluate positively the secular and profane tasks of life in the world."[193]

The particular tragedy in the charismatic withdrawal from developing a social ethic which related to the public world is that it belies the biblical understanding of the gifts of the Spirit. The scriptural promise of a special gift of the Spirit is made only to those Christians who are in confrontation with the public authorities (Mk. 13:11; Mt. 10:19-20; Lk. 12:11-12). Christenson's persistent caricatures of the social-ethical activities of Christians opposing racism, war, injustice, and the like fail to recognize that it is in the courts that the Christian church had and has the opportunity to witness to the world. Stendahl says:

> This line of biblical thinking (to witness before the authorities) strikes me as significant at this time. The concern for the gifts of the Spirit in the charismatic movement has sometimes been seen as being at the opposite end of the spectrum from the exposed place where we find the Berrigans and the conscientious resisters in our land. . . . It seems that the biblical model is the opposite one. In the courts is *the* confrontation that has the promise of the Spirit.[194]

Unfortunately it appears that the charismatic renewal is predominantly interested in socializing its adherents in the dominant values of First World culture.[195]

In concluding this section we would be remiss if we did not call specific attention to an aspect of charismatic social ethics which is

---

[193]McDonnell, "Towards a Critique of the Churches and Charismatic Renewal," 333. Cf. also the similar critique of Ziemer, "In und neben der Kirche," 226.

[194]Stendahl, "The New Testament Evidence," 55.

[195]Cf. Marion Dearman, "Christ and Conformity: A Study of Pentecostal Values," *Journal for the Scientific Study of Religion* 13/4 (1974): 437-53. A recent article in *Time* magazine about Pentecostal and charismatic schools provides the same picture. "A Care for Moral Absolutes," *Time* (June 1981): 34-36. Cf. also Howard Elinson, "The Implications of Pentecostal Religion for Intellectualism, Politics and Race Relations," *The American Journal of Sociology* 70/4 (1965): 403-415.

directed against roughly one-half of the human population—women. Stated baldly: the charismatic renewal, Lutheran and otherwise, is intent on retaining submission of women to male authority. This is in harmony with the charismatic understanding of "Divine Order" exemplified in the normative reading of scriptural passages such as 1 Corinthians 11:3 ("But I wish you to understand that while every man has Christ for his Head, woman's head is man, as Christ's Head is God").[196] At the same time the male chauvinism of the renewal probably also reflects its suspicion of contemporary "secular" concerns and "liberalism." Like the bride in the Song of Solomon women should know their place.[197] Rex Davis, whose sympathies for the renewal are unquestionable, is worth quoting at length on this issue.

> While watching with interest the lay-leadership in much of the charismatic renewal, and particularly the Catholic renewal, there is an inner contradiction which has to be analysed. The suspicion, indeed open hostility to women in leadership roles is very marked in some elements of the North American renewal—so much so that it seems to me to be one of its chronic defects.
>
> I recall visiting Larry Christenson in his study at Trinity Church, San Pedro, to go another cautious step ahead in negotiating for a conference involving the World Council and some leaders in the charismatic renewal. . . . I outlined some of the possible ways we had of bringing people together. Then Larry firmly vetoed the presence of women at what would be, for him, a leaders' meeting. At this still hypothetical level, I tried to make a distinction between a consultation or conference and what I believe we, in the World Council, would designate a "leaders' meeting," and I began to understand quite vividly how deeply felt the judgment about women actually was.
>
> This awareness became more worrying still when I later heard Steve Clark speak on the same theme at a small conference in Belgium.
>
> Others have expressed, at different times, the same uneasiness about this curiously North American fear. I can only say that for me it is another example of what I would call a strangely North American syncretism which unconsciously compromises the Gospel with certain social and cultural developments. And it is very hard to disentangle those elements. So on this score, the charismatic renewal has a stern look about it, almost an obscurantist style, and certainly has become victim to a fundamentalism which seems to imprison the Holy Spirit rather than rejoice in its abundant freedom.[198]

---

[196]Cf. Christenson, *The Christian Family*; Jorstad, *Bold in the Spirit*, 55; Opsahl, *The Holy Spirit in the Life of the Church*, 239, n. 2.

[197]Cf. *SAJS*, 34, 26ff., and 31: "Insofar as the church simply lines up unthinkingly with the latest issue dictated by the secular establishment, she stands in danger of surrendering her distinctive witness, becoming a mere yes-man for the secular culture."

[198]Rex Davis, *Locusts and Wild Honey: The Charismatic Renewal and the Ecumenical Movement* (Geneva: World Council of Churches, 1978) 71f.

The Stephen Clark mentioned above by Davis is the Roman Catholic charismatic coordinator of the Word of God community in Ann Arbor, Michigan. He has written a number of books encouraging charismatic renewal. His most recent book, *Man and Woman in Christ*, is an extended proclamation and argument that women are created by God to be subordinate to men and ought to remain so. We have already seen that Jungkuntz believes that ". . . every woman is to be subordinate to some man, be he her husband, her father, or some surrogate such as her elder or pastor." This attitude toward women is also evident in the European Roman Catholic charismatic movement. On the basis of her participant-observer study, Mennsbrugghe reports that women must cover their heads during prayer, they are not permitted to teach the group, they are sensible to submit to their husbands. If a woman has difficulty receiving the baptism of the Spirit or developing glossolalia it is often attributed to her insufficient submission to her husband.[199] Unfortunately few church reports on the charismatic movement have called attention to this authoritarian element regarding women. One which does, the 1978 Baptist Union of Great Britain and Ireland Report, illustrates that the problem is not confined to North America.[200]

Ecclesiology. In a recent essay Kilian McDonnell has emphasized the importance of community in the charismatic renewal.

> It seems to me that the primary consequence of the resurrection and of Pentecost is not the exercise of the gifts but community formation. This points to the relational nature of Christianity. To be a Christian is to enter into communion, koinonia, with the Father, Son and Holy Spirit. But it is also to enter into deep communion with and commitment to each other. The charismatic community or parish is one expression of this communion which is the Church. The impact of this as central to the renewal of the church has not been sufficiently appreciated.[201]

No one, least of all a theologian, wants to criticize community. After all, from their seminary days pastors and bishops have been exhorted to build community and innumerable projects to develop "koinonia"; these orders being issued from church publishing houses and headquarters alike. At

---

[199]Cf. the review of Stephen Clark, *Man and Woman in Christ* by Letha Scanzoni, "Human and Mrs. Human," *The Christian Century* (11 March 1981) 268-73.

[200]Cf. *PPP*, 2:390. McDonnell, "Towards a Critique of the Churches and Charismatic Renewal," 333 obliquely refers to the issue of women's ordination.

[201]McDonnell, "Towards a Critique of the Churches and Charismatic Renewal," 331f.

times it has seemed that "koinonia" has become the shibboleth for successful ministry and authentic church life. Nevertheless charismatic literature prompts a number of critical questions about the form and style of its community. For the renewal is the charismatic parish one expression or *the* expression of the communion which is the church? What kind of community is this? Is a community which consciously insists upon the subordination of women faithful to the biblical image of the church? Is a community which advocates a simplistic separation from the world with primary concern for its own members a reflection of the body of Christ? To what extent may the charismatic community be understood in terms of a gathering of the "like-minded" or better, "like-experienced"? And in this regard, what does the charismatic community regard as constitutive of the church? Does the charismatic community understand the *communio sanctorum* to be the gathering of forgiven sinners through and around Word and sacrament or a group of those whose reception of the charismata guides their way toward sanctification? Is the charismatic modeling of Christian community upon the New Testament a restorationist construction of the church? Is the renewals' emphasis upon the charismatic experience as an essential part of the fulfillment of baptism a kind of "donatism-of-the-believer" which is also reflected in the ministry as well?

A central clue to the charismatic understanding of this new community, is, as we have mentioned above, the theology of the restoration of the primitive church. The claim is that God is today restoring the gifts initially manifested at the first Pentecost and in Samaria, Caesarea, Ephesus, and Corinth (Acts 2, 8, 10, 19; 1 Cor. 12-14). This restorationist view makes normative for today the experiences of the apostolic period. A critical problem is how to know whether contemporary experiences such as glossolalia are identical with the experiences of the early church.[202] A literalistic reading of the Bible, uncomplicated by biblical criticism which by and large is not acceptable to charismatics, supports the renewals' argument that Scripture establishes a definite pattern of occurrences which can be followed today. But "(e)ven if we could deter-

---

[202]"The baffling question remains: how can Pentecostals . . . be sure that what goes on in tongue-speaking circles today is the same thing that went on in New Testament days?" A. Hoekema, *What About Tongue-Speaking?* (Grand Rapids MI: Eerdmans, 1966) 83, quoted by Packer, "Theological Reflections," 122, n. 63.

mine what the experience of the early Christians really was, are we in fact privileged, or doomed, to repeat it?" Hendrix goes on to say,

> The necessity for a uniform blueprint of church renewal leads to the invention of a primitive church which runs on Holy Spirit baptism and the gift of tongues. By using Scripture in such an uneven and uncritical manner to draw up this blueprint for the restoration of the New Testament church, charismatics make Christianity simpler than the "whole Bible" allows it to be.[203]

As Packer says, the charismatic movement gratuitously models first-century experience on its own.[204]

The problem with a restorationist view of the church is that it bears the seeds of division. "The demand that the present church be made into a replica of the primitive church implies that existing structures are illegitimate insofar as they deviate from the New Testament pattern which serves as normative."[205] Although most commentators acknowledge the charismatic avowal of loyalty to their churches, the potential for marginalization or formation of a new church is also noted. McDonnell speaks of the former danger in terms of "isolation from the church."[206] Certainly the mainline churches have contributed to charismatic marginalization, but the response of some within the renewal to the church's cold or even negative reception is also less than helpful. With loss of hope in the possibilities of restoring the church to its original form, the renewal tends to turn in upon itself becoming either an alternative lifestyle within the church, a prayer group or a covenant community on its outer edge. Such a lack of structural vision leaves the renewal in a charismatic ghetto or else concentrates on being a renewal of the renewal.

The latter possibility of forming new ecclesial structures may be seen in the missionary activities of the renewal which take form in conferences, publishing houses, and national and international charismatic organizations. Among Lutheran charismatics there has been an expansion from the Lutheran Charismatic Renewal Services and the *Lutheran Charismatic Renewal Newsletter* to an international organization, The International Lutheran Center for Church Renewal, which is strategizing charismatic mission and development throughout the world. Four U. S.

---

[203]Hendrix, "Charismatic Renewal," 161f. Cf. ST, 31ff.

[204]Packer, "Theological Reflections," 108; cf. also 13, 104, 109, 112.

[205]Hendrix, "Charismatic Renewal," 165.

[206]McDonnell, "Towards a Critique of the Churches and Charismatic Renewal," 333ff.

Lutheran charismatic leaders have been released from parish responsibilities "to fulfill apostolic roles in the development of renewal leadership."[207] At the same time this Center has developed a quarterly journal as part of its ministry, *Lutheran Renewal International*. That these concerns are on the minds of Lutheran charismatics is illustrated by an article in this journal titled, "Renewal—for the whole church or just a remnant?" which discusses both conscious withdrawal to the margins of the church as well as the possibility of becoming an organized entity within the traditional denomination. The latter would be a variation on the Pietist "ecclesiola in ecclesia."[208] In the short history of this journal this is a constant issue.

> We are presently at a crucial juncture of the renewal movement and the denominational church. For many, the question is whether to commit their lives to a new life for the church or whether to abandon the institutional church. For the church, the issue is to accept or reject renewal influences in the congregations and denominations.[209]

From a theological point of view these developments are related to the issue of what is constitutive of the church for charismatics. Certainly it would be a rare Lutheran charismatic who would deny the centrality of Word and sacraments for the constitution of the church. Thus Jungkuntz warns fellow charismatics of the danger of falling into sectarian attitudes by limiting the true church to Christians "whom they understand to have received baptism in the Spirit and consequently to have received a new baptism beyond water baptism, thus putting them beyond the Jordan, taking the Promised Land, whereas by their definition other 'Christians' are still wandering about and dying back in the wilderness."[210] Nevertheless, in spite of the frequent assertions by Lutheran charismatics that the renewal understands itself as a movement within the church, the suspicion remains that the charismatic movement has an ecclesiology at

---

[207]Cf. W. Dennis Pederson, "Moving Toward a Renewal Strategy," *LRI* 1/2 (1980): 20ff.

[208]By Morris G. C. Vaagenes, Jr., "Vision for the 80's," *LRI* 1/1 (1980): 5-8; "The charismatic renewal can either seek to establish a separate denomination or sacrifice its life for the institutional church and the unregenerate world. We are at the crossroad!" p. 7. In September 1982 Vaagenes opened the North Heights School of Lay Ministry with a full-time staff of three persons.

[209]"Editorial," *LRI* 2/1 (1981): 4.

[210]"Incarnational And/Or Spiritual," *LCRN* 3/10 (1977): 2.

variance with Lutheran theology. Until Lutheran charismatics expressly articulate their understanding of the church we shall, as with other theological motifs, be limited to drawing an analysis from their writings on other topics. Widespread reading in charismatic literature certainly gives support however to Kilian McDonnell's statement that "the renewal is saying that the Holy Spirit is constitutive of the Church."[211] But who, what, and where is this Holy Spirit?

The charismatic answer, in praxis if not always in theory, is to point to charismatic experiences as the expression of the presence and identity of the Holy Spirit. The charismata are not adiaphora to the church but are understood as an integral element of the church which ought to be present and if absent ought to be prayerfully requested and expected. Lack of the charismata is an impoverishment of the church.

> As a Luthercostal, let me state that every baptized believer has the Holy Spirit and that the Baptism with the Holy Spirit is not necessary for salvation. However, if God has anything for us, then not wanting or not seeking it would be an insult to His grace. . . . If you are a believer and have been baptized then you are clothed with power from on High but you may not yet have experienced or claimed the fullness of the power. You might live all your life as a poor man and then discover on your deathbed that your name was really Rockefeller.[212]

The Lutheran emphasis upon the connection between Word and sacraments and the Spirit becomes tenuous in light of the charismatic emphasis upon presence and power. The suspicion of ecclesial triumphalism is strengthened when the renewal in the local congregation is oriented not simply upon the expected new community but upon the circle of the renewed as the kernel for spiritual awakening. To those outside this appears as an exclusive community within the congregation. The suspicion arises that the true Christians and the true church exist only within the charismatic group with its emphasized "ecclesialness" (Kirchlichkeit) and arcane discipline. This suspicion is further strengthened when the particular spiritual experiences within the group are supported by tests which are not available to other members of the community and theologians.[213]

---

[211]McDonnell, "Towards a Critique of the Churches and Charismatic Renewal,"329f.

[212]Erwin Prange, "What's Happening in Lutheran Spiritual Renewal," address delivered to the Lutheran Council in the USA, 1972, quoted by J. Elmo Agrimson, *Gifts of the Spirit and the Body of Christ, Perspectives on the Charismatic Movement* (Minneapolis MN: Augsburg, 1974) 106.

[213]Ziemer, "In und neben der Kirche," 223.

In contrast, Luther emphasized both the insoluble connection between the Spirit and the outward means of Word and sacraments, as well as understanding the church in terms not of power but of the theology of the cross. In these perspectives Luther's concerns are not at odds with those of the charismatic movement but his theology is.[214]

We have already seen that Luther maintains the sovereignty of the Spirit to act where and when he wills. Therefore, when Luther emphasized the relationship of Spirit to Word and sacrament, he is not thinking of any inner metaphysical connection which would lead to ex opera operato perspectives. Rather, Word and sacraments are the sign of revelation. God's majestic presence is veiled for our protection under the humanity of Christ. This precludes the speculative attempts by both reason and piety to ascend to God as he is in himself. Rather, God's presence under the veil of outward things such as the incarnation and Word and sacrament reveals God as he who is for us in Christ. This is therefore at the same time an instrumental sign, for in revealing God as he truly is it changes our lives. This is the outward means of the Spirit.

> God may truly be found in the very *definite*, concrete, outward signs chosen by God. External signs—in all their poverty and insignificance, in their concrete appearance as an unimportant straw—obstruct all ways of our own to God, and they only leave open God's own concrete, unforeseen, incalculable, and inexplicable way. Where we depart from these outward signs, such as baptism, preaching, the Lord's Supper, it always means that we are beginning to enter the dangerous way of speculation or work toward *Deus nudus*.[215]

The visibility and outwardness of the signs express the rejection of all efforts to ascend toward God and proclaim God's descent to humankind. Thus Luther can speak of the *certum signum*. The activity of the Spirit through these signs is certain and public in contrast to the uncertainty of human speculation and experiences which are always ambiguous and hidden. Speaking in tongues and other charismata may or may not be signs used by the Holy Spirit, which is precisely their problem—as experiences they are both ambiguous and limited. "When God comes to

---

[214]On this point see the essay by the Norwegian scholar of Pentecostalism, Nils Bloch-Hoell, "Der Heilige Geist in der Pfingstbewegung und in der charismatischen Bewegung," in Pertti Mäki, ed., *Taufe und Heiliger Geist* (Helsinki, 1979) 89-105, 104f.

[215]Prenter, *Spiritus Creator: Luther's Concept of the Holy Spirit* (Philadelphia: Fortress, 1953) 261. Cf. 259ff., and WA 40 II, 329, 7; 42, 10, 3ff.; 11, 19ff.; 625, 7ff.; 635, 11ff.; 44, 95, 31ff.; 96, 2ff.; 16, 179, 1ff.; 210, 4ff.; 212, 6ff.; 424, 7ff.

us he does not hide himself in a corner where only the especially initiated or those especially fortunate may find him."

> As the God of the gospel, God is that God who for our sakes humbled himself so that he put on the poor garment of the sign of revelation, that is, our nature. In this descent to our life God associates with us as his dear children. External signs are as a mask or a veil God puts on, or a lattice through which he shows himself, so that behind such a protecting cover he may be in our midst as our helper and not as the judge who puts us to death. However, that also means that God in his gracious presence cannot be demonstrated or singled out. He can only be *believed*.[216]

In the same sense the church cannot be demonstrated, it too can only be believed. Luther's intention when asserting the hiddenness of the church was not to confront members of the visible church with doubts about whether they belong to the true church. Rather, Luther's assertion of the hiddenness of the church was directed against Rome on the one hand and the Enthusiasts on the other. Luther was rejecting the identification of the church of God with an empirical, organized community whether it takes the shape of equating curial statements with the voice of God or exchanges a human collectivity and self-separation for the divine assembly and separation. Over against both forms of a theology of glory Luther held that the true church and obedience to it is recognized neither in hierarchical nor moralistic signs. Only Christ the shepherd knows his flock and therefore he alone is able to rule his church.[217]

It is not the sheep but the shepherd's word which creates the flock; meaning that there are no certain signs of faith and church which derive from the members of the church. Indeed, it is impossible to recognize the believer. I do not know whether my neighbor believes; I do not even know whether I believe. I only know that I am called to faith; thus I know in whom I believe. For the sake of this calling not for the sake of my believing I know myself to be in the church. Doubts and questions continue to arise but God's calling Word continues also to empower faith.[218]

From Luther's understanding of the church one can derive little sympathy or support for the charismatic's concern for visible manifesta-

---

[216]Prenter, *Spiritus Creator*, 262, 264. Cf. WA 31 II, 655, 6; 45, 522, 7; 33, 189, 32ff.; 45, 184, 9ff.

[217]Cf. WA 21, 331ff.; WA 9, 196, 16.

[218]Paul Althaus, *Communio Sanctorum. Die Gemeinde im lutherischen Kirchenge-danken* (Munich: Kaiser, 1929), 90-94.

tion of the charismata as signs of the church. Such signs of charismatic renewal as glossolalia, baptism with the Spirit, increased membership, tithing, balanced budgets,[219] Luther would regard as manifestations of a theology of glory. The church is equally under the cross and in sin as individual Christians. To know Christ means to renounce the desire to be anything other than a sinner, for Christ dwells only among sinners. This means that God is loved in his immanence not his transcendence. The church arises from the Word of the cross and exists as does all of God's revelation hidden under its opposite.[220] Luther expresses this in his own inimitable way in letters to his friends Spenlein and Melanchthon.

> Therefore, my dear Friar, learn Christ and him crucified. Learn to praise him and, despairing of yourself, say, "Lord Jesus, you are my righteousness, just as I am your sin. You have taken upon yourself what is mine and have given me what is yours. You have taken upon yourself what you were not and have given to me what I was not." Beware of aspiring to such purity that you will not wish to be looked upon as a sinner or to be one. For Christ dwells only in sinners.... Accordingly you will find peace only in him and only when you despair of yourself and your own works.[221]

> If you are a preacher of grace, then preach a true and not a fictitious grace; if grace is true, you must bear a true and not fictitious sin. God does not save people who are only fictitious sinners. Be a sinner and sin boldly, but believe and rejoice in Christ even more boldly, for he is victorious over sin, death, and the world.[222]

Once again we see how Luther's theological perspectives are tightly interwoven to form a coherent whole: in speaking of the church we have taken into account the theology of the cross, his understanding of faith, and anthropology. The church like the individual Christian is sinner and righteous at the same time. This is why God's gracious presence is mediated by signs linked to his promise to be *for* the sinner. Certainly as Luther acknowledged in the controversies over the sacraments, God is present everywhere (ubiquity) but we only know God's presence as a presence *for us* when it is connected with the promise, the Word. Tongues may or may not be signs of God's gracious presence but their

---

[219]Cf. for example, Jan Markell, "Vision and Faith," *LRI* 1/3 (1980): 10-12. Speaking in tongues is credited with nearly everything ranging from quitting smoking to improving family and business life. Cf. for example *ST*, 72-79.

[220]Althaus, *Communio Sanctorum*, 42ff. Cf. WA Br. 1, 33.

[221]LW 48, 12f.; WA Br. 1, 35, 24ff. To George Spenlein, 8 April 1516.

[222]LW 48, 281f.; WA Br. 2, 370-72. To Philip Melanchthon, 1 August 1521.

ambiguity along with the other charismata stimulates the human efforts to prove their value. Thus legalism in one form or another reenters the church. In a similar manner, the church as *simul*, whether this is developed in sinner-righteous or visible-hidden terminology, precludes both Donatist and perfectionist tendencies which are present in the charismatic renewal.[223]

SUMMARY AND CONCLUSIONS

It is clear by now that our presentation has been critical of the charismatic renewal from the standpoint of Luther's theology. In what follows we shall summarize what we regard to be the deficits of the Lutheran charismatic movement. However we hasten to add two points before beginning. The first is the awareness that slivers in another's eye always appear larger and more dangerous than the log in one's own eye. The Lutheran tradition is no mighty fortress without sufficient glass to tempt any would-be stone-thrower. The second is to restate what ought to be obvious—we are attempting to take Lutheran charismatic renewal seriously. If too much of the above appears in the form of criticism, it cannot be implied that we regard the renewal movement as a passing fad or a superficial "awakening" without deep roots in and analogies to prior renewal movements with which the Lutheran tradition (adequately or not) has had to come to terms. Some years ago Lutheran charismatic leaders called for dialogue. This work is an attempt to make a critical response to that request. In the final section we shall highlight the positive contributions the renewal may make to the Lutheran tradition and life.

The Centrality of Experience. It is not necessary to belabor the criticism that the charismatic renewal overemphasizes experience. There are two sides to this coin, both of which have significance for theology. The first is anti-intellectualism. This may seem to be too harsh a judgment to some Lutheran charismatics and we are aware that there are charismatics such as Richard Jensen and Arnold Bittlinger who take theological and biblical studies seriously. Nevertheless we concur with the assessments of McDonnell, Packer,

---

[223]"The legitimation of ministry in the community goes back in a one-sided way to charismatic experience." *PPP*, 2:458, "The Charismatic Movement in the German Democratic Republic, 1978." Cf. DDR report, 21f., 32f.

and others: "Charismatic preoccupation with experience obviously inhibits the long, hard theological and ethical reflection for which the New Testament letters so plainly call."[224] To some extent the lack of theological work within the renewal may be by default; like its forerunner, Pietism, the renewal may be assuming that the received, traditional theology only needs vivification, not reworking. This is, however, to ignore the tensions which an experience-oriented theology creates for the tradition.

The second side of this "experience coin" has yet to be discussed to our knowledge. There is the very real possibility that if and when the renewal begins serious theological reflection, it will move in the very direction it so vigorously and, at times, shrilly attacks—modern liberal theology! Indeed, does the charismatic renewal already sense this implicit problem? Their attacks upon post-Enlightenment theology remind us of the famous line "thou dost protest too much"! In terms of the history of theology it would be instructive for Lutheran charismatics to reflect upon the context and work of Friedrich Schleiermacher. Schleiermacher, named after his grandfather who was accused of enthusiasm, was educated at Moravian schools and then the Pietist University of Halle and later formulated his theology in reaction to the contemporary rationalism and orthodoxy in Germany. It is not our task to evaluate his development of theology as the description of faith then present in the churches but rather to ask whether charismatic theology is but a pale reflection of this without Schleiermacher's intellectual rigor. Is his attempt to develop theology from the standpoint of religious self-consciousness and the "feeling of absolute dependence" (das Gefühl der schlechthinnigen Abhängigkeit) and the present experience of Christ as the power for redemption far removed from the implicit theological orientation of the charismatic renewal? Remember, too, that Schleiermacher's concern for renewal of the church was manifested not only in theological formulation but day-to-day involvement in the community as chaplain and preacher.

In his recent argument for an inductive theology, Peter Berger says that Schleiermacher:

> ... saw his mission in a defense and reformulation of Christian faith in the face of the onslaught of modern scepticism. He was the true father of theological liberalism. ... Schleiermacher's turn to experience was not eccentric or arbitrary but an almost necessary consequence of the modern challenge to traditional

---

[224]Packer, "Theological Reflections," 17. Cf. McDonnell, "Towards a Critique of the Churches and Charismatic Renewal," 334f.

authority. The turning inward of religious reflection must be seen in the context of the social and *ipso facto* psychological weakening of outward authority. Put differently, the quest for certainty on the basis of subjective insights is the result of the frustration of this quest by what is socially available as objective reality-definitions.[225]

Charismatic renewal movements share a similar context and concern. If they get beyond their biblical positivism and fundamentalism, will they not have to wrestle with the modern consequences of an implicitly inductive theology?

It may also be instructive to recall Schleiermacher's intellectual origins in the "romantic circle" of Berlin with its quest for the transcendent as well as his development of what has come to be called culture-religion.[226] It is of interest to note that the charismatic movements have been analyzed as reflections of contemporary culture. "The charismatic movement, like other movements in the church, is something of a chameleon, taking theological and devotional colour from what surrounds it and is brought to it, and capable of changing colour as these factors change."[227]

> Despite its protest against worldliness the charismatic revival movement can be shown to be penetrated by culture religion. First of all, it reflects the current quest for signs and evidences which points to the weakening of true faith. . . . The emphasis upon the bizarre and spectacular is certainly another manifestation of culture religion. The tendency to exaggeration in neo-Pentecostal circles parallels the passion for success in our business society. . . . The fact that the concern of the movement is the edification of the self rather than social justice reflects again that kind of cultural religion current in the middle and upper-middle classes. It cannot be gainsaid that its main emphasis is on the cultivation of individual piety and not on "social holiness" (Wesley). It is strong on evangelism, but like much of latter-day pietism it lacks the prophetic dimension of faith.[228]

The charismatic rejection of dialogue with contemporary knowledge and experience leads in praxis to an unconscious reflection of particularly

---

[225]Berger, *The Heretical Imperative* (New York: Doubleday, 1979) 68f.

[226]In this context cf. the study by Yorich Spiegel, *Theologie der bürgerlichen Gesellschaft. Sozialphilosophie und Glaubenslehre bei Friedrich Schleiermacher* (München: Chr. Kaiser, 1968); and Peter Berger, *The Social Reality of Religion* (London: Faber & Faber, 1967) 157ff.; Packer, "Theological Reflections," 12, refers to "romantic elements" in the charismatic movement.

[227]Packer, "Theological Reflections," 112.

[228]Bloesch, "The Charismatic Revival," 374.

worldly trends which therefore are not critically overcome but only transferred to the spiritual realm.[229]

A Deficient Theology of the First Article. The tendency to reflect contemporary culture and spiritualize its values and perspectives is an indication of the weakness of charismatic theology in relation to God and creation.

> A criticism the Churches could have made of the renewal but generally failed to do is that it only gives diminished attention to the Father. In this respect the renewal represents a bi-theism (Son and the Spirit). . . . Any view of the Christian life which neglects the Father as the Absolute Start, the Personal Source, as well as the goal and consummation of life, has to be a truncated and impoverished view.[230]

This "super-supernaturalism" as Packer terms it results in an exaggerated discontinuity with the natural and reflects a romantically immature grasp of creation as basic to the activity of God. "Charismatic thinking tends to treat glossolalia, in which mind and tongue are deliberately and systematically dissociated, as the paradigm case of spiritual activity, and to expect all God's work in and around his children to involve similar discontinuity with the ordinary regularities of the created world."[231]

"Jesus Only." In spite of the charismatic emphasis upon the Holy Spirit's activity, "there is more danger that the renewal will develop into a Jesus cult than into a cult of the Spirit."[232] The renewal's emphasis upon existential experience of the Spirit is no substitute for its lack of pneumatology[233] and doctrine of creation. This is also reflected in its biblical positivism and uncritical rejection of contemporary theologies which are concerned with the world, hope, liberation, and the like.

In this connection we may mention the Lutheran charismatic renewal's theological deficits in regard to traditional motifs such as justification, the law-gospel dialectic, the theology of the cross, and theological anthropology.

Anthropology. The anthropology implicit in the renewal deserves attention because, as we argued above, the way that problems are set up has a

---

[229]DDR report, 25.

[230]McDonnell, "Towards a Critique of the Churches and Charismatic Renewal," 330.

[231]Packer, "Theological Reflections," 18.

[232]McDonnell, "Towards a Critique of the Churches and Charismatic Renewal," 329.

[233]Cf. DDR report, 6; and Bloesch, "The Charismatic Renewal," 377.

bearing on their proposed solutions. Here the Lutheran tradition's analysis of sin as radical unbelief and pride is displaced by a more optimistic anthropology which, while it varies from author to author, nevertheless is positive about the perfectibility of the person. I am tempted to term this a kind of "charismatic Kantianism"—I ought to be filled with the Spirit and sanctified, therefore I can. This leads to a trivialization of evil and sin with a concomitant eudaemonism. "(T)he regular and expected projection of euphoria from their (charismatic) platforms and pulpits, plus their standard theology of healing, shows that the assumption is there, reflecting and intensifying the 'now-I-am-happy-all-day-and-you-can-be-so-too' ethos of so much evangelical evangelism since D. L. Moody."[234] At the same time the charismatic emphasis upon expecting the gifts of the Spirit creates distress for those who do not receive them. Here again there is the "more" syndrome discussed earlier—baptism is good but baptism with the Holy Spirit is better.

Charismatic anthropology raises the question of a new legalism which in this case is not only related to the conscious articulation of the "third use" of the law but also to the development of a third mark of the church. J.I. Packer has called this "conformism."

> Group pressure is tyrannical at the best of times, never more so than when the group in question believes itself to be super-spiritual, and finds the evidence of its members' spirituality in their power to perform along approved lines Inevitably, peer pressure to perform (hands raised, hands outstretched, glossolalia, prophecy) is strong in charismatic circles; inevitably, too, the moment one starts living to the group and its expectations rather than to the Lord one is enmeshed in a new legalistic bondage, whereby from yet another angle Christian maturity is threatened.[235]

The praxis of spiritual leadership is often involved with a dangerous claim about the penetrability or discernibility of persons. In the movement one knows exactly what's what with persons and what is necessary for their salvation. There is a confusion between being open before God and being open before persons. "God keeps the secrets—both good and evil—of persons until he himself brings them to light."[236] Whether or not the charismatic emphasis upon openness with its accompanying

---

[234]Packer, "Theological Reflections," 18. Cf. DDR report, 21.

[235]Packer, "Theological Reflections," 19.

[236]DDR report, 22.

loss of human dignity is subtly aggressive behavior,[237] its theological deficit is to underestimate the power of sin.

Justification as Empowerment. The marked tendency within the renewal to understand and proclaim justification in terms of empowerment to follow Jesus and lead a new life of discipleship overshadows that of justification as the forgiveness of sins. This leads to a distortion of the law-gospel dialectic (evident also in the devaluation of the first article) and a theology of glory. Verbal disclaimers of being religious virtuosi by virtue of the charismata do not always suffice to keep it at bay. Elitist tendencies are increased by the restorationist ecclesiology "which sees charismatic experience as the New Testament norm for all time and is inevitably judgmental towards non-charismatic Christianity."[238]

Potential for Sectarianism. The above-mentioned tendency toward elitism creates the potential for sectarianism which, as we have noticed, is something Lutheran charismatics themselves are initiating when they say the Lutheran churches are at the crossroads vis-à-vis the renewal. The renewal is marginal not only because the churches' reception has been less than enthusiastic but because the renewal has turned in upon itself creating its own support, such as its own associations and organizations, reading its own literature, and listening to its own speakers, etc. "This is the thin end of the sectarian wedge in practice, however firm one's profession of aiming at catholic unity."[239]

Individualism. McDonnell rightly points out that "the opposite of personal is impersonal, not private."[240] Yet in the renewal's emphasis upon

---

[237]Cf. the insightful and humorous article by Norman D. Roe, "Aggression and Charismatics," *Theology Today* 35 (1978-79): 81-83. Roe describes elements of a charismatic weekend ("Hands up!," "Hug another person," "Lose your dignity," "Listen to my story") as actions which indicate vulnerability (If I don't want my hands up "it makes little difference who tries to force me to lift them: a gun-toting mugger on a dark street or a kinetic Christian in a social hall."), invasion of personal space, questionable theology (are undignified people "more religious than those of us with less glandular activity and stricter upbringing?"), and subtle aggression (expection that others must listen to one's religious experience).

[238]Packer, "Theological Reflections," 16.

[239]Ibid.; McDonnell, "Towards a Critique of the Churches and Charismatic Renewal," 333; Bloesch, "The Charismatic Revival," 367.

[240]McDonnell, "Towards a Critique of the Churches and Charismatic Renewal," 330.

individual reception of the charismata and sanctification and their consequences for social action it is difficult to avoid the conclusion that church
and world are displaced by the individual's experience of salvation and
special experiences of the Spirit. Is the Christian known by spectacular
gifts or ethical fruits? At best the renewal sees social engagement as
peripheral.[241]

An analysis of the charismatic movement's position on the roles of
men and women, its conservative social postures, idealization of the past
both in terms of life styles and a restorationist ecclesiology prompts the
observation that the renewal is fixated on stasis rather than process. If so,
this in itself is subtle denial of the person and work of the Holy Spirit.

Renewal—Past and Present. The charismatic renewal understands itself
to be a "fresh movement of the Spirit," "a result of daring newness."[242]
The organizing principle and heuristic thesis of our study, to the contrary,
is that the charismatic renewal movement is neither unique in terms of
the history of the Christian churches nor a fundamental theological
departure from prior expressions of renewal. As with any attempt to
provide a comprehensive historical-theological overview, our thesis is
open to caveats, especially by scholars expert in the particular movements
under discussion. Not only are all three renewal movements complex in
their own right but they still await the intense and sustained study which,
for example, continues to be devoted to Luther studies. Of our three
renewal movements, that of the Reformation period has received the
most attention by scholars. Studies of Pietism are still in their infancy
although scholarly organizations and journals are arising to stimulate
and promote more study; the charismatic renewal of the present is
largely unanalyzed from the standpoint of historical theology.

Nevertheless, there is a small but responsible group of scholars who
in one way or another support our thesis and point to its value for
increased understanding of renewal movements in the present and past.
Thus Irvin B. Horst, who regards charismatic renewal as "the modern free

---

[241]Cf. DDR report, 23; Bloesch, "The Charismatic Revival," 369; Ziemer, "In und
neben der Kirche," 226.

[242]Reńe Laurentin, "Charismatische Erneuerung: Prophetische Erneuerung oder
Neokonservatismus?" *Concilium* 17/1 (1981): 27-33, 27. Cf. *ST* 13; *CRAL*, 32. At the
same time in the latter book, Christenson states that the renewal belongs to the church's
inheritance: "Thus it brings nothing new to the church," 118.

church movement," looks to the contemporary experience of charismatic Christianity for clues to the Anabaptist movement.

> Taking a look at the rise of Pentecostalism as a whole, John H. Yoder observes: It "is in our century the closest parallel to what Anabaptism was in the sixteenth: expanding so vigorously that it burst the bonds of its own thinking about church order, living from the multiple gifts of the spirit in the total church while holding leaders in great respect, unembarrassed by the language of the layman and the aesthetic tastes of the poor, mobile, zealously single-minded." My own observations pointed to the studies of the Anabaptist movement, especially on the part of American scholars: "We have emphasized Anabaptists as Biblicists" and that it is time now to give more serious attention to "the early Anabaptists as a movement of the Spirit."[243]

Although Lutheran charismatic leaders may feel uncomfortable with the above references, it is significant that these perspectives come from scholars who are themselves the spiritual descendants of the Reformation renewal movements. Thus these comparisons of sixteenth-century *Schwärmer* to charismatic movements are not polemically intended. In fact a recent popular essay by a Lutheran charismatic makes a similar connection.[244]

The analogies between Pietism and the Charismatic renewal have also been made by charismatic and sympathetic non-charismatics.

> Seen historically, the (charismatic) movement belongs to those movements which have grown out of the soil of classical German Pietism. Thus it is characteristic for the charismatic movement that it has returned in a changed form with its impulse of this tradition as it has become effective in the Methodism of England and North America, in the holiness movements and in the Pentecostal movement.[245]

The DDR report makes the same point more extensively. As Packer succinctly states this: "Charismatic experience is less distinctive than is sometimes made out."[246]

---

[243]Irving B. Horst, "The Fellowship in the Spirit," in I. B. Horst, A. F. de Jong, and D. Visser, eds., *De Geest in het geding opstellen Aangeboden aan J.A. Oosterbaan* (Willink, 1978) 99-110; 105, cf. also 100, 102, 104, 106ff. Cf. also in the same Festschrift the essays by C. J. Dyck, "Hermeneutics and Discipleship," 57-72; Walter Klaasen, "Church Discipline and the Spirit in Pilgrim Marpeck," 169-80; and J. H. Yoder, " 'Spirit' and the Varieties of Reformation Radicalism," 301-306.

[244]Cf. Mark Hillmer, "Spiritual Renewal in the Lutheran Family," *LRI* 1/3 (1980): 6-8; we have already referred to the study by Bengt Hoffman who is sympathetic to the renewal.

[245]Ziemer, "In und neben der Kirche," 224; cf. also 221.

[246]Packer, "Theological Reflections," 20.

If this is indeed the case, as we believe, that these three renewal movements share much in common then both Lutheran charismatics and the Lutheran churches need to face the tensions and potential consequences of a renewal movement which has less in common with the Lutheran tradition than charismatics recognize or the churches wish to admit.

For example, if, as some Mennonite scholars claim, the charismatic movement is heir to concerns of Reformation renewal movements then there is an "old-new" wine implicit in charismatic theology which may burst the traditional Lutheran wineskins. For Luther, grace was unconditional. Justification by this grace alone through faith alone throws the shadow of works-righteousness over personal efforts at holiness. This grace, this forgiveness of sin, mediated by Word and sacraments was Luther's answer to his existential quest for a gracious God. However, the renewal movements are characterized by another equally existential quest—for a gracious community. Of course these are not exclusive concerns but the accent is sufficiently different to create different theologies and lifestyles. The renewals' search for a biblically paradigmatic community of faith and a life-style of obedience led to an emphasis upon an ontological change in the life of the believers as opposed to the "simul" anthropology of proleptic or forensic justification. For the renewal movements: "Revelation is indeed received in the midst of disobedience, but for the purpose of repentance and growth in holiness. It is conditional."[247]

There is a crying need for specialized, in-depth studies on this and many other theological topics. Another example is in the area of Scripture. Luther and all the renewal movements agree that the Bible is the sole authority for faith, but the hermeneutical question continues as a source of tension. The Bible is the Word of God but is the Word of God limited to the Bible?[248] Pneumatology is a central issue but there is an astounding lack of studies not only in regard to the renewal movements but to Luther himself.[249] Are the various renewal movements willing to agree with

---

[247]C. J. Dyck, "Hermeneutics and Discipleship," 72.

[248]Ibid., 60-67.

[249]The now classic study on Luther's understanding of the Spirit is by Prenter, *Spiritus Creator.* For a more recent study cf. Klaus Schwarzwäller, "Delecari assertionibus. Zur Struktur von Luthers Pneumatologie," *Luther Jahrbuch* (1971) 26-58. Cf. also I. B. Horst, "The Fellowship in the Spirit," 101f.

Luther that pneumatology "is a doctrine of the God who in Christ justifies the godless"?[250]

It is claimed that today's charismatic movements have a goal similar to that of the great Pietist, Spener: to open up the spiritual dimension of the church. But if scientific theology urgently requires a spiritual dimension, charismatic renewal, if it is to be a healthy Pietism, must take seriously the vocation of theology.[251]

The above are illustrative of the many themes which the churches and the renewal need to consider in mutual dialogue. There may be "historical and political good sense," as Hendrix says, in the church taking a stance of openness to the renewal, but a realistic assessment of its theology in light of earlier renewal movements is also in order.[252] What, for example, may we surmise about the future development of the charismatic renewal in light of Pietism's outcome in the rationalism and psychologism of the Enlightenment on the one hand and the holiness movement on the other? Or, in light of the earlier renewals, is the charismatic movement's concern for restoration of the early church more characteristic of an orientation toward repristination rather than renewal?

---

[250]Cf. Inge Lønning, "Die Reformation und die Schwärmer," *Concilium* 15/10 (1979): 515-18; 517.

[251]Cf. Lorenz Hein, "Philipp Jakob Spener, Ein Theologe des Heiligen Geistes und Prophet der Kirche," in Lorenz Hein, ed., *Die Einheit der Kirche. Dimensionen ihrer Heiligkeit, Katholizität und Apostolizität* (Festgabe Peter Meinhold zum 60. Geburtstag. Wiesbaden: Steiner Vl., 1977) 103-26, 123f.

[252]Hendrix, "Charismatic Renewal," 165f.

6

ECCLESIA REFORMATA SEMPER REFORMANDA

Not long ago Lutheran charismatics addressed their concerns to the Lutheran church and asked "are there fundamental motifs in the Lutheran tradition which would call some or all of these interpretations of religious experience into question"?[1] It should be clear that the answer is "yes." However this affirmative response should not preclude the recognition and serious consideration of the charismatic challenge to renew the church. Together with their Pietist and Reformation predecessors, Lutheran charismatics share a concern and vision for the renewal of the church which calls attention to potential and actual problems of the Lutheran tradition while at the same time they struggle to incarnate and exemplify Luther's description of the church as the communio sanctorum. This final section will address these charismatic challenges and contributions to the Lutheran tradition.

Experience. The first powerful impression upon both participants and observers of the charismatic movement is the central role which personal experience plays in the renewal. The hearts of those in renewal movements from Karlstadt and Müntzer through Arndt and Spener down to

---

[1]Paul D. Opsahl, ed.,*The Holy Spirit in the Life of the Church: From Biblical Times to the Present* (Minneapolis: Augsburg Publishing House, 1978) 232.

present-day charismatics are at the least "strangely warmed" if not set ablaze. Stendahl terms this "high-voltage religion" and says:

> Opening up the full spectrum of religious experience and expression is badly needed in those churches that have suppressed the charismatic dimension. . . . And no religious tradition can renew itself without the infusion of raw and fresh primary religious experience. It could well be that the charismatic movement is given to the churches as one such infusion. We noncharismatics need not become charismatics—glossolalia is a gift, not a goal or an ideal—but we need to have charismatics among us in the church if the church is to receive and express the fullness of the Christian life. Thus *we* need *them*.[2]

The charismatic renewal concurs wholeheartedly that the churches need the infusion of the religious experience which they have discovered through Spirit-baptism.

From the charismatic perspective the churches need "the infusion of raw and fresh primary religious experience" because they have—consciously or not—allowed modern secular consciousness to displace traditional religious authority. It is difficult to find any Lutheran charismatic leader who in one way or another does not express what Jungkuntz succinctly states: "Whereas secularization pushed God experientially further and further out of our lives into a posture of deistic non-involvement, the Charismatic Renewal has stirred in people's hearts a sense of expectancy regarding God's loving desire to be involved with his people. . . ."[3] Regardless of the varying levels of sophistication among charismatics, there is at the very least the dim recognition of the cataclysmic effects of the modern denial or suppression of religious experience. While few among us have experienced the alienation and chill of the world bereft of religious experience to the extent of a Nietzsche or Dostoyevsky, the effects of secularization on all of us cannot be gainsaid. "The modern situation is a world of religious uncertainty, occasionally staved off by more or less precarious constructions of religious affirmation."[4]

The charismatic emphasis upon experience is a salutary reminder to the churches that the corrosive acids of modernity may not be neutralized

---

[2]Krister Stendahl, "The New Testament Evidence," in *The Charismatic Movement*, ed. by. M.P. Hamilton (Grand Rapids: Eerdmans, 1975) 56f.

[3]Theodor Jungkuntz, "A 'How To Do It' Manual on Miracles," *LCRN*, Pastoral Edition, n.d.,1.

[4]Peter Berger, *The Heretical Imperative* (New York: Doubleday, 1979) 28; cf. ch. 1: "Modernity as the Universalization of History," passim and 54ff.

by either denial or appropriation. Insofar as charismatics can avoid tendencies in the direction of the first option with its concomitant obscurantism and authoritarianism, the renewal brings to the churches the acceptance and explosive power of personal religious experience. Personal testimonies, similar to those of the earlier renewal movements, are a prevalent means of sharing and communicating the religious experience of charismatics. These testimonies share a vision of a new irresistible reality that both transcends and illumines ordinary, everyday life. It is no wonder that charismatics see the present struggle of the church for credibility and authority in terms of a spiritual warfare" and categorically reject the idea that the church should take its cues for action from the world. The recent "Hartford Appeal for Theological Affirmation" also rejects the assumptions that modern thought is normative for Christian faith and life and that "the world must set the agenda for the Church," illustrating that an ecumenical spectrum of church persons shares this concern. In other words, there is widespread concern today about the weakening of tradition and authority in the church that may provide a fruitful locus for dialogue between charismatic and non-charismatic. This is being realized by both leadership in the churches and concerned scholars. "To say, then, that the weakening of tradition *must* lead to a new attention to experience is not just a theoretical proposition. Rather, it serves to explain what has actually taken place."⁵

The very dynamism of the religious experience which all renewal movements are impelled to share is a disrupting dynamic. The charismatic, of whatever period, has in some degree been transported outside or beyond the boundaries of the normal institutions of life including the church. The result is a different perception by the charismatic which in turn is disturbing to those who have not experienced it. A fundamental reason for this tension between renewal movements and the established churches is the awareness that religious experience threatens the social order and the very business of living. This was vividly illustrated by Thomas Müntzer and Melchior Hoffman in the Reformation period; and while the socio-political status quo has not been so violently challenged by

---

⁵Ibid., 33. Bishop James Crumley of the LCA has expressed his sympathies for the motivating force of the renewal in correspondence to me, 4 May 1981. Cf. also *SAJS*, 92f., and Peter Berger and Richard Neuhaus, eds., *Against the World for the World: The Hartford Appeal and the Future of American Religion* (New York: The Seabury Press, 1976).

Pietism and the present renewal, there is still the awareness that religious experience may radically relativize ordinary life. Thus, charismatic encounter is most acute in the church because, while religious tradition is grounded in religious experience, its purpose is to domesticate that experience.

> Religious tradition keeps at bay those nights of glory that might otherwise engulf all of life. Whatever else it is, religious experience is dangerous. Its dangers are reduced and routinized by means of institutionalization. Religious ritual, for example, assigns the encounters with sacred reality to certain times and places, and puts them under the control of typically prudent functionaries. By the same token, religious ritual liberates the rest of life from the burden of having to undergo these encounters. The individual, thanks to religious ritual, can now go about his ordinary business—making love, making war, making a living, and so on—without being constantly interrupted by messengers from another world. Looking at the matter in this way makes understandable the Latin root of the very word "religion," which is *relegere*—"to be careful."[6]

The problem of course is that the preservers and bearers of the religious experience that is ensconced in tradition too frequently succeed all too well in domesticating the experience. Thus the charismatic contribution of "raw and fresh primary religious experience" is a needed reminder of both the community's origins and that the Christian faith is not solely an intellectual enterprise. The holistic approach to persons and community reminds us that there is more to life than reason and technique—a salutary and prophetic stance in the context of the West's banalization of manipulative reason and technique in all areas of life.

This charismatic challenge to the view that the world is rational has the potential to produce a more profound insight into sin and evil. The charismatic movement has once again brought to the attention of the church the reality of the demonic, personal evil, and spiritual conflict. This has been expressed through ministries of healing, exorcism, and deliverance. The charismatic renewal has the potential to recall Luther's own insights into the depth, mystery, and numinous character of the holy. Nevertheless, this charismatic potential still appears to lack the tension-filled dialectic expressed by Luther's terming Satan as the "mask of God" as well as "the prince of lies." The charismatic movement shares the same problem as the earlier renewal, the tendency to dualistically separate God and Satan.

---

[6]Berger, *The Heretical Imperative*, 50.

It was Luther's insight that only when the demonic is identical with the wrath of God is there hope that the demonic will be overcome, for the work of Christ satisfies the wrath of God. Luther's insight that the holy expressed itself through the unholy, the infinite through the finite, God through creation, may provide us with the possibility of once more seeing life in its divine-demonic ambiguity, and even more importantly, to be able to accept this tension-filled dynamic of life.[7]

Theology. The Lutheran charismatic emphasis upon experience stands within the Lutheran tradition's emphasis upon the gospel as *viva vox evangeli*, a living word addressed in community from persons to persons. Thus the Christian faith involves the total person, emotionally as well as intellectually, and the renewal reminds us that Lutheran theology which is limited to purely intellectual or logical terms is a departure from our tradition. We have already discussed above what this may mean in terms of theological method but it will be helpful here to expand positively on those comments.

Peter Berger gives us a helpful typology for reflecting about theologizing in the present context of religious pluralism. He speaks of the deductive, reductive, and inductive options for theology. "The deductive option is to reassert the authority of a religious tradition in the face of modern secularity." "The reductive option is to reinterpret the tradition in terms of modern secularity, which in turn is taken to be a compelling necessity of participating in modern consciousness." "The inductive option is to turn to experience as the ground of all religious affirmations—one's own experience, to whatever extent this is possible, and the experience embodied in a particular range of traditions."[8] It is Berger's conviction that only the inductive option has the promise of being able both to face and overcome the challenges of the modern situation. There are, of course, no pure types as such in the world but these typologies aid us in distinguishing various actual orientations. We have been struck by the apparently unconscious orientation of charismatic theology, even in its still undeveloped state, toward the inductive option. Equally striking is the explicit charismatic rejection of reductionism. There remains in charismatic writing, however, strong elements of

---

[7]C. Lindberg, "Mask of God and Prince of Lies: Luther's Theology of the Demonic," in Alan Olsen, ed., *Disguises of the Demonic* (New York: Association Press, 1975) 87-103, 101.

[8]Berger, *The Heretical Imperative*, 60ff.

the deductive approach which are most evident in the charismatic emphasis upon authority and its attacks on modern biblical criticism. Insofar as charismatic theology can distinguish its basic inductive orientation from uncritical dependence upon the deductive, it may be able to contribute freshness and life to theological methodology. With the same caveat in mind, attention should be called to the kerygmatic orientation of charismatic theology. There seems to be recognition that the post-Enlightenment agenda of liberal theology has lost its cutting edge as an apologetic contest with modernity. If Berger is right when he argues, "The much more pressing agenda today is the contestation with the fullness of human religious possibilities,"[9] then the charismatic renewal has a contribution worth exploring.

Indeed charismatic leaders repeatedly do emphasize that the renewal is concerned with the "fullness of human religious possibilities." Somewhat like the earlier renewal movements the Lutheran charismatics see a deficit or impoverishment in the churches which they believe baptism in the Spirit will remedy. When all is said and done about the charismata, what the charismatics see missing in the life of the church is the appropriation of the power to lead a new life. In short, justification is to be followed by sanctification.

As we have seen, there are charismatics who are as critical of the Lutheran churches as Wesley once was of Luther when he said: "Who has wrote more ably than Martin Luther on justification by faith alone? And who was more ignorant of the doctrine of sanctification, or more confused in his conception of it?"[10] In other words, renewal movements from Karlstadt to the present have been concerned that the Lutheran emphasis upon the gospel as unconditional forgiveness is the first step toward a gospel of "cheap grace." This is an important warning and reminder that even the best intended and formulated theological motifs may be perverted. Lutherans may justly prize the theological insights of Luther and their tradition but without a prophetic critique such motifs as law and gospel, and *simul iustus et peccator* may degenerate into defenses of the status quo and quietism.

The charismatic emphasis upon renewal of the whole person may drive all of us back to a reexamination of Luther's stance on the insepara-

---

[9]Ibid., 183.

[10]*The Works of John Wesley*, 7 (London, 1872) 204.

bility of justification and sanctification. In this we may once again discover Luther's dynamic understanding of the Christian life as "an imperfect act, always in part acquired and in part to be acquired, always in the midst of opposites, and standing at the same time at the starting point and at the goal."[11]

We need to remember that the theme of sanctification was no less emphasized by Luther than by his contemporary "charismatic" opponents. The difference as Luther saw it was that his opponents inverted the order of God's relationship to persons. For Luther only the external proclamation of the gospel and the material reception of the sacraments may call a person out of self-work and self-reflection. It is self-help and self-sanctification which is put to an end by God's promise: "I am here for you." Luther saw in Karlstadt the subtle return of justification by the good works of experience which displace the "external" work of God, who comes to us in Word and sacrament. Ever since Luther's attack on Karlstadt there has been a strong Lutheran anxiety that all types of charismatic orientations endanger justification by grace alone. Luther sharply attacked his opponents on the basis of his stereotype of them. Their own sharp responses only served to confirm what Luther's stereotype had led him to expect.[12] Successful dialogue with the contemporary charismatic renewal will be related to maintaining the validity of Luther's insight into justification and sanctification while remaining sensitive to the dangers to understanding caused by stereotyping.

The distinctive emphasis which the charismatic movement contributes to the renewal of the whole person is through recognition of the church as community. McDonnell claims that the churches have "only sporadically" grasped the importance of community in renewal. "Unless the role of community is grasped one has failed to understand what the renewal is saying. It seems to me that the primary consequence of the resurrection and of Pentecost is not the exercise of the gifts but community formation."[13]

There are numerous facets to a revitalized community and we may mention a few of them here. The charismatic movement reminds us

---

[11]First Psalm Lectures, 1513-1515; LW 11, 494; WA 4, 362, 36-38.

[12]Cf. Mark Edwards, *Luther and the False Brethren* (Stanford: Stanford University Press, 1975) 201f., 58-59.

[13]McDonnell, "Towards a Critique of the Churches and Charismatic Renewal," *One in Christ* 16/4 (1980): 331.

again that the community is an honorable and appropriate place for joy and ecstasy. Stendahl suggests a democratizing effect which overcomes the limitation of religious expression to the "professionals." "As a preacher and lecturer, I even wonder if it is not wise to let glossolalia gush forth in the church so that those who are not professional in the shaping of words are free to express fully their overwhelmed praise to the Lord. Actually, in the history of the church the practice of glossolalia has often had a democratizing effect. It has been one of the expressions through which in a certain sense 'the last have become the first.' "[14] This is significant not only to worship but to missions and hermeneutics as well. As form criticism has made clear, the biblical records were long preserved and passed on through oral tradition which today has its parallels in many Third World churches. The well-known scholar of Pentecostalism and Professor of Mission, Walter Hollenweger, has recently been emphasizing the importance of oral theology.

> In these pre-literate or post-literate cultures the medium of communication is, just as in biblical times, not the definition but the description, not the statement but the story, not the doctrine but the testimony, not the book but the parable, not a systematic theology but a song, not the treatise but the television programme, not the articulation of concepts but the celebration of banquets.[15]

> Songs and stories, prayers for the sick, pilgrimages, exorcism, and glossolalia, in short all the expressions of oral theology, function as a system for passing on theological and social values and information in oral societies in a way that can be likened to a modern computer, because the individual memories can be linked together in such a way that, although no one person actively communicates the whole tradition, in principle everybody has access to the total information.[16]

The charismatic renewal throughout the world warns theologians against the too facile identification of a cultural academic sophistication with theological truth or even adequacy. The oral community context also frees hermeneutics from the limitations of the library and classroom and contributes the insight of a communal context analogous to the Scriptures' origins. The locus for hermeneutics is the living community.

Finally but certainly not least is the frequently emphasized contribution to ecumenism. In general the churches have been defensive about the

---

[14]Stendahl, "The New Testament Evidence," 56.

[15]Walter Hollenweger, "Roots and Fruits of the Charismatic Renewal," *Theological Renewal* 14 (1980): 13.

[16]W. Hollenweger, "Charismatic Renewal in the Third World: Implications for Mission." *Occasional Bulletin of Missionary Research* 4/2 (April 1980): 68-75, 68.

ecumenical nature of the charismatic renewal. Instead of seeing it as an opportunity, the churches have seen in it the dangers of obscuring doctrinal distinctions and disruption of ecclesial order. But "for many people, charismatic renewal has provided the first real experience of Christian fellowship across denominational boundaries."[17] What is striking about the ecumenical impact of the charismatic renewal is that it is taking place on the *local* level in contrast to the established ecumenical movement of the World Council of Churches and the bilateral dialogues of the Lutheran World Federation, the Roman Catholic Church, and the others. This local ecumenism has been taking shape in and through ecumenical covenant communities. It is argued by a participant in these communities that the sociological and cultural—non-doctrinal—factors which have arisen through the years of ecclesial separation are overcome by the common experiences of the activity of the Holy Spirit. It should be noted, however, that doctrinal differences are not always overcome such as the mutual participation in the Lord's Supper.[18]

Charismatic leaders from different churches are agreed in their view of the renewal as a new hope and promise for the churches.[19] The World Council of Churches has also come to share this hope and in 1975 formed a Sub-Unit on Renewal and Congregational Life to take responsibility for clarifying and understanding charismatic renewal.[20] This sub-unit held meetings in the USA and the Federal Republic of Germany in 1978 and a major consultation at the Ecumenical Institute in Bossey in 1980. The papers and reports of these meeting are available in the World Council of Churches' publication *The Church is Charismatic*. A major concern of the WCC's Sub-Unit on Renewal is to develop trust and build bridges

---

[17] Peter Hocken, "Charismatic Renewal, the Churches and Unity," *One in Christ* 15/4 (1979): 310-21, 312; 332.

[18] Cf. Theodore Jungkuntz, "Lutherans and Roman Catholics Participate in Ecumenical Covenant Communities," *ReConcile* 2/3 (May 1981): 7-9.

[19] Cf. Arnold Bittlinger, "Charismatic Renewal: An Opportunity for the Church?" *The Ecumenical Review* 31/3 (1979): 247-51; Heribert Mühlen, "Gemeinsame Geist-Erfahrung: Hoffnung für die getrennten Kirchen," *Una Sancta* 36/1 (1981): 20-32.

[20] Cf. the 1978 report, "Towards a Church Renewed and United in the Spirit," *The Ecumenical Review* 31/3 (1979): 305-309; and the 1980 report, "Die Bedeutung der charismatischen Erneuerung für die Kirchen. Bericht einer Konsultation in Bossey," *Una Sancta* 36/1 (1981): 5-10; and Rex Davis, *Locusts and Wild Honey: The Charismatic Renewal and the Ecumenical Movement* (Geneva: WCC, 1978). The recent volume edited by Arnold Bittlinger, *The Church is Charismatic. The World Council of Churches and the Charismatic Renewal* (Geneva: WCC, 1981), discusses the WCC work on the renewal through the 1980 Bossey Consultation.

between the WCC and the charismatic renewal. The report of the Sub-Units' consultant, Arnold Bittlinger, describes the positive work of the Roman Catholic Church's International Charismatic Communication Centre in Brussels with its "unofficial" link to the Vatican through the person of Cardinal Suenens. "It would be of high value if the non-Catholic charismatics could have a similar centre. Besides communication and information this centre could offer ecumenical, theological and experimental training courses for pastors and leaders in Charismatic Renewal."[21] As mentioned above, Lutheran charismatics have established such an international center in Minneapolis with the same purposes in mind. In the United States a national ecumenical renewal organization was set up in January 1981. Representatives of spiritual renewal from five denominations (United Methodist, United Church of Christ, Presbyterian, Episcopal, and Lutheran) met in Tulsa, Oklahoma and created what is to be called the Parish Renewal Council. The Lutheran charismatic leader, Rev. Dr. Dennis Pederson, was elected chairman of the executive committee. The council will sponsor regional and national parish renewal conferences and provide support through intercessory prayer and renewal prayer fellowships.[22]

It is of interest to note that the name "charismatic" appears with less and less frequency in the title of renewal organizations and publications such as the International Lutheran Center for Church Renewal and its publication *Lutheran RENEWAL International.* The deletion of the name "charismatic" from these efforts to provide an international structural base for Lutheran charismatic renewal brings us back to the topic of the definition and self-understanding of the Lutheran charismatic movement. What is in a name? If a rose is a rose is a rose, and if it smells as sweet by another name, then is not a charismatic movement a charismatic movement even when called a renewal movement? Yes and maybe. Charismatic movements have themselves shifted their self-designations from neo-Pentecostal to charismatic to renewal. There are undoubtedly many reasons for this. Certainly one might surmise that the designation "renewal" will be more acceptable or at least less offensive to non-charismatics than the names neo-Pentecostal and charismatic. After all it

[21]Bittlinger, "Report on the Work of the WCC Consultant on Charismatic Renewal," in Bittlinger, ed., *The Church is Charismatic* (Geneva: WCC, 1981): 228.

[22]Cf. "New USA Milestone," *Renewal* (Great Britain) (June/July 1981) 8.

is much more difficult to say you are opposed to renewal than it is to say you do not accept (neo-) Pentecostal fundamentalism or charismatic enthusiasm. "Renewal" does not carry the emotive liabilities of the other names. This shift probably also reflects a growing maturity and self-understanding of the movement itself (and perhaps also a desire for respectability?). At its best this would seem to indicate what more and more charismatics are saying: that the charismata and church renewal are not tied to any particular theology and culture. Indeed, the WCC volume mentioned above proclaims that *The Church is Charismatic.* Arnold Bittlinger asks "What then *is* a charism?" and answers:

> Purely as a phenomenon, nothing whatever is in itself "charismatic" or "spiritual." All phenomena are the realization of possibilities within this world. But everything, however ordinary or extraordinary, can be made use of by God for the neighbor's or the world's salvation, and thereby becomes a charism (there is no Christian who *always* acts charismatically, but there is also no Christian who *never* acts charismatically).[23]

Who can disagree with this? Indeed the term charismatic here appears to be a synonym for the way Luther understood vocation. The question, however, now becomes whether there is anything distinctive enough about charismatic renewal to warrant interest in it, pro or con. Does the type of definition advanced by Bittlinger indicate a domestication of the charismatic movement, or is it a form of "protective coloration" à la Packer's suggestion that the charismatic movement has a chameleon characteristic? While a definitive answer to these questions is probably not forthcoming in the immediate future, Bittlinger's definition does raise the major question of whether the renewal has a distinctive claim or contribution to make in terms of either experience or doctrine. Engelsviken sees this dilemma when he says:

> *Either* the Charismatic Movement is defined solely in terms of experience at the risk of losing both its distinctive Christian character and the possibility of evaluating the experience according to a "doctrinal" norm, *or* the Charismatic Movement has to be defined in terms of experience *and* doctrine to assure its Christian character at the risk of invalidating some "charismatic" experiences, as well as some theological interpretations of it. It seems impossible to understand the Charismatic Movement or Pentecostalism solely as experience and then set out to describe or explain this experience without resorting to "theology" or "doctrine."[24]

---

[23]Ibid., 11.

[24]Tormod Engelsviken, *The Gift of the Spirit. An Analysis and Evaluation of the Charismatic Movement from a Lutheran Theological Perspective.* Unpublished dissertation (Aquinas Institute, Dubuque, IA, 1981) 22.

Be this as it may the concern persistently voiced by the charismatic movement is renewal of persons as well as renewal of the church. In this light there is a curious ring to the Lutheran charismatic use of the phrase "ecclesia reformata semper reformanda" for their concern is for an "ecclesia renovata." Obviously reform and renewal are not mutually exclusive but emphasis upon one over the other reflects a distinct theological orientation. The Reformation formula does not use the verb *renovare* but *reformare*. In other words, Luther's critique of renewal movements is not that they are extreme or radical but that they are not radical enough. Thus when Luther claimed that the renewal movement of his day and the Roman Catholic Church were formally the same he was associating them on the basis of what he saw as similar theological motifs. But there is a historical-genetic linkage here as well which may partially explain why the renewal movement today has found a more welcome reception within the Catholic Church than within the Lutheran churches.[25] In recent studies the sixteenth-century renewal movement has been reassessed as "an internalizing, personalizing, devotional, laicized, ascetic and biblical reform movement related to the ideals of Franciscanism and the *Devotio Moderna*, . . . a Protestant adaption of a Christian ascetic tradition, more right-wing than left, more conservative than radical. . . ."[26] In other words, the motif of renewal (*renovatio*) is more related to the medieval Catholic tradition than it is to the Reformation.

Without wanting to press too hard, we believe there is heuristic value in developing the historical analogies and continuity of concerns between renewal movements. To view the present charismatic renewal movement in light of the history of the church is to relativize its claim to be a *new* movement. This is not to gainsay the freshness of individual charismatic experience but to see that the expression of its meaning for the church stands in the continuity with prior programs of renewal. This historical orientation toward charismatic renewal could lead to a stereo-

---

[25]Cf. the use of *reformatio* and *renovatio* in the Vatican II decree "On Ecumenism," in, for example, Kardinal Jaeger, *Das Konzils Dekret über den Ökumenismus* (Paderborn: Bonifacious, 1965) 73f., 83ff.

[26]Kenneth R. Davis, *Anabaptism and Asceticism* (Scottdale PA: Herald Press, 1974), 297; cf. also note 1, p.348. Cf. also Werner Packull, *Mysticism and the Early South German-Austrian Anabaptist Movement 1525-1531* (Scottdale PA: Herald Press, 1977), passim.

typing of it in terms of precedents and as a consequence, repristination of Luther's critique. However, it has not been and is not now our intention to use church history to "pigeonhole" the renewal in order to dismiss it as a latter day example of Karlstadt swallowing the Holy Spirit, feathers and all. Rather, we believe the historical perspective may be used constructively as well as critically in the following ways.

1. First of all, the illustration through historical theological analysis that the charismatic renewal is not new or sui generis may aid in removing the discussion of the origins and concerns of the charismatic renewal from uncritical affirmation or rejection.

2. Placing the charismatic renewal within the broader historical-theological context of the history of the church may serve to alleviate unfounded anxiety about the movement by non-charismatics. We have argued that there is much in Luther's critique of Karlstadt and Müntzer which may be applied critically to Pietism and the charismatic renewal. Yet we must not forget that these earlier proponents of renewal made important contributions to the life of the church. Unfortunately polemic has too often obscured the positive legacy we have from them. For example, Müntzer's creative liturgical work not only preceded that of Luther but was also free of the subjectivism one might expect from later polemics. Indeed Luther himself voiced approval of Müntzer's liturgical work when it came to him through another. Müntzer's sensitivity to the importance of having a vernacular liturgy for the people was born of profound awareness of the history of worship. This and his emphasis upon conversion and the sanctifying work of the Holy Spirit in doctrine and life, as well as his focus on "costly grace" and discipleship are more and more receiving their due appreciation by contemporary scholarship.[27] Pietism, frequently attacked in its own day by Lutheran Orthodoxy, has similarly left a legacy of hymnody which transcends contemporary denominational lines. All of these earlier expressions of renewal were conscious of the importance of worship and congregational fellowship to the Christian life. Thus without giving up critical analysis of renewal movements in history but indeed through this method, we may appreciate their contributions without undue anxiety and fear of new wine. People have drunk this wine before and the results have, at least in part, been positive and lasting.

---

[27]Cf. Gordon Rupp, *Patterns of Reformation* (Philadelphia: Fortress, 1969) 207, 305-23.

3. At the same time we may see through historical analysis Luther's contribution to a Lutheran neuralgia concerning religious experience. In good part this is an element of Luther's legacy which still needs to be recognized and dealt with. There is no need to renounce or modify Luther's theological motifs in order to recognize that he had the penchant to beat his opponents over the head with them. All too often Luther's vices have become our virtues and thereby clouded our appreciation of renewal movements. Luther's attacks on Karlstadt and the others functioned at least partially as self-fulfilling prophecies and thereby reconfirmed his opinions about them. It is hoped that non-charismatic Lutherans will learn from this historical experience, if not from present encounters, that to use Lutheran theological motifs as a club against charismatic renewal may well be counterproductive both in terms of excluding the renewal's positive contributions and causing backlash.

4. The history of Lutheran encounters with earlier renewal movements may serve therefore as a resource for relating to the present renewal. It is important that charismatic and non-charismatic alike realize this.

> The great asset of a tradition is its provision of a rich resource of accumulated wisdom that gives perspective to the present moment. Its wisdom has been tested and tried in the crucible of life, not once or twice, but many times over. Out of the wisdom and stability of living tradition, it is possible to carry on dialogue or debate with all that is contemporary and new without being tossed about by every new wind that blows. Tradition provides criteria that enable one to test the spirits.[28]

Not only does awareness of the tradition alert us to the potential problems and critical issues raised by the charismatic renewal, it should also remind us of items which have not been resolved in the past. Thus, for example, Eric Beyreuther comments: "If we do not find better answers to the questions of Pietism than it did, then the questions remain and are even more pressing than Pietism itself thought."[29]

5. The advantage of considering the charismatic renewal in light of the history of earlier renewal movements is that it provides a certain

---

[28]John Leith, *An Introduction to the Reformed Tradition: A Way of Being the Christian Community* (Edinburgh: St. Andrew Press, 1977) 30.

[29]Erich Beyreuther, *Der geschichtliche Auftrag des Pietismus in der Gegenwart.* (Stuttgart: Calwer, 1963) 7.

distance. When one is too close to the trees one has difficulty seeing the forest. Distance, or a certain detachment from immediate causes, provides perspective. For example, Spener's famous pious desires for intensified biblical study, practice of universal priesthood through responsible work of the laity within the church, realization of the convictional efficacy of a Christian life, reform of theological studies in light of congregational needs, and direction of the sermon toward missionary and pastoral concerns, are also present in the charismatic renewal and may be discussed and critiqued historically without the heat of battle.

6. Distance without presence of course also has its problems— abstract theorizing, lifelessness. Thus the resources of our tradition need application and translation into the present context so that they may function hermeneutically to understand the present. Conversely, the present charismatic renewal may also function hermeneutically to understand prior renewals. This is especially true in relation to practice, the focal point for all renewals. Since the life and practice of previous renewals are not easily retrievable by the church historian, the present renewal may provide insights about the praxis of the past renewals.

7. The historical hermeneutic for understanding charismatic renewal is a two-way street. This means that just as contemporary biblical exegesis and theology operate with a deficit if they ignore the past 2,000 years of the church's interpretation of Scripture and theological work, it is equally a loss when charismatic Lutherans interpret their present experience of baptism in the Spirit apart from or in ignorance of their own tradition and the history of the church. All too often the charismatic experience has happened to people in a theological vacuum which means that they do not know how to interpret their experience. An understanding of prior relationships of the Lutheran tradition and renewal movements can assist in filling such a vacuum.

8. Finally, historical awareness of the contexts of renewal movements may provide clues to their appeal, orientation, and potential impact and theological profile. Again, we repeat that this is not a substitute for contemporary analysis but a hermeneutical tool.

It is hoped that the type of historical-theological analysis attempted in this study will reduce unnecessary tensions between charismatics and non-charismatics by highlighting the central concerns of the renewal as they have found their major expressions since the Reformation. It is our conviction that setting the charismatic renewal within the long history of Protestant renewal movements will reduce anxieties about their dangers without uncritical endorsing or rejecting. This in turn should assist in the development of a positive atmosphere for dialogue.

The task of providing theological and doctrinal definition and interpretation of the charismatic renewal within the historic Lutheran tradition is a responsibility which belongs to charismatic and non-charismatic alike. It is in this common task that a constructive and creative voice and shape may be given to the renewal and in turn appropriated by the church.

ABBREVIATIONS

ABK	Sider, Ronald, *Andreas Bodenstein von Karlstadt. The Development of his Thought 1517-1525*, Leiden: Brill, 1974.
ARG	*Archiv für Reformationsgeschichte.*
Asheim	Asheim, Ivor, ed., *Kirche, Mystik, Heiligung und das Natürliche bei Luther*, Göttingen: Vandenhoeck & Ruprecht, 1967.
CRAL	Christenson, Larry, *The Charismatic Renewal Among Lutherans*, Minneapolis: Bethany Fellowship, Inc., 1976.
Franz	Franz, Günther, ed., *Thomas Müntzer. Schriften und Briefe. Kritische Gesamtausgabe*, Gütersloh: Gerd Mohn, 1968.
HJV	Horst, de Jong, and Visser, eds., *De Geest in het geding opstellen Aangeboden aan J. A. Oosterbaan*, Willink, 1978.
LRI	*Lutheran Renewal International.*
LCRN	*Lutheran Charismatic Renewal Newsletter.*
LW	Lehman, Helmut T., and Pelikan, Jaroslav, *Luther's Works*, St. Louis, Philadelphia: Concordia/Fortress, 1955ff. Cited as LW vol., p.
MQR	*Mennonite Quarterly Review.*
PPP	McDonnell, Kilian, ed., *Presence, Power, Praise. Documents on the Charismatic Renewal*, 3 vols., Collegeville: The Liturgical Press, 1980.
PuB	Aland, Kurt, ed., *Pietismus und Bibel*, Witten: Luther-Verlag, 1980.

PuMW   Aland, Kurt, ed., *Pietismus und Moderne Welt*, Witten: Luther Verlag, 1974.

RGG   *Religion in Geschichte und Gegenwart*, Dritte Auflage, Tübingen: J. C. B. Mohr, 1957f.

SAJS   Christenson, Larry, *Social Action Jesus Style*, Minneapolis: Dimension Books, 1976[2].

SCJ   *The Sixteenth Century Journal.*

ST   Christenson, Larry, *Speaking in Tongues*, Minneapolis: Dimension Books (1968), 1975.

WA   *D. Martin Luthers Werke*, Kritische Ausgabe, Weimar: Hermann Böhlau, 1883ff. Cited as WA vol., page, line.

WCC   World Council of Churches.

WNM   Schmidt, Martin, *Wiedergeburt und Neuer Mensch: Gesammelte Studien zur Geschichte des Pietismus*, Witten: Luther Verlag, 1969.

BIBLIOGRAPHY

Agrimson, J. Elmo. *Gifts of the Spirit and the Body of Christ. Perspectives on the Charismatic Movement.* Minneapolis MN: Augsburg, 1974.

Ahlstrom, Sydney. *A Religious History of the American People.* New Haven CT: Yale University Press, 1972.

Aland, Kurt. "Bemerkungen zu August Hermann Francke und seinem Bekehrungserlebnis." *Kirchengeschichtliche Entwürfe.* Gütersloh: Gütersloher Verlagshaus, 1960.

Althaus, Paul. *Communio Sanctorum. Die Gemeinde im lutherischen Kirchengedanken.* Munich: Kaiser, 1929.

American Lutheran Church. "A Report on Glossolalia." *Presence, Power, Praise. Documents on the Charismatic Renewal.* 3 vols. (1963): 1:55-63.

Anderson, Robert Mapes. *Vision of the Disinherited: The Making of American Pentecostalism.* New York/Oxford: University Press, 1979.

Ansons, Gunars. "The Charismatics and their churches. Report on Two Conferences." *Dialog* 15/2 (1976): 142-44

Arndt, Johann. *Johann Arndts Sechs Bücher vom Wahren Christentum nebst dessen Parodies-Gärtlein.* 13th ed. Stuttgart: Steinkopf, n.d.

Arnold, Gottfried. *Unparteiische Kirchen-und Ketzerhistorie vom Anfang des Neuen Testaments bis auf das Jahr Christi 1688.* 2 vols. Reprint. Hildesheim: Olms, 1967.

"The Augsburg Confession in the United States." *Currents in Theology and Mission.* 2 July 1980.

Augustine. *The City of God.* New York: Modern Library, 1950.

Barge, Hermann. *Andreas Bodenstein von Karlstadt.* 2 vols. 1905. Reprint. Nieuwkoop: De Graaf, 1968.

Bäumer, Remigius. *Martin Luther und der Papst.* Münster: Aschendorff, 1970.

Bayer, Oswald. *Promissio. Geschichte der reformatorischen Wende in Luthers Theologie.* Göttingen: Vandenhoeck & Ruprecht, 1971.

Berger, Peter. *The Social Reality of Religion.* London: Faber and Faber, 1967.

———. *The Sacred Canopy: Elements of a Sociological Theory of Religion.* New York: Anchor Books, 1969.

———. *The Heretical Imperative: Contemporary Possibilities of Religious Affirmation.* New York: Doubleday, 1979.

Beyreuther, Erich. *Der geschichtliche Auftrag des Pietismus in der Gegenwart.* Stuttgart: Calwer Verlag, 1963.

Bittlinger, Arnold. *Die Bedeutung der Gnadengaben für die Gemeinde Jesu Christi.* Marburg an der Lahn: Edel, 1964.

———. *Glossolalia: Wert und Problematik des Sprachenredens.* Schloß Craheim: Kühne Verlag, 1969³.

———. *Im Kraftfeld des Heiligen Geistes.* Marburg an der Lahn: Edel, 1971⁴.

———. *Gifts and Ministries.* London: Hodder and Stoughton, 1974.

———. "Die charismatische Erneuerung der Kirchen: Aufbruch urchristlichen Erfahrung." In *Erfahrung und Theologie des Heiligen, Geistes.* Edited by C. Heitmann and H. Mühler. Hamburg/München: Rauhen/Kössel, 1974, 19-35.

———. *Papst und Pfingstler. Der römisch katholisch-pfingstliche Dialog und seine ökumenische Relevanz.* Frankfurt am Main: Peter Lang, 1978.

———. "Charismatic Renewal: An Opportunity for the Church?" *The Ecumenical Review* 31/3 (1979): 247-51.

———. "Report on the Work of the WCC Consultant on Charismatic Renewal." In *The Church is Charismatic: The World Council of Churches and the Charismatic Renewal.* Edited by A. Bittlinger. Geneva: WCC, 1981.

———. *The Church is Charismatic. The World Council of Churches and the Charismatic Renewal.* Geneva: WCC, 1981.

Bloch-Hoell, Nils. *The Pentecostal Movement: Its Origins, Development and Distinctive Character.* London/New York: Allen and Unwin/Humanities Press, 1964.

———. "Der Heilige Geist in der Pfingstbewegung und in der charismatischen Bewegung." In *Taufe und Heiliger Geist.* Edited by Pertti Mäki, Helsinki, 1979, 89-105.

Bloesch, Donald G. "The Charismatic Revival: A Theological Critique." *Religion in Life* 35 (1966): 364-80.

Bornkamm, Heinrich. *Luther im Spiegel der deutschen Geistesgeschichte.* 2nd ed. Göttingen: Vandenhoeck & Ruprecht, 1970.

Bornkamm, Heyer and Schindler, eds. *Der Pietismus in Gestalten und Wirkungen.* Bielefeld: Luther Verlag, 1975.

Brady, Thomas A., Jr. *Ruling Class, Regime and Reformation at Strasbourg 1520-1555.* Leiden: E. J. Brill, 1978.

————. " 'Social History of the Reformation.' 'Sozialgeschichte der Reformation.' A Conference at the Deutsches Historisches Institut London, May 25-27, 1978." *The Sixteenth Century Journal* 10/1 (1979): 89-92.

Brecht, Martin. "Christentum als Lebensordnung. Die Frömmigkeit des Pietismus." In *Evangelischer Glaube im Wandel der Zeit*. Stuttgart: Steinkopf Verlag, 1967.

————. "Johann Albrecht Bengel und schwäbische Biblizismus." In *Pietismus und Bibel*, 193-218.

————. "Randbemerkungen in Luthers Ausgaben der 'Deutsche Theologie.' " *Luther Jahrbuch* 47 (1980): 10-32.

Brewster, P. S., ed. *Pentecostal Doctrine*. Gloucestershire, England: Grenehurst Press, 1976.

Bruner, Frederick, D. *A Theology of the Holy Spirit*. Grand Rapids MI: Eerdmans, 1970.

Bubenheimer, Ulrich. *Consonantia Theologia et Jurisprudentiae: Andreas Bodenstein von Karlstadt als Theologe und Jurist zwischen Scholastik und Reformation*. Tübingen: J. C. B. Mohr, 1977.

————. "Andreas Rudolff Bodenstein von Karlstadt." In *Andreas Bodenstein von Karlstadt* 1480-1541. Edited by Wolfgang Merklein. Karlstadt, 1980, 5-58.

Büchsel, Jürgen. *Gottfried Arnold. Sein Verständnis von Kirche und Wiedergeburt*. Witten: Luther Verlag, 1970.

Bund der Evangelischen Kirchen in der DDR, Theologischen Studienabteilung. "Charisma und Heiligen Geist." Beiträge D4, 1977.

————. "Nachträge zu D1-D4." Beiträge D7, 1978.

————. "Dokumente zur charismatischen Bewegung." 1978.

————. "Das Wirken des Heiligen Geistes und die Wirklichkeit der Kirche." Beiträge A2, 1978.

————. "Charismatische Bewegung in der DDR." Beiträge A3, 1978.

————. "Kirche und charismatische Erneuerung. Über Chancen und Probleme einer Bewegung in unseren Kirchen." Beiträge A4, 1979.

Christenson, Larry. *Die Gabe des Zungenredens in der Lutherischen Kirche*. Marburg an der Lahn: Edel, 1963.

————. *Der Dienst der Krankenheilung in der Kirche—Möglichkeit oder Verpflichtung?* Marburg an der Lahn: Edel, 1964.

————. *The Christian Family*. Minneapolis MN: Bethany Fellowship, 1971.

————. *Speaking in Tongues*. Minneapolis MN: Dimension Books, (1968) 1975.

————. *Social Action Jesus Style*. Minneapolis MN: Dimension Books, 1976².

Christie-Murray, David. *Voices from the Gods: Speaking with Tongues*. London: Routledge and Kegan Paul, 1978.

Dalferth, Ingolf. "Luther on the Experience of Faith." *Heythrop Journal* 21/1 (1980): 50-56.

Davis, Kenneth. *Anabaptism and Asceticism*. Scottdale PA: Herald Press, 1974.

_____ . "The Origins of Anabaptism: Ascetic and charismatic elements exemplifying continuity and discontinuity." In *The Origins and Characteristics of Anabaptism*. Edited by Marc Lienhard. The Hague: Martinus Nijhoff, 1977, 27-41.

_____ . "Anabaptism as a Charismatic Movement." *Mennonite Quarterly Review* 53/3 (1979): 219-34.

Davis, Rex. *Locusts and Wild Honey: The Charismatic Renewal and the Ecumenical Movement*. Geneva: World Council of Churches, 1978.

Dearman, Marion. "Christ and Conformity: A Study of Pentecostal Values." *Journal for the Scientific Study of Religion* 13/4 (1974): 437-53.

Del Pino, Jerome King. *Luther's Theology of the Cross as Reflected in Selected Historical Contexts of Social Change from 1521-1525*. Unpublished dissertation, Boston University, 1980.

Deppermann, Klaus. "Melchior Hoffmans letzte Schriften aus dem Jahre 1524." *Archiv für Reformationsgeschichte* 63 (1972): 72-93.

_____ . *Melchior Hoffman. Soziale Unruhen und apokalyptischen Visionen im Zeitalter der Reformation*. Göttingen: Vandenhoeck & Ruprecht, 1979.

_____ . "Melchior Hoffmans Weg von Luther zu den Täufern." In *Umstrittenes Täufertum 1525-1975*. Edited by Hans-Jürgen Goertz. Göttinger: Vandenhoeck & Ruprecht, 1975.

Dickens, A. G. *The German Nation and Martin Luther*. London: Arnold, 1974.

Dülmer, Richard von. *Reformation als Revolution: Soziale Bewegung und religiösen Radikalismus in der deutschen Reformation*. Munich: Deutscher Taschenbuch, 1977.

Dyck, C. J. "Hermeneutics and Discipleship." In *De Geest in het geding opstellen Aangeboder aan J.A. Oosterbaan*. Edited by Horst, de Jong, and Visser. Willink, 1978, 57-72.

Ebeling, Gerhard. *Luther: Einführung in sein Denken*. Tübingen: J. C. B. Mohr, 1964.

_____ . "Luther and the Beginning of the Modern Age." In *Luther and the Dawn of the Modern Era*. Edited by Heiko A. Oberman. Leiden: Brill, 1974.

Ecke, Karl. *Fortsetzung der Reformation: Kaspar von Schwenckfelds Schau einer apostolischen Reformation*. Gladbeck: Schriftenmissions Verlag, 1978.

Edwards, Mark U., Jr. *Luther and the False Brethren*. Stanford CA: Stanford University Press, 1975.

Elinson, Howard. "The Implications of Pentecostal Religion for Intellectualism, Politics, and Race Relations." *The American Journal of Sociology* 70/4 (1965): 403-15.

Elliger, Walter. *Thomas Müntzer. Leben und Werk*. 2nd ed. Göttingen: Vandenhoeck & Ruprecht, 1975.

_____ . *Aussenseiter der Reformation: Thomas Müntzer*. Göttingen: Vandenhoeck & Ruprecht, 1975.

Elton, G. R. *Reformation Europe 1517-1559*. London: Collins, 1963.

Engelsviken, Tormod. *Molo Wongel: A Documentary Report on the Life and History of the Independent Pentecostal Movement in Ethiopia 1960-1975*. Typescript manuscript, Olso, 1975.

_____. *The Gift of the Spirit. An Analysis and Evaluation of the Charismatic Movement from a Lutheran Theological Perspective*. Unpublished dissertation, Aquinas Institute, School of Theology, Dubuque IA, 1981.

Engelsviken, Tormod, Hanssen Ove, and Sannes Kjell, eds. *Den Hellige and I Kirkkens Liv*. Oslo: Luther Forlag, 1981.

Fast, Heinold, ed. *Der Linke Flügel der Reformation*. Bremen: Schünemann, 1962.

Ford, J. Massyngberde. "Neo-Pentecostalism Within the Roman Catholic Communion." *Dialog* 13/1 (1974): 45-50.

Freys, E., and Barge, H. *Verzeichnis der gedruckten Schriften des Andreas Bodenstein von Karlstadt*. 1904. Reprint. Nieuwkoop, 1965.

Friedman, Robert. *The Theology of Anabaptism*. Scottdale PA: Herald Press, 1973.

Friesen, Abraham. *Reformation and Utopia: The Marxist Interpretation of the Reformation and its Antecendents*. Wiesbaden: Steiner, 1974.

Friesen, A., and Goertz, H.-J., eds. *Thomas Müntzer. Wege der Forschung*. Darmstadt, 1978.

Froelich, Karlfried. "Charismatic Manifestations and the Lutheran Incarnational Stance." In *The Holy Spirit in the Life of the Church: From Biblical Times to the Present*. Edited by Paul D. Opsahl. Minneapolis MN: Augsburg Publishing House, 1978, 136-57.

Frøen, Hans J. "What is Baptism in the Holy Spirit?" In *Jesus, Where Are You Taking Us?*. Edited by Norris Wogen. Carol Stream IL: Creation House, 1973.

Gassmann, Günther, and Harding Meyer, eds. *Neue transkonfessionelle Bewegungen*. Frankfurt am Main: Lembeck, 1976.

Goertz, Hans-Jürgen. *Innere und Äussere Ordnung in der Theologie Thomas Müntzers*. Leiden: Brill, 1967.

_____. *Umstrittenes Täufertum, 1525-1975: Neue Forschungen*. Göttingen: Vandenhoeck & Ruprecht, 1975.

Goeters, J. F. G. "Spiritualisten, religiöse." *Religion in Geschichte und Gegenwart*[3], 6:255-57.

Grane, Lief. *Modus Loquendi Theologicus: Luthers Kampf um die Erneuerung der Theologie 1515-1518*. Leiden: Brill, 1975.

Grimm, Harold J. *The Reformation Era 1500-1650*. New York/London: Collier-MacMillan, 1965.

Gritsch, Eric. *Reformer Without a Church*. Philadelphia PA: Fortress Press, 1967.

_____. "Luther und die Schwärmer: Verworfene Anfechtung?" *Luther* 47 (1976): 105-21.

Gritsch, Eric, and Jensen, Robert. *Lutheranism. The Theological Movement and Its Confessional Writings*. Philadelphia PA: Fortress Press, 1976.

Hagen, Kenneth. *A Theology of Testament in the Young Luther. The Lectures on Hebrews*. Leiden: Brill, 1974.

Hägglund, Bengt. "Luther und die Mystik." In Ivor Asheim, ed., *Kirche, Mystik, Heiligung, und das Natürliche bei Luther*. Göttingen: Vandenhoeck & Ruprecht, 1967, 84-94.

Harnack, Adolf von. "Was hat Historie an festen Erkenntnis zur Deutung der Weltgeschichte zu bieten?" In *Reden und Aufsätze*. NF IV. Giessen: Töpelmann, 1923.

Harrisville, Roy A. "Speaking in Tongues—Proof of Transcendence?" *Dialog* 13/1 (1974): 11-18.

Hein, Lorenz. "Philipp Jakob Spener, Ein Theologe des heiligen Geistes und Prophet der Kirche." In *Die Einheit der Kirche. Dimensionen ihrer Heiligkeit, Katholizität und Apostolizität.* Edited by H. Lorenz, Festgabe Peter Meinhold zum 70. Geburtstag. Wiesbaden: Steiner Verlag, 1977, 103-26.

Hendrix, Scott. "Charismatic Renewal. Old Wine in New Skins." In *Currents in Theology and Mission* 4/3 (1977): 158-66.

———. "Reply to Jungkuntz." *Currents in Theology and Mission* 5/1 (1978): 58-60.

Herlihy, David. "Alienation in Medieval Culture and Society." In *Alienation: Concept, Term and Meanings.* Edited by Frank Johnson. New York and London: Seminar Press, 1973, 125-41.

Herte, Adolf. *Der katholische Lutherbild im Banne der Lutherkommentare der Cochläus.* 3 vols. Münster, 1943.

Hillerbrand, Hans J. "Thomas Müntzer's Last Tract Against Martin Luther." *Mennonite Quarterly Review* 38 (1964): 20-36.

———. "Andreas Bodenstein of Carlstadt, Prodigal Reformer." *Church History* 35 (1966): 379-98.

———. "Anabaptism and History." *Mennonite Quarterly Review* 45 (1971): 107-22.

Hirsch, Emanuel. *Geschichte der neuen evangelischen Theologie.* II. Gütersloh: Mohn, 1960.

———. "Schwenckfeld und Luther." In his *Lutherstudien.* II. Gütersloh: Bertelmann, 1954, 35-67.

Hocken, Peter. "Charismatic Renewal, the Churches and Unity." *One in Christ* 15/4 (1979): 310-21.

———. "A Survey of the Worldwide Charismatic Movement." In *The Church is Charismatic: The World Council of Churches and the Charismatic Renewal.* Edited by Arnold Bittlinger. Geneva: World Council of Churches, 1981, 117-47.

Hoerschelmann, Werner. *Christliche Gurus. Darstellung von Selbstverständnis und Funktion idigenen Christseins durch unabhängige, charismatisch geführte Gruppen in Südindien.* Frankfurt am Main: Peter Lang, 1977.

Hof, Otto. "Luthers Unterscheidung zwischen dem Glauben und der Reflexion auf den Glauben." *Kerygma und Dogma* 18 (1972): 296-324.

Hoffman, Bengt R. *Luther and the Mystics: A Re-examination of Luther's Spiritual Experience and his Relationship to the Mystics.* Minneapolis MN: Augsburg Publishing House, 1976.

Hoffman, R. Joseph. "Meméristai ho Christós? Anti-Enthusiast Polemic from Paul to Augustine." *Studia Theologica* 33 (1979): 149-64.

Holl, Karl. *Gesammelte Aufsätze zur Kirchengeschichte.* 1, 7th ed. Tübingen, 1948.

Hollenweger, Walter. *Enthusiastisches Christentum. Die Pfingstbewegung in Geschichte und Gegenwart.* Zürich: Zwingli Verlag, 1969.

———. "Flowers and Songs. A Mexican Contribution to Theological Hermeneutics." *International Review of Mission* 60/238 (1971): 232-44.

———. *Die Pfingstkirchen: Selbstdarstellung Dokumente, Kommentare.* Stuttgart: Evangelisches Verlagswerk, 1971.

———. "Charismatische und pfingstlerische Bewegung als Frage an die Kirchen heute." In *Wiederentdeckung des Heiligen Geistes.* Edited by M. Lienhard and H. Meyer. Frankfurt am Main: Lembeck, 1974, 53-76.

———. "Roots and Fruits of the Charismatic Renewal in the Third World: Implications for Mission." *Theological Renewal* 14 (1980): 11-28.

———. Review of Robert M. Anderson, *Vision of the Disinherited: The Making of American Pentecostalism.* In *Theological Renewal* 14 (1980): 38-40.

———. "Charismatic Renewal in the Third World: Implications for Mission." *Occasional Bulletin of Missionary Research* 4/2 (April 1980): 68-75.

Horst, Irving B. "The Fellowship in the Spirit." In *De Geest in het geding opstellen Aangeboden aan J.A. Oosterbaan.* Edited by Horst, de Jong, and Willink Visser, 1978, 99-110.

Jaeger, Kardinal. *Das Konzils Dekret über den Okumenismus.* Paderborn: Bonifacius, 1965.

Jensen, Peter. "Calvin, Charismatics and Miracles." *The Evangelical Quarterly* 51/3 (1979): 131-44.

Jensen, Richard. *Touched by the Spirit. One Man's Struggle to Understand His Experience of the Holy Spirit.* Minneapolis MI: Augsburg, 1975.

Joest, Wilfried. *Gesetz und Freiheit. Das Problem des Tertius Usus Legis bei Luther und die Neutestamentliche Parainese.* Göttingen: Vandenhoeck & Ruprecht, 1961.

———. *Ontologie der Person bei Luther.* Göttingen: Vandenhoeck & Ruprecht, 1967.

Jorstad, Erling. "A Movement for our Time." *Event Magazine* (Nov.-Dec., 1973).

———. *Bold in the Spirit. Lutheran Charismatic Renewal in America Today.* Minneapolis MI: Augsburg Publishing House, 1974.

Jungkuntz, Theodore. "Secularization Theology, Charismatic Renewal, and Luther's Theology of the Cross." *Concordia Theological Monthly* 42/1 (1971): 5-24.

———. "Charismatic Worship: Challenge or Challenged?" *Response* 16/1 & 2 (1976): 4-10.

———. "A Response." *The Cresset.* Occasional Paper II, 1977.

———. "Sectarian Consequences of Mistranslation in Luther's Smalcald Articles." *Currents in Theology and Mission* 4/3 (1977): 166-67.

———. "Response to Dr. Lazareth." In *Confession and Congregation (The Cresset.* Occasional Paper 3). Valparaiso IN: Valparaiso University Press, 1978, 57-59.

———. "A Response to Scott Hendrix's 'Charismatic Renewal: Old Wine in New Skins.'" *Currents in Theology and Mission* 5/1 (1978): 54-57.

_____ . "Ethics in a Relativizing Society." *The Cresset*. Occasional Paper 3, 1978.

_____ . "The Question of the Ordination of Women." *The Cresset* (Special Issue) 1978-79.

_____ . The Canon, the Charismata and the Cross." *The Cresset* 1979, 25-29.

_____ . "Lutherans and Roman Catholics Participate in Ecumenical Covenant Communities." *ReConcile* 2/3 (May 1981): 7-9.

_____ . *A Lutheran Charismatic Catechism*. Flushing NY: Bread of Life Ministries, 1979.

Kähler, Ernst. *Karlstadt und Augustin: Der Kommentar des Andreas Bodenstein von Karlstadt zu Augustins Schrift De Spiritu et Litera*. Halle (Saale): Niemeyer, 1952.

Karlstadt, Andreas. *Von Abtuhung der Bilder und das keyn Bedtler unther den Christen seyn sollen*, 1522. Edited by Hans Lietzmann, *Kleine Texte* No. 74. Bonn 1911.

_____ . *Karlstadts Schriften aus den Jahren 1523-1525*. Edited by Erich Hertzsch. 2 vols. Hall (Saale): Niemeyer, 1956-1957.

Kinder, Ernst. "Zur Lehre vom Heiligen Geist nach den Lutherischen Bekenntnisschriften." *Fuldaer* Hefte 15 (1964): 7-38.

Klaasen, Walter. "Spiritualization in the Reformation." *Mennonite Quarterly Review* 37 (1963): 67-77.

_____ . "Church Discipline and the Spirit in Pilgrim Marpeck," In *De Geest in het geding opstellen Aangeboden aan J. A. Oosterbaan*. Edited by Horst, de Jong, and Willink Visser. 1978, 169-80.

Koenig, John. "From Mystery to Ministry: Paul as Interpreter of Charismatic Gifts," *Union Seminary Quarterly Review* 33/3 & 4 (1978): 167-74.

Kopfermann, Wolfram, ed. *Charismatische Gemeinde-Erneuerung. Eine Zwischenbilanz*. Hamburg, 1981.

Ladner, G. "Homo Viator: Medieval Ideas on Alienation and Order." *Speculum* 42/2 (1967): 233-59.

Langen, August. *Der Wortschatz des deutschen Pietismus*. Tübingen: Niemeyer, 1968.

Laurentin, René. "Charismatische Erneuerung: Prophetische Erneuerung oder Neokonservatismus?" *Concilium* 17/1 (1981): 27-33.

Lazareth, William. "The Question of the 'Third Use' of the Law." In *Confession and Congregation*. Valparaiso IN, 1977.

Lehmann, Hartmut. *Pietismus und Weltliche Ordnung in Württemburg von 17. bis zum 20. Jahrhundert*. Stuttgart: Kohlhammer, 1969.

Leith, John. *An Introduction to the Reformed Tradition: A Way of Being the Christian Community*. Edinburgh: St. Andrew Press, 1977.

Lensch, Rodney. *My Personal Pentecost*. Kirkwood MO: Impact Books, 1972.

Leube, Hans. *Orthodoxie und Pietismus. Gesammelte Studien*. Bielefeld: Luther Verlag, 1975.

Lienhard, Marc, ed. *Croyants et Sceptiques au XVIe Siècle*. Strasbourg: Librairie Istra, 1981.

Lindberg, Carter. "Theory and Practice: Reformation Models of Ministry as Resource for the Present." *Lutheran Quarterly* 27/1 (1975): 27-35.

———— . "Mask of God and Prince of Lies: Luther's Theology of the Demonic." In *Disguises of the Demonic*. Edited by Alan Olson. New York: Association Press, 1975, 87-103.

———— . "Theology and Politics: Luther the Radical and Müntzer the Reactionary." *Encounter* 37/4 (1976): 356-71.

———— . "There Should Be No Beggars Among Christians: Karlstadt, Luther and the Origins of Protestant Poor Relief." *Church History* 46/3 (1977): 313-34.

———— . "Conflicting Models of Ministry—Luther Karlstadt and Muentzer." *Concordia Theological Quarterly* 41/4 (1977): 35-50.

———— . "Karlstadt's 'Dialogue' on the Lord's Supper." *Mennonite Quarterly Review* 53/1 (1979): 35-77.

———— . "Through a Glass Darkly. A History of the Church's Vision of the Poor and Poverty." *The Ecumenical Review* 33/1 (1981): 37-52.

———— . "La théologie et l'assistance publique, le cas d'Ypres (1525-1531)." In *Revue d'Histoire et de Philosophie Religieuses* 61/1 (1981): 23-36.

Lindt, Andreas. "Pietismus und Okumene." In *Pietismus und Moderne Welt*. Witten: Luther Verlag, 1974, 138-60.

List, Günther. *Chiliastische Utopie und Radikale Reformation*. München: W. Fink, 1973.

Littell, F. H. *The Origins of Sectarian Protestantism*. New York & London, 1964.

———— . *Das Selbstverständnis der Täufer*. Kassel: J. G. Oncken Verlag, 1966. (English original: *The Anabaptist View of the Church.*)

———— . "In Response to Hans Hillerbrand." *Mennonite Quarterly Review* 45 (1971): 377-80.

Loewenich, Walter von. "Luthers Auslegung des Pfingstgeschichte." In *Vierhundertfünfzig Jahre lutherische Reformation 1517-1967. Festschrift für Franz Lau*. Göttingen: Vandenhoeck & Ruprecht, 1967, 181-90.

———— . "Das christliche Menschenbild im Umbruch der Moderne." In *Der Pietismus in Gestalten und Wirkungen*. Bielefeld: Luther Verlag, 1975, 326-42.

———— . *Luther's Theology of the Cross*. Tr. by W. Bowman. Minneapolis MI: Augsburg Publishing House, 1976.

Lohse, Bernhard. "Die Bedeutung Augustins für den jungen Luther." *Kerygma und Dogma* 11 (1965): 116-35.

———— . "Die Stellung der 'Schwärmer' und Täufer in der Reformationsgeschichte." *Archiv für Reformationsgeschichte* 60/1 (1969): 5-26.

Lonning, Inge. "Die Reformation und die Schwärmer." *Concilium* 15/10 (1979): 515-18.

Luther, Martin. *Luther: Lectures on Romans*. Edited by Wilhelm Pauck. Library of Christian Classics 15. London: SCM, 1961.

Lutheran World Federation. *Sent into the World*. Proceedings of the Fifth Assembly (Evian 1970). Geneva: Luthern World Federation, 1970.

MacRae, George. "Reflections on Ecumenism." *Harvard Divinity Bulletin* 11/1 (1980): 11-13.

Manschreck, Clyde, ed. and tr. *Melanchthon on Christian Doctrine*. New York: Oxford, 1965.

Maron, Gottfried. *Individualismus und Gemeinschaft bei Caspar von Schwenckfeld.* Stuttgart: Evangelisches Verlagswerk, 1961.

_____ . "Schwenkfeld." *Religion in Geschichte und Gegenwart.*[3] V. 1620-1621.

_____ . "Thomas Müntzer als Theologe des Gerichts." *Zeitschrift für Kirchengeschichte* 83 (1972): 193-225.

Matzat, Don. *Serving the Renewal. Stories of the Men of Lutheran Charismatic Renewal Services.* Flushing NY: Bread of Life, 1978.

McDonnell, Kilian. "Pentecostal Culture: Protestant and Catholic." *One in Christ* 7/4 (1971): 310-18.

_____ . "The Relationship of the Charismatic Renewal to the Established Denominations." *Dialog* 13/3 (1974): 223-29.

_____ . "Die charismatische Bewegung in der katholischen Kirche." In *Wiederentdeckung des Heiligen Geistes.* Edited by H. Meyer. Frankfurt am Main: Lembeck, 1974.

_____ . *Charismatic Renewal and the Churches.* New York: Seabury Press, 1976.

_____ . *The Charismatic Renewal and Ecumenism.* New York: Paulist Press, 1978.

_____ . "Towards a Critique of the Churches and the Charismatic Renewal." *One in Christ* 16/4 (1980): 329-37.

McDonnell, K., and Bittlinger, A. *The Baptism in the Holy Spirit as an Ecumenical Problem.* Notre Dame IN: Charismatic Renewal Services, Inc., 1972.

McLaughlin, R. Emmet. "Spiritualism and the Bible: The Case of Caspar Schwenckfeld (1489-1561)." *Mennonite Quarterly Review* 53 (1979): 282-98.

Mehl, Roger. "Approche sociologique des mouvements charismatiques." *Bulletin de la Société du Protestantisme Francais* (octobre-novembre-décembre 1974): 555-73.

Mensbrugghe, Françoise van der, *Les Mouvements de Renouveau Charismatique. Retour de l'Esprit? Retour de Dionysos?* Dissertation, Faculté Autonome de Théologie, Université de Genève, 1978.

Meyer, Harding. "Transkonfessionelle Bewegungen—Hoffnung oder Gefahr?" *Beiheft zur Okumenischen Rundschau* 32 (1978): 55f.

Modalsli, Ole. *Das Gericht nach den Werken.* Göttingen: Vandenhoeck & Ruprecht, 1963.

Moeller, Bernd. "Tauler und Luther." In *La mystique Rhénans: Colloque de Strasbourg 16-19 Mai 1961.* Paris, 1963, 157-68.

Morgan R., and Pye, M., eds. *Ernst Troeltsch: Writings on Theology and Religion.* Atlanta GA: Knox, 1977.

Mühlen, Heribert. *Die Erneuerung des christlichen Glaubens. Charisma-Geist-Befreiung.* Munich: Don Boseo Verlag, 1974.

_____ . *Erfahrung mit dem Heiligen Geist.* Mainz: Grünewald Verlag, 1979.

_____ . "Gemeinsame Geist-Erfahrung: Hoffnung für die getrennten Kirchen." *Una Sancta* 36/1 (1981): 20-32.

Mülhaupt, Erwin. "Die Bedeutung Luthers für den Pietismus." *Luther* 37/1 (1966): 19-33.

_____ . "Martin Luther oder Thomas Müntzer—Wer ist der rechte Prophet?" *Luther* (1974): 55-71.

Müller, Gerhard. *Die Rechtfertigungslehre.* Gütersloh: Gerd Mohn, 1977.

Newbigin, Leslie. *The Household of God.* London: SCM Press Ltd., 1953.

Nipperdey, Thomas. "Theologie und Revolution bei Thomas Müntzer." *Archiv für Reformationsgeschichte* 54 (1963): 145-81.

Nygren, Anders. *Agape and Eros.* Philadelphia PA: Westminster Press, 1953.

Obermann, Heiko. A. "Simul Gemitus et Raptus: Luther und die Mystik." In Ivor Asheim, ed., *Kirche, Mystik, Heiligung und das Natürliche bei Luther.* Göttingen: Vandenhoeck & Ruprecht, 1967, 20-59.

————. *The Harvest of Medieval Theology.* Cambridge MA: Harvard University Press, 1963.

————. *Forerunners of the Reformation.* New York: Holt, Rinehart and Winston, 1966.

————. "The Shape of Late Medieval Thought: The Birthpangs of the Modern Era." *Archiv für Reformationsgeschichte* 64 (1973): 13-33.

————. "Reformation: Epoche oder Episode?," *Archiv für Reformationgeschichte* 68 (1977): 56-111.

O'Connor, Edward. *The Pentecostal Movement in the Catholic Church.* Notre Dame IN: Ava Maria Press, 1971.

Olson, William G. *The Charismatic Church.* Minneapolis MI: Bethany Fellowship, 1974.

Opsahl, Paul D., ed. *The Holy Spirit in the Life of the Church: From Biblical Times to the Present.* Minneapolis MN: Augsburg Publishing House, 1978.

Oyer, John, ed. "Problems of Anabaptist History. A Symposium.' *Mennonite Quarterly Review* 53/3 (1979): 175-218.

Ozment, Steven. *Homo Spiritualis: A Comparative Study of the Anthropology of Johannes Tauler, Jean Gerson and Martin Luther (1509-16) in the Context of their Theological Thought.* Leiden: Brill, 1969.

————. "Homo Viator": Luther and Late Medieval Theology." In *The Reformation in Medieval Perspective.* Edited by Steven Ozment, Chicago IL: Quadrangle Books, 1971.

————. *Mysticism and Dissent. Religious Ideology and Social Protest in the Sixteenth Century.* New Haven CT and London: Yale University Press, 1973.

Packer, J. D. "Theological Reflection on the Charismatic Movement." *The Churchman* 94/1 & 2 (1980): 7-25, 103-26.

Packull, Werner O. *Mysticism and the Early South German-Austrian Anabaptist Movement 1525-1531.* Scottdale PA: Herald Press, 1977.

Pater, Calvin, "Melchior Hoffman's Explication of the Songs (!) of Songs." *Archiv für Reformationsgeschichte* 68 (1977): 173-91.

Peschke, Erhard. "August Hermann Francke und die Bibel." In *Pietismus und Bibel.* Edited by K. Aland, 59-88.

————. *Bekehrung und Reform: Ansatz und Wurzeln der Theologie August Hermann Franckes.* Bielefeld: Luther Verlag, 1977.

Petry, Ray C., ed. *Late Medieval Mysticism.* London: SCM Press Ltd., 1957.

Pfitzner, Victor. *Led in the Spirit.* Adelaide: Lutheran Publishing House, 1976.

Prenter, Regin. *Spiritus Creator: Luther's Concept of the Holy Spirit.* Translated by J. M. Jensen. Philadelphia PA: Fortress Press, 1953.

Preus, James S. *Carlstadt's "Ordinaciones" and Luther's Liberty. A Study of the Wittenberg Movement 1521-1522.* Cambridge MA: Harvard University Press, 1974.

Quebedeaux, Richard. *The New Charismatics: The Origins, Development and Significance of Neo-Pentecostalism.* New York: Doubleday & Co., 1976.

Ranaghan, Kevin and Dorothy. *Catholic Pentecostals.* New York: Paulist Press, 1969.

Richter, L. "Mystik," in *Religion in Geschichte und Gegenwart,* 4:1237.

Rifkin, Jeremy, and Ted Howard. *The Emerging Order. God in the Age of Scarcity.* New York: G. P. Putnam's Sons, 1979.

Roe, Norman D. "Aggression and Charismatics." *Theology Today* 35 (1978-1979): 81-83.

Rupp, Gordon. *The Righteousness of God. Luther Studies.* London: Hodder and Stoughton, 1953.

_____ . "Word and Spirit in the First Years of the Reformation." *Archiv für Reformationsgeschichte* 49/1 (1958): 13-22.

_____ . *Patterns of Reformation.* Philadelphia PA: Fortress Press, 1969.

Scharfe, Martin. *Die Religion des Volkes: Kleine Kultur und Sozialgeschichte des Pietismus.* Gütersloh: Gerd Mohn, 1980.

Scheel, Otto. "Taulers Mystik und Luthers reformatorische Entdeckung." In *Festgabe für J. F. Kaften.* Tübingen, 1920, 298-318.

Schmidt, Martin. *John Wesley.* 2 vols. Zürich: Gotthelf Verlag, 1953-1966.

_____ . "Pietismus." *Religion in Geschichte und Gegenwart.* 5:370ff.

_____ . *Pietismus.* Stuttgart: Kohlhammer, 1972.

_____ . "Das Frühchristentum in der evangelisch lutherischen Überlieferung vom 18-20. Jahrhundert, insbesondere in Deutschland." In *Oecumenica* (1971-1972): 88-110.

_____ . "Philipp Jakob Spener und die Bibel." *Pietismus und Bibel.* Edited by K. Aland, 9-58.

_____ . "Epochen der Pietismusforschung." In *Pietism and Reveil,* edited by Berg and Dooren. Leiden: Brill, 1978, 22-79.

Schwarz, Reinhard. *Die apokalyptische Theologie Thomas Müntzers und der Taboriten.* Tübingen: J. C. B. Mohr, 1977.

Schwarzwäller, Klaus. "Delecari assertionibus. Zur Struktur von Luthers Pneumatologie." *Luther Jahrbuch* (1971): 26-58.

Schweizer, Edward. "Was ist der Heilige Geist? Eine bibel-theologische Hinführung." *Concilium* 15/10 (1979): 494-98.

Seguenny, André. *Spiritualistische Philosophie als Antwort auf die religiöse Frage des XVI Jahrhunderts.* Wiesbaden: Franz Steiner, 1978.

_____ . "Histoire Magistra Vitae. Quelques Remarques à propos de la Chronique de Sebastien Franck." In *Horizons Européens de la Réforme en Alsace.* Edited by M. Kroon and M. Lienhard. Strasbourg: Istra, 1980, 107-18.

Sider, Ronald, ed. *Karlstadt's Battle with Luther.* Philadelphia PA: Fortress Press, 1978.

Siggins, Ian. *Martin Luther's Doctrine of Christ.* New Haven CT and London: Yale University Press, 1970.

Sills, Mark. "The Docetic Church." *The Christian Century* (January 1981) 21:37-38.

Smylie, James H. "Testing the Spirits in the American Context. Great Awakenings, Pentecostalism, and the Charismatic Movements." *Interpretation* 33/1 (1979): 32-46.

Spener, Philipp. *Pia Desideria* (1676). Edited by Kurt Aland. Berlin: De Gruyter, 1955.

Spittler, Russel P., ed., *Perspectives on the New Pentecostalism.* Grand Rapids MI: Baker Book House, 1976.

Spitz, L. W. *The Renaissance and Reformation Movements.* Chicago IL: Rand McNally, 1971.

Staehelin, Ernst, ed., *Die Verkündigung des Reich Gottes in der Kirche Jesu Christi. Zeugnisse aus allen Jahrhunderten und allen Konfessionen.* 4. Basel: Reinhardt, 1957.

Stayer, James. "Thomas Müntzer's Theology and Revolution in Recent Non-Marxist Interpretation." *Mennonite Quarterly Review* 43 (1969): 142-52.

Steck, Karl. *Luther und die Schwärmer.* Zürich: Zollikon, 1955.

Steinmetz, David. "Religious Ecstasy in Staupitz and the Young Luther." *The Sixteenth Century Journal* 11/1 (1980): 23-37.

Stendahl, Krister. "The New Testament Evidence." In *The Charismatic Movement.* Edited by M. P. Hamilton. Grand Rapids MI: Eerdmans, 1975, 49-59.

Stephan, Horst. *Luther in den Wandlungen seiner Kirche.* Berlin: Töpelmann, 1951.

Stoeffler, F. Ernest. *The Rise of Evangelical Pietism.* Leiden: E. J. Brill, 1971.

Strauss, Gerald, ed. *Manifestations of Discontent in Germany on the Eve of the Reformation.* Bloomington IN, 1972.

Strauss, Gerald. *Luther's House of Learning. Indoctrination of the Young in the German Reformation.* Baltimore MD and London: Johns Hopkins University Press, 1978.

Stupperich, R., ed. *Martin Bucers Deutsche Schriften.* 1, Gütersloh: Mohn, 1960.

Synan, Vinson. *The Holiness-Pentecostal Movement in the United States.* Grand Rapids MI: Eerdmans, 1971.

Tappert, Theodore, ed. *The Book of Concord.* Philadelphia PA: Fortress Press, 1959.

Theissen, Gerd. *Studien zur Soziologie der Urchristentums.* Tübingen: J. C. B. Mohr, 1979.

Tinney, James S. "Exclusivist Tendencies in Pentecostal Self-Definition: A Critique from Black Theology." *Journal of Religious Thought* 36/1 (1979): 32-49.

Vetter, Ferdinand, ed. *Die Predigten Taulers.* Berlin: Weidmann, 1910.

Vogelsang, Erich. "Die unio mystica bei Luther." *Archiv für Reformationsgeschichte* 35, (1935): 63-80.

―――― . "Luther und die Mystik." *Luther Jahrbuch* 19 (1937): 32-54.

Walch, Johann Georg. *Historische und Theologische Einleitung in die Religionsstreitigkeiten der Evangelisch-Lutherischen Kirch.* 2. 1733.

Wallmann, Johannes. "Wiedergeburt und Erneuerung bei Philipp Jakob Spener: Ein Diskussions-Beitrag." In *Pietismus und Neuzeit* (Jahrbücher zur Geschichte des Pietismus, 3). Edited by Lindt and Deppermann. Bielefeld: Luther Verlag, 1977, 7-31.

Wappler, Paul. *Thomas Müntzer in Zwickau und die "Zwickau Propheten."* Gütersloh, 1966.

Weigelt, Horst. *Pietismus-Studien. Der Spener-hallische Pietismus.* Stuttgart: Calwer, 1965.

_____ . *Sebastian Franck und die lutherische Reformation.* Gütersloh: Gerd Mohn, 1972.

_____ . *Spiritualistische Tradition im Protestantismus: Das Schwenkfeldertum in Schlesian.* Berlin: De Gruyter, 1973.

Wicks, Jared. *Man Yearning for Grace. Luther's Early Spiritual Teaching.* Wiesbaden: Steiner, 1969.

Wilks, Michael. *The Problem of Sovereignty in the Later Middle Ages.* London: Cambridge University Press, 1963.

Williams, George H., ed. *Spiritual and Anabaptist Writers.* Library of Christian Classics. 25. London: SCM Press, 1957.

_____ . *The Radical Reformation.* Philadelphia PA: Westminster Press, 1962.

_____ . "Sanctification in the Testimony of Several So-Called Schwärmer," In Asheim, 194-211.

_____ . "German Mysticism in the Polarization of Ethical Behavior in Luther and the Anabaptists." *Mennonite Quarterly Review* 48 (1974): 275-304.

Williams, George, and Edith Waldvogel. "A History of Speaking in Tongues and Related Gifts." In *The Charismatic Movement.* Edited by Michael Hamilton. Grand Rapids MI: Eerdmans, 1975, 61-113.

Wood, Lawrence W. *Pentecostal Grace.* Wilmore KY: Asbury Publishing Co., 1980.

World Council of Churches. "Towards a Church Renewed and United in the Spirit." *The Ecumenical Review* 31/3 (1979): 305-309.

_____ . "Die Bedeutung der charismatischen Erneuerung für die Kirchen. Bericht einer Konsultation in Bossey." *Una Sancta* 36/1 (1981): 5-10.

Yoder, J. H. "Anabaptism and History. 'Restitution' and the Possibility of Renewal." In Goertz, *Umstrittenes Täufertum,* 244-58.

_____ . " 'Spirit' and the Varieties of Reformation Radicalism." In *De Geest in het geding opstellin Aangeboden aan J. A. Oosterbaan.* Edited by Horst, de Jong, and Visser, 301-306.

Zaepernick, Gertraud. "Welt und Mensch bei Sebastien Franck." In *Pietismus und Neuzeit.* Edited by Lindt, Andreas, and K. Deppermann. Bielefeld: Luther Verlag, 1974, 9-24.

Zeeden, Ernst. *Martin Luther und die Reformation im Urteil des deutschen Luthertums.* 2. Freiburg: Herder, 1952.

Ziemer, Christof. "In und neben der Kirche. Charismatische Bewegung der DDR." *Die Zeichen der Zeit* 6 (1979): 218-26.

Zur Mühlen, Karl-Heinz. *Nos Extra Nos. Luthers Theologie zwischen Mystik und Scholastik.* Tübingen: J. C. B. Mohr, 1972.

INDEX

MUP THE THIRD REFORMATION?

Designed by Haywood Ellis

Composition by Omni Composition Services
  text typeface—Garamond; display—Mediaeval Roman
  typeset on an Addressograph Multigraph Comp/Set Phototypesetter
    5404, and paginated on an A/M Comp/Set 4510

Design and production specifications:
  text paper—60-pound Warren's Olde Style
  endpapers—80-pound text
  cover (on .088 boards)—Holliston Crown Linen 13445
  dust jacket—80# text

Printing (offset lithography) was by Omnipress of Macon, Inc.,
  Macon, Georgia.
Binding was by John H. Dekker and Sons, Inc., Grand Rapids, Michigan.